D1647814

THE COLLECTED WORKS OF
G. K. CHESTERTON

II

THE COLLECTED WORKS OF G. K. CHESTERTON

II

ST. FRANCIS OF ASSISI

THE EVERLASTING MAN

ST. THOMAS AQUINAS

IGNATIUS PRESS   SAN FRANCISCO

© 1986 Ignatius Press, San Francisco
All rights reserved
ISBN 978-0-89870-116-6 (HB)
ISBN 978-0-89870-117-3 (SB)
Library of Congress catalogue number 85-81511
Printed in the United States of America

CONTENTS

CONTENTS

GENERAL EDITORS' INTRODUCTION

This is the second of three volumes that will be devoted to Chesterton's theological works. The third volume will encompass G. K. C.'s writings on his conversion to the Roman Catholic Church.

St. Francis of Assisi, published in 1923, was considered by Maisie Ward to be "the highest expression of Gilbert's mysticism". In writing this sketch of St. Francis, Chesterton wanted to address

> the ordinary modern man, sympathetic but sceptical, and I can only rather hazily hope that, by approaching the great saint's story through what is evidently picturesque and popular about it, I may at least leave the reader understanding a little more than he did before of the consistency of a complete character; that by approaching it in this way, we may at least get a glimmering of why the poet who praised his lord the sun, often hid himself in a dark cavern, of why the saint who was so gentle with his Brother the Wolf was so harsh to his Brother the Ass (as he nicknamed his own body), of why the troubadour who said that love set his heart on fire separated himself from women, of why the singer who rejoiced in the strength and gaiety of the fire deliberately rolled himself in the snow, of why the very song which cries with all the passion of a pagan, "Praised be God for our Sister, Mother Earth, which brings forth varied fruits and grass and glowing flowers", ends almost with the words "Praised be God for our Sister, the death of the body."

The Reverend George William Rutler, S.T.D., a priest of the Archdiocese of New York, has served as editor of *St. Francis of Assisi*. Father Rutler's introductory essay examines the influence St. Francis had on Chesterton's youth, on his conversion and when "his deepest misgivings about progressivism were fulfilling themselves".

The Everlasting Man (1925) is considered "the *Orthodoxy* of Chesterton's later life". After the publication of this work, William Lyon Phelps wrote to G. K. C. thanking him for writing "a magnificent work of genius and never more needed than now". This friend continued: "I took out my pencil to mark the most important passages, but I quickly put my pencil in my pocket for I found I had to mark every sentence."

Chesterton wrote *The Everlasting Man* to rebut the evolutionary materialism of H. G. Wells' *The Outline of History*. The work is truly an answer to the atheistic humanism and scientism of the twentieth century.

When Chesterton began dictating *St. Thomas Aquinas* (1933) to his longtime secretary, Dorothy Collins, his research for the project consisted of a very casual perusal of a few books on his subject. Frank Sheed and Maisie Ward, the publishers, were concerned that G. K. C.'s efforts might result in a lightweight treatment of a very complex philosopher. Their concerns were unfounded because Chesterton's *St. Thomas Aquinas* was lauded as a major contribution to the understanding of the "Angelic Doctor".

Étienne Gilson, the leading Thomistic scholar of the twentieth century, wrote:

> I consider it as being without possible comparison the best book ever written on St. Thomas. Nothing short of genius can account for such an achievement. Everybody will no doubt admit that it is a "clever" book, but the few readers who have spent twenty or thirty years in studying St. Thomas Aquinas, and who, perhaps, have themselves published two or three volumes on the subject, cannot fail to perceive that the so-called "wit" of Chesterton has put their scholarship to shame. He has guessed all that which they had tried to demonstrate, and he has said all that which they were more or less clumsily attempting to express in academic formulas. Chesterton was one of the deepest thinkers who ever existed; he was deep because he was right; and he could not help being right; but he could not either help being modest and charitable, so he left it to those who could understand him to know that he was right, and deep; to the others, he apologized for being right, and he made up for being deep by being witty. That is all they can see of him.

Dr. Larry Azar, who edited *The Everlasting Man* and *St. Thomas Aquinas*, is a Thomistic scholar with a strong academic background in the sciences. He earned his doctorate at the Pontifical Institute at the University of Toronto, where he studied under Étienne Gilson.

In his essays, Dr. Azar's analysis supports the thesis of James V. Schall, S.J. that Chesterton "is deceptively dangerous for anyone who succumbs to modern scientism and ancient gnosticism. . . . He is dangerous because he does not allow invalid arguments to stand against the truth, even the truth of revelation which somehow does not contradict reason."

Dr. Raymond Dennehy has written the introduction for *St. Thomas Aquinas*. Dr. Dennehy is professor of philosophy in the St. Ignatius Institute at the University of San Francisco, author of *Reason and Dignity* and president of the American Maritain Association.

GEORGE J. MARLIN
RICHARD P. RABATIN
JOHN L. SWAN
   General Editors

JOSEPH SOBRAN
   Consulting Editor

PATRICIA AZAR
REV. RANDALL PAINE O.S.C.
   Associate Editors

ST. FRANCIS OF ASSISI

1923

INTRODUCTION

By George William Rutler

Chesterton is something of an oriental rug merchant to his readers; he is certainly more than a thread merchant. In the bazaar, he could fling open huge and varied patterns; how the details were woven is a matter for apprentices and sometimes for pedants who write introductions. Conversion to Roman Catholicism was another matter: he already had its vast pattern; now he required its particulars. He learned page by page from the Penny Catechism. This is remarkable in a man who glided effortlessly, so it seemed, over the *Summa*. The reason is plain enough: he had absorbed many things, but he wanted to be absorbed by "The Thing" behind them, the enclosure of eternity and the open door of history known to mankind as the Catholic and apostolic Church.

The day he was received into the fullness of the Church, July 30, 1922, in the dance room of the Railway Hotel which served as the Catholic church for Beaconsfield, he fumbled in his pocket for the Ritual and pulled out a three penny shocker. But he was neither confused nor embarrassed. A three penny shocker and the Ritual were not altogether unlike. Nor was a three penny shocker out of place with the Penny Catechism. Such was what he expected of the Holy Catholic Church.

The reason for converting was just that only the Roman Church could produce a St. Francis of Assisi;

> . . . we find [the counsels of perfection] produced by the same religious system which claims continuity and authority from the scenes in which they first appeared. Any number of philosophies will repeat the platitudes of Christianity. But it is the ancient Church that can again startle the world with the paradoxes of Christianity. *Ubi Petrus ibi Franciscus.*

Rome was the great thriller and the great catechist by means of its sane proportions. St. Francis and St. Thomas Aquinas were models of that scale which, as a theological evidence, is the distributive system of grace.

Glimpses of "The Thing" had been with him from his early years in the form of St. Francis, gradually revealing its implications. He dedicated youthful verses to him in his school magazine "The Debater", (though the Francis for which he won the set-piece prize at school was Xavier). His brother, Cecil, was hasty in reading a Catholic consciousness in any of this; Gilbert was passing through the "various stages" of that modern condition "which can admire [St. Francis] yet hardly accept him, or which can appreciate the saint almost without the sanctity". An essay on St. Francis, along with one on William Morris, was the first publication over the initials "GKC".

St. Francis of Assisi was published shortly after his conversion and just before *The Everlasting Man* (1925). These works were done in a period of respite from certain labors, an interlude between the "New Witness" and the start of *GK's Weekly.* It was also the time when his deepest misgivings about progressivism were fulfilling themselves. His Catholic apologetics, and his studies of Cobbett (1925), Stevenson (1927) and Chaucer (1932), would reach back to older ages for brighter themes; the newer world was truly becoming the "goblin kitchen" of little conceits, making a miniature and a mockery of all that was catholic and Catholic. In a poem "The Convert" he declared: ". . . my name is Lazarus and I live." But the restored living was in the time present; and at times, like his Cobbett, he "only had frantic and fantastic nightmares of things as they are".

He did not go on the defensive. That was typical. He was incapable of defensiveness. Defensive people are inclined to offend. By taking the offensive, he appeared ever more amiable, only frustrating his opponents by his intrusiveness. Frustration increased when he selected St. Francis, everyone's friend, as a means of assault; balanced humanists positively groaned when he juggled the Jongleur de Dieu before their eyes. They had wanted Francis on their admirable terms, a Lake District poet or a selfless Anti-Vivisectionist. Chesterton's rowdy act cheerfully smashed those delicate figurines. Naturalists could not ignore such vandalism, for in their own way they loved Francis, but they loved him as does any modern critic who, in the words of James J. Daly, S.J., "understands Tolstoy and does not love him, and loves Francis and does not understand him".

Some of the responses at the time of publication in 1924 were patronizing. One wrote: "Allowing for Mr. Chesterton's little ways, with which we are all agreeably familiar, we are ready to grant at once that he has written an entertaining and even an edifying book. . . ." It is hard to understand why the *Illustrated London News* considered the style more prolix and less animated than usual or why the *New York Times* called it "more restrained and less paradoxical than previous works". The *Book Digest* thought it "an excellent example of the author's method and style", and the *Literary Digest International Book Review* thought it was "done in Mr. Chesterton's best manner: a happy combination of deftness of touch, lightly veiled irony, happy, illuminating metaphor. . . ."

The Saturday Review was not so content: ". . . the habit of making cheap plays on words has become fatally ingrained in his style." American prejudice cannot be held to account; Chesterton's diction pleases only certain tastes anywhere; his compatriot, Evelyn Waugh, once went so far as to propose that a committee be formed to translate him into readable prose. The *Bookman* complained: "If his prophecies are delivered in the lightning flashes of wit and genial humor, without the terrifying accompaniment of thunder, sensitive readers ought to be duly grateful. But we are afraid it is not so." The sensibilities of the *Nation* were more wounded: "Mr. Chesterton's incessant crackle of fireworks seems to us quite inappropriate. To portray these touchingly simple episodes against a flickering background of paradox and word-play is a little like descanting on the beauties of a landscape to the sputter of a motor-cycle." He had said in *Heretics* (1905):

> they are the kind of people who in the time of the maypole would have thought the maypole vulgar; who in the time of the Canterbury pilgrimage would have thought the Canterbury pilgrimage vulgar; who in the time of the Olympian games would have thought the Olympian games vulgar. Nor can there be any reasonable doubt that they were vulgar. . . . Wherever you have belief you will have hilarity, wherever you have hilarity you will have some dangers.

Reviewers were hard put to say much of significance about the thesis, which was that Francis was a saint and that you have to take him or leave him as such. Critics found it less challenging to point out characteristic inaccuracies: that the author is wrong about the etymology of the word "courage"; or that the Canticle of Creation was composed in a hut a year before the Saint's death and not "in the meadows in the sunnier season of his career"; or that the Saint did not in fact intercede with the Emperor for the birds; or that Joachim of Flora, and not a Franciscan, talked about harps; or that Dante may not have belonged to the Third Order; or that St. Francis and St. Dominic probably met not once but thrice; or that the Portiuncula is in the Spoletan valley and not on a hill. Rarely does a critic tackle more substantial matters: for instance, Chesterton does seem nearly oblivious to the two centuries of lay investiture crises which so colored the ecclesiastical background of the age (though he does name the Gregorian reform as one of the three representative medieval signs).

He is cavalier with facts, not because he meant to be cavalier, but because he wanted to be a cavalier. The pen is not mightier than the sword; it is the sword's sword; and while accuracy scores points in fencing, acuteness is what counts in a real duel. If he is light on some facts, he is heavy on fact; information about St. Francis was less pertinent than the information in St. Francis. A biographer more familiar with Spoletan topography would have described more minutely Francis dying; but he might have given an impression of Francis dying minutely, if he missed the point of Francis dying on the hard ground. That bare floor was Chesterton's only topography; flat as it was, it showed to scale the dimensions of Heaven and Hell.

What motivated nearly his entire literary life was a sense of universal justice far more intense than any claims he might make in its halls on his own behalf. St. Francis was more than a model of justice, a blindfolded allegory with scales in hand; he was "The Pardon of God" with eyes open and arms stretched wide in the dawn; a saint is the sight and balance of justice on display in himself, the just man made perfect. Chesterton held St. Francis up before the moderns who were brooding the dehumanizing calculations which make such fainthearted glances at true justice. St. Francis was the likeliest contradiction of "the perpetual torture of incompetent compassion". A. L. Maycock splendidly located the incompetence in the representative figure, Chesterton's great friend and antithesis:

> The whole essence of Shaw's philosophy was that of a man utterly detached from human proceedings, unable to enter into the feeling and motives of ordinary people in spite of a genuine concern and zeal for their welfare. Shaw hated the poverty, squalor and overcrowding of the slums as violently as any man. He regarded physical suffering as the greatest of all evils but he could discuss such human tragedies as the loss of man's faith or the break-up of his marriage with the most cheerful scepticism. He thought of human life in all its pathetic complexity in terms of problems for which you merely had to find the right solutions; and it was not surprising that his attitude to "the poor" was one of contempt, as a race that did not deserve to survive.

Chesterton's detachment was different, as it was a habit of attachment to everything outside himself. His attachment to his wife was far beyond what Shaw might have thought seemly; his attachment to a lamppost was out of the question for Shaw; his attachment to beef was to Shaw's horror. On the whole, his detachment was pathetic when it came to his cheque books, and here Shaw's contempt for poverty helped rescue him. But the matter is deeper. Chesterton saw in St. Francis the exaltation of all that the modern egoist abhorred; the saint suddenly loomed as a deep and portentous shadow across the lolling gardens and birdbaths of materialist reform. The marks in the saint's body were waved as testimony against the naturalists who had come to regard Francis as more Christian than Christ. Love must know its object, or else it is sentimentalism; and Chesterton insisted that such knowledge affirm what the efficient moderns were resisting to the point of violent unreason: "I have said that St. Francis deliberately did not see the wood for the trees. It is even more true that he deliberately did not see the mob for the men."

Some might answer that these are not the Saint's theories, but Chesterton's. They are the theories of both; Chesterton held them because he found them true on Fleet Street, as Francis had come upon them in Assisi. Neither had created them. They could not have created them for they are more than instant theories; they are the presence of prevenient grace. If Francis displayed them more heroically than Gilbert, they were nonetheless joint evidence of a gift greater than either. This is why the author so roundly condemns the Fraticelli for trying to put Francis in the place of Christ.

But what then? Is there more of Chesterton in the book than Francis? Is Chesterton giving us a medieval Chesterton? Is this Francis of Fleet Street, or Gilbert of Assisi? As with the logic of the famous allusion, that is like saying Caesar and Pompey were very much alike, especially Pompey. If *Orthodoxy* was "a sort of slovenly autobiography", *Saint Francis of Assisi* is a rather more compact one. But it is not any less a life of Saint Francis. It is both because it is chiefly an account of Christ among men. Wiry Francis and lumbering Gilbert are both in the image of God; a nearly daunting indication of God's ubiquitous perfection. And if the two did things differently, they illustrated the endless fecundity of God's unity: St. Francis chatting with the Saracen is no more unlikely a scene than Chesterton discussing the Book of Common Prayer with Mussolini.

When confronted with the fact of St. Francis, the mystified materialist will set him up like a fairy at the bottom of his garden and leave him there; Chesterton will use every fairy tale at his disposal to smash that evasion; even if it means portraying the Pardon of God as a jester. Such a fantasy is not misleading; it is along the lines of the Magdalen mistaking the Risen Christ for a gardener. At least she did not mistake him for a garden ornament. By such means the observer learns the meaning of the primal jest and the world's first garden. And he avoids the cynic's attempt to master creation without serving its Creator. But this description of fantasy is also an account of Franciscan fact. One might understand why Chesterton's lyrical description of the Franciscan life seemed to many to be only an enchantment, instead of a spell to break the enchantment.

Poetry has its place in the book; and St. Francis is presented primarily as a poet, hardly in deference to any lightness or delicacy in the Franciscan view of the world, but because "he was a person who could express his personality." That is a line totally beneath Chesterton if one takes it to mean what psychologists commonly mean by it. But for him it is the thunderous description of grace at work when the personality is manifest as a divine endowment. Thus poetry should not be the avoidance of preciseness; it invokes all the canons of order. Nor is it an exercise in egoism; there is no valid self-expression unless it is a tribute to the divine source of human individuation.

So then, the book is not deficient as serious biography for being poetic. Biographers usually set out to give a portrait of a person; Chesterton calls his a sketch. They are not the same, certainly not if a portrait is supposed to "capture the personality" the way the Chinese thought the ruby had caught a flame. Chesterton's method was to free the flame by means of the "jewel thrown into the sea" — a fantastic craft, but possible. It was not possible by magic; it was possible by sanctifying grace. And Chesterton used every magic poetical device to say so. When he could say no more, he pointed to the Saint who "never either deceived or was deceived by the illusion of mass-suggestion".

He might have said that a saint is the light finally let out in a world whose lights were going out. He did say it in various ways. He felt it first, as early as childhood, when he first heard the story of Assisi. Then it was not the Saint but Brother Fire impressing him with "something of harmony between the hearth and the firelight. . . ." Every other discovery was another light from the first light; and each harmony learned through St. Francis, between the sun and moon, between the fire and the eye, was a gift of the first Giver.

Chesterton had the intuition as long as he could remember; as there was harmony in the light, the sign of the dark was not its darkness but its discord. In words very like his account of the birth of his brother, the advent of St. Francis to the world was "like the birth of a child in a dark house, lifting its gloom". And the prayer of the Saint to the burning coal is the high articulation of what Chesterton had sensed when he first saw the shadow pantomime in the nursery hearth: "Brother Fire, God made you beautiful and strong and useful; I pray you be courteous with me." The coal was courteous because the man of peace could tolerate the fearsome harmony of its brightness. When he died, there passed "an outlook on life like a light that was never after on sea or land; a thing not to be replaced or repeated while earth endures". But he does not vanish from the author: "The figure in the brown habit stands above the hearth in the room where I write, and alone among many such images, at no stage of my pilgrimage has he ever seemed to me a stranger."

This is not the language of a chronicler. Nor was the language of St. Paul about Christ. Portions of *St. Francis* are hymnodic as the lines to the Corinthians. Chesterton would have said the Apostle had the advantage: "It would really require a saint to write the life of a saint." But the Apostle himself knew that the sublimest expressions would seem foolish and scandalous. Chesterton had his own Greeks and Jews; he addresses them in the first chapter, with a certain Paulinity about the reversal of lights and shades: ". . . what the foolish will find as impenetrable as darkness and even many of the wise will find almost as invisible as if it were written in silver upon white".

The course, as usual, was to take the offensive against both the foolish and the wise. We have said that Chesterton shunned portraiture. The hand of Giotto had given the portrait already. Chesterton may have been the first to supply a photograph of St. Francis, even though he preferred to call it a sketch. A photograph after the event is possible, provided someone can catch the light. The photograph is a record of light; and even when the light passed "not to be replaced or repeated", its negative remained. Chesterton declined to produce "what many in our world will regard as a sort of photographic negative". Chesterton had been left a negative by the world's default, and all he had to do was to develop it: like the modern discovery of the secrets in the Shroud of Turin.

He did it by casting St. Francis as the Troubadour and Jongleur; an easy thing to do since the role fit him as it fit the Saint. And once again, it was not a projection, but rather an introspection. The roles are not false or affected, when the whole of life is known to be dramatic. They costume that genius by which "in him even what is negative is positive".

Of the Troubadour and Jongleur, says Chesterton, "A glorious mediaeval romance remains to be written about two such companions wandering through the world." Well, twenty years earlier *The Napoleon of Notting Hill* appeared; in it Adam Wayne says to Auberon Quin: "You have a halberd and I a sword. Let us start our wanderings over the world. For we are its two essentials." Wheels were turning even as the author wrote *St. Francis*; he had begun work on *The Return of Don Quixote* just after the Great War, serialized it in *G.K.'s Weekly* from December, 1925 to November, 1926, and published it the following year. But the theme and complex images were his constantly. His wife had even outfitted him with the sword and cape much earlier. Perhaps the two who roamed the world were to have been Cecil and he; or possibly it was the Chesterbelloc. Or more suitably, like St. Francis, he was to be both in one. Everything else was set: progressive England was the inn to be stormed, Blatchford and Shaw were the windmills. St. Francis roamed his world, and Chesterton his; out of the Dark Ages emerged the Canticles of St. Francis, and from the mud of Flanders another stood to chant it again. The new Fabians were no less foolish, or pernicious, than the old Albigensians; and the new Troubadour would remind society of that, too.

His sheer rightness understandably deserved, and got, a wide audience. There is another reason for the attention he got; and it is worth mentioning here, even though it may seem something of an aside. But there is no harm in saying a word about it, since it rarely seems to be noticed.

It is that Chesterton's contemporaries, even many very misguided ones, appreciated intelligence. And this means intelligence and not the popular simulations of it; and this also means knowledge as wisdom, which is far more vital than the aestheticism of knowledge for the sake of knowledge. Chesterton had not what today is provincially called a university education; though the schooling he did have made him far more literate at the age of sixteen than the typical graduate student now can claim to be. But today he would not have been allowed to teach in a school, for lack of credentials. Within a few years from the publication of *St. Francis*, having previously turned down the offer of a university post at Birmingham, he was nominated to run for the honorary headship of the universities of Glasgow, Edinburgh and Aberdeen. It occurred to no one that he needed other than genius to be so honored. A genius is not as rare as those who recognize him.

It was the interior vision of St. Francis which Chesterton seized precisely by letting his genius loose. Here, G. K. C. on St. Francis is G. K. C. on G. K. C.: "He never saw things to scale in our sense, but with a dizzy disproportion which makes the mind reel. Sometimes it seems merely out of drawing like a gaily coloured mediaeval map; and then again it seems to have escaped from everything like a short cut in the fourth dimension."

Chesterton did not set out merely to give the reader insights into St. Francis, just as he did not offer many insights into ornithology. The book rather bestows something of what the Saint saw outside himself. The author did not completely know all that he was conveying; of St. Francis he might have said what he said about Blake, and which is not so silly as a few have thought: "We always feel that he is saying something very plain and emphatic even when we have not the wildest notion of what it is." *St. Francis of Assisi* is ascetical theology, and, as a map, it is a guide to the brightest recesses of prayer. The form could be located partway between Benedictine prose and Franciscan poetry, both of which had its place, as he said. Chesterton composed a prose litany to St. Francis and, when all was said and done, he offered it as a "brief candle burnt out so quickly before his shrine". The method and aim could be comprehended only by loving what the Saint loved. The critical eccentricity of that remains, as in the case of all the saints, the one eccentricity of "always turning towards the center".

The mediaeval Umbrian turned that way by casting off his motley and vesting in drab; the modern Londoner did it by casting off his drab and donning motley. Each set out on spiritual combat, each assumed the armaments of courtesy in the struggle, and each tested the same truth. The author wrote of it in his life of Blake, a dozen years before his conversion: ". . . if every human being lived a thousand years, every human would end up either in utter pessimistic scepticism or in the Catholic religion." A French philosopher of a certain school put it one way by saying that the worst tragedy is not to be a saint; Chesterton agreed in his own way by saying, in many clarion phrases, that the best comedy is to be one.

I

THE PROBLEM OF ST. FRANCIS

A sketch of St. Francis of Assisi in modern English may be written in one of three ways. Between these the writer must make his selection; and the third way, which is adopted here, is in some respects the most difficult of all. At least, it would be the most difficult if the other two were not impossible.

First, he may deal with this great and most amazing man as a figure in secular history and a model of social virtues. He may describe this divine demagogue as being, as he probably was, the world's one quite sincere democrat. He may say (what means very little) that St. Francis was in advance of his age. He may say (what is quite true) that St. Francis anticipated all that is most liberal and sympathetic in the modern mood; the love of nature; the love of animals; the sense of social compassion; the sense of the spiritual dangers of prosperity and even of property. All those things that nobody understood before Wordsworth were familiar to St. Francis. All those things that were first discovered by Tolstoy had been taken for granted by St. Francis. He could be presented, not only as a human but a humanitarian hero; indeed as the first hero of humanism. He has been described as a sort of morning star of the Renaissance. And in comparison with all these things, his ascetical theology can be ignored or dismissed as a contemporary accident, which was fortunately not a fatal accident. His religion can be regarded as a superstition, but an inevitable superstition, from which not even genius could wholly free itself; in the consideration of which it would be unjust to condemn St. Francis for his self-denial or unduly chide him for his chastity. It is quite true that even from so detached a standpoint his stature would still appear heroic. There would still be a great deal to be said about the man who tried to end the Crusades by talking to the Saracens or who interceded with the Emperor for the birds. The writer might describe in a purely historical spirit the whole of that great Franciscan inspiration that was felt in the painting of Giotto, in the poetry of Dante, in the miracle plays that made possible the modern drama, and in so many other things that are already appreciated by the modern culture. He may try to do it, as others have done, almost without raising any religious question at all. In short, he may try to tell the story of a saint without God; which is like being told to write the life of Nansen[1] and forbidden to mention the North Pole.

Second, he may go to the opposite extreme, and decide, as it were, to be defiantly devotional. He may make the theological enthusiasm as thoroughly the theme as it was the theme of the first Franciscans. He may treat religion as the real thing that it was to the real Francis of Assisi. He can find an austere joy, so to speak, in parading the paradoxes of asceticism and all the holy topsy-turvydom of humility. He can stamp the whole history with the Stigmata, record fasts like fights against a dragon; till in the vague modern mind St. Francis is as dark a figure as St. Dominic. In short he can produce what many in our world will regard as a sort of photographic negative, the reversal of all lights and shades; what the foolish will find as impenetrable as darkness and even many of the wise will find almost as invisible as if it were written in silver upon white. Such a study of St. Francis would be unintelligible to anyone who does not share his religion, perhaps only partly intelligible to anyone who does not share his vocation. According to degrees of judgment, it will be regarded as something too bad or too good for the world. The only difficulty about doing the thing in this way is that it cannot be done. It would really require a saint to write the life of a saint. In the present case the objections to such a course are insuperable.

Third, he may try to do what I have tried to do here; and, as I have already suggested, the course has peculiar problems of its own. The writer may put himself in the position of the ordinary modern outsider and enquirer; as indeed the present writer is still largely and was once entirely in that position. He may start from the standpoint of a man who already admires St. Francis, but only for those things

---

[1] Fridtjof Nansen was a Norwegian explorer. His great achievement was the partial accomplishment of his scheme for reaching the North Pole by letting his ship get frozen into the ice north of Siberia and drift with a current toward Greenland.

which such a man finds admirable. In other words he may assume that the reader is at least as enlightened as Renan[2] or Matthew Arnold;[3] but in the light of that enlightenment he may try to illuminate what Renan and Matthew Arnold left dark. He may try to use what is understood to explain what is not understood. He may say to the modern English reader: "Here is an historical character which is admittedly attractive to many of us already, by its gaiety, its romantic imagination, its spiritual courtesy and camaraderie, but which also contains elements (evidently equally sincere and emphatic) which seem to you quite remote and repulsive. But after all, this man was a man and not half a dozen men. What seems inconsistency to you did not seem inconsistency to him. Let us see whether we can understand, with the help of the existing understanding, these other things that seem now to be doubly dark, by their intrinsic gloom and their ironic contrast." I do not mean, of course, that I can really reach such a pyschological completeness in this crude and curt outline. But I mean that this is the only controversial condition that I shall here assume; that I am dealing with the sympathetic outsider. I shall not assume any more or any less agreement than this. A materialist may not care whether the inconsistencies are reconciled or not. A Catholic may not see any inconsistencies to reconcile. But I am here addressing the ordinary modern man, sympathetic but sceptical, and I can only rather hazily hope that, by approaching the great saint's story through what is evidently picturesque and popular about it, I may at least leave the reader understanding a little more than he did before of the consistency of a complete character; that by approaching it in this way, we may at least get a glimmering of why the poet who praised his lord the sun, often hid himself in a dark cavern, of why the saint who was so gentle with his Brother the Wolf was so harsh to his Brother the Ass (as he nicknamed his own body), of why the troubadour who said that love set his heart on fire separated himself from women, of why the singer who rejoiced in the strength and gaiety of the fire deliberately rolled himself in the snow, of why the very song which cries with all

[2] Ernest Renan (1823–1892), French critic, writer and sceptic.
[3] Matthew Arnold (1822–1888), English critic and poet.

the passion of a pagan, "Praised be God for our Sister, Mother Earth, which brings forth varied fruits and grass and glowing flowers," ends almost with the words "Praised be God for our Sister, the death of the body."

Renan and Matthew Arnold failed utterly at this test. They were content to follow Francis with their praises until they were stopped by their prejudices; the stubborn prejudices of the sceptic. The moment Francis began to do something they did not understand or did not like, they did not try to understand it, still less to like it; they simply turned their backs on the whole business and "walked no more with him." No man will get any further along a path of historical enquiry in that fashion. These sceptics are really driven to drop the whole subject in despair, to leave the most simple and sincere of all historical characters as a mass of contradictions, to be praised on the principle of the curate's egg.[4] Arnold refers to the asceticism of Alverno almost hurriedly, as if it were an unlucky but undeniable blot on the beauty of the story; or rather as if it were a pitiable break-down and bathos at the end of the story. Now this is simply to be stone-blind to the whole point of any story. To represent Mount Alverno as the mere collapse of Francis is exactly like representing Mount Calvary as the mere collapse of Christ. Those mountains are mountains, whatever else they are, and it is nonsense to say (like the Red Queen) that they are comparative hollows or negative holes in the ground. They were quite manifestly meant to be culminations and landmarks. To treat the Stigmata as a sort of scandal, to be touched on tenderly but with pain, is exactly like treating the original five wounds of Jesus Christ as five blots on His character. You may dislike the idea of asceticism; you may dislike equally the idea of martyrdom; for that matter you may have an honest and natural dislike of the whole conception of sacrifice symbolised by the cross. But if it is an intelligent dislike, you will still retain the capacity for

---

[4] "Among the catch-phrases that *Punch* has introduced into the language, 'Good in parts, like the curate's egg' is proverbial. The illustration shows a nervous young curate at his bishop's breakfast table. Asked by his lordship whether the egg is to his liking, he is terrified to say that it is bad and stammers out 'Parts of it are excellent!' " (*Brewer's Dictionary of Phrase and Fable*).

seeing the point of a story; of the story of a martyr or even the story of a monk. You will not be able rationally to read the Gospel and regard the Crucifixion as an afterthought or an anti-climax or an accident in the life of Christ; it is obviously the point of the story like the point of a sword, the sword that pierced the heart of the Mother of God.

And you will not be able rationally to read the story of a man presented as a Mirror of Christ without understanding his final phase as a Man of Sorrows, and at least artistically appreciating the appropriateness of his receiving, in a cloud of mystery and isolation, inflicted by no human hand, the unhealed everlasting wounds that heal the world.

The practical reconciliation of the gaiety and austerity I must leave the story itself to suggest. But since I have mentioned Matthew Arnold and Renan and the rationalistic admirers of St. Francis, I will here give the hint of what it seems to me most advisable for such readers to keep in mind. These distinguished writers found things like the Stigmata a stumbling block because to them a religion was a philosophy. It was an impersonal thing; and it is only the most personal passion that provides here an approximate earthly parallel. A man will not roll in the snow for a stream of tendency by which all things fulfil the law of their being. He will not go without food in the name of something, not ourselves, that makes for righteousness. He will do things like this, or pretty nearly like this, under quite a different impulse. He will do these things when he is in love. The first fact to realise about St. Francis is involved in the first fact with which his story starts; that when he said from the first that he was a Troubadour, and said later that he was a Troubadour of a newer and nobler romance, he was not using a mere metaphor, but understood himself much better than the scholars understand him. He was, to the last agonies of asceticism, a Troubadour. He was a Lover. He was a lover of God and he was really and truly a lover of men; possibly a much rarer mystical vocation. A lover of men is very nearly the opposite of a philanthropist; indeed the pedantry of the Greek word carries something like a satire on itself. A philanthropist may be said to love anthropoids. But as St. Francis did not love humanity but men, so he did not love Christianity but Christ. Say, if you think so, that he was a lunatic loving an imaginary person; but an imaginary person, not an imaginary idea. And for the modern reader the clue to the asceticism and all the rest can best be found in the stories of lovers when they seemed to be rather like lunatics. Tell it as the tale of one of the Troubadours, and the wild things he would do for his lady, and the whole of the modern puzzle disappears. In such a romance there would be no contradiction between the poet gathering flowers in the sun and enduring a freezing vigil in the snow, between his praising all earthly and bodily beauty and then refusing to eat, between his glorifying gold and purple and perversely going in rags, between his showing pathetically a hunger for a happy life and a thirst for a heroic death. All these riddles would easily be resolved in the simplicity of any noble love; only this was so noble a love that nine men out of ten have hardly heard of it. We shall see later that this parallel of the earthly lover has a very practical relation to the problems of his life, as to his relations with his father and with his friends and their families. The modern reader will almost always find that if he could only feel this kind of love as a reality, he could feel this kind of extravagance as a romance. But I only note it here as a preliminary point because, though it is very far from being the final truth in the matter, it is the best approach to it. The reader cannot even begin to see the sense of a story that may well seem to him a very wild one, until he understands that to this great mystic his religion was not a thing like a theory but a thing like a love-affair. And the only purpose of this prefatory chapter is to explain the limits of this present book; which is only addressed to that part of the modern world which finds in St. Francis a certain modern difficulty; which can admire him yet hardly accept him, or which can appreciate the saint almost without the sanctity. And my only claim even to attempt such a task is that I myself have for so long been in various stages of such a condition. Many thousand things that I now partly comprehend I should have thought utterly incomprehensible, many things I now hold sacred I should have scouted as utterly superstitious, many things that seem to me lucid and enlightened now they are seen from the inside I should honestly have called dark and barbarous seen from the outside, when long ago in those days of boyhood my fancy first caught fire with the glory of Francis of Assisi. I too have lived in Arcady; but even in Arcady I met one walking in a brown habit who loved the woods better than Pan. The figure in the brown habit stands above the hearth in the room where I write, and alone among many such images, at no stage of my pilgrimage has he ever seemed to me a stranger. There is something of harmony between the hearth and the firelight and my own first pleasure in his words about his brother fire; for he stands far enough back in my memory to mingle with all those more domestic dreams of the first days. Even the fantastic shadows thrown by fire make a sort of shadow pantomime that belongs to the nursery; yet the shadows were even then the shadows of his favourite beasts and birds, as he saw them, grotesque but haloed with the love of God. His Brother Wolf and Brother Sheep seemed then almost like the Brer Fox and Brer Rabbit of a more Christian Uncle Remus. I have come slowly to see many and more marvellous aspects of such a man, but I have never lost that one. His figure stands on a sort of bridge connecting my boyhood with my conversion to many other things; for the romance of his religion had penetrated even the rationalism of that vague Victorian time. In so far as I have had this experience, I may be able to lead others a little further along that road; but only a very little further. Nobody knows better than I do now that it is a road upon which angels might fear to tread; but though I am certain of failure I am not altogether overcome by fear; for he suffered fools gladly.

THE WORLD ST. FRANCIS FOUND

The modern innovation which has substituted journalism for history, or for that tradition that is the gossip of history, has had at least one definite effect. It has insured that everybody should only hear the end of every story. Journalists are in the habit of printing above the very last chapters of their serial stories (when the hero and heroine are just about to embrace in the last chapter, as only an unfathomable perversity prevented them from doing in the first) the rather misleading words, "You can begin this story here." But even this is not a complete parallel; for the journals do give some sort of a summary of the story, while they never give anything remotely resembling a summary of the history. Newspapers not only deal with news, but they deal with everything as if it were entirely new. Tutankamen, for instance, was entirely new. It is exactly in the same fashion that we read that Admiral Bangs has been shot, which is the first intimation we have that he has ever been born. There is something singularly significant in the use which journalism makes of its stores of biography. It never thinks of publishing the life until it is publishing the death. As it deals with individuals it deals with institutions and ideas. After the Great War our public began to be told of all sorts of nations being emancipated. It had never been told a word about their being enslaved. We were called upon to judge of the justice of the settlements, when we had never been allowed to hear of the very existence of the quarrels. People would think it pedantic to talk about the Serbian epics and they prefer to speak in plain every-day modern language about the Yugo-Slavonic international new diplomacy; and they are quite excited about something they call Czecho-Slovakia without apparently having ever heard of Bohemia. Things that are as old as Europe are regarded as more recent than the very latest claims pegged out on the prairies of America. It is very exciting; like the last act of a play to people who have only come into the theatre just before the curtain falls. But it does not conduce exactly to knowing what it is all about. To those content with the mere fact of a pistol-shot or a passionate embrace, such a leisurely manner of patronising the drama may be recommended. To those tormented by a merely intellectual curiosity about who is kissing or killing whom, and why, it is unsatisfactory.

Most modern history, especially in England, suffers from the same imperfection as journalism. At best it only tells half of the history of Christendom; and that the second half without the first half. Men for whom reason begins with the Revival of Learning, men for whom religion begins with the Reformation, can never give a complete account of anything, for they have to start with institutions whose origin they cannot explain, or generally even imagine. Just as we hear of the admiral being shot but have never heard of his being born, so we all heard a great deal about the dissolution of the monasteries, but we heard next to nothing about the creation of the monasteries. Now this sort of history would be hopelessly insufficient, even for an intelligent man who hated the monasteries. It is hopelessly insufficient in connection with institutions that many intelligent men do in a quite healthy spirit hate. For instance, it is possible that some of us have occasionally seen some mention, by our learned leader-writers, of an obscure institution called the Spanish Inquisition. Well, it really is an obscure institution, according to them and the histories they read. It is obscure because its origin is obscure. Protestant history simply begins with the horrible thing in possession, as the pantomime begins with the demon king in the goblin kitchen. It is likely enough that it was, especially towards the end, a horrible thing that might be haunted by demons; but if we say this was so, we have no notion why it was so. To understand the Spanish Inquisition it would be necessary to discover two things that we have never dreamed of bothering about; what Spain was and what an Inquisition was. The former would bring in the whole great question about the Crusade against the Moors; and by what heroic chivalry a European nation freed itself of an alien domination from Africa. The latter would bring in the whole business of the other Crusade against the Albigensians, and why men loved and hated that nihilistic vision from Asia. Unless we understand that there was in these things originally the rush and romance of a Crusade, we cannot understand how they came to deceive men or drag them on towards evil. The Crusaders doubtless abused their victory, but there was a victory to abuse. And where there is victory there is valour in the field and popularity in the forum. There is some sort of enthusiasm that encourages excesses or covers faults. For instance, I for one have maintained from very early days the responsibility of the English for their atrocious treatment of the Irish. But it would be quite unfair to the English to describe even the devilry of '98[1] and leave out altogether all mention of the war with Napoleon. It would be unjust to suggest that the English mind was bent on nothing but the death of Emmet, when it was more probably full of the glory of the death of Nelson. Unfortunately '98 was very far from being the last date of such dirty work; and only a few years ago our politicians started trying to rule by random robbing and killing, while gently remonstrating with the Irish for their memory of old unhappy far-off things and battles long ago. But however badly we may think of the Black-and-Tan[2] business, it would be unjust to forget that most of us were not thinking of Black-and-Tan but of khaki; and that khaki had just then a noble and national connotation covering many things. To write of the war in Ireland and leave out the war against Prussia, and the English sincerity about it, would be unjust to the English. So to talk about the torture-engine as if it had been a hideous toy is unjust to the Spanish. It does not tell sensibly from the start the story of what the Spaniard did, and why. We may concede to our contemporaries that in any case it is not a story that ends well. We do not insist that in their version it should begin well. What we complain of is that in

[1] The United Irishmen (a society which sought to bring Catholics and Protestants together in the cause of radical political reform and to put an end to religious discrimination) planned an uprising in 1798. After some bitter fighting, accompanied by harsh reprisals by the yeomancy and other military units, the rising was suppressed. Though Robert Emmet was to lead a short-lived outbreak in Dublin in 1803, the militant republican movement was, in effect, brought to an end by the defeats of 1798.

[2] The Black and Tans were members of the irregular force enlisted in England for service in Ireland as auxiliaries to the Royal Irish Constabulary during the disturbances of 1919-1922. They received this name because their original uniform was khaki with black leather accouterments.

their version it does not begin at all. They are only in at the death; or even, like Lord Tom Noddy, too late for the hanging. It is quite true that it was sometimes more horrible than any hanging; but they only gather, so to speak, the very ashes of the ashes; the fag-end of the faggot.

The case of the Inquisition is here taken at random, for it is one among any number illustrating the same thing; and not because it is especially connected with St. Francis, in whatever sense it may have been connected with St. Dominic. It may well be suggested later indeed that St. Francis is unintelligible, just as St. Dominic is unintelligible, unless we do understand something of what the thirteenth century meant by heresy and a crusade. But for the moment I use it as a lesser example for a much larger purpose. It is to point out that to begin the story of St. Francis with the birth of St. Francis would be to miss the whole point of the story, or rather not to tell the story at all. And it is to suggest that the modern tail-foremost type of journalistic history perpetually fails us. We learn about reformers without knowing what they had to reform, about rebels without a notion of what they rebelled against, of memorials that are not connected with any memory and restorations of things that had apparently never existed before. Even at the expense of this chapter appearing disproportionate, it is necessary to say something about the great movements that led up to the entrance of the founder of the Franciscans. It may seem to mean describing a world, or even a universe, in order to describe a man. It will inevitably mean that the world or the universe will be described with a few desperate generalisations in a few abrupt sentences. But so far from its meaning that we see a very small figure under so large a sky, it will mean that we must measure the sky before we can begin to measure the towering stature of the man.

And this phrase alone brings me to the preliminary suggestions that seem necessary before even a slight sketch of the life of St. Francis. It is necessary to realise, in however rude and elementary a fashion, into what sort of a world St. Francis entered and what has been the history of that world, at least in so far as it affected him. It is necessary to have, if only in a few sentences, a sort of preface in the form of an Outline of History, if we may borrow the phrase of Mr.

Wells. In the case of Mr. Wells himself, it is evident that the distinguished novelist suffered the same disadvantage as if he had been obliged to write a novel of which he hated the hero. To write history and hate Rome, both pagan and papal, is practically to hate nearly everything that has happened. It comes very near to hating humanity on purely humanitarian grounds. To dislike both the priest and the soldier, both the laurels of the warrior and the lilies of the saint, is to suffer a division from the mass of mankind for which not all the dexterities of the finest and most flexible of modern intelligences can compensate. A much wider sympathy is needed for the historical setting of St. Francis, himself both a soldier and a saint. I will therefore conclude this chapter with a few generalisations about the world that St. Francis found.

Men will not believe because they will not broaden their minds. As a matter of individual belief, I should of course express it by saying that they are not sufficiently catholic to be Catholic. But I am not going to discuss here the doctrinal truths of Christianity, but simply the broad historical fact of Christianity, as it might appear to a really enlightened and imaginative person even if he were not a Christian. What I mean at the moment is that the majority of doubts are made out of details. In the course of random reading a man comes across a pagan custom that strikes him as picturesque or a Christian action that strikes him as cruel; but he does not enlarge his mind sufficiently to see the main truth about pagan custom or the Christian reaction against it. Until we understand, not necessarily in detail, but in their big bulk and proportion that pagan progress and that Christian reaction, we cannot really understand the point of history at which St. Francis appears or what his great popular mission was all about.

Now everybody knows, I imagine, that the twelfth and thirteenth centuries were an awakening of the world. They were a fresh flowering of culture and the creative arts after a long spell of much sterner and even more sterile experience which we call the Dark Ages. They may be called an emancipation; they were certainly an end; an end of what may at least seem a harsher and more inhuman time. But what was it that was ended? From what was it that men were emancipated? That is where there is a real collision and point at issue between the different philosophies of history. On the merely external and secular side, it has been truly said that men awoke from a sleep; but there had been dreams in that sleep of a mystical and sometimes of a monstrous kind. In that rationalistic routine into which most modern historians have fallen, it is considered enough to say that they were emancipated from mere savage superstition and advanced towards mere civilised enlightenment. Now this is the big blunder that stands as a stumbling-block at the very beginning of our story. Anybody who supposes that the Dark Ages were plain darkness and nothing else, and that the dawn of the thirteenth century was plain daylight and nothing else, will not be able to make head or tail of the human story of St. Francis of Assisi. The truth is that the joy of St. Francis and his Jongleurs de Dieu was not merely an awakening. It was something which cannot be understood without understanding their own mystical creed. The end of the Dark Ages was not merely the end of a sleep. It was certainly not merely the end of a superstitious enslavement. It was the end of something belonging to a quite definite but quite different order of ideas.

It was the end of a penance; or, if it be preferred, a purgation. It marked the moment when a certain spiritual expiation had been finally worked out and certain spiritual diseases had been finally expelled from the system. They had been expelled by an era of asceticism, which was the only thing that could have expelled them. Christianity had entered the world to cure the world; and she had cured it in the only way in which it could be cured.

Viewed merely in an external and experimental fashion, the whole of the high civilisation of antiquity had ended in the learning of a certain lesson; that is, in its conversion to Christianity. But that lesson was a psychological fact as well as a theological faith. That pagan civilisation had indeed been a very high civilisation. It would not weaken our thesis, it might even strengthen it, to say that it was the highest that humanity ever reached. It had discovered its still unrivalled arts of poetry and plastic representation; it had discovered its own permanent political ideals; it had discovered its own clear system of logic and of language. But above all, it had discovered its own mistake.

That mistake was too deep to be ideally defined; the short-hand of it is to call it the mistake of nature-worship. It might almost as truly be called the mistake of being natural; and it was a very natural mistake. The Greeks, the great guides and pioneers of pagan antiquity, started out with the idea of something splendidly obvious and direct; the idea that if man walked straight ahead on the high road of reason and nature, he could come to no harm; especially if he was, as the Greek was, eminently enlightened and intelligent. We might be so flippant as to say that man was simply to follow his nose, so long as it was a Greek nose. And the case of the Greeks themselves is alone enough to illustrate the strange but certain fatality that attends upon this fallacy. No sooner did the Greeks themselves begin to follow their own noses and their own notion of being natural, than the queerest thing in history seems to have happened to them. It was much too queer to be an easy matter to discuss. It may be remarked that our more repulsive realists never give us the benefit of their realism. Their studies of unsavoury subjects never take note of the testimony which they bear to the truths of a traditional morality. But if we had the taste for such things, we could cite thousands of such things as part of the case for Christian morals. And an instance of this is found in the fact that nobody has written, in this sense, a real moral history of the Greeks. Nobody has seen the scale or the strangeness of the story. The wisest men in the world set out to be natural; and the most unnatural thing in the world was the very first thing they did. The immediate effect of saluting the sun and the sunny sanity of nature was a perversion spreading like a pestilence. The greatest and even the purest philosophers could not apparently avoid this low sort of lunacy. Why? It would seem simple enough for the people whose poets had conceived Helen of Troy, whose sculptors had carved the Venus of Milo, to remain healthy on the point. The truth is that people who worship health cannot remain healthy. When Man goes straight he goes crooked. When he follows his nose he manages somehow to put his nose out of joint, or even to cut off his nose to spite his face; and that in accordance with something much deeper in human nature than nature-worshippers could ever understand. It was the discovery of that deeper thing, humanly speaking, that constituted the conversion to Christianity. There is a bias in man like the bias in the bowl; and Christianity was the discovery of how to correct the bias and therefore hit the mark. There are many who will smile at the saying; but it is profoundly true to say that the glad good news brought by the Gospel was the news of original sin.

Rome rose at the expense of her Greek teachers largely because she did not entirely consent to be taught these tricks. She had a much more decent domestic tradition; but she ultimately suffered from the same fallacy in her religious tradition; which was necessarily in no small degree the heathen tradition of nature-worship. What was the matter with the whole heathen civilisation was that there was nothing for the mass of men in the way of mysticism, except that concerned with the mystery of the nameless forces of nature, such as sex and growth and death. In the Roman Empire also, long before the end, we find nature-worship inevitably producing things that are against nature. Cases like that of Nero have passed into a proverb when Sadism sat on a throne brazen in the broad daylight. But the truth I mean is something much more subtle and universal than a conventional catalogue of atrocities. What had happened to the human imagination, as a whole, was that the whole world was coloured by dangerous and rapidly deteriorating passions; by natural passions becoming unnatural passions. Thus the effect of treating sex as only one innocent natural thing was that every other innocent natural thing became soaked and sodden with sex. For sex cannot be admitted to a mere equality among elementary emotions or experiences like eating and sleeping. The moment sex ceases to be a servant it becomes a tyrant. There is something dangerous and disproportionate in its place in human nature, for whatever reason; and it does really need a special purification and dedication. The modern talk about sex being free like any other sense, about the body being beautiful like any tree or flower, is either a description of the Garden of Eden or a piece of thoroughly bad psychology, of which the world grew weary two thousand years ago.

This is not to be confused with mere self-righteous sensationalism about the wickedness of the pagan world. It was not so much that

the pagan world was wicked as that it was good enough to realise
that its paganism was becoming wicked, or rather was on the logical
high road to wickedness. I mean that there was no future for
"natural magic"; to deepen it was only to darken it into black
magic. There was no future for it; because in the past it had only
been innocent because it was young. We might say it had only been
innocent because it was shallow. Pagans were wiser than paganism;
that is why the pagans became Christians. Thousands of them had
philosophy and family virtues and military honour to hold them up;
but by this time the purely popular thing called religion was certainly
dragging them down. When this reaction against the evil is allowed
for, it is true to repeat that it was an evil that was everywhere. In
another and more literal sense its name was Pan.

It was no metaphor to say that these people needed a new heaven
and a new earth; for they had really defiled their own earth and even
their own heaven. How could their case be met by looking at the
sky, when erotic legends were scrawled in stars across it; how could
they learn anything from the love of birds and flowers after the sort
of love stories that were told of them? It is impossible here to multiply evidences, and one small example may stand for the rest. We
know what sort of sentimental associations are called up to us by the
phrase "a garden"; and how we think mostly of the memory of melancholy and innocent romances, or quite as often of some gracious
maiden lady or kindly old parson pottering under a yew hedge, perhaps in sight of a village spire. Then, let anyone who knows a little
Latin poetry recall suddenly what would once have stood in place of
the sun-dial or the fountain, obscene and monstrous in the sun; and
of what sort was the god of their gardens.

Nothing could purge this obsession but a religion that was literally
unearthly. It was no good telling such people to have a natural
religion full of stars and flowers; there was not a flower or even a
star that had not been stained. They had to go into the desert where
they could find no flowers or even into the cavern where they could
see no stars. Into that desert and that cavern the highest human intellect entered for some four centuries; and it was the very wisest
thing it could do. Nothing but the stark supernatural stood up for

its salvation; if God could not save it, certainly the gods could not. The Early Church called the gods of paganism devils; and the Early Church was perfectly right. Whatever natural religion may have had to do with their beginnings, nothing but fiends now inhabited those hollow shrines. Pan was nothing but panic. Venus was nothing but venereal vice. I do not mean for a moment of course, that all the individual pagans were of this character even to the end; but it was as individuals that they differed from it. Nothing distinguishes paganism from Christianity so clearly as the fact that the individual thing called philosophy had little or nothing to do with the social thing called religion. Anyhow it was no good to preach natural religion to people to whom nature had grown as unnatural as any religion. They knew much better than we do what was the matter with them and what sort of demons at once tempted and tormented them; and they wrote across that great space of history the text: "This sort goeth not out but by prayer and fasting."

Now the historic importance of St. Francis and the transition from the twelfth to the thirteenth century, lies in the fact that they marked the end of this expiation. Men at the close of the Dark Ages may have been rude and unlettered and unlearned in everything but wars with heathen tribes, more barbarous than themselves, but they were clean. They were like children; the first beginnings of their rude arts have all the clean pleasure of children. We have to conceive them in Europe as a whole living under little local governments, feudal in so far as they were a survival of fierce wars with the barbarians, often monastic and carrying a more friendly and fatherly character, still faintly imperial in so far as Rome still ruled as a great legend. But in Italy something had survived more typical of the finer spirit of antiquity; the republic. Italy was dotted with little states, largely democratic in their ideals, and often filled with real citizens. But the city no longer lay open as under the Roman peace, but was pent in high walls for defence against feudal war and all the citizens had to be soldiers. One of these stood in a steep and striking position on the wooded hills of Umbria; and its name was Assisi. Out of its deep gate under its high turrets was to come the message that was the gospel of the hour, "Your warfare is accomplished, your iniquity is pardoned." But it was out of all these fragmentary things of feudalism and freedom and remains of Roman Law that there was to rise, at the beginning of the thirteenth century, vast and almost universal, the mighty civilisation of the Middle Ages.

It is an exaggeration to attribute it entirely to the inspiration of any one man, even the most original genius of the thirteenth century. Its elementary ethics of fraternity and fair play had never been entirely extinct and Christendom had never been anything less than Christian. The great truisms about justice and pity can be found in the rudest monastic records of the barbaric transition or the stiffest maxims of the Byzantine decline. And early in the eleventh and twelfth centuries a larger moral movement had clearly begun. But what may fairly be said of it is this, that over all those first movements there was still something of that ancient austerity that came from the long penitential period. It was the twilight of morning; but it was still a grey twilight. This may be illustrated by the mere mention of two or three of these reforms before the Franciscan reform. The monastic institution itself, of course, was far older than all these things; indeed it was undoubtedly almost as old as Christianity. Its counsels of perfection had always taken the form of vows of chastity and poverty and obedience. With these unworldly aims it had long ago civilised a great part of the world. The monks had taught people to plough and sow as well as to read and write; indeed they had taught the people nearly everything that the people knew. But it may truly be said that the monks were severely practical, in the sense that they were not only practical but also severe; though they were generally severe with themselves and practical for other people. All this early monastic movement had long ago settled down and doubtless often deteriorated; but when we come to the first medieval movements this sterner character is still apparent. Three examples may be taken to illustrate the point.

First, the ancient social mould of slavery was already beginning to melt. Not only was the slave turning into the serf, who was practically free as regards his own farm and family life, but many lords were freeing slaves and serfs altogether. This was done under the pressure of the priests; but especially it was done in the spirit of a penance. In one sense, of course, any Catholic society must have an atmosphere of penance; but I am speaking of that rather sterner spirit of penance which had expiated the excesses of paganism. There was about such restitutions the atmosphere of the death-bed; as many of them doubtless were examples of death-bed repentance. A very honest atheist with whom I once debated made use of the expression, "Men have only been kept in slavery by the fear of hell." As I pointed out to him, if he had said that men had only been freed from slavery by the fear of hell, he would at least have been referring to an unquestionable historical fact.

Another example was the sweeping reform of Church discipline by Pope Gregory the Seventh.[3] It really was a reform, undertaken from the highest motives and having the healthiest results; it conducted a searching inquisition against simony or the financial corruptions of the clergy; it insisted on a more serious and self-sacrificing ideal for the life of a parish priest. But the very fact that this largely took the form of making universal the obligation of celibacy will strike the note of something which, however noble, would seem to many to be vaguely negative. The third example is in one sense the strongest of all. For the third example was a war; a heroic war and for many of us a holy war; but still something having all the stark and terrible responsibilities of war. There is no space here to say all that should be said about the true nature of the Crusades. Everybody knows that in the very darkest hour of the Dark Ages a sort of heresy had sprung up in Arabia and become a new religion of a military but nomadic sort, invoking the name of Mahomet. Intrinsically it had a character found in many heresies from the Moslem to the Monist. It seemed to the heretic a sane simplification of religion; while it seems to the Catholic an insane simplification of religion,

[3] St. Gregory VII (1020–1085). He was pope from 1073 to 1085 and he ended lay investiture of the clergy. Gregory excommunicated Henry IV of Germany for suppressing the Church and Henry did penance in the snow before Gregory's palace at Canossa in 1077. Henry was absolved, but in 1078 the pope renewed the excommunication. Henry declared war and captured Rome in 1084. St. Gregory died in exile at Salerno in 1085.

because it simplifies all to a single idea and so loses the breadth and balance of Catholicism. Anyhow its objective character was that of a military danger to Christendom and Christendom had struck at the very heart of it, in seeking to reconquer the Holy Places. The great Duke Godfrey and the first Christians who stormed Jerusalem were heroes if there were ever any in the world; but they were the heroes of a tragedy.

Now I have taken these two or three examples of the earlier medieval movements in order to note about them one general character, which refers back to the penance that followed paganism. There is something in all these movements that is bracing even while it is still bleak, like a wind blowing between the clefts of the mountains. That wind, austere and pure, of which the poet speaks, is really the spirit of the time, for it is the wind of a world that has at last been purified. To anyone who can appreciate atmospheres there is something clear and clean about the atmosphere of this crude and often harsh society. Its very lusts are clean; for they have no longer any smell of perversion. Its very cruelties are clean; they are not the luxurious cruelties of the amphitheatre. They come either of a very simple horror at blasphemy or a very simple fury at insult. Gradually against this grey background beauty begins to appear, as something really fresh and delicate and above all surprising. Love returning is no longer what was once called platonic but what is still called chivalric love. The flowers and stars have recovered their first innocence. Fire and water are felt to be worthy to be the brother and sister of a saint. The purge of paganism is complete at last.

For water itself has been washed. Fire itself has been purified as by fire. Water is no longer that water into which slaves were flung to feed the fishes. Fire is no longer that fire through which children were passed to Moloch. Flowers smell no more of the forgotten garlands gathered in the garden of Priapus; stars stand no more as signs of the far frigidity of gods as cold as those cold fires. They are all like things newly made and awaiting new names, from one who shall come to name them. Neither the universe nor the earth have now any longer the old sinister significance of the world. They await a new reconciliation with man, but they are already capable of being reconciled. Man has stripped from his soul the last rag of nature-worship, and can return to nature.

While it was yet twilight a figure appeared silently and suddenly on a little hill above the city, dark against the fading darkness. For it was the end of a long and stern night, a night of vigil, not unvisited by stars. He stood with his hands lifted, as in so many statues and pictures, and about him was a burst of birds singing; and behind him was the break of day.

III

FRANCIS THE FIGHTER

According to one tale, which if not true would be none the less typical, the very name of St. Francis was not so much a name as a nickname. There would be something akin to his familiar and popular instinct in the notion that he was nicknamed very much as an ordinary schoolboy might be called "Frenchy" at school. According to this version, his name was not Francis at all but John; and his companions called him "Francesco" or "The little Frenchman" because of his passion for the French poetry of the Troubadours. The more probable story is that his mother had named him John when he was born in the absence of his father, who shortly returned from a visit to France, where his commercial success had filled him with so much enthusiasm for French taste and social usage that he gave his son the new name signifying the Frank or Frenchman. In either case the name has a certain significance, as connecting Francis from the first with what he himself regarded as the romantic fairyland of the Troubadours.

The name of the father was Pietro Bernardone and he was a substantial citizen of the guild of the cloth merchants in the town of Assisi. It is hard to describe the position of such a man without some appreciation of the position of such a guild and even of such a town. It did not exactly correspond to anything that is meant in modern times either by a merchant or a man of business or a tradesman, or anything that exists under the conditions of capitalism. Bernardone may have employed people but he was not an employer; that is, he did not belong to an employing class as distinct from an employed class. The person we definitely hear of his employing is his son Francis; who, one is tempted to guess, was about the last person that any man of business would employ if it were convenient to employ anybody else. He was rich, as a peasant may be rich by the work of his own family; but he evidently expected his own family to work in a way almost as plain as a peasant's. He was a prominent citizen, but he belonged to a social order which existed to prevent him being too prominent to be a citizen. It kept all such people on their own simple level, and no prosperity connoted that escape from drudgery by which in modern times the lad might have seemed to be a lord or a fine gentleman or something other than the cloth merchant's son. This is a rule that is proved even in the exception. Francis was one of those people who are popular with everybody in any case; and his guileless swagger as a Troubadour and leader of French fashions made him a sort of romantic ringleader among the young men of the town. He threw money about both in extravagance and benevolence, in a way native to a man who never, all his life, exactly understood what money was. This moved his mother to mingled exultation and exasperation and she said, as any tradesman's wife might say anywhere: "He is more like a prince than our son." But one of the earliest glimpses we have of him shows him as simply selling bales of cloth from a booth in the market; which his mother may or may not have believed to be one of the habits of princes. This first glimpse of the young man in the market is symbolic in more ways than one. An incident occurred which is perhaps the shortest and sharpest summary that could be given of certain curious things which were a part of his character, long before it was transfigured by transcendental faith. While he was selling velvet and fine embroideries to some solid merchant of the town, a beggar came imploring alms; evidently in a somewhat tactless manner. It was a rude and simple society and there were no laws to punish a starving man for expressing his need for food, such as have been established in a more humanitarian age; and the lack of any organised police permitted such persons to pester the wealthy without any great danger. But there was, I believe, in many places a local custom of the guild forbidding outsiders to interrupt a fair bargain; and it is possible that some such thing put the mendicant more than normally in the wrong. Francis had all his life a great liking for people who had been put hopelessly in the wrong. On this occasion he seems to have dealt with the double interview with rather a divided mind; certainly with distraction, possibly with irritation. Perhaps he was all the more uneasy because of the almost fastidious standard of manners

that came to him quite naturally. All are agreed that politeness
flowed from him from the first, like one of the public fountains in
such a sunny Italian market place. He might have written among his
own poems as his own motto that verse of Mr. Belloc's poem —

> 'Of Courtesy, it is much less
> Than courage of heart or holiness,
> Yet in my walks it seems to me
> That the grace of God is in Courtesy.'

Nobody ever doubted that Francis Bernardone had courage of heart,
even of the most ordinary manly and military sort; and a time was to
come when there was quite as little doubt about the holiness and the
grace of God. But I think that if there was one thing about which he
was punctilious, it was punctiliousness. If there was one thing of
which so humble a man could be said to be proud, he was proud of
good manners. Only behind his perfectly natural urbanity were
wider and even wilder possibilities, of which we get the first flash in
this trivial incident. Anyhow Francis was evidently torn two ways
with the botheration of two talkers, but finished his business with
the merchant somehow; and when he had finished it, found the beggar was gone. Francis leapt from his booth, left all the bales of velvet
and embroidery behind him apparently unprotected, and went rac-
ing across the market-place like an arrow from the bow. Still running, he threaded the labyrinth of the narrow and crooked streets of
the little town, looking for his beggar, whom he eventually discovered; and loaded that astonished mendicant with money. Then
he straightened himself, so to speak, and swore before God that he
would never all his life refuse help to a poor man. The sweeping simplicity of this undertaking is extremely characteristic. Never was any
man so little afraid of his own promises. His life was one riot of rash
vows; of rash vows that turned out right.

The first biographers of Francis, naturally alive with the great religious revolution that he wrought, equally naturally looked back to
his first years chiefly for omens and signs of such a spiritual earthquake. But writing at a greater distance, we shall not decrease that
dramatic effect, but rather increase it, if we realise that there was not

at this time any external sign of anything particularly mystical about the young man. He had not anything of that early sense of his vocation that has belonged to some of the saints. Over and above his main ambition to win fame as a French poet, he would seem to have most often thought of winning fame as a soldier. He was born kind; he was brave in the normal boyish fashion; but he drew the line both in kindness and bravery pretty well where most boys would have drawn it; for instance, he had the human horror of leprosy of which few normal people felt any need to be ashamed. He had the love of gay and bright apparel which was inherent in the heraldic taste of medieval times and seems altogether to have been rather a festive figure. If he did not paint the town red, he would probably have preferred to paint it all the colours of the rainbow, as in a medieval picture. But in this story of the young man in gay garments scampering after the vanishing beggar in rags there are certain notes of his natural individuality that must be assumed from first to last.

For instance, there is the spirit of swiftness. In a sense he continued running for the rest of his life, as he ran after the beggar. Because nearly all the errands he ran on were errands of mercy, there appeared in his portraiture a mere element of mildness which was true in the truest sense, but is easily misunderstood. A certain precipitancy was the very poise of his soul. This saint should be represented among the other saints as angels were sometimes represented in pictures of angels; with flying feet or even with feathers; in the spirit of the text that makes angels winds and messengers a flaming fire. It is a curiosity of language that courage actually means running; and some of our sceptics will no doubt demonstrate that courage really means running away. But his courage was running, in the sense of rushing. With all his gentleness, there was originally something of impatience in his impetuosity. The psychological truth about it illustrates very well the modern muddle about the word "practical." If we mean by what is practical what is most immediately practicable, we mean merely what is easiest. In that sense St. Francis was very impractical, and his ultimate aims were very unworldly. But if we mean by practicality a preference for prompt effort and energy over doubt or delay, he was very practical indeed. Some might call him a madman, but he was the very reverse of a dreamer. Nobody would be likely to call him a man of business; but he was very emphatically a man of action. In some of his early experiments he was rather too much of a man of action; he acted too soon and was too practical to be prudent. But at every turn of his extraordinary career we shall find him flinging himself round corners in the most unexpected fashion, as when he flew through the crooked streets after the beggar.

Another element implied in the story, which was already partially a natural instinct, before it became a supernatural ideal, was something that had never perhaps been wholly lost in those little republics of medieval Italy. It was something very puzzling to some people; something clearer as a rule to Southerners than to Northerners, and I think to Catholics than to Protestants; the quite natural assumption of the equality of men. It has nothing necessarily to do with the Franciscan love for men; on the contrary one of its merely practical tests is the equality of the duel. Perhaps a gentleman will never be fully an egalitarian until he can really quarrel with his servant. But it was an antecedent condition of the Franciscan brotherhood; and we feel it in this early and secular incident. Francis, I fancy, felt a real doubt about which he must attend to, the beggar or the merchant; and having attended to the merchant, he turned to attend to the beggar; he thought of them as two men. This is a thing much more difficult to describe, in a society from which it is absent, but it was the original basis of the whole business; it was why the popular movement arose in that sort of place and that sort of man. His imaginative magnanimity afterwards rose like a tower to starry heights that might well seem dizzy and even crazy; but it was founded on this high table-land of human equality.

I have taken this the first among a hundred tales of the youth of St. Francis, and dwelt on its significance a little, because until we have learned to look for the significance there will often seem to be little but a sort of light sentiment in telling the story. St. Francis is not a proper person to be patronised with merely "pretty" stories. There are any number of them; but they are too often used so as to be a sort of sentimental sediment of the medieval world, instead of being, as the saint emphatically is, a challenge to the modern world.

We must take his real human development somewhat more seriously; and the next story in which we get a real glimpse of it is in a very different setting. But in exactly the same way it opens, as if by accident, certain abysses of the mind and perhaps of the unconscious mind. Francis still looks more or less like an ordinary young man; and it is only when we look at him as an ordinary young man, that we realise what an extraordinary young man he must be.

War had broken out between Assisi and Perugia. It is now fashionable to say in a satirical spirit that such wars did not so much break out as go on indefinitely between the city-states of medieval Italy. It will be enough to say here that if one of these medieval wars had really gone on without stopping for a century, it might possibly have come within a remote distance of killing as many people as we kill in a year, in one of our great modern scientific wars between our great modern industrial empires. But the citizens of the medieval republic were certainly under the limitation of only being asked to die for the things with which they had always lived, the houses they inhabited, the shrines they venerated and the rulers and representatives they knew; and had not the larger vision calling them to die for the latest rumours about remote colonies as reported in anonymous newspapers. And if we infer from our own experience that war paralysed civilisation, we must at least admit that these warring towns turned out a number of paralytics who go by the names of Dante and Michael Angelo, Aristo and Titian, Leonardo and Columbus, not to mention Catherine of Siena and the subject of this story. While we lament all this local patriotism as a hubbub of the Dark Ages, it must seem a rather curious fact that about three quarters of the greatest men who ever lived came out of these little towns and were often engaged in these little wars. It remains to be seen what will ultimately come out of our large towns; but there has been no sign of anything of this sort since they became large; and I have sometimes been haunted by a fancy of my youth, that these things will not come till there is a city wall round Clapham and the tocsin is rung at night to arm the citizens of Wimbledon.

Anyhow, the tocsin was rung in Assisi and the citizens armed, and among them Francis the son of the cloth merchant. He went out to fight with some company of lancers and in some fight or foray or other he and his little band were taken prisoners. To me it seems most probable that there had been some tale of treason or cowardice about the disaster; for we are told that there was one of the captives with whom his fellow-prisoners flatly refused to associate even in prison; and when this happens in such circumstances, it is generally because the military blame for the surrender is thrown on some individual. Anyhow, somebody noted a small but curious thing, though it might seem rather negative than positive. Francis, we are told, moved among his captive companions with all his characteristic courtesy and even conviviality, "liberal and hilarious" as somebody said of him, resolved to keep up their spirits and his own. And when he came across the mysterious outcast, traitor or coward or whatever he was called, he simply treated him exactly like all the rest, neither with coldness nor compassion, but with the same unaffected gaiety and good fellowship. But if there had been present in that prison someone with a sort of second sight about the truth and trend of spiritual things, he might have known he was in the presence of something new and seemingly almost anarchic; a deep tide driving out to uncharted seas of charity. For in this sense there was really something wanting in Francis of Assisi, something to which he was blind that he might see better and more beautiful things. All those limits in good fellowship and good form, all those landmarks of social life that divide the tolerable and the intolerable, all those social scruples and conventional conditions that are normal and even noble in ordinary men, all those things that hold many decent societies together, could never hold this man at all. He liked as he liked; he seems to have liked everybody, but especially those whom everybody disliked him for liking. Something very vast and universal was already present in that narrow dungeon; and such a seer might have seen in its darkness that red halo of *caritas caritatum* which marks one saint among saints as well as among men. He might have heard the first whisper of that wild blessing that afterwards took the form of a blasphemy; "He listens to those to whom God himself will not listen."

But though such a seer might have seen such a truth, it is exceedingly doubtful if Francis himself saw it. He had acted out of an unconscious largeness, or in the fine medieval phrase largesse, within himself, something that might almost have been lawless if it had not been reaching out to a more divine law; but it is doubtful whether he yet knew that the law was divine. It is evident that he had not at this time any notion of abandoning the military, still less of adopting the monastic life. It is true that there is not, as pacifists and prigs imagine, the least inconsistency between loving men and fighting them, if we fight them fairly and for a good cause. But it seems to me that there was more than this involved; that the mind of the young man was really running towards a military morality in any case. About this time the first calamity crossed his path in the form of a malady which was to revisit him many times and hamper his headlong career. Sickness made him more serious; but one fancies it would only have made him a more serious soldier, or even more serious about soldiering. And while he was recovering, something rather larger than the little feuds and raids of the Italian towns opened an avenue of adventure and ambition. The crown of Sicily, a considerable centre of controversy at the time, was apparently claimed by a certain Gauthier de Brienne, and the Papal cause to aid which Gauthier was called in aroused enthusiasm among a number of young Assisians, including Francis, who proposed to march into Apulia on the count's behalf; perhaps his French name had something to do with it. For it must never be forgotten that though that world was in one sense a world of little things, it was a world of little things concerned about great things. There was more internationalism in the lands dotted with tiny republics than in the huge homogeneous impenetrable national divisions of to-day. The legal authority of the Assisian magistrates might hardly reach further than a bow-shot from their high embattled city walls. But their sympathies might be with the ride of the Normans through Sicily or the palace of the Troubadours at Toulouse; with the Emperor throned in the German forests or the great Pope[1] dying in the exile of Salerno. Above all, it must be remembered that when the interests of an

[1] See Chapter II, footnote 3, page 43.

age are mainly religious they must be universal. Nothing can be
more universal than the universe. And there are several things about
the religious position at that particular moment which modern people
not unnaturally fail to realise. For one thing, modern people naturally think of people so remote as ancient people, and even early people. We feel vaguely that these things happened in the first ages of
the Church. The Church was already a good deal more than a thousand years old. That is, the Church was then rather older than
France is now, a great deal older than England is now. And she
looked old then; almost as old as she does now; possibly older than
she does now. The Church looked like great Charlemagne with the
long white beard, who had already fought a hundred wars with the
heathen, and in the legend was bidden by an angel to go forth and
fight once more though he was two hundred years old. The Church
had topped her thousand years and turned the corner of the second
thousand; she had come through the Dark Ages in which nothing
could be done except desperate fighting against the barbarians and
the stubborn repetition of the creed. The creed was still being
repeated after the victory or escape; but it is not unnatural to suppose that there was something a little monotonous about the repetition. The Church looked old then as now; and there were some who
thought her dying then as now. In truth orthodoxy was not dead
but it may have been dull; it is certain that some people began to
think it dull. The Troubadours of the Provençal movement had
already begun to take that turn or twist towards Oriental fancies
and the paradox of pessimism, which always come to Europeans as
something fresh when their own sanity seems to be something stale.
It is likely enough that after all those centuries of hopeless war
without and ruthless asceticism within, the official orthodoxy
seemed to be something stale. The freshness and freedom of the first
Christians seemed then as much as now a lost and almost prehistoric
age of gold. Rome was still more rational than anything else; the
Church was really wiser but it may well have seemed wearier than
the world. There was something more adventurous and alluring,
perhaps, about the mad metaphysics that had been blown across out
of Asia. Dreams were gathering like dark clouds over the Midi to

break in a thunder of anathema and civil war. Only the light lay on the great plain round Rome; but the light was blank and the plain was flat; and there was no stir in the still air and the immemorial silence about the sacred town.

High in the dark house of Assisi Francesco Bernardone slept and dreamed of arms. There came to him in the darkness a vision splendid with swords, patterned after the cross in the Crusading fashion, of spears and shields and helmets hung in a high armoury, all bearing the sacred sign. When he awoke he accepted the dream as a trumpet bidding him to the battlefield, and rushed out to take horse and arms. He delighted in all the exercises of chivalry; and was evidently an accomplished cavalier and fighting man by the tests of the tournament and the camp. He would doubtless at any time have preferred a Christian sort of chivalry; but it seems clear that he was also in a mood which thirsted for glory, though in him that glory would always have been identical with honour. He was not without some vision of that wreath of laurel which Caesar has left for all the Latins. As he rode out to war the great gate in the deep wall of Assisi resounded with his last boast, "I shall come back a great prince."

A little way along his road his sickness rose again and threw him. It seems highly probable, in the light of his impetuous temper, that he had ridden away long before he was fit to move. And in the darkness of this second and far more desolating interruption, he seems to have had another dream in which a voice said to him, "You have mistaken the meaning of the vision. Return to your own town." And Francis trailed back in his sickness to Assisi, a very dismal and disappointed and perhaps even derided figure, with nothing to do but to wait for what should happen next. It was his first descent into a dark ravine that is called the valley of humiliation, which seemed to him very rocky and desolate, but in which he was afterwards to find many flowers.

But he was not only disappointed and humiliated; he was also very much puzzled and bewildered. He still firmly believed that his two dreams must have meant something; and he could not imagine what they could possibly mean. It was while he was drifting, one may even say mooning, about the streets of Assisi and the fields outside the city wall, that an incident occurred to him which has not always been immediately connected with the business of the dreams, but which seems to me the obvious culmination of them. He was riding listlessly in some wayside place, apparently in the open country, when he saw a figure coming along the road towards him and halted; for he saw it was a leper. And he knew instantly that his courage was challenged, not as the world challenges, but as one would challenge who knew the secrets of the heart of a man. What he saw advancing was not the banner and spears of Perugia, from which it never occurred to him to shrink; not the armies that fought for the crown of Sicily, of which he had always thought as a courageous man thinks of mere vulgar danger. Francis Bernardone saw his fear coming up the road towards him; the fear that comes from within and not without; though it stood white and horrible in the sunlight. For once in the long rush of his life his soul must have stood still. Then he sprang from his horse, knowing nothing between stillness and swiftness, and rushed on the leper and threw his arms round him. It was the beginning of a long vocation of ministry among many lepers, for whom he did many services; to this man he gave what money he could and mounted and rode on. We do not know how far he rode, or with what sense of the things around him; but it is said that when he looked back, he could see no figure on the road.

IV

FRANCIS THE BUILDER

We have now reached the great break in the life of Francis of Assisi; the point at which something happened to him that must remain greatly dark to most of us, who are ordinary and selfish men whom God has not broken to make anew.

In dealing with this difficult passage, especially for my own purpose of making things moderately easy for the more secular sympathiser, I have hesitated as to the proper course; and have eventually decided to state first of all what happened, with little more than a hint of what I imagine to have been the meaning of what happened. The fuller meaning may be debated more easily afterwards, when it was unfolded in the full Franciscan life. Anyhow what happened was this. The story very largely revolves round the ruins of the Church of St. Damian, an old shrine in Assisi which was apparently neglected and falling to pieces. Here Francis was in the habit of praying before the crucifix during these dark and aimless days of transition that followed the tragical collapse of all his military ambitions, probably made bitter by some loss of social prestige terrible to his sensitive spirit. As he did so he heard a voice saying to him, "Francis, seest thou not that my house is in ruins? Go and restore it for me."

Francis sprang up and went. To go and do something was one of the driving demands of his nature; probably he had gone and done it before he had at all thoroughly thought out what he had done. In any case what he had done was something very decisive and immediately very disastrous for his singular social career. In the coarse conventional language of the uncomprehending world, he stole. From his own enthusiastic point of view, he extended to his venerable father Peter Bernardone the exquisite excitement and inestimable privilege of assisting, more or less unconsciously, in the rebuilding of St. Damian's Church. In point of fact what he did was first to sell his own horse and then to go off and sell several bales of his father's cloth, making the sign of the cross over them to indicate their pious and charitable destination. Peter Bernardone did not see things in this light. Peter Bernardone indeed had not very much light to see by, so far as understanding the genius and temperament of his extraordinary son was concerned. Instead of understanding in what sort of a wind and flame of abstract appetites the lad was living, instead of simply telling him (as the priest practically did later) that he had done an indefensible thing with the best intentions, old Bernardone took up the matter in the hardest style; in a legal and literal fashion. He used absolute political powers like a heathen father, and himself put his son under lock and key as a vulgar thief. It would appear that the cry was caught up among many with whom the unlucky Francis had once been popular; and altogether, in his efforts to build up the house of God he had only succeeded in bringing his own house about his ears and lying buried under the ruins. The quarrel dragged drearily through several stages; at one time the wretched young man seems to have disappeared underground, so to speak, into some cavern or cellar where he remained huddled hopelessly in the darkness. Anyhow, it was his blackest moment; the whole world had turned over; the whole world was on top of him.

When he came out, it was only perhaps gradually that anybody grasped that something had happened. He and his father were summoned in the court of the bishop; for Francis had refused the authority of all legal tribunals. The bishop addressed some remarks to him, full of that excellent common sense which the Catholic Church keeps permanently as the background for all the fiery attitudes of her saints. He told Francis that he must unquestionably restore the money to his father; that no blessing could follow a good work done by unjust methods; and in short (to put it crudely) if the young fanatic would give back his money to the old fool, the incident would then terminate. There was a new air about Francis. He was no longer crushed, still less crawling, so far as his father was concerned; yet his words do not, I think, indicate either just indignation or wanton insult or anything in the nature of a mere continuation of the quarrel. They are rather remotely akin to mysterious utterances of his great model, "What have I to do with thee?" or even the terrible "Touch me not."

He stood up before them all and said, "Up to this time I have called Pietro Bernardone father, but now I am the servant of God. Not only the money but everything that can be called his I will restore to my father, even the very clothes he has given me." And he rent off all his garments except one; and they saw that that was a hair-shirt.

He piled the garments in a heap on the floor and tossed the money on top of them. Then he turned to the bishop, and received his blessing, like one who turns his back on society; and, according to the account, went out as he was into the cold world. Apparently it was literally a cold world at the moment, and snow was on the ground. A curious detail, very deep in its significance, I fancy, is given in the same account of this great crisis in his life. He went out half-naked in his hair-shirt into the winter woods, walking the frozen ground between the frosty trees; a man without a father. He was penniless, he was parentless, he was to all appearance without a trade or a plan or a hope in the world; and as he went under the frosty trees, he burst suddenly into song.

It was apparently noted as remarkable that the language in which he sang was French, or that Provençal which was called for convenience French. It was not his native language; and it was in his native language that he ultimately won fame as a poet; indeed St. Francis is one of the very first of the national poets in the purely national dialects of Europe. But it was the language with which all his most boyish ardours and ambitions had been identified; it was for him pre-eminently the language of romance. That it broke from him in this extraordinary extremity seems to me something at first sight very strange and in the last analysis very significant. What that significance was, or may well have been, I will try to suggest in the subsequent chapter; it is enough to indicate here that the whole philosophy of St. Francis revolved round the idea of a new supernatural light on natural things, which meant the ultimate recovery not the ultimate refusal of natural things. And for the purpose of this purely narrative part of the business, it is enough to record that while he wandered in the winter forest in his hair-shirt, like the very wildest of the hermits, he sang in the tongue of the Troubadours.

Meanwhile the narrative naturally reverts to the problem of the ruined or at least neglected church, which had been the starting point of the saint's innocent crime and beatific punishment. That problem still predominated in his mind and was soon engaging his insatiable activities; but they were activities of a new sort; and he made no more attempts to interfere with the commercial ethics of the town of Assisi. There had dawned on him one of those great paradoxes that are also platitudes. He realised that the way to build a church is not to become entangled in bargains and, to him, rather bewildering questions of legal claim. The way to build a church is not to pay for it, certainly not with somebody else's money. The way to build a church is not even to pay for it with your own money. The way to build a church is to build it.

He went about by himself collecting stones. He begged all the people he met to give him stones. In fact he became a new sort of beggar, reversing the parable; a beggar who asks not for bread but a stone. Probably, as happened to him again and again throughout his extraordinary existence, the very queerness of the request gave it a sort of popularity; and all sorts of idle and luxurious people fell in with the benevolent project, as they would have done with a bet. He worked with his own hands at the rebuilding of the church, dragging the material like a beast of burden and learning the very last and lowest lessons of toil. A vast number of stories are told about Francis at this as at every other period of his life; but for the purpose here, which is one of simplification, it is best to dwell on this definite re-entrance of the saint into the world by the low gate of manual labour. There does indeed run through the whole of his life a sort of double meaning, like his shadow thrown upon the wall. All his action had something of the character of an allegory; and it is likely enough that some leaden-witted scientific historian may some day try to prove that he himself was never anything but an allegory. It is true enough in this sense that he was labouring at a double task, and rebuilding something else as well as the church of St. Damian. He was not only discovering the general lesson that his glory was not to be in overthrowing men in battle but in building up the positive and creative monuments of peace. He was truly building up something else, or beginning to build it up; something that has often enough fallen into ruin but has never been past rebuilding; a church that could always be built anew though it had rotted away to its first foundation-stone, against which the gates of hell shall not prevail.

The next stage in his progress is probably marked by his transferring the same energies of architectural reconstruction to the little church of St. Mary of the Angels at the Portiuncula. He had already done something of the same kind at a church dedicated to St. Peter; and that quality in his life noted above, which made it seem like a symbolical drama, led many of his most devout biographers to note the numerical symbolism of the three churches. There was at any rate a more historical and practical symbolism about two of them. For the original church of St. Damian afterwards became the seat of his striking experiment of a female order, and of the pure and spiritual romance of St. Clare. And the church of the Portiuncula will remain for ever as one of the great historic buildings of the world; for it was there that he gathered the little knot of friends and enthusiasts; it was the home of many homeless men. At this time, however, it is not clear that he had the definite idea of any such monastic developments. How early the plan appeared in his own mind it is of course impossible to say; but on the face of events it first takes the form of a few friends who attached themselves to him one by one because they shared his own passion for simplicity. The account given of the form of their dedication is, however, very significant; for it was that of an invocation of the simplification of life as suggested in the New Testament. The adoration of Christ had been a part of the man's passionate nature for a long time past. But the imitation of Christ, as a sort of plan or ordered scheme of life, may in that sense be said to begin here.

The two men who have the credit, apparently, of having first perceived something of what was happening in the world of the soul were a solid and wealthy citizen named Bernard of Quintavalle and a canon from a neighbouring church named Peter. It is the more to their credit because Francis, if one may put it so, was by this time wallowing in poverty and association with lepers and ragged mendicants; and these two were men with much to give up; the one of comforts in the world and the other of ambition in the Church. Bernard the rich burgher did quite literally and finally sell all he had and give to the poor. Peter did even more; for he descended from a chair of spiritual authority, probably when he was already a man of mature years and therefore of fixed mental habits, to follow an extravagant young eccentric whom most people probably regarded as a maniac. What it was of which they had caught a glimpse, of which Francis had seen the glory, may be suggested later so far as it can be suggested at all. At this stage we need profess to see no more than all Assisi saw, and that something not altogether unworthy of comment. The citizens of Assisi only saw the camel go in triumph through the eye of the needle and God doing impossible things because to him all things were possible; only a priest who rent his robes like the Publican and not like the Pharisee and a rich man who went away joyful, for he had no possessions.

These three strange figures are said to have built themselves a sort of hut or den adjoining the leper hospital. There they talked to each other, in the intervals of drudgery and danger (for it needed ten times more courage to look after a leper than to fight for the crown of Sicily), in the terms of their new life, almost like children talking a secret language. Of these individual elements on their first friendship we can say little with certainty; but it is certain that they remained friends to the end. Bernard of Quintavalle occupies in the story something of the position of Sir Bedivere, "first made and latest left of Arthur's knights," for he reappears again at the right hand of the saint on his deathbed and receives some sort of special blessing. But all those things belong to another historical world and were quite remote from the ragged and fantastic trio in their tumble-down hut. They were not monks except perhaps in the most literal and archaic sense which was identical with hermits. They were, so to speak, three solitaries living together socially, but not as a society. The whole thing seems to have been intensely individual, as seen from the outside doubtless individual to the point of insanity. The stir of something that had in it the promise of a movement or a mission can first be felt as I have said in the affair of the appeal to the New Testament.

It was a sort of *sors virgiliana* applied to the Bible; a practice not unknown among Protestants though open to their criticism, one would think, as being rather a superstition of pagans. Anyhow it seems almost the opposite of searching the Scriptures to open them at random; but St. Francis certainly opened them at random. According to one story, he merely made the sign of the cross over the volume of the Gospel and opened it at three places reading three texts. The first was the tale of the rich young man whose refusal to sell all his goods was the occasion of the great paradox about the camel and the needle. The second was the commandment to the disciples to take nothing with them on their journey, neither scrip nor staff nor any money. The third was that saying, literally to be called crucial, that the follower of Christ must also carry his cross. There is a somewhat similar story of Francis finding one of these texts, almost as accidentally, merely in listening to what happened to be the Gospel of the day. But from the former version at least it would seem that the incident occurred very early indeed in his new life, perhaps soon after his breach with his father; for it was after this oracle, apparently, that Bernard the first disciple rushed forth and scattered all his goods among the poor. If this be so, it would seem that nothing followed it for the moment except the individual ascetical life with the hut for a hermitage. It must of course have been a rather public sort of hermitage, but it was none the less in a very real sense withdrawn from the world. St. Simeon Stylites on the top of his pillar was in one sense an exceedingly public character; but there was something a little singular in his situation for all that. It may be presumed that most people thought the situation of Francis singular, that some even thought it too singular. There was inevitably indeed in any Catholic society something ultimate and even subconscious that was at least capable of comprehending it better than a pagan or puritan society could comprehend it. But we must not at this stage, I think, exaggerate this potential public sympathy. As has already been suggested, the Church and all its institutions had already the air of being old and settled and sensible things, the monastic institutions among the rest. Common sense was commoner in the Middle Ages, I think, than in our own rather jumpy journalistic age; but men like Francis are not common in any age, nor are they to be fully understood merely by the exercise of common sense. The thirteenth century was certainly a progressive period; perhaps the only really progressive period in human history. But it can truly be called progressive precisely because its progress was very orderly. It is really and truly an example of an epoch of reforms without revolutions. But the reforms were not only progressive but very practical; and they were very much to the advantage of highly practical institutions; the towns and the trading guilds and the manual crafts. Now the solid men of town and guild in the time of Francis of Assisi were probably very solid indeed. They were much more economically equal, they were much more justly governed in their own economic environment, than the moderns who struggle madly between starvation and the monopolist prizes of capitalism; but it is likely enough that the majority of such citizens were as hard-headed as peasants. Certainly the behaviour of the venerable Peter Bernardone does not indicate a delicate sympathy with the fine and almost fanciful subtleties of the Franciscan spirit. And we cannot measure the beauty and originality of this strange spiritual adventure, unless we have the humour and human sympathy to put into plain words how it would have looked to such an unsympathetic person at the time when it happened. In the next chapter I shall make an attempt, inevitably inadequate, to indicate the inside of this story of the building of the three churches and the little hut. In this chapter I have but outlined it from the outside. And in concluding that chapter I ask the reader to remember and realise what that story really looked like, when thus seen from the outside. Given a critic of rather coarse common sense, with no feeling about the incident except annoyance, and how would the story seem to stand?

A young fool or rascal is caught robbing his father and selling goods which he ought to guard; and the only explanation he will offer is that a loud voice from nowhere spoke in his ear and told him to mend the cracks and holes in a particular wall. He then declares himself naturally independent of all powers corresponding to the police or the magistrates, and takes refuge with an amiable bishop who is forced to remonstrate with him and tell him he is wrong. He then proceeds to take off his clothes in public and practically throw them at his father; announcing at the same time that his father is not his father at all. He then runs about the town asking everybody he meets to give him fragments of buildings or building materials, apparently with reference to his old monomania about mending the wall. It may be an excellent thing that cracks should be filled up, but preferably not by somebody who is himself cracked; and architectural restoration like other things is not best performed by builders who, as we should say, have a tile loose. Finally the wretched youth relapses into rags and squalor and practically crawls away into the gutter. That is the spectacle that Francis must have presented to a very large number of his neighbours and friends.

How he lived at all must have seemed to them dubious; but presumably he already begged for bread as he had begged for building materials. But he was always very careful to beg for the blackest or worst bread he could get, for the stalest crusts or something rather less luxurious than the crumbs which the dogs eat, and which fall from the rich man's table. Thus he probably fared worse than an ordinary beggar; for the beggar would eat the best he could get and the saint ate the worst he could get. In plain fact he was ready to live on refuse; and it was probably something much uglier as an experience than the refined simplicity which vegetarians and waterdrinkers would call the simple life. As he dealt with the question of food, so he apparently dealt with the question of clothing. He dealt with it, that is, upon the same principle of taking what he could get, and not even the best of what he could get. According to one story he changed clothes with a beggar; and he would doubtless have been content to change them with a scarecrow. In another version he got hold of the rough brown tunic of a peasant, but presumably only because the peasant gave him his very oldest brown tunic, which was probably very old indeed. Most peasants have few changes of clothing to give away; and some peasants are not specially inclined to give them away until it is absolutely necessary. It is said that in place of the girdle which he had flung off (perhaps with the more symbolic scorn because it probably carried the purse or wallet by the fashion of the period) he picked up a rope more or less at random, because it was lying near, and tied it round his waist. He undoubtedly meant it as a shabby expedient; rather as the very destitute tramp will sometimes tie his clothes together with a piece of string. He meant to strike the note of collecting his clothes anyhow, like rags from a succession of dust-bins. Ten years later that make-shift costume was the uniform of five thousand men; and a hundred years later, in that, for a pontifical panoply, they laid great Dante in the grave.

V

LE JONGLEUR DE DIEU

Many signs and symbols might be used to give a hint of what really happened in the mind of the young poet of Assisi. Indeed they are at once too numerous for selection and yet too slight for satisfaction. But one of them may be adumbrated in this small and apparently accidental fact: that when he and his secular companions carried their pageant of poetry through the town, they called themselves Troubadours. But when he and his spiritual companions came out to do their spiritual work in the world, they were called by their leader the Jongleurs de Dieu.

Nothing has been said here at any length of the great culture of the Troubadours as it appeared in Provence or Languedoc, great as was their influence in history and their influence on St. Francis. Something more may be said of them when we come to summarise his relation to history; it is enough to note here in a few sentences the facts about them that were relevant to him, and especially the particular point now in question, which was the most relevant of all. Everybody knows who the Troubadours were; everybody knows that very early in the Middle Ages, in the twelfth and early thirteenth centuries, there arose a civilisation in Southern France which threatened to rival or eclipse the rising tradition of Paris. Its chief product was a school of poetry, or rather more especially a school of poets. They were primarily love-poets, though they were often also satirists and critics of things in general. Their picturesque posture in history is largely due to the fact that they sang their own poems and often played their own accompaniments, on the light musical instruments of the period; they were minstrels as well as men of letters. Allied to their love-poetry were other institutions of a decorative and fanciful kind concerned with the same theme. There was what was called the "Gay Science," the attempt to reduce to a sort of system the fine shades of flirtation and philandering. There were the things called Courts of Love, in which the same delicate subjects were dealt with with legal pomp and pedantry. There is one point in this part of the business that must be remembered in relation to St. Francis. There were manifest moral dangers in all this superb sentimentalism; but it is a mistake to suppose that its only danger of exaggeration was in the direction of sensualism. There was a strain in the southern romance that was actually an excess of spirituality; just as the pessimist heresy it produced was in one sense an excess of spirituality. The love was not always animal; sometimes it was so airy as to be almost allegorical. The reader realises that the lady is the most beautiful being that can possibly exist, only he has occasional doubts as to whether she does exist. Dante owed something to the Troubadours; and the critical debates about his ideal woman are an excellent example of these doubts. We know that Beatrice was not his wife, but we should in any case be equally sure that she was not his mistress; and some critics have even suggested that she was nothing at all, so to speak, except his muse. This idea of Beatrice as an allegorical figure is, I believe, unsound; it would seem unsound to any man who has read the *Vita Nuova* and has been in love. But the very fact that it is possible to suggest it illustrates something abstract and scholastic in these medieval passions. But though they were abstract passions they were very passionate passions. These men could feel almost like lovers, even about allegories and abstractions. It is necessary to remember this in order to realise that St. Francis was talking the true language of a troubadour when he said that he also had a most glorious and gracious lady and that her name was Poverty.

But the particular point to be noted here is not concerned so much with the word Troubadour as with the word Jongleur. It is especially concerned with the transition from one to the other; and for this it is necessary to grasp another detail about the poets of the Gay Science. A jongleur was not the same thing as a troubadour, even if the same man were both a troubadour and a jongleur. More often, I believe, they were separate men as well as separate trades. In many cases apparently the two men would walk the world together like companions in arms, or rather companions in arts. The jongleur was properly a joculator or jester; sometimes he was what we should call a juggler.

This is the point, I imagine, of the tale about Taillefer the Jongleur at the battle of Hastings, who sang of the death of Roland while he tossed up his sword and caught it, as a juggler catches balls. Sometimes he may have been even a tumbler; like that acrobat in the beautiful legend who was called "The Tumbler of Our Lady," because he turned head over heels and stood on his head before the image of the Blessed Virgin, for which he was nobly thanked and comforted by her and the whole company of heaven. In the ordinary way, we may imagine, the troubadour would exalt the company with earnest and solemn strains of love and then the jongleur would do his turn as a sort of comic relief. A glorious medieval romance remains to be written about two such companions wandering through the world. At any rate, if there is one place in which the true Franciscan spirit can be found outside the true Franciscan story, it is in that tale of the Tumbler of Our Lady. And when St. Francis called his followers the Jongleurs de Dieu, he meant something very like the Tumblers of Our Lord.

Somewhere in that transition from the ambition of the Troubadour to the antics of the Tumbler is hidden, as under a parable, the truth of St. Francis. Of the two minstrels or entertainers, the jester was presumably the servant or at least the secondary figure. St. Francis really meant what he said when he said he had found the secret of life in being the servant and the secondary figure. There was to be found ultimately in such service a freedom almost amounting to frivolity. It was comparable to the condition of the jongleur because it almost amounted to frivolity. The jester could be free when the knight was rigid; and it was possible to be a jester in the service which is perfect freedom. This parallel of the two poets or minstrels is perhaps the best preliminary and external statement of the Franciscan change of heart, being conceived under an image with which the imagination of the modern world has a certain sympathy. There was, of course, a great deal more than this involved; and we must endeavour however insufficiently to penetrate past the image to the idea. It is so far like the tumblers that it is really to many people a topsy-turvy idea.

Francis, at the time or somewhere about the time when he disappeared into the prison or the dark cavern, underwent a reversal of a

certain psychological kind; which was really like the reversal of a
complete somersault, in that by coming full circle it came back, or
apparently came back, to the same normal posture. It is necessary to
use the grotesque simile of an acrobatic antic, because there is hardly
any other figure that will make the fact clear. But in the inward
sense it was a profound spiritual revolution. The man who went
into the cave was not the man who came out again; in that sense he
was almost as different as if he were dead, as if he were a ghost or a
blessed spirit. And the effects of this on his attitude towards the actual world were really as extravagant as any parallel can make them.
He looked at the world as differently from other men as if he had
come out of that dark hole walking on his hands.

If we apply this parable of Our Lady's Tumbler to the case, we
shall come very near to the point of it. Now it really is a fact that any
scene such as a landscape can sometimes be more clearly and freshly
seen if it is seen upside down. There have been landscape-painters
who adopted the most startling and pantomimic postures in order to
look at it for a moment in that fashion. Thus that inverted vision, so
much more bright and quaint and arresting, does bear a certain resemblance to the world which a mystic like St. Francis sees every
day. But herein is the essential part of the parable. Our Lady's
Tumbler did not stand on his head *in order* to see flowers and trees as
a clearer or quainter vision. He did not do so; and it would never
have occurred to him to do so. Our Lady's Tumbler stood on his
head to please Our Lady. If St. Francis had done the same thing, as
he was quite capable of doing, it would originally have been from the
same motive; a motive of a purely supernatural thought. It would be
after this that his enthusiasm would extend itself and give a sort of
halo to the edges of all earthly things. This is why it is not true to
represent St. Francis as a mere romantic forerunner of the Renaissance and a revival of natural pleasures for their own sake. The
whole point of him was that the secret of recovering the natural
pleasures lay in regarding them in the light of a supernatural pleasure. In other words, he repeated in his own person that historic
process noted in the introductory chapter; the vigil of asceticism
which ends in the vision of a natural world made new. But in the

personal case there was even more than this; there were elements that make the parallel of the Jongleur or Tumbler even more appropriate than this.

It may be suspected that in that black cell or cave Francis passed the blackest hours of his life. By nature he was the sort of man who has that vanity which is the opposite of pride; that vanity which is very near to humility. He never despised his fellow creatures and therefore he never despised the opinion of his fellow creatures; including the admiration of his fellow creatures. All that part of his human nature had suffered the heaviest and most crushing blows. It is possible that after his humiliating return from his frustrated military campaign he was called a coward. It is certain that after his quarrel with his father about the bales of cloth he was called a thief. And even those who had sympathised most with him, the priest whose church he had restored, the bishop whose blessing he had received, had evidently treated him with an almost humorous amiability which left only too clear the ultimate conclusion of the matter. He had made a fool of himself. Any man who has been young, who has ridden horses or thought himself ready for a fight, who has fancied himself as a troubadour and accepted the conventions of comradeship, will appreciate the ponderous and crushing weight of that simple phrase. The conversion of St. Francis, like the conversion of St. Paul, involved his being in some sense flung suddenly from a horse; but in a sense it was an even worse fall; for it was a warhorse. Anyhow, there was not a rag of him left that was not ridiculous. Everybody knew that at the best he had made a fool of himself. It was a solid objective fact, like the stones in the road, that he had made a fool of himself. He saw himself as an object, very small and distinct like a fly walking on a clear window pane; and it was unmistakably a fool. And as he stared at the word "fool" written in luminous letters before him, the word itself began to shine and change.

We used to be told in the nursery that if a man were to bore a hole through the centre of the earth and climb continually down and down, there would come a moment at the centre when he would seem to be climbing up and up. I do not know whether this is true. The reason I do not know whether it is true is that I never happened to bore a hole through the centre of the earth, still less to crawl through it. If I do not know what this reversal or inversion feels like, it is because I have never been there. And this also is an allegory. It is certain that the writer, it is even possible that the reader, is an ordinary person who has never been there. We cannot follow St. Francis to that final spiritual overturn in which complete humiliation becomes complete holiness or happiness, because we have never been there. I for one do not profess to follow it any further than that first breaking down of the romantic barricades of boyish vanity, which I have suggested in the last paragraph. And even that paragraph, of course, is merely conjectural, an individual guess at what he may have felt; but he may have felt something quite different. But whatever else it was, it was so far analogous to the story of the man making a tunnel through the earth that it did mean a man going down and down until at some mysterious moment he begins to go up and up. We have never gone up like that because we have never gone down like that; we are obviously incapable of saying that it does not happen; and the more candidly and calmly we read human history, and especially the history of the wisest men, the more we shall come to the conclusion that it does happen. Of the intrinsic internal essence of the experience I make no pretence of writing at all. But the external effect of it, for the purpose of this narrative, may be expressed by saying that when Francis came forth from his cave of vision, he was wearing the same word "fool" as a feather in his cap; as a crest or even a crown. He would go on being a fool; he would become more and more of a fool; he would be the court fool of the King of Paradise.

This state can only be represented in symbol; but the symbol of inversion is true in another way. If a man saw the world upside down, with all the trees and towers hanging head downwards as in a pool, one effect would be to emphasise the idea *of dependence*. There is a Latin and literal connection; for the very word dependence only means hanging. It would make vivid the Scriptural text which says that God has hanged the world upon nothing. If St. Francis had seen, in one of his strange dreams, the town of Assisi upside down, it need not have differed in a single detail from itself except in being entirely the other way round. But the point is this: that whereas to the normal eye the large masonry of its walls or the massive foundations of its watchtowers and its high citadel would make it seem safer and more permanent, the moment it was turned over the very same weight would make it seem more helpless and more in peril. It is but a symbol; but it happens to fit the psychological fact. St. Francis might love his little town as much as before, or more than before; but the nature of the love would be altered even in being increased. He might see and love every tile on the steep roofs or every bird on the battlements; but he would see them all in a new and divine light of eternal danger and dependence. Instead of being merely proud of his strong city because it could not be moved, he would be thankful to God Almighty that it had not been dropped; he would be thankful to God for not dropping the whole cosmos like a vast crystal to be shattered into falling stars. Perhaps St. Peter saw the world so, when he was crucified head-downwards.

It is commonly in a somewhat cynical sense that men have said, "Blessed is he that expecteth nothing, for he shall not be disappointed." It was in a wholly happy and enthusiastic sense that St. Francis said, "Blessed is he who expecteth nothing, for he shall enjoy everything." It was by this deliberate idea of starting from zero, from the dark nothingness of his own deserts, that he did come to enjoy even earthly things as few people have enjoyed them; and they are in themselves the best working example of the idea. For there is no way in which a man can earn a star or deserve a sunset. But there is more than this involved, and more indeed than is easily to be expressed in words. It is not only true that the less a man thinks of himself, the more he thinks of his good luck and of all the gifts of God. It is also true that he sees more of the things themselves when he sees more of their origin; for their origin is a part of them and indeed the most important part of them. Thus they become more extraordinary by being explained. He has more wonder at them but less fear of them; for a thing is really wonderful when it is significant and not when it is insignificant; and a monster, shapeless or dumb or merely destructive, may be larger than the mountains, but is still in a literal sense insignificant. For a mystic like St. Francis the monsters had a meaning; that is, they had delivered their message. They spoke no longer in an unknown tongue. That is the meaning of all those stories, whether legendary or historical, in which he appears as a magician speaking the language of beasts and birds. The mystic will have nothing to do with mere mystery; mere mystery is generally a mystery of iniquity.

The transition from the good man to the saint is a sort of revolution; by which one for whom all things illustrate and illuminate God becomes one for whom God illustrates and illuminates all things. It is rather like the reversal whereby a lover might say at first sight that a lady looked like a flower, and say afterwards that all flowers reminded him of his lady. A saint and a poet standing by the same flower might seem to say the same thing; but indeed though they would both be telling the truth, they would be telling different truths. For one the joy of life is a cause of faith, for the other rather a result of faith. But one effect of the difference is that the sense of a divine dependence, which for the artist is like the brilliant levin-blaze, for the saint is like the broad daylight. Being in some mystical sense on the other side of things, he sees things go forth from the divine as children going forth from a familiar and accepted home, instead of meeting them as they come out, as most of us do, upon the roads of the world. And it is the paradox that by this privilege he is more familiar, more free and fraternal, more carelessly hospitable than we. For us the elements are like heralds who tell us with trumpet and tabard that we are drawing near the city of a great king; but he hails them with an old familiarity that is almost an old frivolity. He calls them his Brother Fire and his Sister Water.

So arises out of this almost nihilistic abyss the noble thing that is called Praise; which no one will ever understand while he identifies it with nature-worship or pantheistic optimism. When we say that a poet praises the whole creation, we commonly mean only that he praises the whole cosmos. But this sort of poet does really praise creation, in the sense of the act of creation. He praises the passage or transition from nonentity to entity; there falls here also the shadow of that archetypal image of the bridge, which has given to the priest his archaic and mysterious name. The mystic who passes through the moment when there is nothing but God does in some sense behold the beginningless beginnings in which there was really nothing else. He not only appreciates everything but the nothing of which everything was made. In a fashion he endures and answers even the earthquake irony of the Book of Job; in some sense he is there when the foundations of the world are laid, with the morning stars singing together and the sons of God shouting for joy. That is but a distant adumbration of the reason why the Franciscan, ragged, penniless, homeless and apparently hopeless, did indeed come forth singing such songs as might come from the stars of morning; and shouting, a son of God.

This sense of the great gratitude and the sublime dependence was not a phrase or even a sentiment; it is the whole point that this was the very rock of reality. It was not a fancy but a fact; rather it is true that beside it all facts are fancies. That we all depend in every detail, at every instant, as a Christian would say upon God, as even an agnostic would say upon existence and the nature of things, is not an illusion of imagination; on the contrary, it is the fundamental fact which we cover up, as with curtains, with the illusion of ordinary life. That ordinary life is an admirable thing in itself, just as imagination is an admirable thing in itself. But it is much more the ordinary life that is made of imagination than the contemplative life. He who has seen the whole world hanging on a hair of the mercy of God has seen the truth; we might almost say the cold truth. He who has seen the vision of his city upside-down has seen it the right way up.

Rossetti makes the remark somewhere, bitterly but with great truth, that the worst moment for the atheist is when he is really thankful and has nobody to thank. The converse of this proposition is also true; and it is certain that this gratitude produced, in such men as we are here considering, the most purely joyful moments that have been known to man. The great painter boasted that he mixed all his colours with brains, and the great saint may be said to mix all his thoughts with thanks. All goods look better when they look like gifts. In this sense it is certain that the mystical method establishes a very healthy external relation to everything else. But it must always be remembered that everything else has for ever fallen

into a second place, in comparison with this simple fact of dependence on the divine reality. In so far as ordinary social relations have
in them something that seems solid and self-supporting, some sense
of being at once buttressed and cushioned; in so far as they establish
sanity in the sense of security and security in the sense of self-sufficiency, the man who has seen the world hanging on a hair does
have some difficulty in taking them so seriously as that. In so far as
even the secular authorities and hierarchies, even the most natural
superiorities and the most necessary subordinations, tend at once to
put a man in his place, and to make him sure of his position, the man
who has seen the human hierarchy upside down will always have
something of a smile for its superiorities. In this sense the direct vision of divine reality does disturb solemnities that are sane enough in
themselves. The mystic may have added a cubit to his stature; but he
generally loses something of his status. He can no longer take himself for granted, merely because he can verify his own existence in a
parish register or a family Bible. Such a man may have something of
the appearance of the lunatic who has lost his name while preserving
his nature; who straightway forgets what manner of man he was.
"Hitherto I have called Pietro Bernardone father; but now I am the
servant of God."

All these profound matters must be suggested in short and imperfect phrases; and the shortest statement of one aspect of this illum-
ination is to say that it is the discovery of an infinite debt. It may
seem a paradox to say that a man may be transported with joy to discover that he is in debt. But this is only because in commercial cases
the creditor does not generally share the transports of joy; especially
when the debt is by hypothesis infinite and therefore unrecoverable.
But here again the parallel of a natural love-story of the nobler sort
disposes of the difficulty in a flash. There the infinite creditor does
share the joy of the infinite debtor; for indeed they are both debtors
and both creditors. In other words debt and dependence do become
pleasures in the presence of unspoilt love; the word is used too
loosely and luxuriously in popular simplifications like the present;
but here the word is really the key. It is the key of all the problems
of Franciscan morality which puzzle the merely modern mind; but

above all it is the key of asceticism. It is the highest and holiest of the paradoxes that the man who really knows he cannot pay his debt will be for ever paying it. He will be for ever giving back what he cannot give back, and cannot be expected to give back. He will be always throwing things away into a bottomless pit of unfathomable thanks. Men who think they are too modern to understand this are in fact too mean to understand it; we are most of us too mean to practise it. We are not generous enough to be ascetics; one might almost say not genial enough to be ascetics. A man must have magnanimity of surrender, of which he commonly only catches a glimpse in first love, like a glimpse of our lost Eden. But whether he sees it or not, the truth is in that riddle; that the whole world has, or is, only one good thing; and it is a bad debt.

If ever that rarer sort of romantic love, which was the truth that sustained the Troubadours, falls out of fashion and is treated as fiction, we may see some such misunderstanding as that of the modern world about asceticism. For it seems conceivable that some barbarians might try to destroy chivalry in love, as the barbarians ruling in Berlin destroyed chivalry in war. If that were ever so, we should have the same sort of unintelligent sneers and unimaginative questions. Men will ask what selfish sort of woman it must have been who ruthlessly exacted tribute in the form of flowers, or what an avaricious creature she can have been to demand solid gold in the form of a ring: just as they ask what cruel kind of God can have demanded sacrifice and self-denial. They will have lost the clue to all that lovers have meant by love; and will not understand that it was because the thing was not demanded that it was done. But whether or no any such lesser things will throw a light on the greater, it is utterly useless to study a great thing like the Franciscan movement while remaining in the modern mood that murmurs against gloomy asceticism. The whole point about St. Francis of Assisi is that he certainly was ascetical and he certainly was not gloomy. As soon as ever he had been unhorsed by the glorious humiliation of his vision of dependence on the divine love, he flung himself into fasting and vigil exactly as he had flung himself furiously into battle. He had wheeled his charger clean round, but there was no halt or check in the thundering impetuosity of his charge. There was nothing negative about it; it was not a regimen or a stoical simplicity of life. It was not self-denial merely in the sense of self-control. It was as positive as a passion; it had all the air of being as positive as a pleasure. He devoured fasting as a man devours food. He plunged after poverty as men have dug madly for gold. And it is precisely the positive and passionate quality of this part of his personality that is a challenge to the modern mind in the whole problem of the pursuit of pleasure. There undeniably is the historical fact; and there attached to it is another moral fact almost as undeniable. It is certain that he held on this heroic or unnatural course from the moment when he went forth in his hair-shirt into the winter woods to the moment when he desired even in his death agony to lie bare upon the bare ground, to prove that he had and that he was nothing. And we can say, with almost as deep a certainty, that the stars which passed above that gaunt and wasted corpse stark upon the rocky floor had for once, in all their shining cycles round the world of labouring humanity, looked down upon a happy man.

VI

THE LITTLE POOR MAN

From that cavern, that was a furnace of glowing gratitude and humility, there came forth one of the strongest and strangest and most original personalities that human history has known. He was, among other things, emphatically what we call a character; almost as we speak of a character in a good novel or play. He was not only a humanist but a humorist; a humorist especially in the old English sense of a man always in his humour, going his own way and doing what nobody else would have done. The anecdotes about him have a certain biographical quality of which the most familiar example is Dr. Johnson; which belongs in another way to William Blake or to Charles Lamb. The atmosphere can only be defined by a sort of antithesis; the act is always unexpected and never inappropriate. Before the thing is said or done it cannot even be conjectured; but after it is said or done it is felt to be merely characteristic. It is surprisingly and yet inevitably individual. This quality of abrupt fitness and bewildering consistency belongs to St. Francis in a way that marks him out from most men of his time. Men are learning more and more of the solid social virtues of medieval civilisation; but those impressions are still social rather than individual. The medieval world was far ahead of the modern world in its sense of the things in which all men are at one: Death and the daylight of reason and the common conscience that holds communities together. Its generalisations were saner and sounder than the mad materialistic theories of to-day; nobody would have tolerated a Schopenhauer scorning life or a Nietzsche living only for scorn. But the modern world is more subtle in its sense of the things in which men are not at one; in the temperamental varieties and differentiations that make up the personal problems of life. All men who can think themselves now realize that the great schoolmen had a type of thought that was wonderfully clear; but it was as it were deliberately colourless. All are now agreed that the greatest art of the age was the art of public buildings; the popular and communal art of architecture. But it was not an age for the art of portrait-painting. Yet the friends of St. Francis have really contrived to leave behind a portrait; something almost resembling a devout and affectionate caricature. There are lines and colours in it that are personal almost to the extent of being perverse, if one can use the word perversity of an inversion that was also a conversion. Even among the saints he has the air of a sort of eccentric, if one may use the word of one whose eccentricity consisted in always turning towards the centre.

Before resuming the narrative of his first adventures, and the building of the great brotherhood which was the beginning of so merciful a revolution, I think it well to complete this imperfect personal portrait here; and having attempted in the last chapter a tentative description of the process, to add in this chapter a few touches to describe the result. I mean by the result the real man as he was after his first formative experiences, the man whom men met walking about on the Italian roads in his brown tunic tied with a rope. For that man, saving the grace of God, is the explanation of all that followed; men acted quite differently according to whether they had met him or not. If we see afterwards a vast tumult, an appeal to the Pope, mobs of men in brown habits besieging the seats of authority, Papal pronouncements, heretical sessions, trial and triumphant survival, the world full of a new movement, the friar a household word in every corner of Europe, and if we ask *why* all this happened, we can only approximate to any answer to our own question if we can, in some faint and indirect imaginative fashion, hear one human voice or see one human face under a hood. There is no answer except that Francis Bernardone had happened; and we must try in some sense to see what we should have seen if he had happened to us. In other words, after some groping suggestions about his life from the inside, we must again consider it from the outside; as if he were a stranger coming up the road towards us, along the hills of Umbria, between the olives or the vines.

Francis of Assisi was slight in figure with that sort of slightness which, combined with so much vivacity, gives the impression of smallness. He was probably taller than he looked; middle-sized, his biographers say; he was certainly very active and, considering what he went through, must have been tolerably tough. He was of the brownish Southern colouring, with a dark beard thin and pointed such as appears in pictures under the hoods of elves; and his eyes glowed with the fire that fretted him night and day. There is something about the description of all he said and did which suggests that, even more than most Italians, he turned naturally to a passionate pantomime of gestures. If this was so it is equally certain that with him, even more than with most Italians, the gestures were all gestures of politeness or hospitality. And both these facts, the vivacity and the courtesy, are the outward signs of something that mark him out very distinctively from many who might appear to be more of his kind than they really are. It is truly said that Francis of Assisi was one of the founders of the medieval drama, and therefore of the modern drama. He was the very reverse of a theatrical person in the selfish sense; but for all that he was pre-eminently a dramatic person. This side of him can best be suggested by taking what is commonly regarded as a reposeful quality; what is commonly described as a love of nature. We are compelled to use the term; and it is entirely the wrong term.

St. Francis was not a lover of nature. Properly understood, a lover of nature was precisely what he was not. The phrase implies accepting the material universe as a vague environment, a sort of sentimental pantheism. In the romantic period of literature, in the age of Byron and Scott, it was easy enough to imagine that a hermit in the ruins of a chapel (preferably by moonlight) might find peace and a mild pleasure in the harmony of solemn forests and silent stars, while he pondered over some scroll or illuminated volume, about the liturgical nature of which the author was a little vague. In short, the hermit might love nature as a background. Now for St. Francis nothing was ever in the background. We might say that his mind had no background, except perhaps that divine darkness out of which the divine love had called up every coloured creature one by one. He saw everything as dramatic, distinct from its setting, not all of a piece like a picture but in action like a play. A bird went by him like an arrow; something with a story and a purpose, though it was a purpose of life and not a purpose of death. A bush could stop him

like a brigand; and indeed he was as ready to welcome the brigand as
the bush.

In a word, we talk about a man who cannot see the wood for the
trees. St. Francis was a man who did not want to see the wood for
the trees. He wanted to see each tree as a separate and almost a sacred
thing, being a child of God and therefore a brother or sister of man.
But he did not want to stand against a piece of stage scenery used
merely as a background, and inscribed in a general fashion: "Scene; a
wood." In this sense we might say that he was too dramatic for the
drama. The scenery would have come to life in his comedies; the
walls would really have spoken like Snout the Tinker and the trees
would really have come walking to Dunsinane. Everything would
have been in the foreground; and in that sense in the footlights.
Everything would be in every sense a character. This is the quality in
which, as a poet, he is the very opposite of a pantheist. He did not
call nature his mother; he called a particular donkey his brother or a
particular sparrow his sister. If he had called a pelican his aunt or an
elephant his uncle, as he might possibly have done, he would still
have meant that they were particular creatures assigned by their Creator to particular places; not mere expressions of the evolutionary
energy of things. That is where his mysticism is so close to the common sense of the child. A child has no difficulty about understanding
that God made the dog and the cat; though he is well aware that the
making of dogs and cats out of nothing is a mysterious process beyond
his own imagination. But no child would understand what you meant
if you mixed up the dog and the cat and everything else into one
monster with a myriad legs and called it nature. The child would
resolutely refuse to make head or tail of any such animal. St. Francis
was a mystic, but he believed in mysticism and not in mystification.
As a mystic he was the mortal enemy of all those mystics who melt
away the edges of things and dissolve an entity into its environment.
He was a mystic of the daylight and the darkness; but not a mystic of
the twilight. He was the very contrary of that sort of oriental visionary who is only a mystic because he is too much of a sceptic to be a
materialist. St. Francis was emphatically a realist, using the word
realist in its much more real medieval sense. In this matter he really

was akin to the best spirit of his age, which had just won its victory over the nominalism of the twelfth century. In this indeed there was something symbolic in the contemporary art and decoration of his period; as in the art of heraldry. The Franciscan birds and beasts were really rather like heraldic birds and beasts; not in the sense of being fabulous animals but in the sense of being treated as if they were facts, clear and positive and unaffected by the illusions of atmosphere and perspective. In that sense he did see a bird sable on a field azure or a sheep argent on a field vert. But the heraldry of humility was richer than the heraldry of pride; for it saw all these things that God had given as something more precious and unique than the blazonry that princes and peers had only given to themselves. Indeed out of the depths of that surrender it rose higher than the highest titles of the feudal age; than the laurel of Caesar or the Iron Crown of Lombardy. It is an example of extremes that meet, that the Little Poor Man, who had stripped himself of everything and named himself as nothing, took the same title that has been the wild vaunt of the vanity of the gorgeous Asiatic autocrat, and called himself the Brother of the Sun and Moon.

This quality, of something outstanding and even startling in things as St. Francis saw them, is here important as illustrating a character in his own life. As he saw all things dramatically, so he himself was always dramatic. We have to assume throughout, needless to say, that he was a poet and can only be understood as a poet. But he had one poetic privilege denied to most poets. In that respect indeed he might be called the one happy poet among all the unhappy poets of the world. He was a poet whose whole life was a poem. He was not so much a minstrel merely singing his own songs as a dramatist capable of acting the whole of his own play. The things he said were more imaginative than the things he wrote. The things he did were more imaginative than the things he said. His whole course through life was a series of scenes in which he had a sort of perpetual luck in bringing things to a beautiful crisis. To talk about the art of living has come to sound rather artificial than artistic. But St. Francis did in a definite sense make the very act of living an art, though it was an unpremeditated art. Many of his acts will seem grotesque and puzzling to a rationalistic taste. But they were always acts and not explanations; and they always meant what he meant them to mean. The amazing vividness with which he stamped himself on the memory and imagination of mankind is very largely due to the fact that he was seen again and again under such dramatic conditions. From the moment when he rent his robes and flung them at his father's feet to the moment when he stretched himself in death on the bare earth in the pattern of the cross, his life was made up of these unconscious attitudes and unhesitating gestures. It would be easy to fill page after page with examples; but I will here pursue the method found convenient everywhere in this short sketch, and take one typical example, dwelling on it with a little more detail than would be possible in a catalogue, in the hope of making the meaning more clear. The example taken here occurred in the last days of his life, but it refers back in a rather curious fashion to the first; and rounds off the remarkable unity of that romance of religion.

The phrase about his brotherhood with the sun and moon, and with the water and the fire, occurs of course in his famous poem called the Canticle of the Creatures or the Canticle of the Sun. He sang it wandering in the meadows in the sunnier season of his own career, when he was pouring upwards into the sky all the passions of a poet. It is a supremely characteristic work, and much of St. Francis could be reconstructed from that work alone. Though in some ways the thing is as simple and straightforward as a ballad, there is a delicate instinct of differentiation in it. Notice, for instance, the sense of sex in inanimate things, which goes far beyond the arbitrary genders of a grammar. It was not for nothing that he called fire his brother, fierce and gay and strong, and water his sister, pure and clear and inviolate. Remember that St. Francis was neither encumbered nor assisted by all that Greek and Roman polytheism turned into allegory, which has been to European poetry often an inspiration, too often a convention. Whether he gained or lost by his contempt of learning, it never occurred to him to connect Neptune and the nymphs with the water or Vulcan and the Cyclops with the flame. This point exactly illustrates what has already been suggested; that, so far from being a revival of paganism, the Franciscan renascence was a sort of fresh start and first awakening after a forgetfulness of paganism. Certainly it is responsible for a certain freshness in the thing itself. Anyhow St. Francis was, as it were, the founder of a new folk-lore; but he could distinguish his mermaids from his mermen and his witches from his wizards. In short, he had to make his own mythology; but he knew at a glance the goddesses from the gods. This fanciful instinct for the sexes is not the only example of an imaginative instinct of the kind. There is just the same quaint felicity in the fact that he singles out the sun with a slightly more courtly title besides that of brother; a phrase that one king might use of another, corresponding to "Monsieur notre frère." It is like a faint half ironic shadow of the shining primacy that it had held in the pagan heavens. A bishop is said to have complained of a Nonconformist saying Paul instead of Saint Paul; and to have added "He might at least have called him Mr. Paul." So St. Francis is free of all obligation to cry out in praise or terror on the Lord God Apollo, but in his new nursery heavens, he salutes him as Mr. Sun. Those are the things in which he has a sort of inspired infancy, only to be paralleled in nursery tales. Something of the same hazy but healthy awe makes the story of Brer Fox and Brer Rabbit refer respectfully to Mr. Man.

This poem, full of the mirth of youth and the memories of childhood, runs through his whole life like a refrain, and scraps of it turn up continually in the ordinary habit of his talk. Perhaps the last appearance of its special language was in an incident that has always seemed to me intensely impressive, and is at any rate very illustrative of the great manner and gesture of which I speak. Impressions of that kind are a matter of imagination and in that sense of taste. It is idle to argue about them; for it is the whole point of them that they have passed beyond words; and even when they use words, seem to be completed by some ritual movement like a blessing or a blow. So, in a supreme example, there is something far past all exposition, something like the sweeping movement and mighty shadow of a hand, darkening even the darkness of Gethsemane; "Sleep on now, and take your rest. . . ." Yet there are people who have started to paraphrase and expand the story of the Passion.

St. Francis was a dying man. We might say he was an old man, at the time this typical incident occurred; but in fact he was only prematurely old; for he was not fifty when he died, worn out with his fighting and fasting life. But when he came down from the awful asceticism and more awful revelation of Alverno, he was a broken man. As will be apparent when these events are touched on in their turn, it was not only sickness and bodily decay that may well have darkened his life; he had been recently disappointed in his main mission to end the Crusades by the conversion of Islam; he had been still more disappointed by the signs of compromise and a more political or practical spirit in his own order; he had spent his last energies in protest. At this point he was told that he was going blind. If the faintest hint has been given here of what St. Francis felt about the glory and pageantry of earth and sky, about the heraldic shape and colour and symbolism of birds and beasts and flowers, some notion may be formed of what it meant to him to go blind. Yet the remedy might well have seemed worse than the disease. The remedy, admittedly an uncertain remedy, was to cauterise the eye, and that without any anaesthetic. In other words it was to burn his living eyeballs with a red-hot iron. Many of the tortures of martyrdom, which he envied in martyrology and sought vainly in Syria, can have been no worse. When they took the brand from the furnace, he rose as with an urbane gesture and spoke as to an invisible presence: "Brother Fire, God made you beautiful and strong and useful; I pray you be courteous with me."

If there be any such thing as the art of life, it seems to me that such a moment was one of its masterpieces. Not to many poets has it been given to remember their own poetry at such a moment, still less to live one of their own poems. Even William Blake would have been disconcerted if, while he was re-reading the noble lines "Tiger, tiger, burning bright," a real large live Bengal tiger had put his head in at the window of the cottage in Felpham, evidently with every intention of biting his head off. He might have wavered before politely saluting it, above all by calmly completing the recitation of the poem to the quadruped to whom it was dedicated. Shelley, when he wished to be a cloud or a leaf carried before the wind, might have been mildly surprised to find himself turning slowly head over heels in mid air a thousand feet above the sea. Even Keats, knowing that his hold on life was a frail one, might have been disturbed to discover that the true, the blushful Hippocrene of which he has just partaken freely had indeed contained a drug, which really ensured that he should cease upon the midnight with no pain. For Francis there was no drug; and for Francis there was plenty of pain. But his first thought was one of his first fancies from the songs of his youth. He remembered the time when a flame was a flower, only the most glorious and gaily coloured of the flowers in the garden of God; and when that shining thing returned to him in the shape of an instrument of torture, he hailed it from afar like an old friend, calling it by the nickname which might most truly be called its Christian name.

That is only one incident out of a life of such incidents; and I have selected it partly because it shows what is meant here by that shadow of gesture there is in all his words, the dramatic gesture of the south; and partly because its special reference to courtesy covers the next fact to be noted. The popular instinct of St. Francis, and his perpetual preoccupation with the idea of brotherhood, will be entirely misunderstood if it is understood in the sense of what is often called camaraderie; the back-slapping sort of brotherhood. Frequently from the enemies and too frequently from the friends of the democratic ideal, there has come a notion that this note is necessary to that ideal. It is assumed that equality means all men being equally uncivil, whereas it obviously ought to mean all men being equally civil. Such people have forgotten the very meaning and derivation of the word civility, if they do not see that to be uncivil is to be uncivic. But anyhow that was not the equality which Francis of Assisi encouraged; but an equality of the opposite kind; it was a camaraderie actually founded on courtesy.

Even in that fairy borderland of his mere fancies about flowers and animals and even inanimate things, he retained this permanent posture of a sort of deference. A friend of mine said that somebody was the sort of man who apologises to the cat. St. Francis really would have apologised to the cat. When he was about to preach in a wood full of the chatter of birds, he said, with a gentle gesture, "Little sisters, if you have now had your say, it is time that I also should be heard." And all the birds were silent; as I for one can very easily believe. In deference to my special design of making matters intelligible to average modernity, I have treated separately the subject of the miraculous powers that St. Francis most certainly possessed. But even apart from any miraculous powers, men of that magnetic sort, with that intense interest in animals, often have an extraordinary power over them. St. Francis's power was always exercised with this elaborate politeness. Much of it was doubtless a sort of symbolic joke, a pious pantomime intended to convey the vital distinction in his divine mission, that he not only loved but reverenced God in all his creatures. In this sense he had the air not only of apologising to the cat or to the birds, but of apologising to a chair for sitting on it or to a table for sitting down at it. Anyone who had followed him through life merely to laugh at him, as a sort of lovable lunatic, might easily have had an impression as of a lunatic who bowed to every post or took off his hat to every tree. This was all a part of his instinct for imaginative gesture. He taught the world a large part of its lesson by a sort of divine dumb alphabet. But if there was this ceremonial element even in lighter or lesser matters, its significance became far more serious in the serious work of his life, which was an appeal to humanity, or rather to human beings.

I have said that St. Francis deliberately did not see the wood for the trees. It is even more true that he deliberately did not see the mob for the men. What distinguishes this very genuine democrat from any mere demagogue is that he never either deceived or was deceived by the illusion of mass-suggestion. Whatever his taste in monsters, he never saw before him a many-headed beast. He only saw the image of God multiplied but never monotonous. To him a man was always a man and did not disappear in a dense crowd any more than in a desert. He honoured all men; that is, he not only loved but respected them all. What gave him his extraordinary personal power was this; that from the Pope to the beggar, from the sultan of Syria in his pavilion to the ragged robbers crawling out of the wood, there was never a man who looked into those brown burning eyes without being certain that Francis Bernardone was really interested in *him*; in his own inner individual life from the cradle to the grave; that he himself was being valued and taken seriously, and not merely added to the spoils of some social policy or the names in some clerical document. Now for this particular moral and religious idea there is no external expression except courtesy. Exhortation does not express it, for it is not mere abstract enthusiasm; beneficence does not express it, for it is not mere pity. It can only be conveyed by a certain grand manner which may be called good manners. We may say if we like that St. Francis, in the bare and barren simplicity of his life, had clung to one rag of luxury; the manners of a court. But whereas in a court there is one king and a hundred courtiers, in this story there was one courtier, moving among a hundred kings. For he treated the whole mob of men as a mob of kings. And this was really and truly the only attitude that will appeal to that part of man to which he wished to appeal. It cannot be done by giving gold or even bread; for it is a proverb that any reveller may fling largesse in mere scorn. It cannot even be done by giving time and attention; for any number of philanthropists and benevolent bureaucrats do such work with a scorn far more cold and horrible in their hearts. No plans or proposals or efficient rearrangements will give back to a broken man his self-respect and sense of speaking with an equal. One gesture will do it.

With that gesture Francis of Assisi moved among men; and it was soon found to have something in it of magic and to act, in a double sense, like a charm. But it must always be conceived as a completely natural gesture; for indeed it was almost a gesture of apology. He must be imagined as moving thus swiftly through the world with a sort of impetuous politeness; almost like the movement of a man who stumbles on one knee half in haste and half in obeisance. The eager face under the brown hood was that of a man always going somewhere, as if he followed as well as watched the flight of the birds. And this sense of motion is indeed the meaning of the whole revolution that he made; for the work that has now to be described was of the nature of an earthquake or a volcano, an explosion that drove outwards with dynamic energy the forces stored up by ten centuries in the monastic fortress or arsenal and scattered all its riches recklessly to the ends of the earth. In a better sense than the antithesis commonly conveys, it is true to say that what St. Benedict had stored St. Francis scattered; but in the world of spiritual things what had been stored into the barns like grain was scattered over the world as seed. The servants of God who had been a besieged garrison became a marching army; the ways of the world were filled as with thunder with the trampling of their feet and far ahead of that ever swelling host went a man singing; as simply he had sung that morning in the winter woods, where he walked alone.

VII

THE THREE ORDERS

There is undoubtedly a sense in which two is company and three is none; there is also another sense in which three is company and four is none, as is proved by the procession of historic and fictitious figures moving three deep, the famous trios like the Three Musketeers or the Three Soldiers of Kipling. But there is yet another and a different sense in which four is company and three is none; if we use the word company in the vaguer sense of a crowd or a mass. With the fourth man enters the shadow of a mob; the group is no longer one of three individuals only conceived individually. That shadow of the fourth man fell across the little hermitage of the Portiuncula when a man named Egidio, apparently a poor workman, was invited by St. Francis to enter. He mingled without difficulty with the merchant and the canon who had already become the companions of Francis; but with his coming an invisible line was crossed; for it must have been felt by this time that the growth of that small group had become potentially infinite, or at least that its outline had become permanently indefinite. It may have been in the time of that transition that Francis had another of his dreams full of voices; but now the voices were a clamour of the tongues of all nations, Frenchmen and Italians and English and Spanish and Germans, telling of the glory of God each in his own tongue; a new Pentecost and a happier Babel.

Before describing the first steps he took to regularise the growing group, it is well to have a rough grasp of what he conceived that group to be. He did not call his followers monks; and it is not clear, at this time at least, that he even thought of them as monks. He called them by a name which is generally rendered in English as the Friars Minor; but we shall be much closer to the atmosphere of his own mind if we render it almost literally as The Little Brothers. Presumably he was already resolved, indeed, that they should take the three vows of poverty, chastity and obedience which had always been the mark of a monk. But it would seem that he was not so much afraid of the idea of a monk as of the idea of an abbot. He was afraid that the great spiritual magistracies which had given even to their holiest possessors at least a sort of impersonal and corporate pride, would import an element of pomposity that would spoil his extremely and almost extravagantly simple version of the life of humility. But the supreme difference between his discipline and the discipline of the old monastic system was concerned, of course, with the idea that the monks were to become migratory and almost nomadic instead of stationary. They were to mingle with the world; and to this the more old-fashioned monk would naturally reply by asking how they were to mingle with the world without becoming entangled with the world. It was a much more real question than a loose religiosity is likely to realise; but St. Francis had his answer to it, of his own individual sort; and the interest of the problem is in that highly individual answer.

The good Bishop of Assisi expressed a sort of horror at the hard life which the Little Brothers lived at the Portiuncula, without comforts, without possessions, eating anything they could get and sleeping anyhow on the ground. St. Francis answered him with that curious and almost stunning shrewdness which the unworldly can sometimes wield like a club of stone. He said, "If we had any possessions, we should need weapons and laws to defend them." That sentence is the clue to the whole policy that he pursued. It rested upon a real piece of logic; and about that he was never anything but logical. He was ready to own himself wrong about anything else; but he was quite certain he was right about this particular rule. He was only once seen angry; and that was when there was talk of an exception to the rule.

His argument was this: that the dedicated man might go anywhere among any kind of men, even the worst kind of men, so long as there was nothing by which they could hold him. If he had any ties or needs like ordinary men, he would become like ordinary men. St. Francis was the last man in the world to think any the worse of ordinary men for being ordinary. They had more affection and admiration from him than they are ever likely to have again. But for his own particular purpose of stirring up the world to a new spiritual enthusiasm, he saw with a logical clarity that was quite reverse of fanatical or sentimental, that friars must not become like ordinary men; that the salt must not lose its savour even to turn into human nature's daily food. And the difference between a friar and an ordinary man was really that a friar was freer than an ordinary man. It was necessary that he should be free from the cloister; but it was even more important that he should be free from the world. It is perfectly sound common sense to say that there is a sense in which the ordinary man cannot be free from the world; or rather ought not to be free from the world. The feudal world in particular was one labyrinthine system of dependence; but it was not only the feudal world that went to make up the medieval world nor the medieval world that went to make up the whole world; and the whole world is full of this fact. Family life as much as feudal life is in its nature a system of dependence. Modern trade unions as much as medieval guilds are interdependent among themselves even in order to be independent of others. In medieval as in modern life, even where these limitations do exist for the sake of liberty, they have in them a considerable element of luck. They are partly the result of circumstances; sometimes the almost unavoidable result of circumstances. So the twelfth century had been the age of vows; and there was something of relative freedom in that feudal gesture of the vow; for no man asks vows from slaves any more than from spades. Still, in practice, a man rode to war in support of the ancient house of the Column or behind the Great Dog of the Stairway largely because he had been born in a certain city or countryside. But no man need obey little Francis in the old brown coat unless he chose. Even in his relations with his chosen leader he was in one sense relatively free, compared with the world around him. He was obedient but not dependent. And he was as free as the wind, he was almost wildly free, in his relation to that world around him. The world around him was, as has been noted, a network of feudal and family and other forms of dependence. The whole idea of St. Francis was that the Little Brothers should be like little fishes who could go freely in and out of that net. They could do so precisely because they were small fishes and in that sense even slippery fishes. There was nothing that the world could hold them by; for the world catches us mostly by the fringes of our garments, the futile externals of our lives. One of the Franciscans says later, "A monk should own nothing but his harp"; meaning, I suppose, that he should value nothing but his song, the song with which it was his business as a minstrel to serenade every castle and cottage, the song of the joy of the Creator in his creation and the beauty of the brotherhood of men. In imagining the life of this sort of visionary vagabond, we may already get a glimpse also of the practical side of that asceticism which puzzles those who think themselves practical. A man had to be thin to pass always through the bars and out of the cage; he had to travel light in order to ride so fast and so far. It was the whole calculation, so to speak, of that innocent cunning, that the world was to be outflanked and outwitted by him, and be embarrassed about what to do with him. You could not threaten to starve a man who was ever striving to fast. You could not ruin him and reduce him to beggary, for he was already a beggar. There was a very lukewarm satisfaction even in beating him with a stick, when he only indulged in little leaps and cries of joy because indignity was his only dignity. You could not put his head in a halter without the risk of putting it in a halo.

But one distinction between the old monks and the new friars counted especially in the matter of practicality and especially of promptitude. The old fraternities with their fixed habitations and enclosed existence had the limitations of ordinary householders. However simply they lived there must be a certain number of cells or a certain number of beds or at least a certain cubic space for a certain number of brothers; their numbers therefore depended on their land and building material. But since a man could become a Franciscan by merely promising to take his chance of eating berries in a lane or begging a crust from a kitchen, of sleeping under a hedge or sitting patiently on a doorstep, there was no economic reason why there should not be any number of such eccentric enthusiasts within any short period of time. It must also be remembered that the whole of this rapid development was full of a certain kind of democratic optimism that really was part of the personal character of St. Francis.

His very asceticism was in one sense the height of optimism. He demanded a great deal of human nature not because he despised it but rather because he trusted it. He was expecting a very great deal from the extraordinary men who followed him; but he was also expecting a good deal from the ordinary men to whom he sent them. He asked the laity for food as confidently as he asked the fraternity for fasting. But he counted on the hospitality of humanity because he really did regard every house as the house of a friend. He really did love and honour ordinary men and ordinary things; indeed we may say that he only sent out the extraordinary men to encourage men to be ordinary.

This paradox may be more exactly stated or explained when we come to deal with the very interesting matter of the Third Order, which was designed to assist ordinary men to be ordinary with an extraordinary exultation. The point at issue at present is the audacity and simplicity of the Franciscan plan for quartering its spiritual soldiery upon the population; not by force but by persuasion, and even by the persuasion of impotence. It was an act of confidence and therefore a compliment. It was completely successful. It was an example of something that clung about St. Francis always; a kind of tact that looked like luck because it was as simple and direct as a thunderbolt. There are many examples in his private relations of this sort of tactless tact; this surprise effected by striking at the heart of the matter. It is said that a young friar was suffering from a sort of sulks between morbidity and humility, common enough in youth and hero-worship, in which he had got it into his head that his hero hated or despised him. We can imagine how tactfully social diplomatists would steer clear of scenes and excitements, how cautiously psychologists would watch and handle such delicate cases. Francis suddenly walked up to the young man, who was of course secretive and silent as the grave, and said, "Be not troubled in your thoughts for you are dear to me, and even among the number of those who are most dear. You know that you are worthy of my friendship and society; therefore come to me, in confidence, whensoever you will, and from friendship learn faith." Exactly as he spoke to that morbid boy he spoke to all mankind. He always went to the point; he always seemed at once more right and more simple than the person he was speaking to. He seemed at once to be laying open his guard and yet lunging at the heart. Something in this attitude disarmed the world as it has never been disarmed again. He was better than other men; he was a benefactor of other men; and yet he was not hated. The world came into church by a newer and nearer door; and by friendship it learnt faith.

It was while the little knot of people at the Portiuncula was still small enough to gather in a small room that St. Francis resolved on his first important and even sensational stroke. It is said that there were only twelve Franciscans in the whole world when he decided to march, as it were, on Rome and found a Franciscan order. It would seem that this appeal to remote headquarters was not generally regarded as necessary; possibly something could have been done in a secondary way under the Bishop of Assisi and the local clergy. It would seem even more probable that people thought it somewhat unnecessary to trouble the supreme tribunal of Christendom about what a dozen chance men chose to call themselves. But Francis was obstinate and as it were blind on this point; and his brilliant blindness is exceedingly characteristic of him. A man satisfied with small things, or even in love with small things, he yet never felt quite as we do about the disproportion between small things and large. He never saw things to scale in our sense, but with a dizzy disproportion which makes the mind reel. Sometimes it seems merely out of drawing like a gaily coloured medieval map; and then again it seems to have escaped from everything like a short cut in the fourth dimension. He is said to have made a journey to interview the Emperor, throned among his armies under the eagle of the Holy Roman Empire, to intercede for the lives of certain little birds. He was quite capable of facing fifty emperors to intercede for one bird. He started out with two companions to convert the Mahomedan world. He started out with eleven companions to ask the Pope to make a new monastic world.

Innocent III, the great Pope, according to Bonaventura, was walking on the terrace of St. John Lateran, doubtless revolving the great political questions which troubled his reign, when there appeared abruptly before him a person in peasant costume whom he took to be some sort of shepherd. He appears to have got rid of the shepherd with all convenient speed; possibly he formed the opinion that the shepherd was mad. Anyhow he thought no more about it until, says the great Franciscan biographer, he dreamed that night a strange dream. He fancied that he saw the whole huge ancient temple of St. John Lateran, on whose high terraces he had walked so securely, leaning horribly and crooked against the sky as if all its domes and turrets were stooping before an earthquake. Then he looked again and saw that a human figure was holding it up like a living caryatid; and the figure was that of the ragged shepherd or peasant from whom he had turned away on the terrace. Whether this be a fact or a figure it is a very true figure of the abrupt simplicity with which Francis won the attention and the favour of Rome. His first friend seems to have been the Cardinal Giovanni di San Paolo who pleaded for the Franciscan idea before a conclave of Cardinals summoned for the purpose. It is interesting to note that the doubts thrown upon it seem to have been chiefly doubts about whether the rule was not too hard for humanity, for the Catholic Church is always on the watch against excessive asceticism and its evils. Probably they meant, especially when they said it was unduly hard, that it was unduly dangerous. For a certain element that can only be called danger is what marks the innovation as compared with older institutions of the kind. In one sense indeed the friar was almost the opposite of the monk. The value of the old monasticism had been that there was not only an ethical but an economic repose. Out of that repose had come the works for which the world will never be sufficiently grateful, the preservation of the classics, the beginning of the Gothic, the schemes of science and philosophies, the illuminated manuscripts and the coloured glass. The whole point of a monk was that his economic affairs were settled for good; he knew where he would get his supper, though it was a very plain supper. But the whole point of a friar was that he did not know where he would get his supper. There was always a possibility that he might get no supper. There was an element of what would be called romance, as of the gipsy or adventurer. But there was also an element of potential tragedy, as of the tramp or the casual labourer. So the Cardinals

of the thirteenth century were filled with compassion, seeing a few
men entering of their own free will that estate to which the poor of
the twentieth century are daily driven by cold coercion and moved
on by the police.

Cardinal San Paolo seems to have argued more or less in this manner: it may be a hard life, but after all it is the life apparently described as ideal in the Gospel; make what compromises you think
wise or humane about that ideal; but do not commit yourselves to
saying that men shall *not* fulfil that ideal if they can. We shall see the
importance of this argument when we come to the whole of that
higher aspect of the life of St. Francis which may be called the Imitation of Christ. The upshot of the discussion was that the Pope gave
his verbal approval to the project and promised a more definite en-
dorsement, if the movement should grow to more considerable proportions. It is probable that Innocent, who was himself a man of no
ordinary mentality, had very little doubt that it would do so;
anyhow he was not left long in doubt before it did do so. The next
passage in the history of the order is simply the story of more and
more people flocking to its standard; and as has already been remarked, once it had begun to grow, it could in its nature grow
much more quickly than any ordinary society requiring ordinary
funds and public buildings. Even the return of the twelve pioneers
from their papal audience seems to have been a sort of triumphal
procession. In one place in particular, it is said, the whole population of a town, men, women and children, turned out, leaving their
work and wealth and homes exactly as they stood and begging to be
taken into the army of God on the spot. According to the story, it
was on this occasion that St. Francis first fore-shadowed his idea of
the Third Order which enabled men to share in the movement
without leaving the homes and habits of normal humanity. For the
moment it is most important to regard this story as one example of
the riot of conversion with which he was already filling all the roads
of Italy. It was a world of wandering; friars perpetually coming and
going in all the highways and byways, seeking to ensure that any
man who met one of them by chance should have a spiritual adventure. The First Order of St. Francis had entered history.

This rough outline can only be rounded off here with some description of the Second and Third Orders, though they were founded later and at separate times. The former was an order for women and owed its existence, of course, to the beautiful friendship of St. Francis and St. Clare. There is no story about which even the most sympathetic critics of another creed have been more bewildered and misleading. For there is no story that more clearly turns on that simple test which I have taken as crucial throughout this criticism. I mean that what is the matter with these critics is that they will not believe that a heavenly love can be as real as an earthly love. The moment it is treated as real, like an earthly love, their whole riddle is easily resolved. A girl of seventeen, named Clare and belonging to one of the noble families of Assisi was filled with an enthusiasm for the conventual life; and Francis helped her to escape from her home and to take up the conventual life. If we like to put it so, he helped her to elope into the cloister, defying her parents as he had defied his father. Indeed the scene had many of the elements of a regular romantic elopement; for she escaped through a hole in the wall, fled through a wood and was received at midnight by the light of torches. Even Mrs. Oliphant, in her fine and delicate study of St. Francis, calls it "an incident which we can hardly record with satisfaction."

Now about that incident I will here only say this. If it had really been a romantic elopement and the girl had become a bride instead of a nun, practically the whole modern world would have made her a heroine. If the action of the Friar towards Clare had been the action of the Friar towards Juliet, everybody would be sympathising with her exactly as they sympathise with Juliet. It is not conclusive to say that Clare was only seventeen. Juliet was only fourteen. Girls married and boys fought in battles at such early ages in medieval times; and a girl of seventeen in the thirteenth century was certainly old enough to know her own mind. There cannot be the shadow of a doubt, for any sane person considering subsequent events, that St. Clare did know her own mind. But the point for the moment is that modern romanticism entirely encourages such defiance of parents when it is done in the name of romantic love. For it knows that romantic love is a reality, but it does not know that divine love is a reality. There may have been something to be said for the parents of Clare; there may have been something to be said for Peter Bernardone. So there may have been a great deal to be said for the Montagues or the Capulets; but the modern world does not want it said; and does not say it. The fact is that as soon as we assume for a moment as a hypothesis, what St. Francis and St. Clare assumed all the time as an absolute, that there is a direct divine relation more glorious than any romance, the story of St. Clare's elopement is simply a romance with a happy ending; and St. Francis is the St. George or knight-errant who gave it a happy ending. And seeing that some millions of men and women have lived and died treating this relation as a reality, a man is not much of a philosopher if he cannot even treat it as a hypothesis.

For the rest, we may at least assume that no friend of what is called the emancipation of women will regret the revolt of St. Clare. She did most truly, in the modern jargon, live her own life, the life that she herself wanted to lead, as distinct from the life into which parental commands and conventional arrangements would have forced her. She became the foundress of a great feminine movement which still profoundly affects the world; and her place is with the powerful women of history. It is not clear that she would have been so great or so useful if she had made a runaway match, or even stopped at home and made a *mariage de convenance*. So much any sensible man may well say considering the matter merely from the outside; and I have no intention of attempting to consider it from the inside. If a man may well doubt whether he is worthy to write a word about St. Francis, he will certainly want words better than his own to speak of the friendship of St. Francis and St. Clare. I have often remarked that the mysteries of this story are best expressed symbolically in certain silent attitudes and actions. And I know no better symbol than that found by the felicity of popular legend which says that one night the people of Assisi thought the trees and the holy house were on fire, and rushed up to extinguish the conflagration. But they found all quiet within, where St. Francis broke bread with St. Clare at one of their rare meetings, and talked of the love of God. It would be hard to find a more imaginative image for some sort of utterly pure and disembodied passion, than that red halo round the unconscious figures on the hill; a flame feeding on nothing and setting the very air on fire.

But if the Second Order was the memorial of such an unearthly love, the Third Order was as solid a memorial of a very solid sympathy with earthly loves and earthly lives. The whole of this feature in Catholic life, the lay orders in touch with clerical orders, is very little understood in Protestant countries and very little allowed for in Protestant history. The vision which has been so faintly suggested in these pages has never been confined to monks or even to friars. It has been an inspiration to innumerable crowds of ordinary married men and women; living lives like our own, only entirely different. That morning glory which St. Francis spread over earth and sky has lingered as a secret sunshine under a multitude of roofs and in a multitude of rooms. In societies like ours nothing is known of such a Franciscan following. Nothing is known of such obscure followers; and if possible less is known of the well-known followers. If we imagine passing us in the street a pageant of the Third Order of St. Francis, the famous figures would surprise us more than the strange ones. For us it would be like the unmasking of some mighty secret society. There rides St. Louis, the great king, lord of the higher justice whose scales hang crooked in favour of the poor. There is Dante crowned with laurel, the poet who in his life of passions sang the praises of the Lady Poverty, whose grey garment is lined with purple and all glorious within. All sorts of great names from the most recent and rationalistic centuries would stand revealed; the great Galvani, for instance, the father of all electricity, the magician who has made so many modern systems of stars and sounds. So various a following would alone be enough to prove that St. Francis had no lack of sympathy with normal men, if the whole of his own life did not prove it.

But in fact his life did prove it, and that possibly in a more subtle sense. There is, I fancy, some truth in the hint of one of his modern biographers, that even his natural passions were singularly normal and even noble, in the sense of turning towards things not unlawful in themselves but only unlawful for him. Nobody ever lived of whom we could less fitly use the word "regret" than Francis of

Assisi. Though there was much that was romantic, there was nothing in the least sentimental about his mood. It was not melancholy enough for that. He was of far too swift and rushing a temper to be troubled with doubts and reconsiderations about the race he ran; though he had any amount of self-reproach about not running faster. But it is true, one suspects, that when he wrestled with the devil, as every man must to be worth calling a man, the whispers referred mostly to those healthy instincts that he would have approved for others; they bore no resemblance to that ghastly painted paganism which sent its demoniac courtesans to plague St. Anthony in the desert. If St. Francis had only pleased himself, it would have been with simpler pleasures. He was moved to love rather than lust, and by nothing wilder than wedding-bells. It is suggested in that strange story of how he defied the devil by making images in the snow, and crying out that these sufficed him for a wife and family. It is suggested in the saying he used when disclaiming any security from sin, "I may yet have children"; almost as if it was of the children rather than the woman that he dreamed. And this, if it be true, gives a final touch to the truth about his character. There was so much about him of the spirit of the morning, so much that was curiously young and clean, that even what was bad in him was good. As it was said of others that the light in their body was darkness, so it may be said of this luminous spirit that the very shadows in his soul were of light. Evil itself could not come to him save in the form of a forbidden good; and he could only be tempted by a sacrament.

VIII

THE MIRROR OF CHRIST

No man who has been given the freedom of the Faith is likely to fall into those hole-and-corner extravagances in which later degenerate Franciscans, or rather Fraticelli, sought to concentrate entirely on St. Francis as a second Christ, the creator of a new gospel. In fact any such notion makes nonsense of every motive in the man's life; for no man would reverently magnify what he was meant to rival, or only profess to follow what he existed to supplant. On the contrary, as will appear later, this little study would rather specially insist that it was really the papal sagacity that saved the great Franciscan movement for the whole world and the universal Church, and prevented it from petering out as that sort of stale and second-rate sect that is called a new religion. Everything that is written here must be understood not only as distinct from but diametrically opposed to the idolatry of the Fraticelli. The difference between Christ and St. Francis was the difference between the Creator and the creature; and certainly no creature was ever so conscious of that colossal contrast as St. Francis himself. But subject to this understanding, it is perfectly true and it is vitally important that Christ was the pattern on which St. Francis sought to fashion himself; and that at many points their human and historical lives were even curiously coincident; and above all, that compared to most of us at least St. Francis is a most sublime approximation to his Master, and, even in being an intermediary and a reflection, is a splendid and yet a merciful Mirror of Christ. And this truth suggests another, which I think has hardly been noticed; but which happens to be a highly forcible argument for the authority of Christ being continuous in the Catholic Church.

Cardinal Newman wrote in his liveliest controversial work a sentence that might be a model of what we mean by saying that his creed tends to lucidity and logical courage. In speaking of the ease with which truth may be made to look like its own shadow or sham, he said, "And if Antichrist is like Christ, Christ I suppose is like

Antichrist." Mere religious sentiment might well be shocked at the end of the sentence; but nobody could object to it except the logician who said that Caesar and Pompey were very much alike, especially Pompey. It may give a much milder shock if I say here, what most of us have forgotten, that if St. Francis was like Christ, Christ was to that extent like St. Francis. And my present point is that it is really very enlightening to realise that Christ was like St. Francis. What I mean is this; that if men find certain riddles and hard sayings in the story of Galilee, and if they find the answers to those riddles in the story of Assisi, it really does show that a secret has been handed down in one religious tradition and no other. It shows that the casket that was locked in Palestine can be unlocked in Umbria; for the Church is the keeper of the keys.

Now in truth while it has always seemed natural to explain St. Francis in the light of Christ, it has not occurred to many people to explain Christ in the light of St. Francis. Perhaps the word "light" is not here the proper metaphor; but the same truth is admitted in the accepted metaphor of the mirror. St. Francis is the mirror of Christ rather as the moon is the mirror of the sun. The moon is much smaller than the sun, but it is also much nearer to us; and being less vivid it is more visible. Exactly in the same sense St. Francis is nearer to us, and being a mere man like ourselves is in that sense more imaginable. Being necessarily less of a mystery, he does not, for us, so much open his mouth in mysteries. Yet as a matter of fact, many minor things that seem mysteries in the mouth of Christ would seem merely characteristic paradoxes in the mouth of St. Francis. It seems natural to re-read the more remote incidents with the help of the more recent ones. It is a truism to say that Christ lived before Christianity; and it follows that as an historical figure He is a figure in heathen history. I mean that the medium in which He moved was not the medium of Christendom but of the old pagan empire; and from that alone, not to mention the distance of time, it follows that His circumstances are more alien to us than those of an Italian monk such as we might meet even to-day. I suppose the most authoritative commentary can hardly be certain of the current or conventional weight of all His words or phrases; of which of them would then have seemed a common allusion and which a strange fancy. This archaic setting has left many of the sayings standing like hieroglyphics and subject to many and peculiar individual interpretations. Yet it is true of almost any of them that if we simply translate them into the Umbrian dialect of the first Franciscans, they would seem like any other part of the Franciscan story; doubtless in one sense fantastic, but quite familiar. All sorts of critical controversies have revolved round the passage which bids men consider the lilies of the field and copy them in taking no thought for the morrow. The sceptic has alternated between telling us to be true Christians and do it, and explaining that it is impossible to do. When he is a communist as well as an atheist, he is generally doubtful whether to blame us for preaching what is impracticable or for not instantly putting it into practice. I am not going to discuss here the point of ethics and economics; I merely remark that even those who are puzzled at the saying of Christ would hardly pause in accepting it as a saying of St. Francis. Nobody would be surprised to find that he had said, "I beseech you, little brothers, that you be as wise as Brother Daisy and Brother Dandelion; for never do they lie awake thinking of tomorrow, yet they have gold crowns like kings and emperors or like Charlemagne in all his glory." Even more bitterness and bewilderment has arisen about the command to turn the other cheek and to give the coat to the robber who has taken the cloak. It is widely held to imply the wickedness of war among nations; about which, in itself, not a word seems to have been said. Taken thus literally and universally, it much more clearly implies the wickedness of all law and government. Yet there are many prosperous peacemakers who are much more shocked at the idea of using the brute force of soldiers against a powerful foreigner than they are at using the brute force of policemen against a poor fellow-citizen. Here again I am content to point out that the paradox becomes perfectly human and probable if addressed by Francis to Franciscans. Nobody would be surprised to read that Brother Juniper did then run after the thief that had stolen his hood, beseeching him to take his gown also; for so St. Francis had commanded him. Nobody would be surprised if St. Francis told a young noble about to be admitted to his company, that so far from pursuing a brigand to recover his shoes, he ought to pursue him to make him a present of his stockings. We may like or not the atmosphere these things imply; but we know what atmosphere they do imply. We recognise a certain note as natural and clear as the note of a bird; the note of St. Francis. There is in it something of gentle mockery of the very idea of possessions; something of a hope of disarming the enemy by generosity; something of a humorous sense of bewildering the worldly with the unexpected; something of the joy of carrying an enthusiastic conviction to a logical extreme. But anyhow we have no difficulty in recognising it, if we have read any of the literature of the Little Brothers and the movement that began in Assisi. It seems reasonable to infer that if it was this spirit that made such strange things possible in Umbria, it was the same spirit that made them possible in Palestine. If we hear the same unmistakable note and sense the same indescribable savour in two things at such a distance from each other, it seems natural to suppose that the case that is more remote from our experience was like the case that is closer to our experience. As the thing is explicable on the assumption that Francis was speaking to Franciscans, it is not an irrational explanation to suggest that Christ also was speaking to some dedicated band that had much the same function as Franciscans. In other words, it seems only natural to hold, as the Catholic Church has held, that these counsels of perfection were part of a particular vocation to astonish and awaken the world. But in any case it is important to note that when we do find these particular features with their seemingly fantastic fitness, reappearing after more than a thousand years, we find them produced by the same religious system which claims continuity and authority from the scenes in which they first appeared. Any number of philosophies will repeat the platitudes of Christianity. But it is the ancient Church that can again startle the world with the paradoxes of Christianity. *Ubi Petrus ibi Franciscus.*[1]

But if we understand that it was truly under the inspiration of his divine Master that St. Francis did these merely quaint or eccentric

[1] "Where Peter is, there is Francis."

acts of charity, we must understand that it was under the same inspiration that he did acts of self-denial and austerity. It is clear that these more or less playful parables of the love of men were conceived after a close study of the Sermon on the Mount. But it is evident that he made an even closer study of the silent sermon on that other mountain; the mountain that was called Golgotha. Here again he was speaking the strict historical truth, when he said that in fasting or suffering humiliation he was but trying to do something of what Christ did; and here again it seems probable that as the same truth appears at the two ends of a chain of tradition, the tradition has preserved the truth. But the import of this fact at the moment affects the next phase in the personal history of the man himself.

For as it becomes clearer that his great communal scheme is an accomplished fact and past the peril of an early collapse, as it becomes evident that there already is such a thing as an Order of the Friars Minor, this more individual and intense ambition of St. Francis emerges more and more. So soon as he certainly has followers, he does not compare himself with his followers, towards whom he might appear as a master; he compares himself more and more with his Master, towards whom he appears only as a servant. This, it may be said in passing, is one of the moral and even practical conveniences of the ascetical privilege. Every other sort of superiority may be superciliousness. But the saint is never supercilious, for he is always by hypothesis in the presence of a superior. The objection to an aristocracy is that it is a priesthood without a god. But in any case the service to which St. Francis had committed himself was one which, about this time, he conceived more and more in terms of sacrifice and crucifixion. He was full of the sentiment that he had not suffered enough to be worthy even to be a distant follower of his suffering God. And this passage in his history may really be roughly summarised as the Search for Martyrdom.

This was the ultimate idea in the remarkable business of his expedition among the Saracens in Syria. There were indeed other elements in his conception, which are worthy of more intelligent understanding than they have often received. His idea, of course, was to bring the Crusades in a double sense to their end; that is, to reach their conclusion and to achieve their purpose. Only he wished to do it by conversion and not by conquest; that is, by intellectual and not material means. The modern mind is hard to please; and it generally calls the way of Godfrey ferocious and the way of Francis fanatical. That is, it calls any moral method unpractical, when it has just called any practical method immoral. But the idea of St. Francis was far from being a fanatical or necessarily even an unpractical idea; though perhaps he saw the problem as rather too simple, lacking the learning of his great inheritor Raymond Lully,[2] who understood more but has been quite as little understood. The way he approached the matter was indeed highly personal and peculiar; but that was true of almost everything he did. It was in one way a simple idea, as most of his ideas were simple ideas. But it was not a silly idea; there was a great deal to be said for it and it might have succeeded. It was, of course, simply the idea that it is better to create Christians than to destroy Moslems. If Islam had been converted, the world would have been immeasurably more united and happy; for one thing, three quarters of the wars of modern history would never have taken place. It was not absurd to suppose that this might be effected, without military force, by missionaries who were also martyrs. The Church had conquered Europe in that way and may yet conquer Asia or Africa in that way. But when all this is allowed for, there is still another sense in which St. Francis was not thinking of Martyr-dom as a means to an end, but almost as an end in itself; in the sense that to him the supreme end was to come closer to the example of Christ. Through all his plunging and restless days ran the refrain: I have not suffered enough; I have not sacrificed enough; I am not yet worthy even of the shadow of the crown of thorns. He wandered about the valleys of the world looking for the hill that has the outline of a skull.

A little while before his final departure for the East a vast and tri-umphant assembly of the whole order had been near the Portiuncula;

[2] Lully, Raymond (c. 1232–1316). Known as "Doctor Illuminatus" he was a Spanish Franciscan theologian, philosopher and author. Lully sought to reestablish the unification of truth in theology and philosophy in opposition to the "double-truth" theory of rationalists such as Boethius and Siger of Brabant.

and called The Assembly of the Straw Huts, from the manner in which that mighty army encamped in the field. Tradition says that it was on this occasion that St. Francis met St. Dominic for the first and last time. It also says, what is probable enough, that the practical spirit of the Spaniard was almost appalled at the devout irresponsibility of the Italian, who had assembled such a crowd without organising a commissariat. Dominic the Spaniard was, like nearly every Spaniard, a man with the mind of a soldier. His charity took the practical form of provision and preparation. But, apart from the disputes about faith which such incidents open, he probably did not understand in this case the power of mere popularity produced by mere personality. In all his leaps in the dark, Francis had an extraordinary faculty of falling on his feet. The whole countryside came down like a landslide to provide food and drink for this sort of pious picnic. Peasants brought waggons of wine and game; great nobles walked about doing the work of footmen. It was a very real victory for the Franciscan spirit of a reckless faith not only in God but in man. Of course there is much doubt and dispute about the whole story and the whole relation of Francis and Dominic; and the story of the Assembly of the Straw Huts is told from the Franciscan side. But the alleged meeting is worth mentioning, precisely because it was immediately before St. Francis set forth on his bloodless crusade that he is said to have met St. Dominic, who has been so much criticised for lending himself to a more bloody one. There is no space in this little book to explain how St. Francis, as much as St. Dominic, would ultimately have defended the defence of Christian unity by arms. Indeed it would need a large book instead of a little book to develop that point alone from its first principles. For the modern mind is merely a blank about the philosophy of toleration; and the average agnostic of recent times has really had no notion of what he meant by religious liberty and equality. He took his own ethics as self-evident and enforced them; such as decency or the error of the Adamite heresy. Then he was horribly shocked if he heard of anybody else, Moslem or Christian, taking *his* ethics as self-evident and enforcing *them*; such as reverence or the error of the Atheist heresy. And then he wound up by taking all this lop-sided illogical

deadlock, of the unconscious meeting the unfamiliar, and called it
the liberality of his own mind. Medieval men thought that if a social
system was founded on a certain idea it must fight for that idea,
whether it was as simple as Islam or as carefully balanced as Catholicism. Modern men really think the same thing, as is clear when
communists attack their ideas of property. Only they do not think it
so clearly, because they have not really thought out their idea of
property. But while it is probable that St. Francis would have reluctantly agreed with St. Dominic that war for the truth was right in
the last resort, it is certain that St. Dominic did enthusiastically
agree with St. Francis that it was far better to prevail by persuasion
and enlightenment if it were possible. St. Dominic devoted himself
much more to persuading than to persecuting; but there was a difference in the methods simply because there was a difference in the
men. About everything St. Francis did there was something that
was in a good sense childish, and even in a good sense wilful. He
threw himself into things abruptly, as if they had just occurred to
him. He made a dash for his Mediterranean enterprise with something of the air of a schoolboy running away to sea.

In the first act of that attempt he characteristically distinguished
himself by becoming the Patron Saint of Stowaways. He never
thought of waiting for introductions or bargains or any of the considerable backing that he already had from rich and responsible people. He simply saw a boat and threw himself into it, as he threw
himself into everything else. It has all the air of running a race which
makes his whole life read like an escapade or even literally an escape.
He lay like lumber among the cargo, with one companion whom he
had swept with him in his rush; but the voyage was apparently unfortunate and erratic and ended in an enforced return to Italy. Apparently it was after this first false start that the great re-union took
place at the Portiuncula, and between this and the final Syrian journey there was also an attempt to meet the Moslem menace by
preaching to the Moors in Spain. In Spain indeed several of the first
Franciscans had already succeeded gloriously in being martyred. But
the great Francis still went about stretching out his arms for such
torments and desiring that agony in vain. No one would have said

more readily than he that he was probably less like Christ than those others who had already found their Calvary; but the thing remained with him like a secret; the strangest of the sorrows of man.

His later voyage was more successful, so far as arriving at the scene of operations was concerned. He arrived at the headquarters of the Crusade which was in front of the besieged city of Damietta, and went on in his rapid and solitary fashion to seek the headquarters of the Saracens. He succeeded in obtaining an interview with the Sultan; and it was at that interview that he evidently offered, and as some say proceeded, to fling himself into the fire as a divine ordeal, defying the Moslem religious teachers to do the same. It is quite certain that he would have done so at a moment's notice. Indeed throwing himself into the fire was hardly more desperate, in any case, than throwing himself among the weapons and tools of torture of a horde of fanatical Mahomedans and asking them to renounce Mahomet. It is said further that Mahomedan muftis showed some coldness towards the proposed competition, and that one of them quietly withdrew while it was under discussion; which would also appear credible. But for whatever reason Francis evidently returned as freely as he came. There may be something in the story of the individual impression produced on the Sultan, which the narrator represents as a sort of secret conversion. There may be something in the suggestion that the holy man was unconsciously protected among half-barbarous orientals by the halo of sanctity that is supposed in such places to surround an idiot. There is probably as much or more in the more generous explanation of that graceful though capricious courtesy and compassion which mingled with wilder things in the stately Soldans of the type and tradition of Saladin. Finally, there is perhaps something in the suggestion that the tale of St. Francis might be told as a sort of ironic tragedy and comedy called The Man Who Could Not Get Killed. Men liked him too much for himself to let him die for his faith; and the man was received instead of the message. But all these are only converging guesses at a great effort that is hard to judge, because it broke off short like the beginning of a great bridge that might have united East and West, and remains one of the great might-have-beens of history.

Meanwhile the great movement in Italy was making giant strides. Backed now by papal authority as well as popular enthusiasm, and creating a kind of comradeship among all classes, it had started a riot of reconstruction on all sides of religious and social life; and especially began to express itself in that enthusiasm for building which is the mark of all the resurrections of Western Europe. There had notably been established at Bologna a magnificent mission house of the Friars Minor; and a vast body of them and their sympathisers surrounded it with a chorus of acclamation. Their unanimity had a strange interruption. One man alone in that crowd was seen to turn and suddenly denounce the building as if it had been a Babylonian temple; demanding indignantly since when the Lady Poverty had thus been insulted with the luxury of palaces. It was Francis, a wild figure, returned from his Eastern Crusade; and it was the first and last time that he spoke in wrath to his children.

A word must be said later about this serious division of sentiment and policy, about which many Franciscans, and to some extent Francis himself, parted company with the more moderate policy which ultimately prevailed. At this point we need only note it as another shadow fallen upon his spirit after his disappointment in the desert; and as in some sense the prelude to the next phase of his career, which is the most isolated and the most mysterious. It is true that everything about this episode seems to be covered with some cloud of dispute, even including its date; some writers putting it much earlier in the narrative than this. But whether or no it was chronologically it was certainly logically the culmination of the story, and may best be indicated here. I say indicated for it must be a matter of little more than indication; the thing being a mystery both in the higher moral and the more trivial historical sense. Anyhow the conditions of the affair seem to have been these. Francis and a young companion, in the course of their common wandering, came past a great castle all lighted up with the festivities attending a son of the house receiving the honour of knighthood. This aristocratic mansion, which took its name from Monte Feltro, they entered in their beautiful and casual fashion and began to give their own sort of good news. There were some at least who listened to the saint "as if

he had been an angel of God"; among them a gentleman named
Orlando of Chiusi, who had great lands in Tuscany, and who proceeded to do St. Francis a singular and somewhat picturesque act of
courtesy. He gave him a mountain; a thing somewhat unique
among the gifts of the world. Presumably the Franciscan rule which
forbade a man to accept money had made no detailed provision
about accepting mountains. Nor indeed did St. Francis accept it save
as he accepted everything, as a temporary convenience rather than a
personal possession; but he turned it into a sort of refuge for the ere-
mitical rather than the monastic life; he retired there when he
wished for a life of prayer and fasting which he did not ask even his
closest friends to follow. This was Alverno of the Apennines, and
upon its peak there rests for ever a dark cloud that has a rim or halo
of glory.

What it was exactly that happened there may never be known.
The matter has been, I believe, a subject of dispute among the most
devout students of the saintly life as well as between such students
and others of the more secular sort. It may be that St. Francis never
spoke to a soul on the subject; it would be highly characteristic, and
it is certain in any case that he said very little; I think he is only alleged to have spoken of it to one man. Subject however to such truly
sacred doubts, I will confess that to me personally this one solitary
and indirect report that has come down to us reads very like the
report of something real; of some of those things that are more real
than what we call daily realities. Even something as it were double
and bewildering about the image seems to carry the impression of an
experience shaking the senses; as does the passage in Revelations
about the supernatural creatures full of eyes. It would seem that St.
Francis beheld the heavens above him occupied by a vast winged being like a seraph spread out like a cross. There seems some mystery
about whether the winged figure was itself crucified or in the posture of crucifixion, or whether it merely enclosed in its frame of
wings some colossal crucifix. But it seems clear that there was some
question of the former impression; for St. Bonaventura distinctly
says that St. Francis doubted how a seraph could be crucified, since
those awful and ancient principalities were without the infirmity of

the Passion. St. Bonaventura suggests that the seeming contradiction may have meant that St. Francis was to be crucified as a spirit since he could not be crucified as a man; but whatever the meaning of the vision, the general idea of it is very vivid and overwhelming. St. Francis saw above him, filling the whole heavens, some vast immemorial unthinkable power, ancient like the Ancient of Days, whose calm men had conceived under the forms of winged bulls or monstrous cherubim, and all that winged wonder was in pain like a wounded bird. This seraphic suffering, it is said, pierced his soul with a sword of grief and pity; it may be inferred that some sort of mounting agony accompanied the ecstasy. Finally after some fashion the apocalypse faded from the sky and the agony within subsided; and silence and the natural air filled the morning twilight and settled slowly in the purple chasms and cleft abysses of the Apennines.

The head of the solitary sank, amid all that relaxation and quiet in which time can drift by with the sense of something ended and complete; and as he stared downwards, he saw the marks of nails in his own hands.

IX

MIRACLES AND DEATH

The tremendous story of the Stigmata of St. Francis, which was the end of the last chapter, was in some sense the end of his life. In a logical sense, it would have been the end even if it had happened at the beginning. But truer traditions refer it to a later date and suggest that his remaining days on the earth had something about them of the lingering of a shadow. Whether St. Bonaventura was right in his hint that St. Francis saw in that seraphic vision something almost like a vast mirror of his own soul, that could at least suffer like an angel though not like a god, or whether it expressed under an imagery more primitive and colossal than common Christian art the primary paradox of the death of God, it is evident from its traditional consequences that it was meant for a crown and for a seal. It seems to have been after seeing this vision that he began to go blind.

But the incident has another and much less important place in this rough and limited outline. It is the natural occasion for considering briefly and collectively all the facts or fables of another aspect of the life of St. Francis; an aspect which is, I will not say more disputable, but certainly more disputed. I mean all that mass of testimony and tradition that concerns his miraculous powers and supernatural experiences, with which it would have been easy to stud and bejewel every page of the story; only that certain circumstances necessary to the conditions of this narration make it better to gather, somewhat hastily, all such jewels into a heap.

I have here adopted this course in order to make allowance for a prejudice. It is indeed to a great extent a prejudice of the past; a prejudice that is plainly disappearing in days of greater enlightenment, and especially of a greater range of scientific experiment and knowledge. But it is a prejudice that is still tenacious in many of an older generation and still traditional in many of the younger. I mean, of course, what used to be called the belief "that miracles do not happen," as I think Matthew Arnold expressed it, in expressing the standpoint of so many of our Victorian uncles and great-uncles. In other words it was the remains of that sceptical simplification by which some of the philosophers of the early eighteenth century had popularised the impression (for a very short time) that we had discovered the regulations of the cosmos like the works of a clock, of so very simple a clock that it was possible to distinguish almost at a glance what could or could not have happened in a human experience. It should be remembered that these real sceptics, of the golden age of scepticism, were quite scornful of the first fancies of science as of the lingering legends of religion. Voltaire, when he was told that a fossil fish had been found on the peaks of the Alps, laughed openly at the tale and said that some fasting monk or hermit had dropped his fish-bones there; possibly in order to effect another monkish fraud. Everybody knows by this time that science has had its revenge on scepticism. The border between the credible and the incredible has not only become once more as vague as in any barbaric twilight; but the credible is obviously increasing and the incredible shrinking. A man in Voltaire's time did not know what miracle he would next have to throw up. A man in our time does not know what miracle he will next have to swallow.

But long before these things had happened, in those days of my boyhood when I first saw the figure of St. Francis far away in the distance and drawing me even at that distance, in those Victorian days which did seriously separate the virtues from the miracles of the saints—even in those days I could not help feeling vaguely puzzled about how this method could be applied to history. Even then I did not quite understand, and even now I do not quite understand, on what principle one is to pick and choose in the chronicles of the past which seem to be all of a piece. All our knowledge of certain historical periods, and notably of the whole medieval period, rest on certain connected chronicles written by people who are some of them nameless and all of them dead, who cannot in any case be cross-examined and cannot in some cases be corroborated. I have never been quite clear about the nature of the right by which historians accepted masses of detail from them as definitely true, and suddenly denied their truthfulness when one detail was preternatural. I do not complain of their being sceptics; I am puzzled about why the sceptics are not more sceptical. I can understand their saying that these details would never have been included in a chronicle except by lunatics or liars; but in that case the only inference is that the chronicle was written by liars or lunatics. They will write for instance: "Monkish fanaticism found it easy to spread the report that miracles were already being worked at the tomb of Thomas Becket." Why should they not say equally well, "Monkish fanaticism found it easy to spread the slander that four knights from King Henry's court had assassinated Thomas Becket in the cathedral"? They would write something like this: "The credulity of the age readily believed that Joan of Arc had been inspired to point out the Dauphin although he was in disguise." Why should they not write on the same principle: "The credulity of the age was such as to suppose that an obscure peasant girl could get an audience at the court of the Dauphin"? And so, in the present case, when they tell us there is a wild story that St. Francis flung himself into the fire and emerged scathless, upon what precise principle are they forbidden to tell us of a wild story that St. Francis flung himself into the camp of the ferocious Moslems and returned safe? I only ask for information; for I do not see the rationale of the thing myself. I will undertake to say there was not a word written of St. Francis by any contemporary who was himself incapable of believing and telling a miraculous story. Perhaps it is all monkish fables and there never was any St. Francis or any St. Thomas Becket or any Joan of Arc. This is undoubtedly a *reductio ad absurdum*; but it is a *reductio ad absurdum* of the view which thought all miracles absurd.

And in abstract logic this method of selection would lead to the wildest absurdities. An intrinsically incredible story could only mean that the authority was unworthy of credit. It could not mean that other parts of his story must be received with complete credulity. If somebody said he had met a man in yellow trousers, who proceeded to jump down his own throat, we should not exactly take our Bible oath or be burned at the stake for the statement that he wore yellow trousers. If somebody claimed to have gone up in a blue balloon and found that the moon was made of green cheese, we should not exactly take an affidavit that the balloon was blue any more than that the moon was green. And the really logical conclusion from throwing doubts on all tales like the miracles of St. Francis was to throw doubts on the existence of men like St. Francis. And there really was a modern moment, a sort of high-water mark of insane scepticism, when this sort of thing was really said or done. People used to go about saying that there was no such person as St. Patrick; which is every bit as much of a human and historical howler as saying there was no such person as St. Francis. There was a time, for instance, when the madness of mythological explanation had dissolved a large part of solid history under the universal and luxuriant warmth and radiance of the Sun-Myth. I believe that that particular sun has already set, but there have been any number of moons and meteors to take its place.

St. Francis, of course, would make a magnificent Sun-Myth. How could anybody miss the chance of being a Sun-Myth when he is actually best known by a song called The Canticle of the Sun? It is needless to point out that the fire in Syria was the dawn in the East and the bleeding wounds in Tuscany the sunset in the West. I could expound this theory at considerable length; only, as so often happens to such fine theorists, another and more promising theory occurs to me. I cannot think how everybody, including myself, can have overlooked the fact that the whole tale of St. Francis is of Totemistic origin. It is unquestionably a tale that simply swarms with totems. The Franciscan woods are as full of them as any Red Indian fable. Francis is made to call himself an ass, because in the original mythos Francis was merely the name given to the real four-footed donkey, afterwards vaguely evolved into a half-human god or hero. And that, no doubt, is why I used to feel that the Brother Wolf and Sister Bird of St. Francis were somehow like the Brer Fox and Sis Cow of Uncle Remus. Some say there is an innocent stage of infancy in which we do really believe that a cow talked or a fox made a tar baby. Anyhow there is an innocent period of intellectual growth in which we do sometimes really believe that St. Patrick was a Sun-Myth or St. Francis a Totem. But for the most of us both those phases of paradise are past.

As I shall suggest in a moment, there is one sense in which we can for practical purposes distinguish between probable and improbable

things in such a story. It is not so much a question of cosmic criticism about the nature of the event as of literary criticism about the
nature of the story. Some stories are told much more seriously than
others. But apart from this, I shall not attempt here any definite differentiation between them. I shall not do so for a practical reason affecting the utility of the proceeding; I mean the fact that in a practical
sense the whole of this matter is again in the melting pot, from
which many things may emerge moulded into what rationalism
would have called monsters. The fixed points of faith and philosophy do indeed remain always the same. Whether a man believes
that fire in one case could fail to burn, depends on why he thinks it
generally does burn. If it burns nine sticks out of ten because it is its
nature or doom to do so, then it will burn the tenth stick as well. If
it burns nine sticks because it is the will of God that it should, then
it might be the will of God that the tenth should be unburned. Nobody can get behind that fundamental difference about the reason of
things; and it is as rational for a theist to believe in miracles as for an
atheist to disbelieve in them. In other words there is only one intelligent reason why a man does not believe in miracles and that is that he
does believe in materialism. But these fixed points of faith and philosophy are things for a theoretical work and have no particular place
here. And in the matter of history and biography, which have their
place here, nothing is fixed at all. The world is in a welter of the possible and impossible, and nobody knows what will be the next scientific
hypothesis to support some ancient superstition. Three-quarters of the
miracles attributed to St. Francis would already be explained by psychologists, not indeed as a Catholic explains them, but as a materialist
must necessarily refuse to explain them. There is one whole department of the miracles of St. Francis; the miracles of healing. What is
the good of a superior sceptic throwing them away as unthinkable, at
the moment when faith-healing is already a big booming Yankee
business like Barnum's Show? There is another whole department
analogous to the tales of Christ "perceiving men's thoughts." What is
the use of censoring them and blacking them out because they are
marked "miracles," when thought-reading is already a parlour game
like musical chairs? There is another whole department, to be studied

separately if such scientific study were possible, of the well-attested wonders worked from his relics and fragmentary possessions. What is the use of dismissing all that as inconceivable, when even these common psychical parlour tricks turn perpetually upon touching some familiar object or holding in the hand some personal posses- sion? I do not believe, of course, that these tricks are of the same type as the good works of the saint; save perhaps in the sense of *Diabolus simius Dei*.[1] But it is not a question of what I believe and why, but of what the sceptic disbelieves and why. And the moral for the practical biographer and historian is that he must wait till things settle down a little more, before he claims to disbelieve anything.

This being so he can choose between two courses; and not with- out some hesitation, I have here chosen between them. The best and boldest course would be to tell the whole story in a straightforward way, miracles and all, as the original historians told it. And to this sane and simple course the new historians will probably have to re- turn. But it must be remembered that this book is avowedly only an introduction to St. Francis or the study of St. Francis. Those who need an introduction are in their nature strangers. With them the object is to get them to listen to St. Francis at all; and in doing so it is perfectly legitimate so to arrange the order of the facts that the fa- miliar come before the unfamiliar and those they can at once under- stand before those they have a difficulty in understanding. I should only be too thankful if this thin and scratchy sketch contains a line or two that attracts men to study St. Francis for themselves; and if they do study him for themselves, they will soon find that the super- natural part of the story seems quite as natural as the rest. But it was necessary that my outline should be a merely human one, since I was only presenting his claim on all humanity, including sceptical humanity. I therefore adopted the alternative course, of showing first that nobody but a born fool could fail to realise that Francis of Assisi was a very real historical human being; and then summarising briefly in this chapter the superhuman powers that were certainly a part of that history and humanity. It only remains to say a few

---

[1] "The Devil an ape of God."

words about some distinctions that may reasonably be observed in the matter by any man of any views; that he may not confuse the point and climax of the saint's life with the fancies or rumours that were really only the fringes of his reputation.

There is so immense a mass of legends and anecdotes about St. Francis of Assisi, and there are so many admirable compilations that cover nearly all of them, that I have been compelled within these narrow limits to pursue a somewhat narrow policy; that of following one line of explanation and only mentioning one anecdote here or there because it illustrates that explanation. If this is true about all the legends and stories, it is especially true about the miraculous legends and the supernatural stories. If we were to take some stories as they stand, we should receive a rather bewildered impression that the biography contains more supernatural events than natural ones. Now it is clean against Catholic tradition, co-incident in so many points with common sense, to suppose that this is really the proportion of these things in practical human life. Moreover, even considered as supernatural or preternatural stories, they obviously fall into certain different classes, not so much by our experience of miracles as by our experience of stories. Some of them have the character of fairy stories, in their form even more than their incident. They are obviously tales told by the fire to peasants or the children of peasants, under conditions in which nobody thinks he is propounding a religious doctrine to be received or rejected, but only rounding off a story in the most symmetrical way, according to that sort of decorative scheme or pattern that runs through all fairy stories. Others are obviously in their form most emphatically evidence; that is they are testimony that is truth or lies; and it will be very hard for any judge of human nature to think they are lies.

It is admitted that the story of the Stigmata is not a legend but can only be a lie. I mean that it is certainly not a late legendary accretion added afterwards to the fame of St. Francis; but is something that started almost immediately with his earliest biographers. It is practically necessary to suggest that it was a conspiracy; indeed there has been some disposition to put the fraud upon the unfortunate Elias, whom so many parties have been disposed to treat as a useful universal villain. It has been said, indeed, that these early biographers, St. Bonaventura and Celano and the Three Companions, though they declare that St. Francis received the mystical wounds, do not say that they themselves saw those wounds. I do not think this argument conclusive; because it only arises out of the very nature of the narrative. The Three Companions are not in any case making an affidavit; and therefore none of the admitted parts of their story are in the form of an affidavit. They are writing a chronicle of a comparatively impersonal and very objective description. They do not say, "I saw St. Francis's wounds"; they say, "St. Francis received wounds." But neither do they say, "I saw St. Francis go into the Portiuncula"; they say, "St. Francis went into the Portiuncula." But I still cannot understand why they should be trusted as eye-witnesses about the one fact and not trusted as eye-witnesses about the other. It is all of a piece; it would be a most abrupt and abnormal interruption in their way of telling the story if they suddenly began to curse and to swear, and give their names and addresses, and take their oath that they themselves saw and verified the physical facts in question. It seems to me, therefore, that this particular discussion goes back to the general question I have already mentioned; the question of why these chronicles should be credited at all, if they are credited with abounding in the incredible. But that again will probably be found to revert, in the last resort, to the mere fact that some men cannot believe in miracles because they are materialists. That is logical enough; but they are bound to deny the preternatural as much in the testimony of a modern scientific professor as in that of a medieval monkish chronicler. And there are plenty of professors for them to contradict by this time.

But whatever may be thought of such supernaturalism in the comparatively material and popular sense of supernatural acts, we shall miss the whole point of St. Francis, especially of St. Francis after Alverno, if we do not realise that he was living a supernatural life. And there is more and more of such supernaturalism in his life as he approaches towards his death. This element of the supernatural did not separate him from the natural; for it was the whole point of his position that it united him more perfectly to the natural. It did not make him dismal or dehumanised; for it was the whole meaning of his message that such mysticism makes a man cheerful and humane. But it was the whole point of his position, and it was the whole meaning of his message, that the power that did it was a supernatural power. If this simple distinction were not apparent from the whole of his life, it would be difficult for anyone to miss it in reading the account of his death.

In a sense he may be said to have wandered as a dying man, just as he had wandered as a living one. As it became more and more apparent that his health was failing, he seems to have been carried from place to place like a pageant of sickness or almost like a pageant of mortality. He went to Rieti, to Nursia, perhaps to Naples, certainly to Cortona by the lake of Perugia. But there is something profoundly pathetic, and full of great problems, in the fact that at last, as it would seem, his flame of life leapt up and his heart rejoiced when they saw afar off on the Assisian hill the solemn pillars of the Portiuncula. He who had become a vagabond for the sake of a vision, he who had denied himself all sense of place and possession, he whose whole gospel and glory it was to be homeless, received like a Parthian shot from nature, the sting of the sense of home. He also had his *maladie du clocher*, his sickness of the spire; though his spire was higher than ours. "Never," he cried with the sudden energy of strong spirits in death, "never give up this place. If you would go anywhere or make any pilgrimage, return always to your home; for this is the holy house of God." And the procession passed under the arches of his home; and he laid down on his bed and his brethren gathered round him for the last long vigil. It seems to me no moment for entering into the subsequent disputes about which successors he blessed or in what form and with what significance. In that one mighty moment he blessed us all.

After he had taken farewell of some of his nearest and especially some of his oldest friends, he was lifted at his own request off his own rude bed and laid on the bare ground; as some say clad only in a hair-shirt, as he had first gone forth into the wintry woods from the presence of his father. It was the final assertion of his great fixed idea; of praise and thanks springing to their most towering height out of nakedness and nothing. As he lay there we may be certain that his seared and blinded eyes saw nothing but their object and their origin. We may be sure that the soul, in its last inconceivable isolation, was face to face with nothing less than God Incarnate and Christ Crucified. But for the men standing around him there must have been other thoughts mingling with these; and many memories must have gathered like ghosts in the twilight, as that day wore on and that great darkness descended in which we all lost a friend.

For what lay dying there was not Dominic of the Dogs of God,[2] a leader in logical and controversial wars that could be reduced to a plan and handed on like a plan; a master of a machine of democratic discipline by which others could organise themselves. What was passing from the world was a person; a poet; an outlook on life like a light that was never after on sea or land; a thing not to be replaced or repeated while the earth endures. It has been said that there was only one Christian, who died on the cross; it is truer to say in this sense that there was only one Franciscan, whose name was Francis. Huge and happy as was the popular work he left behind him, there was something that he could not leave behind, any more than a landscape painter can leave his eyes in his will. It was an artist in life who was here called to be an artist in death; and he had a better right than Nero, his anti-type, to say *Qualis artifex pereo*.[3] For Nero's life was full of posing for the occasion like that of an actor; while the Umbrian's had a natural and continuous grace like that of an athlete. But St. Francis had better things to say and better things to think about, and his thoughts were caught upwards where we cannot follow them, in divine and dizzy heights to which death alone can lift us up.

Round about him stood the brethren in their brown habits, those that had loved him even if they afterwards disputed with each other. There was Bernard his first friend and Angelo who had served as his secretary and Elias his successor, whom tradition tried to turn into a sort of Judas, but who seems to have been little worse than an official in the wrong place. His tragedy was that he had a Franciscan

---

[2] The symbol for the Dominican order is the dog. A pun on *Domini canes* —hounds of the Lord.

[3] "As an actor do I die."

habit without a Franciscan heart, or at any rate with a very un-Franciscan head. But though he made a bad Franciscan, he might have made a decent Dominican. Anyhow, there is no reason to doubt that he loved Francis, for ruffians and savages did that. Anyhow he stood among the rest as the hours passed and the shadow lengthened in the house of the Portiuncula; and nobody need think so ill of him as to suppose that his thoughts were then in the tumultuous future, in the ambitions and controversies of his later years.

A man might fancy that the birds must have known when it happened; and made some motion in the evening sky. As they had once, according to the tale, scattered to the four winds of heaven in the pattern of a cross at his signal of dispersion, they might now have written in such dotted lines a more awful augury across the sky. Hidden in the woods perhaps were little cowering creatures never again to be so much noticed and understood; and it has been said that animals are sometimes conscious of things to which man their spiritual superior is for the moment blind. We do not know whether any shiver passed through all the thieves and the outcasts and the outlaws, to tell them what had happened to him who never knew the nature of scorn. But at least in the passages and porches of the Portiuncula there was a sudden stillness, where all the brown figures stood like bronze statues; for the stopping of the great heart that had not broken till it held the world.

X

THE TESTAMENT OF ST. FRANCIS

In one sense doubtless it is a sad irony that St. Francis, who all his life had desired all men to agree, should have died amid increasing disagreements. But we must not exaggerate this discord, as some have done, so as to turn it into a mere defeat of all his ideals. There are some who represent his work as having been merely ruined by the wickedness of the world, or what they always assume to be the even greater wickedness of the Church.

This little book is an essay on St. Francis and not on the Franciscan Order, still less on the Catholic Church or the Papacy or the policy pursued towards the extreme Franciscans or the Fraticelli. It is therefore only necessary to note in a very few words what was the general nature of the controversy that raged after the great saint's death, and to some extent troubled the last days of his life. The dominant detail was the interpretation of the vow of poverty, or the refusal of all possessions. Nobody so far as I know ever proposed to interfere with the vow of the individual friar that he would have no individual possessions. Nobody, that is, proposed to interfere with his negation of private property. But some Franciscans, invoking the authority of Francis on their side, went further than this and further I think than anybody else has ever gone. They proposed to abolish not only private property but property. That is, they refused to be corporately responsible for anything at all; for any buildings or stores or tools; they refused to own them collectively even when they used them collectively. It is perfectly true that many, especially among the first supporters of this view, were men of a splendid and selfless spirit, wholly devoted to the great saint's ideal. It is also perfectly true that the Pope and the authorities of the Church did not think this conception was a workable arrangement, and went so far in modifying it as to set aside certain clauses in the great saint's will. But it is not at all easy to see that it *was* a workable arrangement or even an arrangement at all; for it was really a refusal to arrange anything. Everybody knew of course that Franciscans were communists; but this was not so much being a communist as being an anarchist. Surely upon any argument somebody or something must be answerable for what happened to or in or concerning a number of historic edifices and ordinary goods and chattels. Many idealists of a socialistic sort, notably of the school of Mr. Shaw or Mr. Wells, have treated this dispute as if it were merely a case of the tyranny of wealthy and wicked pontiffs crushing the true Christianity of Christian Socialists. But in truth this extreme ideal was in a sense the very reverse of Socialist, or even social. Precisely the thing which these enthusiasts refused was that social ownership on which Socialism is built; what they primarily refused to do was what Socialists primarily exist to do; to own legally in their corporate capacity. Nor is it true that the tone of the Popes towards the enthusiasts was merely harsh and hostile. The Pope maintained for a long time a compromise which he had specially designed to meet their own conscientious objections; a compromise by which the Papacy itself held the property in a kind of trust for the owners who refused to touch it. The truth is that this incident shows two things which are common enough in Catholic history, but very little understood by the journalistic history of industrial civilisation. It shows that the Saints were sometimes great men when the Popes were small men. But it also shows that great men are sometimes wrong when small men are right. And it will be found, after all, very difficult for any candid and clear-headed outsider to deny that the Pope was right, when he insisted that the world was not made only for Franciscans.

For that was what was behind the quarrel. At the back of this particular practical question there was something much larger and more momentous, the stir and wind of which we can feel as we read the controversy. We might go so far as to put the ultimate truth thus. St. Francis was so great and original a man that he had something in him of what makes the founder of a religion. Many of his followers were more or less ready, in their hearts, to treat him as the founder of a religion. They were willing to let the Franciscan spirit escape from Christendom as the Christian spirit had escaped from Israel. They were willing to let it eclipse Christendom as the Christian spirit had eclipsed Israel. Francis, the fire that ran through the roads of Italy, was to be the beginning of a conflagration in which the old Christian civilisation was to be consumed. That was the point the Pope had to settle; whether Christendom should absorb Francis or Francis Christendom. And he decided rightly, apart from the duties of his place; for the Church could include all that was good in the Franciscans and the Franciscans could not include all that was good in the Church.

There is one consideration which, though sufficiently clear in the whole story, has not perhaps been sufficiently noted, especially by those who cannot see the case for a certain Catholic common sense larger even than Franciscan enthusiasm. Yet it arises out of the very merits of the man whom they so rightly admire. Francis of Assisi, as has been said again and again, was a poet; that is, he was a person who could express his personality. Now it is everywhere the mark of this sort of man that his very limitations make him larger. He is what he is, not only by what he has, but in some degree by what he has not. But the limits that make the lines of such a personal portrait cannot be made the limits of all humanity. St. Francis is a very strong example of this quality in the man of genius, that in him even what is negative is positive, because it is part of a character. An excellent example of what I mean may be found in his attitude towards learning and scholarship. He ignored and in some degree discouraged books and book-learning; and from his own point of view and that of his own work in the world he was absolutely right. The whole point of his message was to be so simple that the village idiot could understand it. The whole point of his point of view was that it looked out freshly upon a fresh world, that might have been made that morning. Save for the great primal things, the Creation and the Story of Eden, the first Christmas and the first Easter, the world had no history. But is it desired or desirable that the whole Catholic Church should have no history?

It is perhaps the chief suggestion of this book that St. Francis walked the world like the Pardon of God. I mean that his appearance marked the moment when men could be reconciled not only to God but to nature and, most difficult of all, to themselves. For it marked the moment when all the stale paganism that had poisoned the ancient world was at last worked out of the social system. He opened the gates of the Dark Ages as of a prison of purgatory, where men had cleansed themselves as hermits in the desert or heros in the barbarian wars. It was in fact his whole function to tell men to start afresh and, in that sense, to tell them to forget. If they were to turn over a new leaf and begin a fresh page with the first large letters of the alphabet, simply drawn and brilliantly coloured in the early medieval manner, it was clearly a part of that particular childlike cheerfulness that they should paste down the old page that was all black and bloody with horrid things. For instance, I have already noted that there is not a trace in the poetry of this first Italian poet of all that pagan mythology which lingered long after paganism. The first Italian poet seems the only man in the world who has never even heard of Virgil. This was exactly right for the special sense in which he is the first Italian poet. It is quite right that he should call a nightingale a nightingale, and not have its song spoilt or saddened by the terrible tales of Itylus or Procne.[1] In short, it is really quite right and quite desirable that St. Francis should never have heard of Virgil. But do we really desire that Dante should never have heard of Virgil? Do we really desire that Dante should never have read any pagan mythology? It has been truly said that the use that Dante makes of such fables is altogether part of a deeper orthodoxy; that his huge heathen fragments, his gigantic figures of Minos or of Charon only give a hint of some enormous natural religion behind all history and from the first foreshadowing the Faith. It is well to have the Sybil as well as David in the Dies Irae. That St. Francis would have burned all the leaves of all the books of the Sybil, in exchange for one fresh leaf from the nearest tree, is perfectly true; and perfectly proper to St. Francis. But it is good to have the Dies Irae as well as the Canticle of the Sun.

By this thesis, in short, the coming of St. Francis was like the birth of a child in a dark house, lifting its doom; a child that grows up unconscious of the tragedy and triumphs over it by his innocence.

---

[1] Procne cooked her son Itylus and served him to her husband Tereus for dinner. Procne was changed into a swallow.

In him it is necessarily not only innocence but ignorance. It is the essence of the story that *he* should pluck at the green grass without knowing it grows over a murdered man or climb the apple-tree without knowing it was the gibbet of a suicide. It was such an amnesty and reconciliation that the freshness of the Franciscan spirit brought to all the world. But it does not follow that it ought to impose its ignorance on all the world. And I think it would have tried to impose it on all the world. For some Franciscans it would have seemed right that Franciscan poetry should expel Benedictine prose. For the symbolic child it was quite rational. It was right enough that for such a child the world should be a large new nursery with blank white-washed walls, on which he could draw his own pictures in chalk in the childish fashion, crude in outline and gay in colour; the beginnings of all our art. It was right enough that to him such a nursery should seem the most magnificent mansion of the imagination of man. But in the Church of God are many mansions.

Every heresy has been an effort to narrow the Church. If the Franciscan movement had turned into a new religion, it would after all have been a narrow religion. In so far as it did turn here and there into a heresy, it was a narrow heresy. It did what heresy always does; it set the mood against the mind. The mood was indeed originally the good and glorious mood of the great St. Francis, but it was not the whole mind of God or even of man. And it is a fact that the mood itself degenerated, as the mood turned into a monomania. A sect that came to be called the Fraticelli declared themselves the true sons of St. Francis and broke away from the compromises of Rome in favour of what they would have called the complete programme of Assisi. In a very little while these loose Franciscans began to look as ferocious as Flagellants. They launched new and violent vetos; they denounced marriage; that is, they denounced mankind. In the name of the most human of saints they declared war upon humanity. They did not perish particularly through being persecuted; many of them were eventually persuaded; and the unpersuadable rump of them that remained remained without producing anything in the least calculated to remind anybody of the real St. Francis. What was the matter with these people was that they were mystics; mystics and nothing else but mystics; and not Catholics; mystics and not Christians; mystics and not men. They rotted away because, in the most exact sense, they would not listen to reason. And St. Francis, however wild and romantic his gyrations might appear to many, always hung on to reason by one invisible and indestructible hair.

The great saint was sane; and with the very sound of the word sanity, as at a deeper chord struck upon a harp, we come back to something that was indeed deeper than everything about him that seemed an almost elvish eccentricity. He was not a mere eccentric because he was always turning towards the centre and heart of the maze; he took the queerest and most zigzag short cuts through the wood, but he was always going home. He was not only far too humble to be an heresiarch, but he was far too human to desire to be an extremist, in the sense of an exile at the ends of the earth. The sense of humour which salts all the stories of his escapades alone prevented him from ever hardening into the solemnity of sectarian self-righteousness. He was by nature ready to admit that he was wrong; and if his followers had on some practical points to admit that he was wrong, they only admitted that he was wrong in order to prove that he was right. For it is they, his real followers, who have really proved that he was right and even in transcending some of his negations have triumphantly extended and interpreted his truth. The Franciscan order did not fossilise or break off short like something of which the true purpose has been frustrated by official tyranny or internal treason. It was this, the central and orthodox trunk of it, that afterwards bore fruit for the world. It counted among its sons Bonaventura the great mystic and Bernardino the popular preacher, who filled Italy with the very beatific buffooneries of a Jongleur de Dieu. It counted Raymond Lully with his strange learning and his large and daring plans for the conversion of the world; a man intensely individual exactly as St. Francis was intensely individual. It counted Roger Bacon, the first naturalist whose experiments with light and water had all the luminous quaintness that belongs to the beginnings of natural history; and whom even the most material scientists have hailed as a father of science. It is not merely true that these were great men who did great work for the world; it is also true that they were a certain kind of men keeping the spirit and savour of a certain kind of man, that we can recognise in them a taste and tang of audacity and simplicity, and know them for the sons of St. Francis.

For that is the full and final spirit in which we should turn to St. Francis; in the spirit of thanks for what he has done. He was above all things a great giver; and he cared chiefly for the best kind of giving which is called thanksgiving. If another great man wrote a grammar of assent, he may well be said to have written a grammar of acceptance; a grammar of gratitude. He understood down to its very depths the theory of thanks; and its depths are a bottomless abyss. He knew that the praise of God stands on its strongest ground when it stands on nothing. He knew that we can best measure the towering miracle of the mere fact of existence if we realise that but for some strange mercy we should not even exist. And something of that larger truth is repeated in a lesser form in our own relations with so mighty a maker of history. He also is a giver of things we could not have even thought of for ourselves; he also is too great for anything but gratitude. From him came a whole awakening of the world and a dawn in which all shapes and colours could be seen anew. The mighty men of genius who made the Christian civilisation that we know appear in history almost as his servants and imitators. Before Dante was, he had given poetry to Italy; before St. Louis ruled, he had risen as the tribune of the poor; and before Giotto had painted the pictures, he had enacted the scenes. That great painter who began the whole human inspiration of European painting had himself gone to St. Francis to be inspired. It is said that when St. Francis staged in his own simple fashion a Nativity Play of Bethlehem, with kings and angels in the stiff and gay medieval garments and the golden wigs that stood for haloes, a miracle was wrought full of the Franciscan glory. The Holy Child was a wooden doll or bambino, and it was said that he embraced it and that the image came to life in his arms. He assuredly was not thinking of lesser things; but we may at least say that one thing came to life in his arms; and that was the thing that we call the drama. Save for his intense individual love of song, he did not perhaps himself embody this spirit in any of these arts. He was the spirit that was embodied. He was the spiritual essence and substance that walked the world, before anyone had seen these things in visible forms derived from it: a wandering fire as if from nowhere, at which men more material could light both torches and tapers. He was the soul of medieval civilisation before it even found a body. Another and quite different stream of spiritual inspiration derives largely from him; all that reforming energy of medieval and modern times that goes to the burden of *Deus est Deus Pauperum*.[2] His abstract ardour for human beings was in a multitude of just medieval laws against the pride and cruelty of riches; it is to-day behind much that is loosely called Christian Socialist and can more correctly be called Catholic Democrat. Neither on the artistic nor the social side would anybody pretend that these things would not have existed without him; yet it is strictly true to say that we cannot now imagine them without him; since he has lived and changed the world.

And something of that sense of impotence which was more than half his power will descend on anyone who knows what that inspiration has been in history, and can only record it in a series of straggling and meagre sentences. He will know something of what St. Francis meant by the great and good debt that cannot be paid. He will feel at once the desire to have done infinitely more and the futility of having done anything. He will know what it is to stand under such a deluge of dead man's marvels, and have nothing in return to establish against it; to have nothing to set up under the overhanging, overwhelming arches of such a temple of time and eternity, but this brief candle burnt out so quickly before his shrine.

[2] "God is the God of the poor."

THE EVERLASTING MAN

1925

INTRODUCTION

By Larry Azar, Ph.D.

We can dig into the past and find pictures of reindeer drawn by prehistoric man, but we would have to dig for ever before coming across a picture of a man drawn by a prehistoric reindeer. Such obvious truisms, which we find on every page of Chesterton, arrest the reader and suddenly dissipate the atmospheric trends of thought which elsewhere harden into the common wisdom—more properly the common folly. Man differs from the other animals in *kind*, not merely in degree, and Chesterton's insistence on this theme is an enduring rebuke to a recurring fallacy.

Today, the American Civil Liberties Union, in defending evolution, will not even permit the use of the word "kind", for it insists that there is no difference in kind between man and other animals. And the winner of two Nobel prizes, Albert Szent-Gyorgyi, categorically maintained, "There is no *real* difference between cabbages and kings" (*The Cell and Protoplasm*, page 160). Chesterton shows that such a stance stems from a prejudgment, for if the facts were honestly investigated, they would clearly show that man is, not an evolution, but a revolution. For when the evidence is considered, we do find pictures in caves drawn by genuine artists. Nowhere do we find pictures of dogs drawn by cats; indeed, "it sounds like a joke to say that the most intelligent monkey drew a picture of a man." As a matter of fact, "art is the signature of man." And the existence of art alone, Chesterton observes, shows clearly that man is not only a creature, but a creator as well: "Man is the image of God."

And Chesterton sets the comparative religionists against the evolutionists (though they are usually the same person). If all religions can be reduced to one common abstraction, just as all men and animals can be reduced to one grey genus, then how can it be that no animals are religious *at all* while all men (with the statistically insignificant exception of the students of comparative religions) are?

There are, of course, other exclusively human characteristics:

Man "cannot sleep in his own skin. . . . He is wrapped in artificial bandages called clothes; he is propped up on artificial crutches called furniture"; he laughs and buries his dead. Evolution, of course, explains none of these characteristics; indeed it explains nothing whatsoever of what everyone admits most clearly describes man: his mind.

Would anyone claim that Adam was a pre-Adamite? Yet anthropologists speak without hesitation of "the history of pre-historic man". Or worse, they conclude that pre-historic man wore no clothing, and they base this conclusion on the fact that there is no evidence that he did. But, asks Chesterton, what kind of clothes would he have had to wear if his vestments were to survive the ravages of time? Did the scientist expect to find "a stone hat as well as a stone hatchet . . . iron hats and trousers"?

There really is evidence for the evolution of society as there is not for the evolution of the individual. Only all the evidence supports an evolution in exactly the reverse direction of the evolutionary hypothesis. The known history of Egypt shows that ". . . it is emphatically not true that it was most despotic in the earliest age and grew more liberal in a later age; the practical process of history is exactly the reverse." Or if this evolution was not a retrogression, it was at best a standstill. "There is not a grain of evidence that primitive government was despotic and tyrannical." On the contrary, all the records we have indicate that humanity had always been civilized: "Barbarism and civilisation were not successive stages in the progress of the world." This is clearly seen in the histories of Egypt and Babylon, the only societies "of which we have any reliable and detailed record".

While sympathizing with the men who made the myths (and the men made by the myths) Chesterton insists that the myths themselves must be distinguished from religion. Mythology sought God through the imagination—philosophy sought God through the intellect. But pagan antiquity never could (or at least never did) unite these two halves of the human mind. Religion, which simultaneously satisfied the mythological desire for a story and the philosophical demand for the truth with the first and last true story of God's love for man, only appeared with the Christian Church:

poets and philosophers were joined. Outside of Christianity, myth and philosophy were never united.

Chesterton's remark that the greatest of all philosophers was Aristotle may permit us to note that a type of intellectual schizophrenia is discoverable in that ancient thinker, according to whose religion the supreme God, Zeus, was quite human, having a human body and desires; the God of Aristotle's philosophy, however, was completely non-material and indifferent to human affairs. As the supreme being, God performed the noblest act: He thought. And when he did so, he thought of the best thing: himself. Hence, God is properly described as thought thinking thought. Neither the prayers of men nor the providence of God have any meaning. Obviously, then, in such a milieu where "the philosopher was a rival of the priest . . . religion was one thing and philosophy quite another."

In Part II of *The Everlasting Man*, Chesterton observes that, unlike other religions, Christianity joins "two ideas that most of mankind must regard as remote from each other": a child and a sustainer of the universe. In this fashion, "divinity and infancy", like "omnipotence and impotence" are united in one and the same being. Which pagans, Chesterton asks, would consider a child superior to a man? And why have some non-Christian religions denied nature, or posited two supreme principles of the universe, or even declared war on life itself? Such facts reinforce Chesterton's earlier view that all religions are *not* the same. Indeed, even if the teaching of the Catholic Church on the divinity of Christ were wrong, it would yet remain true that no other religion even made such a claim. No Moslem ever taught that its founder, Mohammed, was divine; no Jew ever insisted that Moses possessed a divine nature.

Another of Chesterton's apparently effortless and incidental insights is that the doctrine "God is Love" is practically identical to the doctrine of the eternal nature of the Word. For if the Supreme Principle of the universe were a single person, what could God have loved before the creation of the universe if "there was nothing to be loved"? From this it becomes apparent why, outside of the Christian tradition, it has been next to impossible to account for human freedom. The philosophical notion that the good is diffusive led many thinkers to maintain that God, the Supreme Good, *had* to create the universe. But if the highest principle of existing things lacks freedom — if God is not free — how could humans be? But the Christian God, who is triune and therefore love, remains free to create the universe or not. And so he remains free to bestow freedom (and so prayer and responsibility) upon his creatures. The God of the (mere) philosophers cannot be the God of Abraham. As Chesterton observes, "in every age and country outside Christendom, there has been a feud for ever between the philosopher and the priest".

Chesterton seems often to digress or to repeat himself. But upon examination one sees that the fragments are related, converge from a hundred different angles, illuminate the same truths as by a summer sky full of disparate stars scattered from horizon to horizon.

Finally there is a unity of purpose as well as style as Chesterton tells the "short story of mankind". Man stands up like a miracle (or else like a monster) among the animals that surround him. And Christ (and his Church) stand out from mankind and his social forms like Charles Williams'

> A light that shone from behind the sun; the sun
> Was not so fierce as to pierce where that light could.

PREFATORY NOTE

This book needs a preliminary note that its scope be not misunderstood. The view suggested is historical rather than theological, and does not deal directly with a religious change which has been the chief event of my own life; and about which I am already writing a more purely controversial volume. It is impossible, I hope, for any Catholic to write any book on any subject, above all this subject, without showing that he is a Catholic; but this study is not specially concerned with the differences between a Catholic and a Protestant. Much of it is devoted to many sorts of Pagans rather than any sort of Christians; and its thesis is that those who say that Christ stands side by side with similar myths, and his religion side by side with similar religions, are only repeating a very stale formula contradicted by a very striking fact. To suggest this I have not needed to go much beyond matters known to us all; I make no claim to learning; and have to depend for some things, as has rather become the fashion, on those who are more learned. As I have more than once differed from Mr. H. G. Wells in his view of history, it is the more right that I should here congratulate him on the courage and constructive imagination which carried through his vast and varied and intensely interesting work; but still more on having asserted the reasonable right of the amateur to do what he can with the facts which the specialists provide.

INTRODUCTION

THE PLAN OF THIS BOOK

There are two ways of getting home; and one of them is to stay there. The other is to walk round the whole world till we come back to the same place; and I tried to trace such a journey in a story I once wrote. It is, however, a relief to turn from that topic to another story that I never wrote. Like every book I never wrote, it is by far the best book I have ever written. It is only too probable that I shall never write it, so I will use it symbolically here; for it was a symbol of the same truth. I conceived it as a romance of those vast valleys with sloping sides, like those along which the ancient White Horses of Wessex are scrawled along the flanks of the hills. It concerned some boy whose farm or cottage stood on such a slope, and who went on his travels to find something, such as the effigy and grave of some giant; and when he was far enough from home he looked back and saw that his own farm and kitchen-garden, shining flat on the hill-side like the colours and quarterings of a shield, were but parts of some such gigantic figure, on which he had always lived, but which was too large and too close to be seen. That, I think, is a true picture of the progress of any really independent intelligence today; and that is the point of this book.

The point of this book, in other words, is that the next best thing to being really inside Christendom is to be really outside it. And a particular point of it is that the popular critics of Christianity are not really outside it. They are on a debatable ground, in every sense of the term. They are doubtful in their very doubts. Their criticism has taken on a curious tone; as of a random and illiterate heckling. Thus they make current and anti-clerical cant as a sort of small-talk. They will complain of parsons dressing like parsons; as if we should be any more free if all the police who shadowed or collared us were plain-clothes detectives. Or they will complain that a sermon cannot be interrupted, and call a pulpit a coward's castle; though they do not call an editor's office a coward's castle. It would be unjust both to journalists and priests; but it would be much truer of journalists. The clergyman appears in person and could easily be kicked as he came out of church; the journalist conceals even his name so that nobody can kick him. They write wild and pointless articles and letters in the press about why the churches are empty, without even going there to find out if they are empty, or which of them are empty. Their suggestions are more vapid and vacant than the most insipid curate in a three-act farce, and move us to comfort him after the manner of the curate in the Bab Ballads; 'Your mind is not so blank as that of Hopley Porter.' So we may truly say to the very feeblest cleric: 'Your mind is not so blank as that of Indignant Layman or Plain Man or Man in the Street, or any of your critics in the newspapers; for they have not the most shadowy notion of what they want themselves, let alone of what you ought to give them.' They will suddenly turn round and revile the Church for not having prevented the War, which they themselves did not want to prevent; and which nobody had ever professed to be able to prevent, except some of that very school of progressive and cosmopolitan sceptics who are the chief enemies of the Church. It was the anti-clerical and agnostic world that was always prophesying the advent of universal peace; it is that world that was, or should have been, abashed and confounded by the advent of universal war. As for the general view that the Church was discredited by the War — they might as well say that the Ark was discredited by the Flood. When the world goes wrong, it proves rather that the Church is right. The Church is justified, not because her children do not sin, but because they do. But that marks their mood about the whole religious tradition: they are in a state of reaction against it. It is well with the boy when he lives on his father's land; and well with him again when he is far enough from it to look back on it and see it as a whole. But these people have got into an intermediate state, have fallen into an intervening valley from which they can see neither the heights beyond them nor the heights behind. They cannot get out of the penumbra of Christian controversy. They cannot be Christians and they cannot leave off being Anti-Christians. Their whole atmosphere is the atmosphere of a reaction: sulks, perversity, petty criticism. They still live in the shadow of the faith and have lost the light of the faith.

Now the best relation to our spiritual home is to be near enough to love it. But the next best is to be far enough away not to hate it. It is the contention of these pages that while the best judge of Christianity is a Christian, the next best judge would be something more like a Confucian. The worst judge of all is the man now most ready with his judgments; the ill-educated Christian turning gradually into the ill-tempered agnostic, entangled in the end of a feud of which he never understood the beginning, blighted with a sort of hereditary boredom with he knows not what, and already weary of hearing what he has never heard. He does not judge Christianity calmly as a Confucian would; he does not judge it as he would judge Confucianism. He cannot by an effort of fancy set the Catholic Church thousands of miles away in strange skies of morning and judge it as impartially as a Chinese pagoda. It is said that the great St. Francis Xavier, who very nearly succeeded in setting up the Church there as a tower overtopping all pagodas, failed partly because his followers were accused by their fellow missionaries of representing the Twelve Apostles with the garb or attributes of Chinamen. But it would be far better to see them as Chinamen, and judge them fairly as Chinamen, than to see them as featureless idols merely made to be battered by iconoclasts; or rather as cockshies to be pelted by empty-handed cockneys. It would be better to see the whole thing as a remote Asiatic cult; the mitres of its bishops as the towering headdresses of mysterious bonzes; its pastoral staffs as the sticks twisted like serpents carried in some Asiatic procession; to see the prayer-book as fantastic as the prayer-wheel and the Cross as crooked as the Swastika. Then at least we should not lose our temper as some of the sceptical critics seem to lose their temper, not to mention their wits. Their anti-clericalism has become an atmosphere, an atmosphere of negation and hostility from which they cannot escape. Compared with that, it would be better to see the whole thing as something belonging to another continent, or to another planet. It would be more philosophical to stare indifferently at bonzes than to be perpetually and pointlessly grumbling at bishops. It would be better to walk past a church as if it were a pagoda than to stand permanently in the porch, impotent either to go inside and help or to go outside and forget. For those in whom a mere reaction has thus become an obsession, I do seriously recommend the imaginative effort of conceiving the Twelve Apostles as Chinamen. In other words, I recommend these critics to try to do as much justice to Christian saints as if they were Pagan sages.

But with this we come to the final and vital point. I shall try to show in these pages that when we *do* make this imaginative effort to see the whole thing from the outside, we find that it really looks like what is traditionally said about it inside. It is exactly when the boy gets far enough off to see the giant that he sees that he really is a giant. It is exactly when we do at last see the Christian Church afar under those clear and level eastern skies that we see that it is really the Church of Christ. To put it shortly, the moment we are really impartial about it, we know why people are partial to it. But this second proposition requires more serious discussion; and I shall here set myself to discuss it.

As soon as I had clearly in my mind this conception of something solid in the solitary and unique character of the divine story, it struck me that there was exactly the same strange and yet solid character in the human story that had led up to it; because that human story also had a root that was divine. I mean that just as the Church seems to grow more remarkable when it is fairly compared with the common religious life of mankind, so mankind itself seems to grow more remarkable when we compare it with the common life of nature. And I have noticed that most modern history is driven to something like sophistry, first to soften the sharp transition from animals to men, and then to soften the sharp transition from heathens to Christians. Now the more we really read in a realistic spirit of those two transitions the sharper we shall find them to be. It is because the critics are *not* detached that they do not see this detachment; it is because they are not looking at things in a dry light that they cannot see the difference between black and white. It is because they are in a particular mood of reaction and revolt that they have a motive for making out that all the white is dirty grey and the black not so black as it is painted. I do not say there are not human excuses for their revolt; I do not say it is not in some ways sympathetic; what I say is that it is not in any way scientific. An iconoclast may be indignant; an iconoclast may be justly indignant; but an iconoclast is not impartial. And it is stark hypocrisy to pretend that nine-tenths of the higher critics and scientific evolutionists and professors of comparative religion are in the least impartial. Why should they be impartial, what is being impartial, when the whole world is at war about whether one thing is a devouring superstition or a divine hope? I do not pretend to be impartial in the sense that the final act of faith fixes a man's mind because it satisfies his mind. But I do profess to be a great deal more impartial than they are; in the sense that I can tell the story fairly, with some sort of imaginative justice to all sides; and they cannot. I do profess to be impartial in the sense that I should be ashamed to talk such nonsense about the Lama of Thibet as they do about the Pope of Rome, or to have as little sympathy with Julian the Apostate as they have with the Society of Jesus. They are not impartial; they never by any chance hold the historical scales even; and above all they are never impartial upon this point of evolution and transition. They suggest everywhere the grey gradations of twilight, because they believe it is the twilight of the gods. I propose to maintain that whether or no it is the twilight of gods, it is not the daylight of men.

I maintain that when brought out into the daylight these two things look altogether strange and unique; and that it is only in the false twilight of an imaginary period of transition that they can be made to look in the least like anything else. The first of these is the creature called man and the second is the man called Christ. I have therefore divided this book into two parts: the former being a sketch of the main adventure of the human race in so far as it remained heathen; and the second a summary of the real difference that was made by it becoming Christian. Both motives necessitate a certain method, a method which is not very easy to manage, and perhaps even less easy to define or defend.

In order to strike, in the only sane or possible sense, the note of impartiality, it is necessary to touch the nerve of novelty. I mean that in one sense we see things fairly when we see them first. That, I may remark in passing, is why children generally have very little difficulty about the dogmas of the Church. But the Church, being a highly practical thing for working and fighting, is necessarily a thing for men and not merely for children. There must be in it for working purposes a great deal of tradition, of familiarity, and even of routine. So long as its fundamentals are sincerely felt, this may even be the saner condition. But when its fundamentals are doubted, as at present, we must try to recover the candour and wonder of the child; the unspoilt realism and objectivity of innocence. Or if we cannot do that, we must try at least to shake off the cloud of mere custom and see the thing as new, if only by seeing it as unnatural. Things that may well be familiar so long as familiarity breeds affection had much better become unfamiliar when familiarity breeds contempt. For in connection with things so great as are here considered, whatever our view of them, contempt must be a mistake. Indeed contempt must be an illusion. We must invoke the most wild and soaring sort of imagination; the imagination that can see what is there.

The only way to suggest the point is by an example of something, indeed of almost anything, that has been considered beautiful or wonderful. George Wyndham once told me that he had seen one of the first aeroplanes rise for the first time and it was very wonderful; but not so wonderful as a horse allowing a man to ride on him. Somebody else has said that a fine man on a fine horse is the noblest bodily object in the world. Now, so long as people feel this in the right way, all is well. The first and best way of appreciating it is to come of people with a tradition of treating animals properly; of men in the right relation to horses. A boy who remembers his father who rode a horse, who rode it well and treated it well, will know that the relation can be satisfactory and will be satisfied. He will be all the more indignant at the ill-treatment of horses because he knows how they ought to be treated; but he will see nothing but what is normal in a man riding on a horse. He will not listen to the great modern philosopher who explains to him that the horse ought to be riding on the man. He will not pursue the pessimist fancy of Swift and say that men must be despised as monkeys and horses worshipped as gods. And horse and man together making an image that is to him human and civilised, it will be easy, as it were, to lift horse and man together into something heroic or symbolical; like a vision of St. George in the clouds. The fable of the winged horse will not be wholly unnatural to him: and he will know why Ariosto set many a Christian hero in such an airy saddle, and made him the rider of the sky. For the horse has really been lifted up along with the man in the wildest fashion in the very word we use when we speak 'chivalry.' The very name of the horse has been given to the highest mood and moment of the man; so that we might almost say that the handsomest compliment to a man is to call him a horse.

But if a man has got into a mood in which he is *not* able to feel this sort of wonder, then his cure must begin right at the other end. We must now suppose that he has drifted into a dull mood, in which somebody sitting on a horse means no more than somebody sitting on a chair. The wonder of which Wyndham spoke, the beauty that made the thing seem an equestrian statue, the meaning of the more chivalric horseman, may have become to him merely a convention and a bore. Perhaps they have been merely a fashion; perhaps they have gone out of fashion; perhaps they have been talked about too much or talked about in the wrong way; perhaps it was then difficult to care for horses without the horrible risk of being horsy. Anyhow, he has got into a condition when he cares no more for a horse than for a towel-horse. His grandfather's charge at Balaclava seems to him as dull and dusty as the album containing such family portraits. Such a person has not really become enlightened about the album; on the contrary, he has only become blind with the dust. But when he has reached *that* degree of blindness, he will not be able to look at a horse or a horseman at all until he has seen the whole thing as a thing entirely unfamiliar and almost unearthly.

Out of some dark forest under some ancient dawn there must come towards us, with lumbering yet dancing motions, one of the very queerest of the prehistoric creatures. We must see for the first time the strangely small head set on a neck not only longer but thicker than itself, as the face of a gargoyle is thrust out upon a gutter-spout, the one disproportionate crest of hair running along the ridge of that heavy neck like a beard in the wrong place; the feet, each like a solid club of horn, alone amid the feet of so many cattle; so that the true fear is to be found in showing, not the cloven, but the uncloven hoof. Nor is it mere verbal fancy to see him thus as a unique monster; for in a sense a monster means what is unique, and he is really unique. But the point is that when we thus see him as the first man saw him, we begin once more to have some imaginative sense of what it meant when the first man rode him. In such a dream he may seem ugly, but he does not seem unimpressive; and certainly that two-legged dwarf who could get on top of him will not seem unimpressive. By a longer and more erratic road we shall come back to the same marvel of the man and the horse; and the marvel will be, if possible, even more marvellous. We shall have again a glimpse of St. George; the more glorious because St. George is not riding on the horse, but rather riding on the dragon.

In this example, which I have taken merely because it is an example, it will be noted that I do not say that the nightmare seen by the first man of the forest is either more true or more wonderful than the normal mare of the stable seen by the civilised person who can appreciate what is normal. Of the two extremes, I think on the whole that the traditional grasp of truth is the better. But I say that the truth is found at one or other of these two extremes, and is lost in the intermediate condition of mere fatigue and forgetfulness of tradition. In other words, I say it is better to see a horse as a monster than to see it only as a slow substitute for a motor-car. If we have got into *that* state of mind about a horse as something stale, it is far better to be frightened of a horse because it is a good deal too fresh.

Now, as it is with the monster that is called a horse, so it is with the monster that is called a man. Of course the best condition of all, in my opinion, is always to have regarded man as he is regarded in my philosophy. He who holds the Christian and Catholic view of human nature will feel certain that it is a universal and therefore a sane view, and will be satisfied. But if he has lost the pose to strike wherever possible this note of what is new and strange, and for that reason the style even on so serious a subject may sometimes be deliberately grotesque and fanciful. I do desire to help the reader to see Christendom from the outside in the sense of seeing it as a whole, against the background of other historic things; just as I desire him to see humanity as a whole against the background of natural things. And I say that in both cases, when seen thus, they stand out from their background like supernatural things. They do *not* fade into the rest with the colours of impressionism; they stand out from the rest with the colours of heraldry; as vivid as a red cross on a white shield or a black lion on a ground of gold. So stands the Red Clay against the green field of nature, or the White Christ against the red clay of his race.

But in order to see them clearly we have to see them as a whole. We have to see how they developed as well as how they began; for the most incredible part of the story is that things which began thus should have developed thus. Anyone who chooses to indulge in mere imagination can imagine that other things might have happened or other entities evolved. Anyone thinking of what might have happened may conceive a sort of evolutionary equality; but anyone facing what did happen must face an exception and a prodigy. If there was ever a moment when man was only an animal, we can if we choose make a fancy picture of his career transferred to some other animal. An entertaining fantasia might be made in which elephants built in elephantine architecture, with towers and turrets like tusks and trunks, cities beyond the scale of any colossus. A pleasant fable might be conceived in which a cow had developed a costume, and put on four boots and two pairs of trousers. We could imagine a Supermonkey more marvellous than any Superman, a quadrumanous creature carving and painting with his hands and cooking and carpentering with his feet. But if we are considering what did happen, we shall certainly decide that man has distanced everything else with a distance like that of the astronomical spaces and a speed like that of the still thunderbolt of the light. And in the same fashion, while we can if we choose see the Church amid a mob of Mithraic or Manichean superstitions squabbling and killing each other at the end of the Empire, while we can if we choose imagine the Church killed in the struggle and some other chance cult taking its place, we shall be the more surprised (and possibly puzzled) if we meet it two thousand years afterwards rushing through the ages as the winged thunderbolt of thought and everlasting enthusiasm; a thing without rival or resemblance; and still as new as it is old.

PART I

On the Creature Called Man

I

THE MAN IN THE CAVE

Far away in some strange constellation in skies infinitely remote, there is a small star, which astronomers may some day discover. At least I could never observe in the faces or demeanour of most astronomers or men of science any evidence that they have discovered it; though as a matter of fact they were walking about on it all the time. It is a star that brings forth out of itself very strange plants and very strange animals; and none stranger than the men of science. That at least is the way in which I should begin a history of the world, if I had to follow the scientific custom of beginning with an account of the astronomical universe. I should try to see even this earth from the outside, not by the hackneyed insistence of its relative position to the sun, but by some imaginative effort to conceive its remote position for the dehumanised spectator. Only I do not believe in being dehumanised in order to study humanity. I do not believe in dwelling upon the distances that are supposed to dwarf the world; I think there is even something a trifle vulgar about this idea of trying to rebuke spirit by size. And as the first idea is not feasible, that of making the earth a strange planet so as to make it significant, I will not stoop to the other trick of making it a small planet in order to make it insignificant. I would rather insist that we do not even know that it is a planet at all, in the sense in which we know that it is a place; and a very extraordinary place too. That is the note which I wish to strike from the first, if not in the astronomical, then in some more familiar fashion.

One of my first journalistic adventures, or misadventures, concerned a comment on Grant Allen, who had written a book about the Evolution of the Idea of God. I happened to remark that it would be much more interesting if God wrote a book about the evolution of the idea of Grant Allen. And I remember that the editor objected to my remark on the ground that it was blasphemous; which naturally amused me not a little. For the joke of it was, of course, that it never occurred to him to notice the title of the book itself, which really was blasphemous; for it was, when translated into English, 'I will show you how this nonsensical notion that there is a God grew up among men.' My remark was strictly pious and proper; confessing the divine purpose even in its most seemingly dark or meaningless manifestations. In that hour I learned many things, including the fact that there is something purely acoustic in much of that agnostic sort of reverence. The editor had not seen the point, because in the title of the book the long word came at the beginning and the short word at the end; whereas in my comments the short word came at the beginning and gave him a sort of shock. I have noticed that if you put a word like God into the same sentence with a word like dog, these abrupt and angular words affect people like pistol-shots. Whether you say that God made the dog or the dog made God does not seem to matter; that is only one of the sterile disputations of the too subtle theologians. But so long as you begin with a long word like evolution the rest will roll harmlessly past; very probably the editor had not read the whole of the title, for it is rather a long title and he was rather a busy man.

But this little incident has always lingered in my mind as a sort of parable. Most modern histories of mankind begin with the word evolution, and with a rather wordy exposition of evolution, for much the same reason that operated in this case. There is something slow and soothing and gradual about the word and even about the idea. As a matter of fact, it is not, touching these primary things, a very practical word or a very profitable idea. Nobody can imagine how nothing could turn into something. Nobody can get an inch nearer to it by explaining how something could turn into something else. It is really far more logical to start by saying 'In the beginning God created heaven and earth' even if you only mean 'In the beginning some unthinkable power began some unthinkable process.' For God is by its nature a name of mystery, and nobody ever supposed that man could imagine how a world was created any more than he could create one. But evolution really is mistaken for explanation. It has the fatal quality of leaving on many minds the impression that they do understand it and everything else; just as many of them live under a sort of illusion that they have read the *Origin of Species*.

But this notion of something smooth and slow, like the ascent of a slope, is a great part of the illusion. It is an illogicality as well as an illusion; for slowness has really nothing to do with the question. An event is not any more intrinsically intelligible or unintelligible because of the pace at which it moves. For a man who does not believe in a miracle, a slow miracle would be just as incredible as a swift one. The Greek witch may have turned sailors to swine with a stroke of the wand. But to see a naval gentleman of our acquaintance looking a little more like a pig every day, till he ended with four trotters and a curly tail, would not be any more soothing. It might be rather more creepy and uncanny. The medieval wizard may have flown through the air from the top of a tower; but to see an old gentleman walking through the air, in a leisurely and lounging manner, would still seem to call for some explanation. Yet there runs through all the rationalistic treatment of history this curious and confused idea that difficulty is avoided, or even mystery eliminated, by dwelling on mere delay or on something dilatory in the processes of things. There will be something to be said upon particular examples elsewhere; the question here is the false atmosphere of facility and ease given by the mere suggestion of going slow; the sort of comfort that might be given to a nervous old woman travelling for the first time in a motor-car.

Mr. H. G. Wells has confessed to being a prophet; and in this matter he was a prophet at his own expense. It is curious that his first fairy-tale was a complete answer to his last book of history. The Time Machine destroyed in advance all comfortable conclusions founded on the mere relativity of time. In that sublime nightmare the hero saw trees shoot up like green rockets, and vegetation spread visibly like a green conflagration, or the sun shoot across the sky from east to west with the swiftness of a meteor. Yet in his sense these things were quite as natural when they went swiftly; and in our sense they are quite as supernatural when they go slowly. The ultimate question is why they go at all; and anybody who really understands that question will know that it always has been and always will be a religious question; or at any rate a philosophical or metaphysical question. And most certainly he will not think the question answered by some substitution of gradual for abrupt change; or, in other words by a merely relative question of the same story being spun out or rattled rapidly through, as can be done with any story at a cinema by turning a handle.

Now what is needed for these problems of primitive existence is something more like a primitive spirit. In calling up this vision of the first things, I would ask the reader to make with me a sort of experiment in simplicity. And by simplicity I do not mean stupidity, but rather the sort of clarity that sees things like life rather than words like evolution. For this purpose it would really be better to turn the handle of the Time Machine a little more quickly and see the grass growing and the trees springing up into the sky, if that experiment could contract and concentrate and make vivid the upshot of the whole affair. What we know, in a sense in which we know nothing else, is that the trees and the grass did grow and that a number of other extraordinary things do in fact happen; that queer creatures support themselves in the empty air by beating it with fans of various fantastic shapes; that other queer creatures steer themselves about alive under a load of mighty waters; that other queer creatures walk about on four legs, and that the queerest creature of all walks about on two. These are things and not theories; and compared with them evolution and the atom and even the solar system are merely theories. The matter here is one of history and not of philosophy; so that it need only be noted that no philosopher denies that a mystery still attaches to the two great transitions: the origin of the universe itself and the origin of the principle of life itself. Most philosophers have the enlightenment to add that a third mystery attaches to the origin of man himself. In other words, a third bridge was built across a third abyss of the unthinkable when there came into the world what we call reason and what we call will. Man is not merely an evolution but rather a revolution. That he has a backbone or other parts upon a similar pattern to birds and fishes is an obvious fact, whatever be the meaning of the fact. But if we attempt to regard him, as it were, as a quadruped standing on his hind legs, we shall find what follows far more fantastic and subversive than if he were standing on his head.

I will take one example to serve for an introduction to the story of man. It illustrates what I mean by saying that a certain childish directness is needed to see the truth about the childhood of the world. It illustrates what I mean by saying that a mixture of popular science and journalistic jargon have confused the facts about the first things, so that we cannot see which of them really comes first. It illustrates, though only in one convenient illustration, all that I mean by the necessity of seeing the sharp differences that give its shape to history, instead of being submerged in all these generalisations about slowness and sameness. For we do indeed require, in Mr. Wells's phrase, an outline of history. But we may venture to say, in Mr. Mantalini's phrase, that this evolutionary history has no outline or is a demd outline. But, above all, it illustrates what I mean by saying that the more we really look at man as an animal, the less he will look like one.

To-day all our novels and newspapers will be found swarming with numberless allusions to a popular character called a Cave-Man. He seems to be quite familiar to us, not only as a public character but as a private character. His psychology is seriously taken into account in psychological fiction and psychological medicine. So far as I can understand, his chief occupation in life was knocking his wife about, or treating women in general with what is, I believe, known in the world of the film as 'rough stuff.' I have never happened to come upon the evidence for this idea; and I do not know on what primitive diaries or prehistoric divorce-reports it is founded. Nor, as I have explained elsewhere, have I ever been able to see the probability of it, even considered a priori. We are always told without any explanation or authority that primitive man waved a club and knocked the woman down before he carried her off. But on every animal analogy, it would seem an almost morbid modesty and reluctance, on the part of the lady, always to insist on being knocked down before consenting to be carried off. And I repeat that I can never comprehend why, when the male was so very rude, the female should have been so very refined. The cave-man may have been a brute, but there is no reason why he should have been more brutal than the brutes. And the loves of the giraffes and the river romance of the hippopotami are effected without any of this preliminary fracas or shindy. The cave-man may have been no better that the cave-bear;

but the child she-bear, so famous in hymnology, is not trained with any such bias for spinsterhood. In short these details of the domestic life of the cave puzzle me upon either the revolutionary or the static hypothesis; and in any case I should like to look into the evidence for them; but unfortunately I have never been able to find it. But the curious thing is this: that while ten thousand tongues of more or less scientific or literary gossip seemed to be talking at once about this unfortunate fellow, under the title of the cave-man, the one connection in which it is really relevant and sensible to talk about him as the cave-man has been comparatively neglected. People have used this loose term in twenty loose ways; but they have never even looked at their own term for what could really be learned from it.

In fact, people have been interested in everything about the cave-man except what he did in the cave. Now there does happen to be some real evidence of what he did in the cave. It is little enough, like all the prehistoric evidence, but it is concerned with the real cave-man and his cave and not the literary cave-man and his club. And it will be valuable to our sense of reality to consider quite simply what that real evidence is, and not to go beyond it. What was found in the cave was not the club, the horrible gory club notched with the number of women it had knocked on the head. The cave was not a Bluebeard's Chamber filled with the skeletons of slaughtered wives; it was not filled with female skulls all arranged in rows and all cracked like eggs. It was something quite unconnected, one way or the other, with all the modern phrases and philosophical implications and literary rumours which confuse the whole question for us. And if we wish to see as it really is this authentic glimpse of the morning of the world, it will be far better to conceive even the story of its discovery as some such legend of the land of morning. It would be far better to tell the tale of what was really found as simply as the tale of heroes finding the Golden Fleece or the Gardens of the Hesperides, if we could so escape from a fog of controversial theories into the clear colours and clean-cut outlines of such a dawn. The old epic poets at least knew how to tell a story, possibly a tall story but never a twisted story, never a story tortured out of its own shape to fit theories and philosophies invented centuries afterwards. It would be well if modern investigators could describe their discoveries in the bald narrative style of the earliest travellers, and without any of these long allusive words that are full of irrelevant implication and suggestion. Then we might realise exactly what we do know about the cave-man, or at any rate about the cave.

A priest and a boy entered sometime ago a hollow in the hills and passed into a sort of subterranean tunnel that led into a labyrinth of such sealed and secret corridors of rock. They crawled through cracks that seemed almost impassable, they crept through tunnels that might have been made for moles, they dropped into holes as hopeless as wells, they seemed to be burying themselves alive seven times over beyond the hope of resurrection. This is but the commonplace of all such courageous exploration; but what is needed here is some one who shall put such stories in the primary light, in which they are not commonplace. There is, for instance, something strangely symbolic in the accident that the first intruders into that sunken world were a priest and a boy, the types of the antiquity and of youth of the world. But here I am even more concerned with the symbolism of the boy than with that of the priest. Nobody who remembers boyhood needs to be told what it might be to a boy to enter like Peter Pan under a roof of the roots of all the trees and go deeper and deeper, till he reach what William Morris called the very roots of the mountains. Suppose somebody, with that simple and unspoilt realism that is a part of innocence, to pursue that journey to its end, not for the sake of what he could deduce or demonstrate in some dusty magazine controversy, but simply for the sake of what he could see. What he did see at last was a cavern so far from the light of day that it might have been the legendary Domdaniel cavern[1] that was under the floor of the sea. This secret chamber of rock, when illuminated after its long night of unnumbered ages, revealed on its walls large and sprawling outlines diversified with coloured earths; and when they followed the lines of them they recognised, across that vast void of ages, the movement and the gesture of a man's hand. They were drawings or paintings of animals; and they were drawn or painted not only by a man but by an artist. Under whatever archaic

---

[1] A fabled submarine hall, located under the sea near Tunis, where a magician or sorcerer met with his disciples. It first appears in Chaves and Gazotte's *Continuation of the Arabian Nights* (1788–1793).

limitations, they showed that love of the long sweeping or the long wavering line which any man who has ever drawn or tried to draw will recognise; and about which no artist will allow himself to be contradicted by any scientist. They showed the experimental and adventurous spirit of the artist, the spirit that does not avoid but attempts difficult things; as where the draughtsman had represented the action of the stag when he swings his head clean round and noses towards his tail, an action familiar enough in the horse. But there are many modern animal-painters who would set themselves something of a task in rendering it truly. In this and twenty other details it is clear that the artist had watched animals with a certain interest and presumably a certain pleasure. In that sense it would seem that he was not only an artist but a naturalist; the sort of naturalist who is really natural.

Now it is needless to note, except in passing, that there is nothing whatever in the atmosphere of that cave to suggest the bleak and pessimistic atmosphere of that journalistic cave of the winds, that blows and bellows about us with countless echoes concerning the cave-man. So far as any human character can be hinted at by such traces of the past, that human character is quite human and even humane. It is certainly not the ideal of an inhuman character, like the abstraction invoked in popular science. When novelists and educationists and psychologists of all sorts talk about the cave-man, they never conceive him in connection with anything that is really in the cave. When the realist of the sex novel writes, 'Red sparks danced in Dagmar Doubledick's brain; he felt the spirit of the cave-man rising within him,' the novelist's readers would be very much disappointed if Dagmar only went off and drew large pictures of cows on the drawing-room wall. When the psycho-analyst writes to a patient, 'The submerged instincts of the cave-man are doubtless prompting you to gratify a violent impulse,' he does not refer to the impulse to paint in water-colours; or to make conscientious studies of how cattle swing their heads when they graze. Yet we do know for a fact that the cave-man did these mild and innocent things; and we have not the most minute speck of evidence that he did any of the violent and ferocious things. In other words the cave-man as commonly presented to us is simply a myth or rather a muddle; for a myth has at least an imaginative outline of truth. The whole of the current way of talking is simply a confusion and a misunderstanding, founded on no sort of scientific evidence and valued only as an excuse for a very modern mood of anarchy. If any gentleman wants to knock a woman about, he can surely be a cad without taking away the character of the cave-man, about whom we know next to nothing except what we can gather from a few harmless and pleasing pictures on a wall.

But this is not the point about the pictures or the particular moral here to be drawn from them. That moral is something much larger and simpler, so large and simple that when it is first stated it will sound childish. And indeed it is in the highest sense childish; and that is why I have in this apologue in some sense seen it through the eyes of a child. It is the biggest of all the facts really facing the boy in the cavern; and is perhaps too big to be seen. If the boy was one of the flock of the priest, it may be presumed that he had been trained in a certain quality of common sense; that common sense that often comes to us in the form of tradition. In that case he would simply recognise the primitive man's work as the work of a man, interesting but in no way incredible in being primitive. He would see what was there to see; and he would not be tempted into seeing what was not there, by any evolutionary excitement or fashionable speculation. If he had heard of such things he would admit, of course, that the speculations might be true and were not incompatible with the facts that were true. The artist may have had another side to his character besides that which he has alone left on record in his works of art. The primitive man may have taken a pleasure in beating women as well as in drawing animals; all we can say is that the drawings record the one but not the other. It may be true that when the cave-man's finished jumping on his mother, or his wife as the case may be, he loves to hear the little brook a-gurgling, and also to watch the deer as they come down to drink at the brook. These things are not impossible, but they are irrelevant. The common sense of the child could confine itself to learning from the facts what the facts have to teach; and the pictures in the cave are very nearly all the facts there are. So far as that evidence goes, the child would be justified in assuming that a man had represented animals with rock and red ochre for the same reason as he himself was in the habit of trying to represent animals with charcoal and red chalk. The man had drawn a stag just as the child had drawn a horse; because it was fun. The man had drawn a stag with his head turned as the child had drawn a pig with his eyes shut; because it was difficult. The child and the man, being both human, would be united by the brotherhood of men; and the brotherhood of men is even nobler when it bridges the abyss of ages than when it bridges only the chasm of class. But anyhow he would see no evidence of the cave-man of crude evolutionism; because there is none to be seen. If somebody told him that the pictures had all been drawn by St. Francis of Assisi out of pure and saintly love of animals, there would be nothing in the cave to contradict it.

Indeed I once knew a lady who half-humorously suggested that the cave was a crèche, in which the babies were put to be specially safe, and that coloured animals were drawn on the walls to amuse them; very much as diagrams of elephants and giraffes adorn a modern infant school. And though this was but a jest, it does draw attention to some of the other assumptions that we make only too readily. The pictures do not prove even that the cave-men lived in caves, any more than the discovery of a wine-cellar in Balham (long after that suburb had been destroyed by human or divine wrath) would prove that the Victorian middle classes lived entirely underground. The cave might have had a special purpose like the cellar; it might have been a religious shrine or a refuge in war or the meeting-place of a secret society or all sorts of things. But it is quite true that its artistic decoration has much more of the atmosphere of a nursery than of any of these nightmares of anarchical fury and fear. I have conceived a child as standing in the cave; and it is easy to conceive any child, modern or immeasurably remote, as making a living gesture as if to pat the painted beasts upon the wall. In that gesture there is a foreshadowing, as we shall see later, of another cavern and another child.

But suppose the boy had not been taught by a priest but by a professor, by one of the professors who simplify the relation of men and beasts to a mere evolutionary variation. Suppose the boy saw himself, with the same simplicity and sincerity, as a mere Mowgli[2] running with the pack of nature and roughly indistinguishable from the rest save by a relative and recent variation. What would be for him the simplest lesson of that strange stone picture-book? After all, it would come back to this; that he had dug very deep and found the place where a man had drawn the picture of a reindeer. But he would dig a good deal deeper before he found a place where a reindeer had drawn a picture of a man. That sounds like a truism, but in this connection it is really a very tremendous truth. He might descend to depths unthinkable, he might sink into sunken continents as strange as remote stars, he might find himself in the inside of the world as far from men as the other side of the moon; he might see in those cold chasms or colossal terraces of stone, traced in the faint hieroglyphic of the fossil, the ruins of lost dynasties of biological life, rather like the ruins of successive creations and separate universes than the stages in the story of one. He would find the trail of monsters blindly developing in directions outside all our common imagery of fish and bird; groping and grasping and touching life with every extravagant elongation of horn and tongue and tenacle; growing a forest of fantastic caricatures of the claw and the fin and the finger. But nowhere would he find one finger that had traced one significant line upon the sand; nowhere one claw that had even begun to scratch the faint suggestion of a form. To all appearance, the thing would be as unthinkable in all those countless cosmic variations of forgotten aeons as it would be in the beasts and birds before our eyes. The child would no more expect to see it than to see the cat scratch on the wall a vindictive caricature of the dog. The childish common sense would keep the most evolutionary child from expecting to see anything like that; yet in the traces of the rude and recently evolved ancestors of humanity he would have seen exactly that. It must surely strike him as strange that men so remote from him should be so near, and that beasts so near to him should be so remote. To his simplicity it must seem at least odd that he could not find any trace of the beginning of any arts among any animals. That

[2] In Rudyard Kipling's *Jungle Books* (1894), a native boy reared by wolves in the jungles of India.

is the simplest lesson to learn in the cavern of the coloured pictures; only it is too simple to be learnt. It is the simple truth that man does differ from the brutes in kind and not in degree; and the proof of it is here; that it sounds like a truism to say that the most primitive man drew a picture of a monkey and that it sounds like a joke to say that the most intelligent monkey drew a picture of a man. Something of division and disproportion has appeared; and it is unique. Art is the signature of man.

That is the sort of simple truth with which a story of the beginnings ought really to begin. The evolutionist stands staring in the painted cavern at the things that are too large to be seen and too simple to be understood. He tries to deduce all sorts of other indirect and doubtful things from the details of the pictures, because he cannot see the primary significance of the whole; thin and theoretical deductions about the absence of religion or the presence of superstition; about tribal government and hunting and human sacrifice and heaven knows what. In the next chapter I shall try to trace in a little more detail the much disputed question about these prehistoric origins of human ideas and especially of the religious idea. Here I am only taking this one case of the cave as a sort of symbol of the simpler sort of truth with which the story ought to start. When all is said, the main fact that the record of the reindeer men attests, along with all other records, is that the reindeer man could draw and the reindeer could not. If the reindeer man was as much an animal as the reindeer, it was all the more extraordinary that he could do what all other animals could not. If he was an ordinary product of biological growth, like any other beast or bird, then it is all the more extraordinary that he was not in the least like any other beast or bird. He seems rather more supernatural as a natural product than as a supernatural one.

But I have begun this story in the cave, like the cave of the speculations of Plato, because it is a sort of model of the mistake of merely evolutionary introductions and prefaces. It is useless to begin by saying that everything was slow and smooth and a mere matter of development and degree. For in the plain matter like the pictures there is in fact not a trace of any such development or degree. Monkeys did not begin pictures and men finish them; Pithecanthropus did not draw a reindeer badly and Homo Sapiens draw it well. The higher animals did not draw better and better portraits; the dog did not paint better in his best period than in his early bad manner as a jackal; the wild horse was not an Impressionist and the race-horse a Post-Impressionist. All we can say of this notion of reproducing things in shadow or representative shape is that it exists nowhere in nature except in man; and that we cannot even talk about it without treating man as something separate from nature. In other words, every sane sort of history must begin with man as man, a thing standing absolute and alone. How he came there, or indeed how anything else came there, is a thing for theologians and philosophers and scientists and not for historians. But an excellent test case of this isolation and mystery is the matter of the impulse of art. This creature was truly different from all other creatures; because he was a creator as well as a creature. Nothing in that sense could be made in any other image but the image of man. But the truth is so true that, even in the absence of any religious belief, it must be assumed in the form of some moral or metaphysical principle. In the next chapter we shall see how this principle applies to all the historical hypotheses and evolutionary ethics now in fashion; to the origins of tribal government or mythological belief. But the clearest and most convenient example to start with is this popular one of what the cave-man really did in his cave. It means that somehow or other a new thing had appeared in the cavernous night of nature, a mind that is like a mirror. It is like a mirror because it is truly a thing of reflection. It is like a mirror because in it alone all the other shapes can be seen like shining shadows in a vision. Above all, it is like a mirror because it is the only thing of its kind. Other things may resemble it or resemble each other in various ways; other things may excel it or excel each other in various ways; just as in the furniture of a room a table may be round like a mirror or a cupboard may be larger than a mirror. But the mirror is the only thing that can contain them all. Man is the microcosm; man is the measure of all things; man is the image of God. These are the only real lessons to be learnt in the cave, and it is time to leave it for the open road.

It will be well in this place, however, to sum up once and for all what is meant by saying that man is at once the exception to everything and the mirror and the measure of all things. But to see man as he is, it is necessary once more to keep close to that simplicity that can clear itself of accumulated clouds of sophistry. The simplest truth about man is that he is a very strange being; almost in the sense of being a stranger on the earth. In all sobriety, he has much more of the external appearance of one bringing alien habits from another land than of a mere growth of this one. He has an unfair advantage and an unfair disadvantage. He cannot sleep in his own skin; he cannot trust his own instincts. He is at once a creator moving miraculous hands and fingers and a kind of cripple. He is wrapped in artificial bandages called clothes; he is propped on artificial crutches called furniture. His mind has the same doubtful liberties and the same wild limitations. Alone among the animals, he is shaken with the beautiful madness called laughter; as if he had caught sight of some secret in the very shape of the universe hidden from the universe itself. Alone among the animals he feels the need of averting his thought from the root realities of his own bodily being; of hiding them as in the presence of some higher possibility which creates the mystery of shame. Whether we praise these things as natural to man or abuse them as artificial in nature, they remain in the same sense unique. This is realised by the whole popular instinct called religion, until disturbed by pedants, especially the laborious pedants of the Simple Life. The most sophistical of all sophists are gymnosophists.

It is not natural to see man as a natural product. It is not common sense to call man a common object of the country or the seashore. It is not seeing straight to see him as an animal. It is not sane. It sins against the light; against that broad daylight of proportion which is the principle of all reality. It is reached by stretching a point, by making out a case, by artificially selecting a certain light and shade, by bringing into prominence the lesser or lower things which may happen to be similar. The solid thing standing in the sunlight, the thing we can walk round and see from all sides, is quite different. It is also quite extraordinary; and the more sides we see of it the more extraordinary it seems. It is emphatically not a thing that follows or flows naturally from anything else. If we imagine that an inhuman or impersonal intelligence could have felt from the first the general nature of the non-human world sufficiently to see that things would evolve in whatever way they did evolve, there would have been nothing whatever in all that natural world to prepare such a mind for such an unnatural novelty. To such a mind, man would most certainly not have seemed something like one herd out of a hundred herds finding richer pasture; or one swallow out of a hundred swallows making a summer under a strange sky. It would not be in the same scale and scarcely in the same dimension. We might as truly say that it would not be in the same universe. It would be more like seeing one cow out of a hundred cows suddenly jump over the moon or one pig out of a hundred pigs grow wings in a flash and fly. It would not be a question of the cattle finding their own grazing-ground but of their building their own cattle-sheds, not a question of one swallow making a summer but of his making a summer-house. For the very fact that birds do build nests is one of those similarities that sharpen the startling difference. The very fact that a bird can get as far as building a nest, and cannot get any farther, proves that he has not a mind as man has a mind; it proves it more completely than if he built nothing at all. If he built nothing at all, he might possibly be a philosopher of the Quietist or Buddhistic school, indifferent to all but the mind within. But when he builds as he does build and is satisfied and sings aloud with satisfaction, then we know there is really an invisible veil like a pane of glass between him and us, like the window on which a bird will beat in vain. But suppose our abstract onlooker saw one of the birds begin to build as men build. Suppose in an incredibly short space of time there were seven styles of architecture for one style of nest. Suppose the bird carefully selected forked twigs and pointed leaves to express the piercing piety of Gothic, but turned to broad foliage and black mud when he sought in a darker mood to call up the heavy columns of Bel and Ashtaroth; making his nest indeed one of the hanging gardens of Babylon. Suppose the bird made little clay statues of birds celebrated in letters or politics and stuck them up in front of the nest. Suppose that one bird out of a thousand birds began to do one of the thousand things that man had already done even in the morning of the world; and we can be quite certain that the onlooker would not regard such a bird as a mere evolutionary variety of the other birds; he would regard it as a very fearful wild-fowl indeed; possibly as a bird of ill-omen, certainly as an omen. That bird would tell the augurs, not of something that would happen, but of something that had happened. That something would be the appearance of a mind with a new dimension of depth; a mind like that of man. If there be no God, no other mind could conceivably have foreseen it.

Now, as a matter of fact, there is not a shadow of evidence that *this* thing was evolved at all. There is not a particle of proof that *this* transition came slowly, or even that it came naturally. In a strictly scientific sense, we simply know nothing whatever about how it grew, or whether it grew, or what it is. There may be a broken trail of stone and bone faintly suggesting the development of the human body. There is nothing even faintly suggesting such a development of this human mind. It was not and it was; we know not in what instant or in what infinity of years. Something happened; and it has all the appearance of a transaction outside of time. It has therefore nothing to do with history in the ordinary sense. The historian must take it or something like it for granted; it is not his business as a historian to explain it. But if he cannot explain it as a historian, he will not explain it as a biologist. In neither case is there any disgrace to him in accepting it without explaining it; for it is a reality, and history and biology deal with realities. He is quite justified in calmly confronting the pig with wings and the cow that jumped over the moon, merely because they have happened. He can reasonably accept man as a freak, because he accepts man as a fact. He can be perfectly comfortable in a crazy and disconnected world, or in a world that can produce such a crazy and disconnected thing. For reality is a thing in which we can all repose, even if it hardly seems related to anything else. The thing is there; and that is enough for most of us. But if we do indeed want to know how it can conceivably have come there, if we do indeed wish to see it related realistically to other things, if we do insist on seeing it evolved before our very eyes from an environment nearer to its own nature, then assuredly it is to very different things that we must go. We must stir very strange memories and return to very simple dreams, if we desire some origin that can make man other than a monster. We shall have discovered very different causes before he becomes a creature of causation; and invoked other authority to turn him into something reasonable, or even into anything probable. That way lies all that is at once awful and familiar and forgotten, with dreadful faces thronged and fiery arms. We can accept man as a fact, if we are content with an unexplained fact. We can accept him as an animal, if we can live with a fabulous animal. But if we must needs have sequence and necessity, then indeed we must provide a prelude and crescendo of mounting miracles, that ushered in with unthinkable thunders in all the seven heavens of another order, a man may be an ordinary thing.

II

PROFESSORS AND PREHISTORIC MEN

Science is weak about these prehistoric things in a way that has hardly been noticed. The science whose modern marvels we all admire succeeds by incessantly adding to its data. In all practical inventions, in most natural discoveries, it can always increase evidence by experiment. But it cannot experiment in making men; or even in watching to see what the first men make. An inventor can advance step by step in the construction of an aeroplane, even if he is only experimenting with sticks and scraps of metal in his own back-yard. But he cannot watch the Missing Link evolving in his own backyard. If he has made a mistake in his calculations, the aeroplane will correct it by crashing to the ground. But if he has made a mistake about the arboreal habitat of his ancestor, he cannot see his arboreal ancestor falling off the tree. He cannot keep a cave-man like a cat in the back-yard and watch him to see whether he does really practice cannibalism or carry off his mate on the principles of marriage by capture. He cannot keep a tribe of primitive men like a pack of hounds and notice how far they are influenced by the herd instinct. If he sees a particular bird behave in a particular way, he can get other birds and see if they behave in that way; but if he finds a skull, or the scrap of a skull, in the hollow of a hill, he cannot multiply it into a vision of the valley of dry bones. In dealing with a past that has almost entirely perished, he can only go by evidence and not by experiment. And there is hardly enough evidence to be even evidential. Thus while most science moves in a sort of curve, being constantly corrected by new evidence, this science flies off into space in a straight line uncorrected by anything. But the habit of forming conclusions, as they can really be formed in more fruitful fields, is so fixed in the scientific mind that it cannot resist talking like this. It talks about the idea suggested by one scrap of bone as if it were something like the aeroplane which is constructed at last out of whole scrapheaps of scraps of metal. The trouble with the professor of the prehistoric is that he cannot scrap his scrap. The marvellous and triumphant aeroplane is made out of a hundred mistakes. The student of origins can only make one mistake and stick to it.

We talk very truly of the patience of science; but in this department it would be truer to talk of the impatience of science. Owing to the difficulty above described, the theorist is in far too much of a hurry. We have a series of hypotheses so hasty that they may well be called fancies, and cannot in any case be further corrected by facts. The most empirical anthropologist is here as limited as an antiquary. He can only cling to a fragment of the past and has no way of increasing it for the future. He can only clutch his fragment of fact, almost as the primitive man clutched his fragment of flint. And indeed he does deal with it in much the same way and for much the same reason. It is his tool and his only tool. It is his weapon and his only weapon. He often wields it with a fanaticism far in excess of anything shown by men of science when they can collect more facts from experience and even add new facts by experiment. Sometimes the professor with his bone becomes almost as dangerous as a dog with his bone. And the dog at least does not deduce a theory from it, proving that mankind is going to the dogs—or that it came from them.

For instance, I have pointed out the difficulty of keeping a monkey and watching it evolve into a man. Experimental evidence of such an evolution being impossible, the professor is not content to say (as most of us would be ready to say) that such an evolution is likely enough anyhow. He produces his little bone, or little collection of bones, and deduces the most marvellous things from it. He found in Java a piece of a skull, seeming by its contour to be smaller than the human. Somewhere near it he found an upright thigh-bone and in the same scattered fashion some teeth that were not human. If they all form part of one creature, which is doubtful, our conception of the creature would be almost equally doubtful. But the effect on popular science was to produce a complete and even complex figure, finished down to the last details of hair and habits. He was given a name as if he were an ordinary historical character. People talked of Pithecanthropus as of Pitt or Fox or Napoleon. Popular histories published portraits of him like the portraits of Charles the First and George the Fourth. A detailed drawing was reproduced, carefully shaded, to show that the very hairs of his head were all numbered. No uninformed person looking at its carefully lined face and wistful eyes would imagine for a moment that this was the portrait of a thigh-bone; or of a few teeth and a fragment of a cranium. In the same way people talked about him as if he were an individual whose influence and character were familiar to us all. I have just read a story in a magazine about Java, and how modern white inhabitants of that island are prevailed on to misbehave themselves by the personal influence of poor old Pithecanthropus. That the modern inhabitants of Java misbehave themselves I can very readily believe; but I do not imagine that they need any encouragement from the discovery of a few highly doubtful bones. Anyhow, those bones are far too few and fragmentary and dubious to fill up the whole of the vast void that does in reason and in reality lie between man and his bestial ancestors, if they were his ancestors. On the assumption of that evolutionary connection (a connection which I am not in the least concerned to deny), the really arresting and remarkable fact is the comparative absence of any such remains recording that connection at that point. The sincerity of Darwin really admitted this; and that is how we came to use such a term as the Missing Link. But the dogmatism of Darwinians has been too strong for the agnosticism of Darwin; and men have insensibly fallen into turning this entirely negative term into a positive image. They talk of searching for the habits and habitat of the Missing Link; as if one were to talk of being on friendly terms with the gap in a narrative or the hole in an argument, of taking a walk with a *non-sequitur* or dining with an undistributed middle.

In this sketch, therefore, of man in his relation to certain religious and historical problems, I shall waste no further space on these speculations on the nature of man before he became man. His body may have been evolved from the brutes; but we know nothing of any such transition that throws the smallest light upon his soul as it has shown itself in history. Unfortunately the same school of writers pursue the same style of reasoning when they come to the first real evidence about the first real men. Strictly speaking of course we know nothing about prehistoric man, for the simple reason that he was prehistoric. The history of prehistoric man is a very obvious contradiction in terms. It is the sort of unreason in which only rationalists are allowed to indulge. If a parson had casually observed that the Flood was ante-diluvian, it is possible that he might be a little chaffed about his logic. If a bishop were to say that Adam was Preadamite, we might think it a little odd. But we are not supposed to notice such verbal trifles when sceptical historians talk of the part of history that is prehistoric. The truth is that they are using the terms historic and prehistoric without any clear test or definition in their minds. What they mean is that there are traces of human lives before the beginning of human stories; and in that sense we do at least know that humanity was before history.

Human civilisation is older than human records. That is the sane way of stating our relations to these remote things. Humanity has left examples of its other arts earlier than the art of writing; or at least of any writing that we can read. But it is certain that the primitive arts were arts; and it is in every way probable that the primitive civilisations were civilisations. The man left a picture of the reindeer, but he did not leave a narrative of how he hunted the reindeer; and therefore what we say of him is hypothesis and not history. But the art he did practice was quite artistic; his drawing was quite intelligent and there is no reason to doubt that his story of the hunt would be quite intelligent, only if it exists it is not intelligible. In short, the prehistoric period need not mean the primitive period, in the sense of the barbaric or bestial period. It does not mean the time before civilisation or the time before arts and crafts. It simply means the time before any connected narratives that we can read. This does indeed make all the practical difference between remembrance and forgetfulness; but it is perfectly possible that there were all sorts of forgotten forms of civilisation, as well as all sorts of forgotten forms of barbarism. And in any case everything indicated that many of these forgotten or half-forgotten social stages were much more civilised and much less barbaric than is vulgarly imagined today. But even about these unwritten histories of humanity, when humanity was quite certainly human, we can only conjecture with the greatest doubt and caution. And unfortunately doubt and caution are the last things commonly encouraged by the loose evolutionism of current culture. For that culture is full of curiosity; and the one thing that it cannot endure is the agony of agnosticism. It was in the Darwinian age that the word first became known and the thing first became impossible.

It is necessary to say plainly that all this ignorance is simply covered by impudence. Statements are made so plainly and positively that men have hardly the moral courage to pause upon them and find that they are without support. The other day a scientific summary of the state of a prehistoric tribe began confidently with the words 'They wore no clothes.' Not one reader in a hundred probably stopped to ask himself how we should come to know whether clothes had once been worn by people of whom everything has perished except a few chips of bone and stone. It was doubtless hoped that we should find a stone hat as well as a stone hatchet. It was evidently anticipated that we might discover an everlasting pair of trousers of the same substance as the everlasting rock. But to persons of a less sanguine temperament it will be immediately apparent that people might wear simple garments, or even highly ornamental garments, without leaving any more traces of them than these people have left. The plaiting of rushes and grasses, for instance, might have become more and more elaborate without in the least becoming more eternal. One civilisation might specialise in things that happened to be perishable, like weaving and embroidery, and not in things that happen to be more permanent, like architecture and sculpture. There have been plenty of examples of such specialist societies. A man of the future finding the ruins of our factory machinery might as fairly say that we were acquainted with iron and with no other substance; and announce the discovery that the proprietor and manager of the factory undoubtedly walked about naked—or possibly wore iron hats and trousers.

It is not contended here that these primitive men did wear clothes any more than they did weave rushes; but merely that we have not enough evidence to know whether they did or not. But it may be worth while to look back for a moment at some of the very few things that we do know and that they did do. If we consider them, we shall certainly not find them inconsistent with such ideas as dress and decoration. We do not know whether they decorated other things. We do not know whether they had embroideries, and if they had the embroideries could not be expected to have remained. But we do know that they did have pictures; and the pictures have remained. And there remains with them, as already suggested, the testimony to something that is absolute and unique; that belongs to man and to nothing else except man; that is a difference of kind and not a difference of degree. A monkey does not draw clumsily and a man cleverly; a monkey does not begin the art of representation and a man carry it to perfection. A monkey does not do it at all; he does not begin to do it at all; he does not begin to begin to do it at all. A line of some kind is crossed before the first faint line can begin.

Another distinguished writer, again, in commenting on the cave-drawings attributed to the neolithic men of the reindeer period, said that none of their pictures appeared to have any religious purpose; and he seemed almost to infer that they had no religion. I can hardly imagine a thinner thread of argument than this which reconstructs the very inmost moods of the pre-historic mind from the fact that somebody who has scrawled a few sketches on a rock, from what motive we do not know, for what purpose we do not know, acting under what customs or conventions we do not know, may possibly have found it easier to draw reindeer than to draw religion. He may have drawn it because it was his religious symbol. He may have drawn it because it was not his religious symbol. He may have drawn anything except his religious symbol. He may have drawn his real religious symbol somewhere else; or it may have been deliberately destroyed when it was drawn. He may have done or not done half a million things; but in any case it is an amazing leap of logic to infer that he had no religious symbol, or even to infer from his having no religious symbol that he had no religion. Now this particular case happens to illustrate the insecurity of these guesses very clearly. For a little while afterwards, people discovered not only paintings but sculptures of animals in the caves. Some of these were said to be damaged with dints or holes supposed to be the marks of arrows; and the damaged images were conjectured to be the remains of some magic rite of killing the beasts in effigy; while the undamaged images were explained in connection with another magic rite invoking fertility upon the herds. Here again there is something faintly humorous about the scientific habit of having it both ways. If the image is damaged it proves one superstition and if it is undamaged it proves another. Here again there is a rather reckless jumping to conclusions; it has hardly occurred to the speculators that a crowd of hunters imprisoned in winter in a cave might conceivably have aimed at a mark for fun, as a sort of primitive parlour game. But in any case, if it was done out of superstition, what has become of the thesis that it had nothing to do with religion? The truth is that all this guesswork has nothing to do with anything. It is not half such a good parlour game as shooting arrows at a carved reindeer, for it is shooting them into the air.

Such speculators rather tend to forget, for instance, that men in the modern world also sometimes make marks in caves. When a crowd of trippers is conducted through the labyrinth of the Marvelous Grotto or the Magic Stalactite Cavern, it has been observed that hieroglyphics spring into sight where they have passed; initials and inscriptions which the learned refuse to refer to any remote date. But the time will come when these inscriptions will really be of remote date. And if the professors of the future are anything like the professors of the present, they will be able to deduce a vast number of very vivid and interesting things from these cave-writings of the twentieth century. If I know anything about the breed, and if they have not fallen away from the full-blooded confidence of their fathers, they will be able to discover the most fascinating facts about us from the initials left in the Magic Grotto by 'Arry and 'Arriet, possibly in the form of two intertwined A's. From this alone they will know (1) That as the letters are rudely chipped with a blunt pocket-knife, the twentieth century possessed no delicate graving-tools and was unacquainted with the art of sculpture. (2) That as the letters are capital letters, our civilisation never evolved any small letters or anything like a running hand. (3) That because initial consonants stand together in an unpronounceable fashion, our language was possibly akin to Welsh or more probably of the early Semitic type that ignored vowels. (4) That as the initials of 'Arry and 'Arriet do not in any special fashion profess to be religious symbols, our civilisation possessed no religion. Perhaps the last is about the nearest to the truth; for a civilisation that had religion would have a little more reason.

It is commonly affirmed, again, that religion grew in a very slow and evolutionary manner; and even that it grew not from one cause; but from a combination that might be called a coincidence. Generally speaking, the three chief elements in the combination are, first, the fear of the chief of the tribe (whom Mr. Wells insists on calling, with regrettable familiarity, the Old Man), second, the phenomena of dreams, and third, the sacrificial associations of the harvest and the resurrection symbolised in the growing corn. I may remark in passing that it seems to me very doubtful psychology to refer one living and single spirit to three dead and disconnected causes, if they were merely dead and disconnected causes. Suppose Mr. Wells, in one of his fascinating novels of the future, were to tell us that there would arise among men a new and as yet nameless passion, of which men will dream as they dream of first love, for which they will die as they die for a flag and a fatherland. I think we should be a little puzzled if he told us that this singular sentiment would be a combination of the habit of smoking Woodbines, the increase of the income tax and the pleasure of a motorist in exceeding the speed limit. We could not easily imagine this, because we could not imagine any connection between the three or any common feeling that could include them all. Nor could anyone imagine any connection between corn and dreams and an old chief with a spear, unless there was already a common feeling to include them all. But if there was such a common feeling it could only be the religious feeling; and these things could not be the beginnings of a religious feeling that existed already. I think anybody's common sense will tell him that it is far more likely that this sort of mystical sentiment did exist already; and that in the light of it dreams and kings and corn-fields could appear mystical then, as they can appear mystical now.

For the plain truth is that all this is a trick of making things seem distant and dehumanised, merely by pretending not to understand things that we do understand. It is like saying that prehistoric men had an ugly and uncouth habit of opening their mouths wide at intervals and stuffing strange substances into them, as if we had never heard of eating. It is like saying that the terrible Troglodytes of the Stone Age lifted alternate legs in rotation, as if we never heard of walking. If it were meant to touch the mystical nerve and awaken us to the wonder of walking and eating, it might be a legitimate fancy. As it is here intended to kill the mystical nerve and deaden us to the wonder of religion, it is irrational rubbish. It pretends to find something incomprehensible in the feelings that we all comprehend. Who does *not* find dreams mysterious, and feel that they lie on the dark borderland of being? Who does *not* feel the death and resurrection of the growing things of the earth as something near to the secret of the universe? Who does *not* understand that there must always be the savour of something sacred about authority and the solidarity that is the soul of the tribe? If there be any anthropologist who really finds these things remote and impossible to realise, we can say nothing of that scientific gentleman except that he has not got so large and enlightened a mind as a primitive man. To me it seems obvious that nothing but a spiritual sentiment already active could have clothed these separate and diverse things with sanctity. To say that religion came *from* reverencing a chief or sacrificing at a harvest is to put a highly elaborate cart before a really primitive horse. It is like saying that the impulse to draw pictures came from the contemplation of the pictures of reindeers in the cave. In other words, it is explaining painting by saying that it arose out of the work of painters; or accounting for art by saying that it arose out of art. It is even more like saying that the thing we call poetry arose as the result of certain customs; such as that of an ode being officially composed to celebrate the advent of spring; or that of a young man rising at a regular hour to listen to the skylark and then writing his report on a piece of paper. It is quite true that young men often become poets in the spring; and it is quite true that when once there are poets, no mortal power can restrain them from writing about the skylark.

But the poems did not exist before the poets. The poetry did not arise out of the poetic forms. In other words, it is hardly an adequate explanation of how a thing appeared for the first time to say it existed already. Similarly, we cannot say that religion arose out of the religious forms, because that is only another way of saying that it only arose when it existed already. It needed a certain sort of mind to see that there was anything mystical about the dreams or the dead, as it needed a particular sort of mind to see that there was anything poetical about the skylark or the spring. That mind was presumably what we call the human mind, very much as it exists to this day; for mystics still meditate upon death and dreams as poets still write about spring and skylarks. But there is not the faintest hint to suggest that anything short of the human mind we know feels any of these mystical associations at all. A cow in a field seems to derive no lyrical impulse or instruction from her unrivalled opportunities for listening to the skylark. And similarly there is no reason to suppose that live sheep will ever begin to use dead sheep as the basis of a system of elaborate ancestor-worship. It is true that in the spring a young quadruped's fancy may lightly turn to thoughts of love, but no succession of springs has ever led it to turn however lightly to thoughts of literature. And in the same way, while it is true that a dog has dreams, while most other quadrupeds do not seem even to have that, we have waited a long time for the dog to develop his dreams into an elaborate system or religious ceremonial. We have waited so long that we have really ceased to expect it; and we no more look to see a dog apply his dreams to ecclesiastical construction than to see him examine his dreams by the rules of psycho-analysis. It is obvious, in short, that for some reason or other these natural experiences, and even natural excitements, never do pass the line that separates them from creative expression like art and religion, in any creature except man. They never do, they never have, and it is now to all appearance very improbable that they ever will. It is not impossible, in the sense of self-contradictory, that we should see cows fasting from grass every Friday or going on their knees as in the old legend about Christmas Eve. It is not in that sense impossible that cows should contemplate death until they can lift up a sublime psalm of lamentation to the tune the old cow died of. It is not in that sense impossible that they should express their hopes of a heavenly career in a symbolic dance, in honour of the cow that jumped over the moon. It may be that the dog will at last have laid in a sufficient store of dreams to enable him to build a temple to Cerberus as a sort of canine trinity. It may be that his dreams have already begun to turn into visions capable of verbal expression, in some revelation about the Dog Star as the spiritual home for lost dogs. These things are logically possible, in the sense that it is logically difficult to prove the universal negative which we call an impossibility. But all that instinct for the probable, which we call common sense, must long ago have told us that the animals are not to all appearance evolving in that sense; and that, to say the least, we are not likely to have any personal evidence of their passing from the animal experience to the human experiments. But spring and death and even dreams, considered merely as experiences, are their experiences as much as ours. The only possible conclusion is that these experiences, considered as experiences, do not generate anything like a religious sense in any mind except a mind like ours. We come back to the fact of a certain kind of mind that was already alive and alone. It was unique and it could make creeds as it could make cave-drawings. The materials for religion had lain there for countless ages like the materials for everything else; but the power of religion was in the mind. Man could already see in these things the riddles and hints and hopes that he still sees in them. He could not only dream but dream about dreams. He could not only see the dead but see the shadow of death; and was possessed with that mysterious mystification that forever finds death incredible.

It is quite true that we have even these hints chiefly about man when he unmistakably appears as man. We cannot affirm this or anything else about the alleged animal originally connecting man and the brutes. But that is only because he is not an animal but an allegation. We cannot be certain the Pithecanthropus ever worshipped, because we cannot be certain that he ever lived. He is only a vision called up to fill the void that does in fact yawn between the first creatures who were certainly men and any other creatures that are certainly apes or other animals. A few very doubtful fragments are scraped together to suggest such an intermediate creature because it is required by a certain philosophy; but nobody supposes that these are sufficient to establish anything philosophical even in support of that philosophy. A scrap of skull found in Java cannot establish anything about religion or about the absence of religion. If there ever was any such ape-man, he may have exhibited as much ritual in religion as a man or as much simplicity in religion as an ape. He may have been a mythologist or he may have been a myth. It might be interesting to inquire whether this mystical quality appeared in a transition from the ape to the man, if there were really any types of the transition to inquire about. In other words, the missing link might or might not be mystical if he were not missing. But compared with the evidence we have of real human beings, we have no evidence that he was a human being or a half-human being or a being at all. Even the most extreme evolutionists do not attempt to deduce any evolutionary views about the origin of religion from *him.* Even in trying to prove that religion grew slowly from rude or irrational sources, they begin their proof with the first men who were men. But their own proof only proves that the men who were already men were already mystics. They used the rude and irrational elements as only men and mystics can use them. We come back once more to the simple truth; that at sometime too early for these critics to trace, a transition had occurred to which bones and stones cannot in their nature bear witness; and man became a living soul.

Touching this matter of the origin of religion, the truth is that those who are thus trying to explain it are trying to explain it away. Subconsciously they feel that it looks less formidable when thus lengthened out into a gradual and almost invisible process. But in fact this perspective entirely falsifies the reality of experience. They bring together two things that are totally different, the stray hints of evolutionary origins and the solid and self-evident block of humanity, and try to shift their standpoint till they see them in a single foreshortened line. But it is an optical illusion. Men do not in fact stand related to monkeys or missing links in any such chain as that in which men stand related to men. There may have been intermediate creatures whose faint traces can be found here and there in the

huge gap. Of these beings, if they ever existed, it may be true that
they were things very unlike men or men very unlike ourselves. But
of prehistoric men, such as those called the cave-men or the reindeer
men, it is not true in any sense whatever. Prehistoric men of that
sort were things exactly like men and men exceedingly like ourselves. They only happened to be men about whom we do not know
much, for the simple reason that they have left no records or chronicles; but all that we do know about them makes them just as human
and ordinary as men in a medieval manor or a Greek city.

Looking from our human standpoint up the long perspective of
humanity, we simply recognise this thing as human. If we had to
recognise it as animal we should have had to recognise it as abnormal. If we chose to look through the other end of the telescope, as I
have done more than once in these speculations, if we chose to project the human figure forward out of an unhuman world, we could
only say that one of the animals had obviously gone mad. But seeing
the thing from the right end, or rather from the inside, we know it
is sanity; and we know that these primitive men were sane. We hail
a certain human freemasonry wherever we see it, in savages, in foreigners or in historical characters. For instance, all we can infer from
primitive legend, and all we know of barbaric life, supports a certain
moral and even mystical idea of which the commonest symbol is
clothes. For clothes are very literally vestments and man wears them
because he is a priest. It is true that even as an animal he is here different from the animals. Nakedness is not nature to him; it is not his
life but rather his death; even in the vulgar sense of his death of cold.
But clothes are worn for dignity or decency or decoration where
they are not in any way wanted for warmth. It would sometimes appear that they are valued for ornament before they are valued for use.
It would almost always appear that they are felt to have some connection with decorum. Conventions of this sort vary a great deal
with various times and places; and there are some who cannot get
over this reflection, and for whom it seems a sufficient argument for
letting all conventions slide. They never tire of repeating, with simple wonder, that dress is different in the Cannibal Islands and in
Camden Town; they cannot get any further and throw up the

whole idea of decency in despair. They might as well say that because there have been hats of a good many different shapes, and some
rather eccentric shapes, therefore hats do not matter or do not exist.
They would probably add that there is no such thing as sunstroke or
going bald. Men have felt everywhere that certain forms were
necessary to fence off and protect certain private things from contempt or coarse misunderstanding; and the keeping of those forms,
whatever they were, made for dignity and mutual respect. The fact
that they mostly refer, more or less remotely, to the relations of the
sexes illustrates the two facts that must be put at the very beginning
of the record of the race. The first is the fact that original sin is really
original. Not merely in theology but in history it is a thing rooted in
the origins. Whatever else men have believed, they have all believed
that there is something the matter with mankind. This sense of sin has
made it impossible to be natural and have no clothes, just as it has
made it impossible to be natural and have no laws. But above all it is
to be found in that other fact, which is the father and mother of all
laws as it is itself founded on a father and mother; the thing that is before all thrones and even all commonwealths.

That fact is the family. Here again we must keep the enormous
proportions of a normal thing clear of various modifications and degrees and doubts more or less reasonable, like clouds clinging about
a mountain. It may be that what we call the family had to fight
its way from or through various anarchies and aberrations; but it
certainly survived them and is quite as likely as not to have also preceded them. As we shall see in the case of communism and nomadism, more formless things could and did lie on the flank of societies
that had taken a fixed form; but there is nothing to show that the
form did not exist before the formlessness. What is vital is that form
is more important than formlessness; and that the material called
mankind has taken this form. For instance, of the rules revolving
round sex, which were recently mentioned, none is more curious
than the savage custom commonly called the *couvade*. That seems
like a law out of topsyturvydom; by which the father is treated as if
he were the mother. In any case it clearly involves the mystical sense
of sex; but many have maintained that it is really a symbolic

act by which the father accepts the responsibility of fatherhood. In that case that grotesque antic is really a very solemn act; for it is the foundation of all we call the family and all we know as human society. Some groping in these dark beginnings have said that mankind was once under a matriarchy; I suppose that under a matriarchy it would not be called mankind but womankind. But others have conjectured that what is called matriarchy was simply moral anarchy, in which the mother alone remained fixed because all the fathers were fugitive and irresponsible. Then came the moment when the man decided to guard and guide what he had created. So he became the head of the family, not as a bully with a big club to beat women with, but rather as a respectable person trying to be a responsible person. Now all that might be perfectly true, and might even have been the first family act, and it would still be true that man then for the first time acted like a man, and therefore for the first time became fully a man. But it might quite as well be true that the matriarchy or moral anarchy, or whatever we call it, was only one of the hundred social dissolutions or barbaric backslidings which may have occurred at intervals in prehistoric as they certainly did in historic times. A symbol like the *couvade*, if it was really such a symbol, may have commemorated the suppression of a heresy rather than the first rise of a religion. We cannot conclude with any certainty about these things, except in their big results in the building of mankind, but we can say in what style the bulk of it and the best of it is built. We can say that the family is the unit of the state; that it is the cell that makes up the formation. Round the family do indeed gather the sanctities that separate men from ants and bees. Decency is the curtain of that tent; liberty is the wall of that city; property is but the family farm; honour is but the family flag. In the practical proportions of human history, we come back to that fundamental of the father and the mother and the child. It has been said already that if this story cannot start with religious assumptions, it must none the less start with some moral or metaphysical assumptions, or no sense can be made of the story of man. And this is a very good instance of that alternative necessity. If we are not of those who begin by invoking a divine Trinity, we must none the less invoke a human Trinity; and see that triangle repeated everywhere in the pattern of the world. For the highest event in history, to which all history looks forward and leads up, is only something that is at once the reversal and the renewal of that triangle. Or rather it is the one triangle superimposed so as to intersect the other, making a sacred pentacle of which, in a mightier sense than that of the magicians, the fiends are afraid. The old Trinity was of father and mother and child and is called the human family. The new is of child and mother and father and has the name of the Holy Family. It is in no way altered except in being entirely reversed; just as the world which is transformed was not in the least different, except in being turned upside-down.

III

THE ANTIQUITY OF CIVILISATION

The modern man looking at the most ancient origins has been like a man watching for daybreak in a strange land; and expecting to see that dawn breaking behind bare uplands or solitary peaks. But that dawn is breaking behind the black bulk of great cities long builded and lost for us in the original night; colossal cities like the houses of giants, in which even the carved ornamental animals are taller than the palm-trees; in which the painted portrait can be twelve times the size of the man; with tombs like mountains of man set four-square and pointing to the stars; with winged and bearded bulls standing and staring enormous at the gates of temples; standing still eternally as if a stamp would shake the world. The dawn of history reveals a humanity already civilized. Perhaps it reveals a civilisation already old. And among other more important things, it reveals the folly of most of the generalisations about the previous and unknown period when it was really young. The two first human societies of which we have any reliable and detailed record are Babylon and Egypt. It so happens that these two vast and splendid achievements of the genius of the ancients bear witness against two of the commonest and crudest assumptions of the culture of the moderns. If we want to get rid of half the nonsense about nomads and cave-men and the old man of the forest, we need only look steadily at the two solid and stupendous facts called Egypt and Babylon.

Of course most of these speculators who are talking about primitive men are thinking about modern savages. They prove their progressive evolution by assuming that a great part of the human race has not progressed or evolved; or even changed in any way at all. I do not agree with their theory of change; nor do I agree with their dogma of things unchangeable. I may not believe that civilised man has had so rapid and recent a progress; but I cannot quite understand why uncivilised man should be so mystically immortal and immutable. A somewhat simpler mode of thought and speech seems to me to be needed throughout this inquiry. Modern savages cannot be exactly like primitive man, because they are not primitive. Modern savages are not ancient because they are modern. Something has happened to their race as much as to ours, during the thousands of years of our existence and endurance on the earth. They have had some experiences, and have presumably acted on them if not profited by them, like the rest of us. They have had some environment, and even some change of environment, and have presumably adapted themselves to it in a proper and decorous evolutionary manner. This would be true even if the experiences were mild or the environment dreary; for there is an effect in mere time when it takes the moral form of monotony. But it has appeared to a good many intelligent and well-informed people quite as probable that the experience of the savages has been that of a decline from civilisation. Most of those who criticise this view do not seem to have any very clear notion of what a decline from civilisation would be like. Heaven help them, it is likely enough that they will soon find out. They seem to be content if cave-men and cannibal islanders have some things in common, such as certain particular implements. But it is obvious on the face of it that any peoples reduced for any reason to a ruder life would have some things in common. If we lost all our firearms we should make bows and arrows; but we should not necessarily resemble in every way the first men who made bows and arrows. It is said that the Russians in their great retreat were so short of armament that they fought with clubs cut in the wood. But a professor of the future would err in supposing that the Russian army of 1916 was a naked Scythian tribe that had never been out of the wood. It is like saying that a man in his second childhood must exactly copy his first. A baby is bald like an old man; but it would be an error for one ignorant of infancy to infer that the baby had a long white beard. Both a baby and an old man walk with difficulty; but he who shall expect the old gentleman to lie on his back, and kick joyfully instead, will be disappointed.

It is therefore absurd to argue that the first pioneers of humanity must have been identical with some of the last and most stagnant leavings of it. There were almost certainly some things, there were probably many things, in which the two were widely different or flatly contrary. An example of the way in which this distinction works, and an example essential to our argument here, is that of the nature and origin of government. I have already alluded to Mr. H. G. Wells and the Old Man, with whom he appears to be on such intimate terms. If we considered the cold facts of prehistoric evidence for this portrait of the prehistoric chief of the tribe, we could only excuse it by saying that its brilliant and versatile author simply forgot for a moment that he was supposed to be writing a history, and dreamed he was writing one of his own very wonderful and imaginative romances. At least I cannot imagine how he can possibly know that the prehistoric ruler was called the Old Man or that court etiquette requires it to be spelt with capital letters. He says of the same potentate, 'No one was allowed to touch his spear or to sit in his seat.' I have difficulty in believing that anybody has dug up a prehistoric spear with a prehistoric label, 'Visitors are Requested not to Touch,' or a complete throne with the inscription, 'Reserved for the Old Man.' But it may be presumed that the writer, who can hardly be supposed to be merely making up things out of his own head, was merely taking for granted this very dubious parallel between the prehistoric and the decivilised man. It may be that in certain savage tribes the chief is called the Old Man and nobody is allowed to touch his spear or sit on his seat. It may be that in those cases he is surrounded with superstitious and traditional terrors; and it may be that in those cases, for all I know, he is despotic and tyrannical. But there is not a grain of evidence that primitive government was despotic and tyrannical. It may have been, of course, for it may have been anything or even nothing; it may not have existed at all. But the despotism in certain dingy and decayed tribes in the twentieth century does not prove that the first men were ruled despotically. It does not even suggest it; it does not even begin to hint at it. If there is one fact we really can prove, from the history that we really do know, it is that despotism can be a development, often a late development and very often indeed the end of societies that have been highly democratic. A despotism may almost be defined as a tired democracy. As fatigue falls on a community, the citizens are less inclined for that eternal vigilance which has truly been called the price of liberty; and they prefer to arm only one single sentinel to watch the city while they sleep. It is also true that they sometimes needed him for some sudden and militant act of reform; it is equally true that he often took advantage of being the strong man armed to be a tyrant like some of the Sultans of the East. But I cannot see why the Sultan should have appeared any earlier in history than many other human figures. On the contrary, the strong man armed obviously depends upon the superiority of his armour; and armament of that sort comes with more complex civilisation. One man may kill twenty with a machine-gun; it is obviously less likely that he could do it with a piece of flint. As for the current cant about the strongest man ruling by force and fear, it is simply a nursery fairy-tale about a giant with a hundred hands. Twenty men could hold down the strongest strong man in any society, ancient or modern. Undoubtedly they might *admire*, in a romantic and poetical sense, the man who was really the strongest; but that is quite a different thing, and is as purely moral and even mystical as the admiration for the purest or the wisest. But the spirit that endures the mere cruelties and caprices of an established despot is the spirit of an ancient and settled and probably stiffened society, not the spirit of a new one. As his name implies, the Old Man is the ruler of an old humanity.

It is far more probable that a primitive society was something like a pure democracy. To this day the comparatively simple agricultural communities are by far the purest democracies. Democracy is a thing which is always breaking down through the complexity of civilisation. Anyone who likes may state it by saying that democracy is the foe of civilisation. But he must remember that some of us really prefer democracy to civilisation, in the sense of preferring democracy to complexity. Anyhow, peasants tilling patches of their own land in a rough equality, and meeting to vote directly under a village tree, are the most truly self-governing of men. It is surely as likely as not that such a simple idea was found in the first condition of even simpler men. Indeed the despotic vision is exaggerated, even if we do not regard the men as men. Even on an evolutionary assumption of the most materialistic sort, there is really no reason why men should not have had at least as much camaraderie as rats or rooks. Leadership of some sort they doubtless had, as have the gregarious animals; but leadership implies no such irrational servility as that attributed to the superstitious subjects of the Old Man. There was doubtless somebody corresponding, to use Tennyson's expression, to the many-wintered crow that leads the clanging rookery home. But I fancy that if that venerable fowl began to act after the fashion of some Sultans in ancient and decayed Asia, it would become a very clanging rookery and the many-wintered crow would not see many more winters. It may be remarked, in this connection, but even among animals it would seem that something else is respected more than bestial violence, if it be only the familiarity which in men is called tradition or the experience which in men is called wisdom. I do not know if crows really follow the oldest crow, but if they do they are certainly not following the strongest crow. And I do know, in the human case, that if some ritual of seniority keeps savages reverencing somebody called Old Man, then at least they have not our own servile sentimental weakness for worshipping the Strong Man.

It may be said then that primitive government, like primitive art and religion and everything else, is very imperfectly known or rather guessed at; but that it is at least as good a guess to suggest that it was as popular as a Balkan or Pyrenean village as that it was as capricious and secret as a Turkish divan. Both the mountain democracy and the oriental palace are modern in the sense that they are still there, or are some sort of growth of history; but of the two the palace has much more the look of being an accumulation and a corruption, the village much more the look of being a really unchanged and primitive thing. But my suggestions at this point do not go beyond expressing a wholesome doubt about the current assumption. I think it interesting, for instance, that liberal institutions have been traced even by moderns back to barbarians or undeveloped states, when it happened to be convenient for the support of some race or nation or philosophy. So the Socialists profess that their ideal of communal property existed in very early times. So the Jews are proud of the Jubilees or juster redistributions under their ancient law. So the Teutonists boasted of tracing parliaments and juries and various popular things among the Germanic tribes of the north. So the Celtophiles and those testifying to the wrongs of Ireland have pleaded the more equal justice of the clan system, to which the Irish chiefs bore witness before Strongbow.[1] The strength of the case varies in the different cases; but as there is some case for all of them, I suspect there is some case for the general proposition that popular institutions of some sort were by no means uncommon in early and simple societies. Each of these separate schools were making the admission to prove a particular modern thesis; but taken together they suggest a more ancient and general truth, that there was something more in prehistoric councils than ferocity and fear. Each of these separate theorists had his own axe to grind, but he was willing to use a stone axe; and he manages to suggest that the stone axe might have been as republican as the guillotine.

But the truth is that the curtain rises upon the play already in progress. In one sense it is a true paradox that there was history before history. But it is not the irrational paradox implied in prehistoric history; for it is a history we do not know. Very probably it was exceedingly like the history we do know, except in the one detail that we do not know it. It is thus the very opposite of the pretentious prehistoric history, which professes to trace everything in a consistent course from the amoeba to the anthropoid and from the anthropoid to the agnostic. So far from being a question of our knowing all about queer creatures very different from ourselves, they were very probably people very like ourselves, except that we know nothing about them. In other words, our most ancient records only reach back to a time when humanity had long been human, and even long been civilised. The most ancient records we have not only mention but take for granted things like kings and priests and princes and assemblies of the people; they describe communities that are roughly recognisable as communities in our own sense. Some of them are despotic; but we cannot tell that they have always been despotic. Some of them may be already decadent and nearly all are

[1] Strongbow (c. 1130–76) is the name by which Richard, 2nd Earl of Pembroke, was known. He succeeded to great estates in Normandy, England, and Wales. Made the custos of Ireland by Henry II.

mentioned as if they were old. We do not know what really happened in the world before those records; but the little we do know would leave us anything but astonished if we learnt that it was very much like what happens in this world now. There would be nothing inconsistent or confounding about the discovery that those unknown ages were full of republics collapsing under monarchies and rising again as republics, empires expanding and finding colonies and then losing colonies, kingdoms combining again into world-states and breaking up again into small nationalities, classes selling themselves into slavery and marching out once more into liberty; all that procession of humanity which may or may not be a progress but is most assuredly a romance. But the first chapters of the romance have been torn out of the book; and we shall never read them.

It is so also with the more special fancy about evolution and social stability. According to the real records available, barbarism and civilisation were not successive states in the progress of the world. They were conditions that existed side by side, as they still exist side by side. There were civilisations then as there are civilisations now; there are savages now as there were savages then. It is suggested that all men passed through a nomadic stage; but it is certain that there are some who have never passed out of it, and it seems not unlikely that there were some who never passed into it. It is probable that from very primitive times the static tiller of the soil and the wandering shepherd were two distinct types of men; and the chronological rearrangement of them is but a mark of that mania for progressive stages that has largely falsified history. It is suggested that there was a communist stage, in which private property was everywhere unknown, a whole humanity living on the negation of property; but the evidences of this negation are themselves rather negative. Redistributions of property, jubilees, and agrarian laws, occur at various intervals and in various forms; but that humanity inevitably passed through a communist stage seems as doubtful as the parallel proposition that humanity will inevitably return to it. It is chiefly interesting as evidence that the boldest plans for the future invoke the authority of the past; and that even a revolutionary seeks to satisfy himself that he is also a reactionary. There is an amusing parallel example in the case of what is called feminism. In spite of all the pseudo-scientific gossip about marriage by capture and the cave-man beating the cave-woman with a club, it may be noted that as soon as feminism became a fashionable cry, it was insisted that human civilisation in its first stage had been a matriarchy. Apparently it was the cave-woman who carried the club. Anyhow all these ideas are little better than guesses; they have a curious way of following the fortune of modern theories and fads. In any case they are not history in the sense of record; and we may repeat that when it comes to record, the broad truth is that barbarism and civilisation have always dwelt side by side in the world, the civilisation sometimes spreading to absorb the barbarians, sometimes decaying into relative barbarism, and in almost all cases possessing in a more finished form certain ideas and institutions which the barbarians possess in a ruder form; such as government or social authority, the arts and especially the decorative arts, mysteries and taboos of various kinds especially surrounding the matter of sex, and some form of that fundamental thing which is the chief concern of this enquiry; the thing that we call religion.

Now Egypt and Babylon, those two primeval monsters, might in this matter have been specially provided as models. They might almost be called working models to show how these modern theories do not work. The two great truths we know about these two great cultures happen to contradict flatly the two current fallacies which have just been considered. The story of Egypt might have been invented to point the moral that man does not necessarily begin with despotism because he is barbarous, but very often finds his way to despotism because he is civilised. He finds it because he is experienced; or, what is often much the same thing, because he is exhausted. And the story of Babylon might have been invented to point the moral that man need not be a nomad or a communist before he becomes a peasant or a citizen; and that such cultures are not always in successive stages but often in contemporary states. Even touching these great civilisations with which our written history begins there is a temptation of course to be too ingenious or too cocksure. We can read the bricks of Babylon in a very different sense from that in which we guess about the Cup and Ring stones[2]; and we do definitely know what is meant by the animals in the Egyptian hieroglyphic as we know nothing of the animal in the neolithic cave. But even here the admirable archeologists who have deciphered line after line of miles of hieroglyphics may be tempted to read too much between the lines; even the real authority on Babylon may forget how fragmentary is his hard-won knowledge; may forget that Babylon has only heaved half a brick at him, though half a brick is better than no cuneiform. But some truths, historic and not prehistoric, dogmatic and not evolutionary, facts and not fancies, do indeed emerge from Egypt and Babylon; and these two truths are among them.

Egypt is a green ribbon along the river edging the dark red desolation of the desert. It is a proverb, and one of vast antiquity, that it is created by the mysterious bounty and almost sinister benevolence of the Nile. When we first hear of Egyptians they are living as in a string of river-side villages, in small and separate but co-operative communities along the bank of the Nile. Where the river branched into the broad Delta there was traditionally the beginning of a somewhat different district or people; but this need not complicate the main truth. These more or less independent though interdependent peoples were considerably civilised already. They had a sort of heraldry; that is, decorative art used for symbolic and social purposes; each sailing the Nile under its own ensign representing some bird or animal. Heraldry involves two things of enormous importance to normal humanity; the combination of the two making that noble thing called co-operation; on which rest all peasantries and peoples that are free. The art of heraldry means independence; an image chosen by the imagination to express the individuality. The science of heraldry means interdependence; an agreement between different bodies to recognise different images; a science of imagery. We have here therefore exactly that compromise of co-operation between free families or groups which is the most normal mode of life for humanity

[2] Stones with small artificial depressions within concentric rings thought to have been in use from the late Neolithic to the late Bronze Age. Imaginative, far-fetched and often contradictory hypotheses about their use prompted more sober archaeologists to an admission of ignorance.

and is particularly apparent wherever men own their own land and live on it. With the very mention of the image of bird and beast the student of mythology will murmur the word 'totem' almost in his sleep. But to my mind much of the trouble arises from his habit of saying such words as if in his sleep. Throughout this rough outline I have made a necessarily inadequate attempt to keep on the inside rather than the outside of such things; to consider them where possible in terms of thought and not merely in terms of terminology. There is very little value in talking about totems unless we have some feeling of what it really felt like to have a totem. Granted that they had totems and we have no totems; was it because they had more fear of animals or more familiarity with animals? Did a man whose totem was a wolf feel like a were-wolf or like a man running away from a were-wolf? Did he feel like Uncle Remus about Brer Wolf or like St. Francis about his brother the wolf, or like Mowgli about his brothers the wolves? Was a totem a thing like the British lion or a thing like the British bull-dog? Was the worship of a totem like the feeling of niggers about Mumbo Jumbo, or of children about Jumbo? I have never read any book of folk-lore, however learned, that gave me any light upon this question, which I think by far the most important one. I will confine myself to repeating that the earliest Egyptian communities had a common understanding about the images that stood for their individual states; and that this amount of communication is prehistoric in the sense that it is already there at the beginning of history. But as history unfolds itself, this question of communication is clearly the main question of these riverside communities. With the need of communication comes the need of a common government and the growing greatness and spreading shadow of the king. The other binding force besides the king, and perhaps older than the king, is the priesthood; and the priesthood has presumably even more to do with these ritual symbols and signals by which men can communicate. And here in Egypt arose probably the primary and certainly the typical invention to which we owe all history, and the whole difference between the historic and the prehistoric: the archetypal script, the art of writing.

The popular pictures of these primeval empires are not half so popular as they might be. There is shed over them the shadow of an exaggerated gloom, more than the normal and even healthy sadness of heathen men. It is part of the same sort of secret pessimism that loves to make primitive man a crawling creature, whose body is filth and whose soul is fear. It comes of course from the fact that men are moved most by their religion; especially when it is irreligion. For them anything primary and elemental must be evil. But it is the curious consequence that while we have been deluged with the wildest experiments in primitive romance, they have all missed the real romance of being primitive. They have described scenes that are wholly imaginary, in which the men of the Stone Age are men of stone like walking statues; in which the Assyrians or Egyptians are as stiff or as painted as their own most archaic art. But none of these makers of imaginary scenes have tried to imagine what it must really have been like to see those things as fresh which we see as familiar. They have not seen a man discovering fire like a child discovering fireworks. They have not seen a man playing with the wonderful invention called the wheel, like a boy playing at putting up a wireless station. They have never put the spirit of youth into their descriptions of the youth of the world. It follows that amid all their primitive or prehistoric fancies there are no jokes. There are not even practical jokes, in connection with the practical inventions. And this is very sharply defined in the particular case of hieroglyphics; for there seems to be serious indication that the whole high human art of scripture or writing began with a joke.

There are some who will learn with regret that it seems to have begun with a pun. The king or the priests or some responsible persons, wishing to send a message up the river in that inconveniently long and narrow territory, hit on the idea of sending it in picture-writing, like that of the Red Indian. Like most people who have written picture-writing for fun, he found the words did not always fit. But when the word for taxes sounded rather like the word for pig, he boldly put down a pig as a bad pun and chanced it. So a modern hieroglyphist might represent 'at once' by unscrupulously drawing a hat followed by a series of upright numerals. It was good enough for the Pharaohs and ought to be good enough for him. But it must have been great fun to write or even to read these messages, when writing and reading were really a new thing. And if people must write romances about ancient Egypt (and it seems that neither prayers nor tears nor curses can withhold them from the habit), I suggest that scenes like this would really remind us that the ancient Egyptians were human beings. I suggest that somebody should describe the scene of the great monarch sitting among his priests, and all of them roaring with laughter and bubbling over with suggestions as the royal puns grew more and more wild and indefensible. There might be another scene of almost equal excitement about the decoding of this cipher; the guesses and clues and discoveries having all the popular thrill of a detective story. That is how primitive romance and primitive history really ought to be written. For whatever was the quality of the religious or moral life of remote times, and it was probably much more human than is conventionally supposed, the scientific interest of such a time must have been intense. Words must have been more wonderful than wireless telegraphy; and experiments with common things a series of electric shocks. We are still waiting for somebody to write a lively story of primitive life. The point is in some sense a parenthesis here; but it is connected with the general matter of political development, by the institution which was most active in these first and most fascinating of all the fairy-tales of science.

It is admitted that we owe most of this science to the priests. Modern writers like Mr. Wells cannot be accused of any weakness of sympathy with a pontifical hierarchy; but they agree at least in recognising what pagan priesthoods did for the arts and sciences. Among the more ignorant of the enlightened there was indeed a convention of saying that priests had obstructed progress in all ages; and a politician once told me in a debate that I was resisting modern reforms exactly as some ancient priest probably resisted the discovery of wheels. I pointed out, in reply, that it was far more likely that the ancient priest made the discovery of the wheels. It is overwhelmingly probable that the ancient priest had a great deal to do with the discovery of the art of writing. It is obvious enough in the fact that the very word hieroglyphic is akin to the word hierarchy.

The religion of these priests was apparently a more or less tangled polytheism of a type that is more particularly described elsewhere. It passed through a period when it cooperated with the king, another period when it was temporarily destroyed by the king, who happened to be a prince with a private theism of his own, and a third period when it practically destroyed the king and ruled in his stead. But the world has to thank it for many things which it considers common and necessary; and the creators of those common things ought really to have a place among the heroes of humanity. If we were at rest in a real paganism, instead of being restless in a rather irrational reaction from Christianity, we might pay some sort of pagan honour to these nameless makers of mankind. We might have veiled statues of the man who first found fire or the man who first made a boat or the man who first tamed a horse. And if we brought them garlands or sacrifices, there would be more sense in it than in disfiguring our cities with cockney statues of stale politicians and philanthropists. But one of the strange marks of the strength of Christianity is that, since it came, no pagan in our civilisation has been able to be really human.

The point is here, however, that the Egyptian government, whether pontifical or royal, found it more and more necessary to establish communication; and there always went with communication a certain element of coercion. It is not necessarily an indefensible thing that the state grew more despotic as it grew more civilised; it is arguable that it had to grow more despotic in order to grow more civilised. That is the argument for autocracy in every age; and the interest lies in seeing it illustrated in the earliest age. But it is emphatically not true that it was most despotic in the earliest age and grew more liberal in a later age; the practical process of history is exactly the reverse. It is not true that the tribe began in the extreme of terror of the Old Man and his seat and spear; it is probable, at least in Egypt, that the Old Man was rather a New Man armed to attack new conditions. His spear grew longer and longer and his throne rose higher and higher, as Egypt rose into a complex and complete civilisation. That is what I mean by saying that the history of the Egyptian territory is in this the history of the earth; and directly denies the vulgar assumption that terrorism can only come at the beginning and cannot come at the end. We do not know what was the very first condition of the more or less feudal amalgam of landowners, peasants and slaves in the little commonwealths beside the Nile; but it may have been a peasantry of an even more popular sort. What we do know is that it was by experience and education that little commonwealths lose their liberty; that absolute sovereignty is something not merely ancient but rather relatively modern; and it is at the end of the path called progress that men return to the king.

Egypt exhibits, in that brief record of its remotest beginnings, the primary problem of liberty and civilisation. It is the fact that men actually lose variety by complexity. We have not solved the problem properly any more than they did; but it vulgarises the human dignity of the problem itself to suggest that even tyranny has no motive save in tribal terror. And just as the Egyptian example refutes the fallacy about despotism and civilisation, so does the Babylonian example refute the fallacy about civilisation and barbarism. Babylon also we first hear of when it is already civilised; for the simple reason that we cannot hear of anything until it is educated enough to talk. It talks to us in what is called cuneiform; that strange and stiff triangular symbolism that contrasts with the picturesque alphabet of Egypt. However relatively rigid Egyptian art may be, there is always something different from the Babylonian spirit which was too rigid to have any art. There is always a living grace in the lines of the lotus and something of rapidity as well as rigidity in the movement of the arrows and the birds. Perhaps there is something of the restrained but living curve of the river, which makes us in talking of the serpent of old Nile almost think of the Nile as a serpent. Babylon was a civilisation of diagrams rather than of drawings. Mr. W. B. Yeats who has a historical imagination to match his mythological imagination (and indeed the former is impossible without the latter) wrote truly of the men who watched the stars 'from their pedantic Babylon.' The cuneiform was cut upon bricks, of which all their architecture was built up; the bricks were of baked mud and perhaps the material had something in it forbidding the sense of form to develop in sculpture or relief. Theirs was a static but a scientific civilisation, far advanced in the machinery of life and in some ways highly modern. It is said that they had much of the modern cult of the higher spinsterhood and recognised an official class of independent working women. There is perhaps something in that mighty stronghold of hardened mud that suggests the utilitarian activity of a huge hive. But though it was huge it was human; we see many of the same social problems as in ancient Egypt or modern England; and whatever its evils this also was one of the earliest masterpieces of man. It stood, of course, in the triangle formed by the almost legendary rivers of Tigris and Euphrates, and the vast agriculture of its empire, on which its towns depended, was perfected by a highly scientific system of canals. It had by tradition a high intellectual life, though rather philosophic than artistic; and there preside over its primal foundation those figures who have come to stand for the star-gazing wisdom of antiquity; the teachers of Abraham; the Chaldees.

Against this solid society, as against some vast bare wall of brick, there surged age after age the nameless armies of the Nomads. They came out of the deserts where the nomadic life had been lived from the beginning and where it is still lived to-day. It is needless to dwell on the nature of that life; it was obvious enough and even easy enough to follow a herd or a flock which generally found its own grazing-ground and to live on the milk or meat it provided. Nor is there any reason to doubt that this habit of life could give almost every human thing except a home. Many such shepherds or herdsmen may have talked in the earliest time of all the truths and enigmas of the Book of Job; and of these were Abraham and his children, who have given to the modern world for an endless enigma the almost mono-maniac monotheism of the Jews. But they were a wild people without comprehension of complex social organisation; and a spirit like the wind within them made them wage war on it again and again. The history of Babylonia is largely the history of its defence against the desert hordes; who came on at intervals of a century or two and generally retreated as they came. Some say that an admixture of nomad invasion built at Nineveh the arrogant kingdom of the Assyrians, who carved great monsters upon their temples, bearded bulls with wings like cherubim, and who sent forth many military conquerors who stamped the world as if with such colossal hooves. Assyria was an imperial interlude; but it was an interlude. The main story of all that land is the war between the wandering peoples and the state that was truly static. Presumably in prehistoric times, and certainly in historic times, those wanderers went westward to waste whatever they could find. The last time they came they found Babylon vanished; but that was in historic times and the name of their leader was Mahomet.

Now it is worth while to pause upon that story because, as has been suggested, it directly contradicts the impression still current that nomadism is merely a prehistoric thing and social settlement a comparatively recent thing. There is nothing to show that the Babylonians had ever wandered; there is very little to show that the tribes of the desert ever settled down. Indeed it is probable that this notion of a nomadic stage followed by a static stage has already been abandoned by the sincere and genuine scholars to whose researches we all owe so much. But I am not at issue in this book with sincere and genuine scholars, but with a vast and vague public opinion which has been prematurely spread from certain imperfect investigations, and which has made fashionable a false notion of the whole history of humanity. It is the whole vague notion that a monkey evolved into a man and in the same way a barbarian evolved into a civilised man and therefore at every stage we have to look back to barbarism and forward to civilisation. Unfortunately this notion is in a double sense entirely in the air. It is an atmosphere in which men live rather than a thesis which they defend. Men in that mood are more easily answered by objects than by theories; and it will be well if anyone tempted to make that assumption, in some trivial turn of talk or writing, can be checked for a moment by shutting his eyes and seeing for an instant, vast and vaguely crowded, like a populous precipice, the wonder of the Babylonian wall.

One fact does certainly fall across us like its shadow. Our glimpses of both these early empires show that the first domestic relation had been complicated by something which was less human, but was often regarded as equally domestic. The dark giant called Slavery had been called up like a genii and was labouring on gigantic works of brick and stone. Here again we must not too easily assume that what was backward was barbaric; in the matter of manumission the earlier servitude seems in some ways more liberal than the later; perhaps more liberal than the servitude of the future. To insure food for humanity by forcing part of it to work was after all a very human expedient; which is why it will probably be tried again. But in one sense there is a significance in the old slavery. It stands for one fundamental fact about all antiquity before Christ; something to be assumed from first to last. It is the insignificance of the individual before the State. It was as true of the most democratic City State in Hellas as of any despotism in Babylon. It is one of the signs of this spirit that a whole class of individuals could be insignificant or even invisible. It must be normal because it was needed for what would now be called 'social service.' Somebody said, 'The Man is nothing and the Work is all,' meaning it for a breezy Carlylean commonplace. It was the sinister motto of the heathen Servile State. In that sense there is truth in the traditional vision of vast pillars and pyramids going up under those everlasting skies for ever by the labour of numberless and nameless men, toiling like ants and dying like flies, wiped out by the work of their own hands.

But there are two other reasons for beginning with the two fixed points of Egypt and Babylon. For one thing they are fixed in tradition as the types of antiquity; and history without tradition is dead. Babylon is still the burden of a nursery rhyme, and Egypt (with its enormous population of princesses awaiting reincarnation) is still the topic of an unnecessary number of novels. But a tradition is generally a truth; so long as the tradition is sufficiently popular; even if it is almost vulgar. And there is a significance in this Babylonian and Egyptian element in nursery rhymes and novels; even the newspapers, normally so much behind the times, have already got as far as the reign of Tutankhamen. The first reason is full of the commonsense of popular legend; it is the simple fact that we do know more of these traditional things than of other contemporary things; and that we always did. All travellers from Herodotus to Lord Carnarvon[3] follow this route. Scientific speculations of to-day do indeed

[3] Lord Carnarvon (1866–1923) was a British Egyptologist and collector of antiquities; in 1922, with archaeologist Howard Carter, he discovered the tomb of Tutankhamen.

spread out a map of the whole primitive world, with streams of racial emigration or admixture marked in dotted lines everywhere; over spaces which the unscientific medieval map-maker would have been content to call 'Terra incognita,' if he did not fill the inviting blank with a picture of a dragon, to indicate the probable reception given to pilgrims. But these speculations are only speculations at the best; and at the worst the dotted lines can be far more fabulous than the dragon.

There is unfortunately one fallacy here into which it is very easy for men to fall, even those who are most intelligent and perhaps especially those who are most imaginative. It is the fallacy of suppositing that because an idea is greater in the sense of larger, therefore it is greater in the sense of more fundamental and fixed and certain. If a man lives alone in a straw hut in the middle of Thibet, he may be told that he is living in the Chinese Empire; and the Chinese Empire is certainly a splendid and spacious and impressive thing. Or alternatively he may be told that he is living in the British Empire, and be duly impressed. But the curious thing is that in certain mental states he can feel much more certain about the Chinese Empire that he cannot see than about the straw hut that he can see. He has some strange magical juggle in his mind, by which his argument begins with the empire though his experience begins with the hut. Sometimes he goes mad and appears to be proving that a straw hut cannot exist in the domains of the Dragon Throne; that it is impossible for such a civilisation as he enjoys to contain such a hovel as he inhabits. But his insanity arises from the intellectual slip of supposing that because China is a large and all-embracing hypothesis, therefore it is something more than a hypothesis. Now modern people are perpetually arguing in this way; and they extend it to things much less real and certain than the Chinese Empire. They seem to forget, for instance, that a man is not even certain of the Solar System as he is certain of the South Downs. The Solar System is a deduction, and doubtless a true deduction; but the point is that it is a very vast and far-reaching deduction and therefore he forgets that it is a deduction at all and treats it as a first principle. He *might* discover that the whole calculation is a mis-calculation; and the sun and stars and street-lamps would look exactly the same. But he has forgotten that it is a calculation, and is almost ready to contradict the sun if it does not fit into the solar system. If this is a fallacy even in the case of facts pretty well ascertained, such as the Solar System and the Chinese Empire, it is an even more devastating fallacy in connection with theories and other things that are not really ascertained at all. Thus history, especially prehistoric history, has a horrible habit of beginning with certain generalisations about races. I will not describe the disorder and misery this inversion has produced in modern politics. Because the race is vaguely supposed to have produced the nation, men talk as if the nation were something vaguer than the race. Because they have themselves invented a reason to explain a result, they almost deny the result in order to justify the reason. They first treat a Celt as an axiom and then treat an Irishman as an inference. And then they are surprised that a great fighting, roaring Irishman is angry at being treated as an inference. They cannot see that the Irish are Irish whether or no they are Celtic, whether or no there ever were any Celts. And what misleads them once more is the *size* of the theory; the sense that the fancy is bigger than the fact. A great scattered Celtic race is supposed to contain the Irish, so of course the Irish must depend for their very existence upon it. The same confusion, of course, has eliminated the English and the Germans by swamping them in the Teutonic race; and some tried to prove from the races being at one that the nations could not be at war. But I only give these vulgar and hackneyed examples in passing, as more familiar examples of the fallacy; the matter at issue here is not its application to these modern things but rather to the most ancient things. But the more remote and unrecorded was the racial problem, the more fixed was this curious inverted certainty in the Victorian man of science. To this day it gives a man of those scientific traditions the same sort of shock to question these things, which were only the last inferences when he turned them into first principles. He is still more certain that he is an Aryan even than that he is an Anglo-Saxon, just as he is more certain that he is an Anglo-Saxon than that he is an Englishman. He has never really discovered that he is a European. But he has never doubted that he is an Indo-European. These Victorian theories have shifted a great deal in their shape and scope; but this habit of a rapid hardening of a hypothesis into a theory, and of a theory into an assumption, has hardly yet gone out of fashion. People cannot easily get rid of the mental confusion of feeling that the foundations of history must surely be secure; that the first steps must be safe; that the biggest generalisation must be obvious. But though the contradiction may seem to them a paradox, this is the very contrary of the truth. It is the large thing that is secret and invisible; it is the small thing that is evident and enormous.

Every race on the face of the earth has been the subject of these speculations, and it is impossible even to suggest an outline of the subject. But if we take the European race alone, its history, or rather its prehistory, has undergone many retrospective revolutions in the short period of my own lifetime. It used to be called the Caucasian race; and I read in childhood an account of its collision with the Mongolian race; it was written by Bret Harte and opened with the query 'Or is the Caucasian played out?' Apparently the Caucasian was played out, for in a very short time he had been turned into the Indo-European man; sometimes, I regret to say, proudly presented as the Indo-Germanic man. It seems that the Hindu and the German have similar words for mother or father; there were other similarities between Sanskrit and various Western tongues; and with that all superficial differences between a Hindu and a German seemed suddenly to disappear. Generally this composite person was more conveniently described as the Aryan, and the really important point was that he had marched westward out of those high lands of India where fragments of his language could still be found. When I read this as a child, I had the fancy that after all the Aryan need not have marched westward and left his language behind him; he might also have marched eastward and taken his language with him. If I were to read it now, I should content myself with confessing my ignorance of the whole matter. But as a matter of fact I have great difficulty in reading it now, because it is not being written now. It looks as if the Aryan is also played out. Anyhow he has not merely changed his name but changed his address; his starting-place and his route of travel. One new theory maintains that our race did not come to its present home from the East but from the South. Some say the

Europeans did not come from Asia but from Africa. Some have even had the wild idea that the Europeans came from Europe; or rather that they never left it.

Then there is a certain amount of evidence of a more or less prehistoric pressure from the North, such as that which seems to have brought the Greeks to inherit the Cretan culture and so often brought the Gauls over the hills into the fields in Italy. But I merely mention this example of European ethnology to point out that the learned have pretty well boxed the compass by this time; and that I, who am not one of the learned, cannot pretend for a moment to decide where such doctors disagree. But I can use my own common sense, and I sometimes fancy that theirs is a little rusty from want of use. The first act of common sense is to recognise the difference between a cloud and a mountain. And I will affirm that nobody knows any of these things, in the sense that we all know of the existence of the Pyramids of Egypt.

The truth, it may be repeated, is that what we really see, as distinct from what we may reasonably guess, in this earliest phase of history is darkness covering the earth and great darkness the peoples, with a light or two gleaming here and there on chance patches of humanity; and that two of these flames do burn upon two of these tall primeval towns; upon the high terraces of Babylon and the huge pyramids of the Nile. There are indeed other ancient lights, or lights that may be conjectured to be very ancient, in very remote parts of that vast wilderness of night. Far away to the east there is a high civilisation of vast antiquity in China; there are the remains of civilisations in Mexico and South America and other places, some of them apparently so high in civilisation as to have reached the most refined forms of devil-worship. But the difference lies in the element of tradition; the tradition of these lost cultures has been broken off, and though the tradition of China still lives, it is doubtful whether we know anything about it. Moreover, a man trying to measure the Chinese antiquity has to use Chinese traditions of measurement; and he has a strange sensation of having passed into another world under other laws of time and space. Time is telescoped outwards and centuries assume the slow and stiff movement of aeons; the white man trying to see it as the yellow man sees, feels as if his head were turning round and wonders wildly whether it is growing a pigtail. Anyhow he cannot take in a scientific sense that queer perspective that leads up to the primeval pagoda of the first of the Sons of Heaven. He is the real antipodes; the only true alternative world to Christendom; and he is after a fashion walking upside down. I have spoken of the medieval map-maker and his dragon; but what medieval traveller, however much interested in monsters, would expect to find a country where a dragon is a benevolent and amiable being? Of the more serious side of Chinese tradition something will be said in another connection; but I am only talking of tradition and the test of antiquity. And I only mention China as an antiquity that is not for us reached by a bridge of tradition; and Babylon and Egypt as antiquities that are. Herodotus is a human being, in a sense in which a Chinaman in a billy-cock hat, sitting opposite to us in a London tea-shop, is hardly human. We feel as if we knew what David and Isaiah felt like, in a way in which we never were quite certain what Li Hung Chang[4] felt like. The very sins that snatched away Helen or Bathsheba have passed into a proverb of private human weakness, of pathos and even of pardon. The very virtues of the Chinaman have about them something terrifying. This is the difference made by the destruction or preservation of a continuous historical inheritance; as from ancient Egypt to modern Europe. But when we ask what was that world that we inherit, and why those particular people and places seem to belong to it, we are led to the central fact of civilised history.

That centre was the Mediterranean; which was not so much a piece of water as a world. But it was a world with something of the character of such a water; for it became more and more a place of unification in which the streams of strange and very diverse cultures met. The Nile and the Tiber alike flow into the Mediterranean; so did the Egyptian and the Etrurian alike contribute to a Mediterranean

[4] A Chinese statesman who was the organizer of China's first body of modern soldiers, founder of her modern navy, and builder of her first railway. In 1871, a flood caused serious damage to the province of Chihli, and on this occasion Li Hung-Chang distinguished himself by offering propitiatory prayers to a water-snake which had been caught and identified as the River god.

civilisation. The glamour of the great sea spread indeed very far inland and the unity was felt among the Arabs alone in the deserts and the Gauls beyond the northern hills. But the gradual building up of a common culture running round all the coasts of this inner sea is the main business of antiquity. As will be seen, it was sometimes a bad business as well as a good business. In that *orbis terrarum* or circle of lands there were the extremes of evil and of piety, there were contrasted races and still more contrasted religions. It was the scene of an endless struggle between Asia and Europe from the flight of the Persian ships at Salamis to the flight of the Turkish ships at Lepanto. It was the scene, as will be more especially suggested later, of a supreme spiritual struggle between the two types of paganism, confronting each other in the Latin and the Phoenician cities; in the Roman forum and the Punic mart. It was the world of war and peace, the world of good and evil, the world of all that matters most; with all respect to the Aztecs and the Mongols of the Far East, they did not matter as the Mediterranean tradition mattered and still matters. Between it and the Far East there were, of course, interesting cults and conquests of various kinds, more or less in touch with it, and in proportion as they were so intelligible also to us. The Persians came riding in to make an end of Babylon; and we are told in a Greek story how these barbarians learned to draw the bow and tell the truth. Alexander the great Greek marched with his Macedonians into the sunrise and brought back strange birds coloured like the sunrise clouds and strange flowers and jewels from the gardens and treasuries of nameless kings. Islam went eastward into that world and made it partly imaginable to us; precisely because Islam itself was born in that circle of lands that fringed our own ancient and ancestral sea. In the Middle Ages the empire of the Moguls increased its majesty without losing its mystery; the Tartars conquered China and the Chinese apparently took very little notice of them. All these things are interesting in themselves; but it is impossible to shift the centre of gravity to the inland spaces of Asia from the inland sea of Europe. When all is said, if there were nothing in the world but what was said and done and written and built in the lands lying round the Mediterranean, it would still be in all the most vital and

valuable things the world in which we live. When that southern
culture spread to the north-west it produced many very wonderful
things; of which doubtless we ourselves are the most wonderful.
When it spread thence to colonies and new countries, it was still the
same culture so long as it was culture at all. But round that little sea
like a lake were the things themselves, apart from all extensions and
echoes and commentaries on the things; the Republic and the
Church; the Bible and the heroic epics; Islam and Israel and the
memories of the lost empires; Aristotle and the measure of all
things. It is because the first light upon *this* world is really light, the
daylight in which we are still walking to-day, and not merely the
doubtful visitation of strange stars, that I have begun here with noting where that light first falls on the towered cities of the eastern
Mediterranean.

But though Babylon and Egypt have thus a sort of first claim, in
the very fact of being familiar and traditional, fascinating riddles to
us but also fascinating riddles to our fathers, we must not imagine
that they were the only old civilisations on the southern sea; or that
all the civilisation was merely Sumerian or Semitic or Coptic, still
less merely Asiatic or African. Real research is more and more exalting the ancient civilisation of Europe and especially of what we may
still vaguely call the Greeks. It must be understood in the sense that
there were Greeks before the Greeks, as in so many of their mythologies there were gods before the gods. The island of Crete was the
centre of the civilisation now called Minoan, after the Minos who
lingered in ancient legend and whose labyrinth was actually discovered by modern archeology. This elaborate European society,
with its harbours and its drainage and its domestic machinery, seems
to have gone down before some invasion of its northern neighbours,
who made or inherited the Hellas we know in history. But that earlier period did not pass till it had given to the world gifts so great
that the world has ever since been striving in vain to repay them, if
only by plagiarism.

Somewhere along the Ionian coast opposite Crete and the islands
was a town of some sort, probably of the sort that we should call a
village or hamlet with a wall. It was called Ilion but it came to be

called Troy, and the name will never perish from the earth. A poet who may have been a beggar and a ballad-monger, who may have been unable to read and write, and was described by tradition as blind, composed a poem about the Greeks going to war with this town to recover the most beautiful woman in the world. That the most beautiful woman in the world lived in that one little town sounds like a legend; that the most beautiful poem in the world was written by somebody who knew of nothing larger than such little towns is a historical fact. It is said that the poem came at the end of the period; that the primitive culture brought it forth in its decay; in which case one would like to have seen that culture in its prime. But anyhow it is true that this, which is our first poem, might very well be our last poem too. It might well be the last word as well as the first word spoken by man about his mortal lot, as seen by merely mortal vision. If the world becomes pagan and perishes, the last man left alive would do well to quote the Iliad and die.

But in this one great human revelation of antiquity there is another element of great historical importance; which has hardly I think been given its proper place in history. The poet has so conceived the poem that his sympathies apparently, and those of his reader certainly, are on the side of the vanquished rather than of the victor. And this is a sentiment which increases in the poetical tradition even as the poetical origin itself recedes. Achilles had some status as a sort of demigod in pagan times; but he disappears altogether in later times. But Hector grows greater as the ages pass; and it is his name that is the name of a Knight of the Round Table and his sword that legend puts into the hand of Roland, laying about him with the weapon of the defeated Hector in the last ruin and splendour of his own defeat. The name anticipates all the defeats through which our race and religion were to pass; that survival of a hundred defeats that is its triumph.

The tale of the end of Troy shall have no ending; for it is lifted up forever into living echoes, immortal as our hopelessness and our hope. Troy standing was a small thing that may have stood nameless for ages. But Troy falling has been caught up in a flame and suspended in an immortal instant of annihilation; and because it was destroyed with fire the fire shall never be destroyed. And as with the city so with the hero; traced in archaic lines in that primeval twilight is found the first figure of the Knight. There is a prophetic coincidence in his title; we have spoken of the word chivalry and how it seems to mingle the horseman with the horse. It is almost anticipated ages before in the thunder of the Homeric hexameter, and that long leaping word with which the Iliad ends. It is that very unity for which we can find no name but the holy centaur of chivalry. But there are other reasons for giving in this glimpse of antiquity the flame upon the sacred town. The sanctity of such towns ran like a fire round the coasts and islands of the northern Mediterranean; the high-fenced hamlet for which heroes died. From the smallness of the city came the greatness of the citizen. Hellas with her hundred statues produced nothing statelier than that walking statue; the ideal of the self-commanding man. Hellas of the hundred statues was one legend and literature; and all that labyrinth of little walled nations resounding with the lament of Troy.

A later legend, an afterthought but not an accident, said that stragglers from Troy founded a republic on the Italian shore. It was true in spirit that republican virtue had such a root. A mystery of honour, that was not born of Babylon or the Egyptian pride, there shone like the shield of Hector, defying Asia and Africa; till the light of a new day was loosened, with the rushing of the eagles and the coming of the name; the name that came like a thunderclap when the world woke to Rome.

IV

GOD AND COMPARATIVE RELIGION

I was once escorted over the Roman foundations of an ancient British city by a professor, who said something that seems to me a satire on a good many other professors. Possibly the professor saw the joke, though he maintained an iron gravity, and may or may not have realised that it was a joke against a great deal of what is called comparative religion. I pointed out a sculpture of the head of the sun with the usual halo of rays, but with the difference that the face in the disc, instead of being boyish like Apollo, was bearded like Neptune or Jupiter. 'Yes,' he said with a certain delicate exactitude, 'that is supposed to represent the local god Sul. The best authorities identify Sul with Minerva; but this has been held to show that the identification is not complete.'

That is what we call a powerful understatement. The modern world is madder than any satires on it; long ago Mr. Belloc made his burlesque don say that a bust of Ariadne had been proved by modern research to be a Silenus. But that is not better than the real appearance of Minerva as the Bearded Woman of Mr. Barnum. Only both of them are very like many identifications by 'the best authorities' on comparative religion; and when Catholic creeds are identified with various wild myths, I do not laugh or curse or misbehave myself; I confine myself decorously to saying that the identification is not complete.

In the days of my youth the Religion of Humanity was a term commonly applied to Comtism, the theory of certain rationalists who worshipped corporate mankind as a Supreme Being. Even in the days of my youth, I remarked that there was something slightly odd about despising and dismissing the doctrine of the Trinity as a mystical and even maniacal contradiction; and then asking us to adore a deity who is a hundred million persons in one God, neither confounding the persons nor dividing the substance.

But there is another entity, more or less definable and much more

214

imaginable than the many-headed and monstrous idol of mankind. And it has a much better right to be called, in a reasonable sense, the religion of humanity. Man is not indeed the idol; but man is almost everywhere the idolator. And these multitudinous idolatries of mankind have something about them in many ways more human and sympathetic than modern metaphysical abstractions. If an Asiatic god has three heads and seven arms, there is at least in it an idea of material incarnation bringing an unknown power nearer to us and not farther away. But if our friends Brown, Jones, and Robinson, when out for a Sunday walk, were transformed and amalgamated into an Asiatic idol before our eyes, they would surely seem farther away. If the arms of Brown and the legs of Robinson waved from the same composite body, they would seem to be waving something of a sad farewell. If the heads of all three gentlemen appeared smiling on the same neck, we should hesitate even by what name to address our new and somewhat abnormal friend. In the many-headed and many-handed Oriental idol there is a certain sense of mysteries becoming at least partly intelligible; of formless forces of nature taking some dark but material form, but though this may be true of the multiform god it is not so of the multiform man. The human beings become less human by becoming less separate; we might say less human in being less lonely. The human beings become less intelligible as they become less isolated; we might say with strict truth that the closer they are to us the farther they are away. An Ethical Hymn-book of this humanitarian sort of religion was carefully selected and expurgated on the principle of preserving anything human and eliminating anything divine. One consequence was that a hymn appeared in the amended form of 'Nearer Mankind to Thee, Nearer to Thee.' It always suggested to me the sensations of a strap-hanger during a crush on the Tube. But it is strange and wonderful how far away the souls of men can seem, when their bodies are so near as all that.

The human unity with which I deal here is not to be confounded with this modern industrial monotony and herding, which is rather a congestion than a communion. It is a thing to which human groups left to themselves, and even human individuals left to themselves, have everywhere tended by an instinct that may truly be called human. Like all healthy human things, it has varied very much within the limits of a general character; for that is characteristic of everything belonging to that ancient land of liberty that lies before and around the servile industrial town. Industrialism actually boasts that its products are all of one pattern; that men in Jamaica or Japan can break the same seal and drink the same bad whiskey, that a man at the North Pole and another at the South might recognise the same optimistic label on the same dubious tinned salmon. But wine, the gift of gods to men, can vary with every valley and every vineyard, can turn into a hundred wines without any wine once reminding us of whiskey; and cheeses can change from county to county without forgetting the difference between chalk and cheese. When I am speaking of this thing, therefore, I am speaking of something that doubtless includes very wide differences; nevertheless I will here maintain that it is one thing. I will maintain that most of the modern botheration comes from not realising that it is really one thing. I will advance the thesis that before all talk about comparative religion and the separate religious founders of the world, the first essential is to recognise this thing as a whole, as a thing almost native and normal to the great fellowship that we call mankind. This thing is Paganism; and I propose to show in these pages that it is the one real rival to the Church of Christ.

Comparative religion is very comparative indeed. That is, it is so much a matter of degree and distance and difference that it is only comparatively successful when it tries to compare. When we come to look at it closely we find it comparing things that are really quite incomparable. We are accustomed to see a table or catalogue of the world's great religions in parallel columns, until we fancy they are really parallel. We are accustomed to see the names of the great religious founders all in a row: Christ; Mahomet; Buddha; Confucius. But in truth this is only a trick; another of these optical illusions by which any objects may be put into a particular relation by shifting to a particular point of sight. Those religions and religious founders, or rather those whom we choose to lump together as religions and religious founders, do not really show any common character. The illusion is partly produced by Islam coming immediately after Christianity in the list; as Islam did come after Christianity and was largely an imitation of Christianity. But the other eastern religions, or what we call religions, not only do not resemble the Church but do not resemble each other. When we come to Confucianism at the end of the list, we come to something in a totally different world of thought. To compare the Christian and Confucian religions is like comparing a theist with an English squire or asking whether a man is a believer in immortality or a hundred-per-cent American. Confucianism may be a civilisation but it is not a religion.

In truth the Church is too unique to prove herself unique. For most popular and easy proof is by parallel; and here there is no parallel. It is not easy, therefore, to expose the fallacy by which a false classification is created to swamp a unique thing, when it really is a unique thing. As there is nowhere else exactly the same fact, so there is nowhere else exactly the same fallacy. But I will take the nearest thing I can find to such a solitary social phenomenon, in order to show how it is thus swamped and assimilated. I imagine most of us would agree that there is something unusual and unique about the position of the Jews. There is nothing that is quite in the same sense an international nation; an ancient culture scattered in different countries but still distinct and indestructible. Now this business is like an attempt to make a list of Nomadic Nations in order to soften the strange solitude of the Jew. It would be easy enough to do it, by the same process of putting a plausible approximation first, and then tailing off into totally different things thrown in somehow to make up the list. Thus in the new list of nomadic nations the Jews would be followed by the Gypsies; who at least are really nomadic if they are not really national. Then the professor of the new science of Comparative Nomadics could pass easily on to something different; even if it was very different. He could remark on the wandering adventure of the English who had scattered their colonies over so many seas; and call *them* nomads. It is quite true that a great many Englishmen seem to be strangely restless in England. It is quite true that not all of them have left their country for their country's good. The moment we mention the wandering empire of the English, we must add the strange exiled empire of the Irish. For it is a curious fact, to be noted in our imperial literature, that the same ubiquity and un-rest which is a proof of English enterprise and triumph is a proof of Irish futility and failure. Then the professor of Nomadism would look round thoughtfully and remember that there was great talk re-cently of German waiters, German barbers, German clerks, Ger-mans naturalising themselves in England and the United States and the South American republics. The Germans would go down as the fifth nomadic race; the words Wanderlust and Folk-Wandering would come in very useful here. For there really have been historians who explained the Crusades by suggesting that the Germans were found wandering (as the police say) in what happened to be the neighbourhood of Palestine. Then the professor, feeling he was now near the end, would make a last leap in desperation. He would recall the fact that the French army has captured nearly every capital in Europe, that it marched across countless conquered lands under Charlemagne or Napoleon; and *that* would be wanderlust and *that* would be the note of a nomadic race. Thus he would have his six no-madic nations all compact and complete, and would feel that the Jew was no longer a sort of mysterious and even mystical exception. But people with more common sense would probably realise that he had only extended nomadism by extending the meaning of nomadism; and that he had extended that until it really had no meaning at all. It is quite true that the French soldier has made some of the finest marches in all military history. But it is equally true, and far more self-evident, that if the French peasant is not a rooted reality there is no such thing as a rooted reality in the world; or in other words, if he is a nomad there is nobody who is not a nomad.

Now that is the sort of trick that has been tried in the case of com-parative religion and the world's religious founders all standing re-spectably in a row. It seeks to classify Jesus as the other would classify Jews, by inventing a new class for the purpose and filling up the rest of it with stop-gaps and second-rate copies. I do not mean that these other things are not often great things in their own real character and class. Confucianism and Buddhism are great things, but it is not true to call them Churches; just as the French and English are great peoples, but it is nonsense to call them nomads. There are some points of resemblance between Christendom and its imitation in Islam; for that matter there are some points of resemblance between Jews and Gypsies. But after that the lists are made up of anything that comes to hand; of anything that can be put in the same catalogue without being in the same category.

In this sketch of religious history, with all decent deference to men much more learned than myself, I propose to cut across and disregard this modern method of classification, which I feel sure has falsified the facts of history. I shall here submit an alternative classification of religion or religions, which I believe would be found to cover all the facts and, what is quite as important here, all the fancies. Instead of dividing religion geographically and as it were vertically, into Christian, Moslem, Brahmin, Buddhist, and so on, I would divide it psychologically and in some sense horizontally; into the strata of spiritual elements and influences that could sometimes exist in the same country, or even in the same man. Putting the Church apart for the moment, I should be disposed to divide the natural religion of the mass of mankind under such headings as these: God; the Gods; the Demons; the Philosophers. I believe some such classification will help us to sort out the spiritual experiences of men much more successfully than the conventional business of comparing religions; and that many famous figures will naturally fall into their place in this way who are only forced into their place in the other. As I shall make use of these titles or terms more than once in narrative and allusion, it will be well to define at this stage for what I mean them to stand. And I will begin with the first, the simplest and the most sublime, in this chapter.

In considering the elements of pagan humanity, we must begin by an attempt to describe the indescribable. Many get over the difficulty of describing it by the expedient of denying it, or at least ignoring it; but the whole point of it is that it was something that was never quite eliminated even when it was ignored. They are obsessed by their evolutionary monomania that every great thing grows from a seed, or something smaller than itself. They seem to forget that every seed comes from a tree, or something larger than itself. Now there is very good ground for guessing that religion did not originally come from some detail that was forgotten, because it was too small to be traced. Much more probably it was an idea that was abandoned because it was too large to be managed. There is very good reason to suppose that many people did begin with the simple but overwhelming idea of one God who governs all; and afterwards fell away into such things as demon-worship almost as a sort of secret dissipation. Even the test of savage beliefs, of which the folk-lore students are so fond, is admittedly often found to support such a view. Some of the very rudest savages, primitive in every sense in which anthropologists use the word, the Australian aborigines for instance, are found to have a pure monotheism with a high moral tone. A missionary was preaching to a very wild tribe of polytheists, who had told him all their polytheistic tales, and telling them in return of the existence of the one good God who is a spirit and judges men by spiritual standards. And there was a sudden buzz of excitement among these stolid barbarians, as at somebody who was letting out a secret, and they cried to each other, 'Atahocan! He is speaking of Atahocan!'

Probably it was a point of politeness and even decency among those polytheists not to speak of Atahocan. The name is not perhaps so much adapted as some of our own to direct and solemn religious exhortation; but many other social forces are always covering up and confusing such simple ideas. Possibly the old god stood for an old morality found irksome in more expansive moments; possibly intercourse with demons was more fashionable among the best people, as in the modern fashion of Spiritualism. Anyhow, there are any number of similar examples. They all testify to the unmistakable psychology of a thing taken for granted, as distinct from a thing talked about. There is a striking example in a tale taken down word for word from a Red Indian in California, which starts out with hearty legendary and literary relish: 'The sun is the father and ruler of the heavens. He is the big chief. The moon is his wife and the stars are their children'; and so on through a most ingenious and complicated story, in the middle of which is a sudden parenthesis saying that the sun and moon have to do something because 'It is ordered that way by the Great Spirit Who lives above the place of all.' That is exactly the attitude of most paganism towards God. He is something assumed and forgotten and remembered by accident; a habit possibly not peculiar to pagans. Sometimes the higher deity is remembered in the higher moral grades and is a sort of mystery. But always, it has been truly said, the savage is talkative about his mythology and taciturn about his religion. The Australian savages, indeed, exhibit a topsyturveydom such as the ancients might have thought truly worthy of the antipodes. The savage who thinks nothing of tossing off such a trifle as a tale of the sun and moon being the halves of a baby chopped in two, or dropping into small-talk about a colossal cosmic cow milked to make the rain, merely in order to be sociable, will then retire to secret caverns sealed against women and white men, temples of terrible initiation where to the thunder of the bull-roarer and the dripping of sacrificial blood, the priest whispers the final secrets, known only to the initiate: that honesty is the best policy, that a little kindness does nobody any harm, that all men are brothers and that there is but one God, the Father Almighty, maker of all things visible and invisible.

In other words, we have here the curiosity of religious history that the savage seems to be parading all the most repulsive and impossible parts of his belief and concealing all the most sensible and creditable parts. But the explanation is that they are not in that sense parts of his belief; or at least not parts of the same sort of belief. The myths are merely tall stories, though as tall as the sky, the waterspout, or the tropic rain. The mysteries are true stories, and are taken secretly that they may be taken seriously. Indeed it is only too easy to forget that there is a thrill in theism. A novel in which a number of separate characters all turned out to be the same character would certainly be a sensational novel. It is so with the idea that sun and tree and river are the disguises of one god and not of many. Alas, we also find it only too easy to take Atahocan for granted. But whether he is allowed to fade into a truism or preserved as a sensation by being preserved as a secret, it is clear that he is always either an old truism or an old tradition. There is nothing to show that he is an improved product of the mere mythology and everything to show that he preceded it. He is worshipped by the simplest tribes with no trace of ghosts or grave-offerings, or any of the complications in which Herbert Spencer and Grant Allen sought the origin of the simplest of all ideas. Whatever else there was, there was never any such thing as the Evolution of the Idea of God. The idea was concealed, was avoided, was almost forgotten, was even explained away; but it was never evolved.

There are not a few indications of this change in other places. It is implied, for instance, in the fact that even polytheism seems often the combination of several monotheisms. A god will gain only a minor seat on Mount Olympus, when he had owned earth and heaven and all the stars while he lived in his own little valley. Like many a small nation melting in a great empire, he gives up local universality only to come under universal limitation. The very name of Pan suggests that he became a god of the wood when he had been a god of the world. The very name of Jupiter is almost a pagan translation of the words 'Our Father which art in heaven.' As with the Great Father symbolised by the sky, so with the Great Mother whom we still call Mother Earth. Demeter and Ceres and Cybele often seem to be almost capable of taking over the whole business of godhood, so that men should need no other gods. It seems reasonably probable that a good many men did have no other gods but one of these, worshipped as the author of all.

Over some of the most immense and populous tracts of the world, such as China, it would seem that the simpler idea of the Great Father has never been very much complicated with rival cults, though it may have in some sense ceased to be a cult itself. The best authorities seem to think that though Confucianism is in one sense agnosticism, it does not directly contradict the old theism, precisely because it has become a rather vague theism. It is one in which God is called Heaven, as in the case of polite persons tempted to swear in drawing-rooms. But Heaven is still overhead, even if it is very far overhead. We have all the impression of a simple truth that has receded, until it was remote without ceasing to be true. And this phrase alone would bring us back to the same idea even in the pagan mythology of the West. There is surely something of this very notion of the withdrawal of some higher power, in all those mysterious and very imaginative myths about the separation of earth and sky. In a hundred forms we are told that heaven and earth were once lovers, or were once at one, when some upstart thing, often some undutiful child, thrust them apart; and the world was built on an abyss; upon a division and a parting. One of its grossest versions was given by Greek civilisation in the myth of Uranus and Saturn. One of its most charming versions was that of some savage niggers, who say that a little pepper-plant grew taller and taller and lifted the whole sky like a lid; a beautiful barbaric vision of daybreak for some of our painters who love that tropical twilight. Of myths, and the highly mythical explanations which the moderns offer of myths, something will be said in another section; for I cannot but think that most mythology is on another and more superficial plane. But in this primeval vision of the rending of one world into two there is surely something more of ultimate ideas. As to what it means, a man will learn far more about it by lying on his back in a field, and merely looking at the sky, than by reading all the libraries even of the most learned and valuable folklore. He will know what is meant by saying that the sky ought to be nearer to us than it is, that perhaps it was once nearer than it is, that it is not a thing merely alien and abysmal but in some fashion sundered from us and saying farewell. There will creep across his mind the curious suggestion that after all, perhaps, the myth-maker was not merely a moon-calf or village idiot thinking he could cut up the clouds like a cake, but had in him something more than it is fashionable to attribute to the Troglodyte; that it is just possible that Thomas Hood[1] was not talking like a Troglodyte when he said that, as time went on, the tree-tops only told him he was further off from heaven than when he was a boy. But anyhow the legend of Uranus the Lord of Heaven dethroned by Saturn the Time Spirit would mean something to the author of that poem. And it would mean, among other things, this banishment of the first fatherhood. There is the idea of God in the very notion that there were gods before the gods. There is an idea of greater simplicity in all the allusions to that more ancient order. The suggestion is supported by the process of propagation we see in historic times. Gods

---

[1] Thomas Hood (1799–1845) was an English poet noted for his humor.

and demigods and heroes breed like herrings before our very eyes, and suggest of themselves that the family may have had one founder; mythology grows more and more complicated, and the very complication suggests that at the beginning it was more simple. Even on the external evidence, of the sort called scientific, there is therefore a very good case for the suggestion that man began with monotheism before it developed or degenerated into polytheism. But I am concerned rather with an internal than an external truth; and, as I have already said, the internal truth is almost indescribable. We have to speak of something of which it is the whole point that people did not speak of it; we have not merely to translate from a strange tongue or speech, but from a strange silence.

I suspect an immense implication behind all polytheism and paganism. I suspect we have only a hint of it here and there in these savage creeds or Greek origins. It is not exactly what we mean by the presence of God; in a sense it might more truly be called the absence of God. But absence does not mean non-existence; and a man drinking the toast of absent friends does not mean that from his life all friendship is absent. It is a void but it is not a negation; it is something as positive as an empty chair. It would be an exaggeration to say that the pagan saw higher than Olympus an empty throne. It would be nearer the truth to take the gigantic imagery of the Old Testament, in which the prophet saw God from behind; it was as if some immeasureable presence had turned its back on the world. Yet the meaning will again be missed, if it is supposed to be anything so conscious and vivid as the monotheism of Moses and his people. I do not mean that the pagan peoples were in the least overpowered by this idea merely because it is overpowering. On the contrary, it was so large that they all carried it lightly, as we all carry the load of the sky. Gazing at some detail like a bird or a cloud, we can all ignore its awful blue background; we can neglect the sky; and precisely because it bears down upon us with an annihilating force it is felt as nothing. A thing of this kind can only be an impressing and a rather subtle impression; but to me it is a very strong impression made by pagan literature and religion. I repeat that in our special sacramental sense there is, of course, the absence of the presence of God. But there is in a very real sense the presence of the absence of God. We feel it in the unfathomable sadness of pagan poetry; for I doubt if there was ever in all the marvellous manhood of antiquity a man who was happy as St. Francis was happy. We feel it in the legend of a Golden Age and again in the vague implication that the gods themselves are ultimately related to something else, even when that Unknown God has faded into a Fate. Above all we feel it in those immortal moments when the pagan literature seems to return to a more innocent antiquity and speak with a more direct voice, so that no word is worthy of it except our own monotheistic monosyllable. We cannot say anything but 'God' in a sentence like that of Socrates bidding farewell to his judges: 'I go to die and you remain to live; and God alone knows which of us goes the better way.' We can use no other word even for the best moments of Marcus Aurelius: 'Can they say dear city of Cecrops,[2] and canst thou not say dear city of God?' We can use no other word in that mighty line in which Virgil spoke to all who suffer with the veritable cry of a Christian before Christ: 'O you that have borne things more terrible, to this also God shall give an end.'

In short, there is a feeling that there is something higher than the gods; but because it is higher it is also further away. Not yet could even Virgil have read the riddle and the paradox of that other divinity, who is both higher and nearer. For them what was truly divine was very distant, so distant that they dismissed it more and more from their minds. It had less and less to do with the mere mythology of which I shall write later. Yet even in this there was a sort of tacit admission of its intangible purity, when we consider what most of the mythology is like. As the Jews would not degrade it by images, so the Greeks did not degrade it even by imaginations. When the gods were more and more remembered only by pranks and profligacies, it was relatively a movement of reverence. It was an act of piety to forget God. In other words, there is something in the whole tone of the time suggesting that men had accepted a lower level, and still were half conscious that it was a lower level. It is hard to find words

[2] Traditionally the first king of Attica in ancient Greece, he was represented as human in his upper body and a dragon in the lower body.

for these things; yet the one really just word stands ready. These men were conscious of the Fall if they were conscious of nothing else; and the same is true of all heathen humanity. Those who have fallen may remember the fall, even when they forget the height. Some such tantalising blank or break in memory is at the back of all pagan sentiment. There is such a thing as the momentary power to remember that we forget. And the most ignorant of humanity know by the very look of earth that they have forgotten heaven. But it remains true that even for these men there were moments, like the memories of childhood, when they heard themselves talking with a simpler language; there were moments when the Roman, like Virgil in the line already quoted, cut his way with a sword-stroke of song out of the tangle of the mythologies; the motley mob of gods and goddesses sank suddenly out of sight and the Sky-Father was alone in the sky.

This latter example is very relevant to the next step in the process. A white light as of a lost morning still lingers on the figure of Jupiter, of Pan or of the elder Apollo; and it may well be, as already noted, that each was once a divinity as solitary as Jehovah or Allah. They lost this lonely universality by a process it is here very necessary to note; a process of amalgamation very like what was afterwards called syncretism. The whole pagan world set itself to build a Pantheon. They admitted more and more gods, gods not only of the Greeks but of the barbarians; gods not only of Europe but of Asia and Africa. The more the merrier, though some of the Asian and African ones were not very merry. They admitted them to equal thrones with their own; sometimes they identified them with their own. They may have regarded it as an enrichment of their religious life; but it meant the final loss of all that we now call religion. It meant that ancient light of simplicity, that had a single source like the sun, finally fades away in a dazzle of conflicting lights and colours. God is really sacrificed to the Gods; in a very literal sense of the flippant phrase, they have been too many for him.

Polytheism, therefore, was really a sort of pool; in the sense of the pagans having consented to the pooling of their pagan religions. And this point is very important in many controversies ancient and modern. It is regarded as a liberal and enlightened thing to say that the god of the stranger may be as good as our own; and doubtless the pagans thought themselves very liberal and enlightened when they agreed to add to the gods of the city or the hearth some wild and fantastic Dionysus coming down from the mountains or some shaggy and rustic Pan creeping out of the woods. But exactly what it lost by these larger ideas is the largest idea of all. It is the idea of the fatherhood that makes the whole world one. And the converse is also true. Doubtless those more antiquated men of antiquity who clung to their solitary statues and their single sacred names were regarded as superstitious savages benighted and left behind. But these superstitious savages were preserving something that is much more like the cosmic power as conceived by philosophy, or even as conceived by science. This paradox by which the rude reactionary was a sort of prophetic progressive has one consequence very much to the point. In a purely historical sense, and apart from any other controversies in the same connection, it throws a light, a single and a steady light, that shines from the beginning on a little and lonely people. In this paradox, as in some riddle of religion of which the answer was sealed up for centuries, lies the mission and the meaning of the Jews.

It is true in this sense, humanly speaking, that the world owes God to the Jews. It owes that truth to much that is blamed on the Jews, possibly to much that is blameable in the Jews. We have already noted the nomadic position of the Jews amid the other pastoral peoples upon the fringe of the Babylonian Empire, and something of that strange erratic course of theirs blazed across the dark territory of extreme antiquity, as they passed from the seat of Abraham and the shepherd princes into Egypt and doubled back into the Palestinian hills and held them against the Philistines from Crete and fell into captivity in Babylon; and yet again returned to their mountain city by the Zionist policy of the Persian conquerors; and so continued that amazing romance of restlessness of which we have not yet seen the end. But through all their wanderings, and especially through all their early wanderings, they did indeed carry the fate of the world in that wooden tabernacle, that held perhaps a featureless symbol and

certainly an invisible god. We may say that one most essential feature was that it was featureless. Much as we may prefer that creative
liberty which the Christian culture has declared and by which it has
eclipsed even the arts of antiquity, we must not underrate the deter-
mining importance at the time of the Hebrew inhibition of images. It
is a typical example of one of those limitations that did in fact preserve and perpetuate enlargement, like a wall built round a wide
open space. The God who could not have a statue remained a spirit.
Nor would his statue in any case have had the disarming dignity and
grace of the Greek statues then or the Christian statues afterwards.
He was living in a land of monsters. We shall have occasion to consider more fully what those monsters were, Moloch and Dagon[3] and
Tanit[4] the terrible goddess. If the deity of Israel had ever had an image, he would have had a phallic image. By merely giving him a
body they would have brought in all the worst elements of mythology; all the polygamy of polytheism; the vision of the harem in
heaven. This point about the refusal of art is the first example of the
limitations which are often adversely criticised, only because the critics themselves are limited. But an even stronger case can be found in
the other criticism offered by the same critics. It is often said with a
sneer that the God of Israel was only a God of Battles, 'a mere barbaric Lord of Hosts' pitted in rivalry against other gods only as their
envious foe. Well it is for the world that he was a God of Battles.
Well it is for us that he was to all the rest only a rival and a foe. In
the ordinary way, it would have been only too easy for them to have
achieved the desolate disaster of conceiving him as a friend. It would
have been only too easy for them to have seen him stretching out his
hands in love and reconciliation, embracing Baal and kissing the
painted face of Astarte, feasting in fellowship with the gods; the last
god to sell his crown of stars for the Soma[5] of the Indian pantheon or

[3] The Semitic god of crop fertility, worshipped extensively throughout the Far East. An
especially important god to the Philistines, he was supposedly the father of the god Baal.

[4] The chief goddess of Carthage. As mother goddess, she was connected with fertility and child sacrifice to her was practiced.

[5] An unidentified plant, the juice of which was used as an offering in the Vedic
sacrifices of ancient India.

the nectar of Olympus or the mead of Valhalla. It would have been easy enough for his worshippers to follow the enlightened course of Syncretism and the pooling of all the pagan traditions. It is obvious indeed that his followers were always sliding down this easy slope; and it required the almost demoniac energy of certain inspired demagogues, who testified to the divine unity in words that are still like winds of inspiration and ruin. The more we really understand of the ancient conditions that contributed to the final culture of the Faith, the more we shall have a real and even a realistic reverence for the greatness of the Prophets of Israel. As it was, while the whole world melted into this mass of confused mythology, this Deity who is called tribal and narrow, precisely because he was what is called tribal and narrow, preserved the primary religion of all mankind. He was tribal enough to be universal. He was as narrow as the universe.

In a word, there was a popular pagan god called Jupiter-Ammon. There was never a god called Jehovah-Ammon. There was never a god called Jehovah-Jupiter. If there had been, there would certainly have been another called Jehovah-Moloch. Long before the liberal and enlightened amalgamators had got so far afield as Jupiter, the image of the Lord of Hosts would have been deformed out of all suggestion of a monotheistic maker and ruler and would have become an idol far worse than any savage fetish; for he might have been as civilised as the gods of Tyre and Carthage. What that civilisation meant we shall consider more fully in the chapter that follows; when we note how the power of demons nearly destroyed Europe and even the heathen health of the world. But the world's destiny would have been distorted still more fatally if monotheism had failed in the Mosaic tradition. I hope in a subsequent section to show that I am not without sympathy with all that health in the heathen world that made its fairy-tales and its fanciful romances of religion. But I hope also to show that these were bound to fail in the long run; and the world would have been lost if it had been unable to return to that great original simplicity of a single authority in all things. That we do preserve something of that primary simplicity, that poets and philosophers can still indeed in some sense say an Universal Prayer, that we live in a large and serene world under a sky that stretches paternally over all the peoples of the earth, that philosophy and philanthropy are truisms in a religion of reasonable men, all that we do most truly owe, under heaven, to a secretive and restless nomadic people; who bestowed on men the supreme and serene blessing of a jealous God.

The unique possession was not available or accessible to the pagan world, because it was also the possession of a jealous people. The Jews were unpopular, partly because of this narrowness already noted in the Roman world, partly perhaps because they had already fallen into that habit of merely handling things for exchange instead of working to make them with their hands. It was partly also because polytheism had become a sort of jungle in which solitary monotheism could be lost; but it is strange to realise how completely it really was lost. Apart from more disputed matters, there were things in the tradition of Israel which belong to all humanity now, and might have belonged to all humanity then. They had one of the colossal corner-stones of the world: the Book of Job. It obviously stands over against the Iliad and the Greek tragedies; and even more than they it was an early meeting and parting of poetry and philosophy in the morning of the world. It is a solemn and uplifting sight to see those two eternal fools, the optimist and the pessimist, destroyed in the dawn of time. And the philosophy really perfects the pagan tragic irony, precisely because it is more monotheistic and therefore more mystical. Indeed the Book of Job avowedly only answers mystery with mystery. Job is comforted with riddles; but he is comforted. Herein is indeed a type, in the sense of a prophecy, of things speaking with authority. For when he who doubts can only say 'I do not understand,' it is true that he who knows can only reply or repeat 'You do not understand.' And under that rebuke there is always a sudden hope in the heart; and the sense of something that would be worth understanding. But this mighty monotheistic poem remained unremarked by the whole world of antiquity, which was thronged with polytheistic poetry. It is a sign of the way in which the Jews stood apart and kept their tradition unshaken and unshared, that they should have kept a thing like the Book of Job out of the whole intellectual world of antiquity. It is as if the Egyptians had modestly concealed the Great Pyramid. But there were other reasons for a cross-purpose and an impasse, characteristic of the whole of the end of paganism. After all, the tradition of Israel had only got hold of one-half of the truth, even if we use the popular paradox and call it the bigger half. I shall try to sketch in the next chapter that love of locality and personality that ran through mythology; here it need only be said that there was a truth in it that could not be left out, though it were a lighter and less essential truth. The sorrow of Job had to be joined with the sorrow of Hector; and while the former was the sorrow of the universe the latter was the sorrow of the city; for Hector could only stand pointing to heaven as the pillar of holy Troy. When God speaks out of the whirlwind he may well speak in the wilderness. But the monotheism of the nomad was not enough for all that varied civilisation of fields and fences and walled cities and temples and towns; and the turn of these things also was to come, when the two could be combined in a more definite and domestic religion. Here and there in all that pagan crowd could be found a philosopher whose thought ran of pure theism; but he never had, or supposed that he had, the power to change the customs of the whole populace. Nor is it easy even in such philosophies to find a true definition of this deep business of the relation of polytheism and theism. Perhaps the nearest we can come to striking the note, or giving the thing a name, is in something far away from all that civilisation and more remote from Rome than the isolation of Israel. It is in a saying I once heard from some Hindu tradition; that gods as well as men are only the dreams of Brahma; and will perish when Brahma wakes. There is indeed in such an image something of the soul of Asia which is less sane than the soul of Christendom. We should call it despair, even if they would call it peace. This note of nihilism can be considered later in a fuller comparison between Asia and Europe. It is enough to say here that there is more of disillusion in that idea of a divine awakening than is implied for us in the passage from mythology to religion. But the symbol is very subtle and exact in one respect; that it does suggest the disproportion and even disruption between the very ideas of mythology and religion; the chasm between the two categories. It is really the collapse of comparative religion that there is no comparison between God and the gods.

There is no more comparison than there is between a man and the men who walked about in his dreams. Under the next heading some attempt will be made to indicate the twilight of that dream in which the gods walk about like men. But if anyone fancies the contrast of monotheism and polytheism is only a matter of some people having one god and others a few more, for him it will be far nearer the truth to plunge into the elephantine extravagance of Brahmin cosmology; that he may feel a shudder going through the veil of things, the many-handed creators, and the throned and haloed animals and all the network of entangled stars and rulers of the night, as the awful eyes of Brahma open like dawn upon the death of all.

V

MAN AND MYTHOLOGIES

What are here called the Gods might almost alternatively be called the Day-Dreams. To compare them to dreams is not to deny that dreams can come true. To compare them to travellers' tales is not to deny that they may be true tales, or at least truthful tales. In truth they are the sort of tales the traveller tells to himself. All this mythological business belongs to the poetical part of men. It seems strangely forgotten nowadays that a myth is a work of imagination and therefore a work of art. It needs a poet to make it. It needs a poet to criticise it. There are more poets than non-poets in the world, as is proved by the popular origin of such legends. But for some reason I have never heard explained, it is only the minority of unpoetical people who are allowed to write critical studies of these popular poems. We do not submit a sonnet to a mathematician or a song to a calculating boy; but we do indulge the equally fantastic idea that folk-lore can be treated as a science. Unless these things are appreciated artistically they are not appreciated at all. When the Professor is told by the Polynesian that once there was nothing except a great feathered serpent, unless the learned man feels a thrill and a half temptation to wish it were true, he is no judge of such things at all. When he is assured, on the best Red Indian authority, that a primitive hero carried the sun and moon and stars in a box, unless he clasps his hands and almost kicks his legs as a child would at such a charming fancy, he knows nothing about the matter. This test is not nonsensical; primitive children and barbaric children do laugh and kick like other children; and we must have a certain simplicity to repicture the childhood of the world. When Hiawatha was told by his nurse that a warrior threw his grandmother up to the moon, he laughed like any English child told by his nurse that a cow jumped over the moon. The child sees the joke as well as most men, and better than some scientific men. But the ultimate test even of the fantastic is the appropriateness of the inappropriate. And the test must appear

233

merely arbitrary because it is merely artistic. If any student tells me that the infant Hiawatha only laughed out of respect for tribal custom of sacrificing the aged to economical housekeeping, I say he did not. If any scholar tells me that the cow jumped over the moon only because a heifer was sacrificed to Diana, I answer that it did not. It happened because it is obviously the right thing for a cow to jump over the moon. Mythology is a lost art, one of the few arts that really are lost; but it is an art. The horned moon and the horned mooncalf make a harmonious and almost a quiet pattern. And throwing your grandmother into the sky is not good behaviour; but it is perfectly good taste.

Thus scientists seldom understand, as artists understand, that one branch of the beautiful is the ugly. They seldom allow for the legitimate liberty of the grotesque. And they will dismiss a savage myth as merely coarse and clumsy and an evidence of degradation, because it has not all the beauty of the herald Mercury new lighted on a heaven-kissing hill; when it really has the beauty of the Mock Turtle or the Mad Hatter. It is the supreme proof of a man being prosaic that he always insists on poetry being poetical. Sometimes the humour is in the very subject as well as the style of the fable. The Australian aborigines, regarded as the rudest of savages, have a story about a giant frog who had swallowed the sea and all the waters of the world; and who was only forced to spill them by being made to laugh. All the animals with all their antics passed before him and, like Queen Victoria, he was not amused. He collapsed at last before an eel who stood delicately balanced on the tip of its tail, doubtless with a rather desperate dignity. Any amount of fine fantastic literature might be made out of that fable. There is philosophy in that vision of the dry world before the beatific Deluge of laughter. There is imagination in the mountainous monster erupting like an aqueous volcano; there is plenty of fun in the thought of his goggling visage as the pelican or the penguin passed by. Anyhow the frog laughed; but the folk-lore student remains grave.

Moreover, even where the fables are inferior as art, they cannot be properly judged by science; still less properly judged as science. Some myths are very crude and queer like the early drawings of children;

but the child is trying to draw. It is none the less an error to treat his drawing as if it were a diagram, or intended to be a diagram. The student cannot make a scientific statement about the savage, because the savage is not making a scientific statement about the world. He is saying something quite different; what might be called the gossip of the gods. We may say, if we like, that it is believed before there is time to examine it. It would be truer to say it is accepted before there is time to believe it.

I confess I doubt the whole theory of the dissemination of myths or (as it commonly is) of one myth. It is true that something in our nature and conditions makes many stories similar; but each of them may be original. One man does not borrow the story from the other man, though he may tell it from the same motive as the other man. It would be easy to apply the whole argument about legend to literature; and turn it into a vulgar monomania of plagiarism. I would undertake to trace a notion like that of the Golden Bough through individual modern novels as easily as through communal and antiquated myths. I would undertake to find something like a bunch of flowers figuring again and again from the fatal bouquet of Becky Sharpe to the spray of roses sent by the Princess of Ruritania. But though these flowers may spring from the same soil, it is not the same faded flower that is flung from hand to hand. Those flowers are always fresh.

The true origin of all the myths has been discovered much too often. There are too many keys to mythology, as there are too many cryptograms in Shakespeare. Everything is phallic; everything is totemistic; everything is seed-time and harvest; everything is ghosts and grave-offerings; everything is the golden bough of sacrifice; everything is the sun and moon; everything is everything. Every folk-lore student who knew a little more than his own monomania, every man of wider reading and critical culture like Andrew Lang, has practically confessed that the bewilderment of these things left his brain spinning. Yet the whole trouble comes from a man trying to look at these stories from the outside, as if they were scientific objects. He has only to look at them from the inside, and ask himself how he would begin a story. A story may start with anything and go anywhere. It may start with a bird without the bird being a totem; it may start with the sun without being a solar myth. It is said there are only ten plots in the world; and there will certainly be common and recurrent elements. Set ten thousand children talking at once, and telling tarradiddles about what they did in the wood, and it will not be hard to find parallels suggesting sun-worship or animal-worship. Some of the stories may be pretty and some silly and some perhaps dirty; but they can only be judged as stories. In the modern dialect, they can only be judged aesthetically. It is strange that aesthetics, or mere feeling, which is now allowed to usurp where it has no rights at all, to wreck reason with pragmatism and morals with anarchy, is apparently not allowed to give a purely aesthetic judgment on what is obviously a purely aesthetic question. We may be fanciful about everything except fairy-tales.

Now the first fact is that the most simple people have the most subtle ideas. Everybody ought to know that, for everybody has been a child. Ignorant as a child is, he knows more than he can say and feels not only atmospheres but fine shades. And in this matter there are several fine shades. Nobody understands it who has not had what can only be called the ache of the artist to find some sense and some story in the beautiful things he sees; his hunger for secrets and his anger at any tower or tree escaping with its tale untold. He feels that nothing is perfect unless it is personal. Without that the blind unconscious beauty of the world stands in its garden like a headless statue. One need only be a very minor poet to have wrestled with the tower or the tree until it spoke like a titan or a dryad. It is often said that pagan mythology was a personification of the powers of nature. The phrase is true in a sense, but it is very unsatisfactory; because it implies that the forces are abstractions and the personification is artificial. Myths are not allegories. Natural powers are not in this case abstractions. It is not as if there were a God of Gravitation. There may be a genius of the waterfall; but not of mere falling, even less than of mere water. The impersonation is not of something impersonal. The point is that the personality perfects the water with significance. Father Christmas is not an allegory of snow and holly; he is not merely the stuff called snow afterwards artificially given a human form, like a snow man. He is something that gives a new meaning to the white world and the evergreens; so that snow itself seems to be warm rather than cold. The test therefore is purely imaginative. But imaginative does not mean imaginary. It does not follow that it is all what the moderns call subjective, when they mean false. Every true artist does feel, consciously or unconsciously, that he is touching transcendental truths; that his images are shadows of things seen through the veil. In other words, the natural mystic does know that there is something *there*; something behind the clouds or within the trees; but he believes that the pursuit of beauty is the way to find it; that imagination is a sort of incantation that can call it up.

Now we do not comprehend this process in ourselves, far less in our most remote fellow-creatures. And the danger of these things being classified is that they may seem to be comprehended. A really fine work of folklore, like *The Golden Bough*, will leave too many readers with the idea, for instance, that this or that story of a giant's or wizard's heart in a casket or a cave only 'means' some stupid and static superstition called 'the external soul.' But we do not know what these things mean, simply because we do not know what we ourselves mean when we are moved by them. Suppose somebody in a story says 'Pluck this flower and a princess will die in a castle beyond the sea,' we do not know why something stirs in the subconsciousness, or why what is impossible seems almost inevitable. Suppose we read 'And in the hour when the king extinguished the candle his ships were wrecked far away on the coast of Hebrides.' We do not know why the imagination has accepted that image before the reason can reject it; or why such correspondences seem really to correspond to something in the soul. Very deep things in our nature, some dim sense of the dependence of great things upon small, some dark suggestion that the things nearest to us stretch far beyond our power, some sacramental feeling of the magic in material substances, and many more emotions past finding out, are in an idea like that of the external soul. The power even in the myths of savages is like the power in the metaphors of poets. The soul of such a metaphor is often very emphatically an external soul. The best critics have remarked that in the best poets the simile is often a picture that seems quite separate from the text. It is as irrelevant as the remote castle to the flower or the Hebridean coast to the candle. Shelley compares the skylark to a young woman on a turret, to a rose embedded in thick foliage, to a series of things that seem to be about as unlike a skylark in the sky as anything we can imagine. I suppose the most potent piece of pure magic in English literature is the much-quoted passage in Keats's *Nightingale* about the casements opening on the perilous foam. And nobody notices that the image seems to come from nowhere; that it appears abruptly after some almost equally irrelevant remarks about Ruth; and that it has nothing in the world to do with the subject of the poem. If there is one place in the world where nobody could reasonably expect to find a nightingale, it is on a window-sill at the seaside. But it is only in the same sense that nobody would expect to find a giant's heart in a casket under the sea. Now, it would be very dangerous to classify the metaphors of the poets. When Shelley says that the cloud will rise 'like a child from the womb, like a ghost from the tomb,' it would be quite possible to call the first a case of the coarse primitive birth-myth and the second a survival of the ghost-worship which became ancestor-worship. But it is the wrong way of dealing with a cloud; and is liable to leave the learned in the condition of Polonius, only too ready to think it like a weasel, or very like a whale.

Two facts follow from this psychology of day-dreams, which must be kept in mind throughout their development in mythologies and even religions. First, these imaginative impressions are often strictly local. So far from being abstractions turned into allegories, they are often images almost concentrated into idols. The poet feels the mystery of a particular forest; not of the science of afforestation or the department of woods and forests. He worships the peak of a particular mountain, not the abstract idea of altitude. So we find the god is not merely water but often one special river; he may be the sea because the sea is single like a stream; the river that runs round the world. Ultimately doubtless many deities are enlarged into elements; but they are something more than omnipresent. Apollo does not merely dwell wherever the sun shines; his home is on the rock of Delphi. Diana is great enough to be in three places at once, earth and heaven and hell, but greater is Diana of the Ephesians. This localised feeling has its lowest form in the mere fetish or talisman, such as millionaires put on their motor-cars. But it can also harden into something like a high and serious religion, where it is connected with high and serious duties; into the gods of the city or even the gods of the hearth.

The second consequence is this; that in these pagan cults there is every shade of sincerity — and insincerity. In what sense exactly did an Athenian really think he had to sacrifice to Pallas Athene? What scholar is really certain of the answer? In what sense did Dr. Johnson really think that he had to touch all the posts in the street or that he had to collect orange-peel? In what sense does a child really think that he ought to step on every alternate paving-stone? Two things are at least fairly clear. First, in simpler and less self-conscious times these forms could become more solid without really becoming more serious. Day-dreams could be acted in broad daylight, with more liberty of artistic expression; but still perhaps with something of the light step of the somnambulist. Wrap Dr. Johnson in an antique mantle, crown him (by his kind permission) with a garland, and he will move in state under those ancient skies of morning; touching a series of sacred posts carved with the heads of the strange terminal gods, that stand at the limits of the land and of the life of man. Make the child free of the marbles and mosaics of some classic temple, to play on a whole floor inlaid with squares of black and white; and he will willingly make this fulfilment of his idle and drifting daydream the clear field for a grave and graceful dance. But the posts and the paving-stones are little more and little less real than they are under modern limits. They are not really much more serious for being taken seriously. They have the sort of sincerity that they always had; the sincerity of art as a symbol that expresses very real spiritualities under the surface of life. But they are only sincere in the same sense as art; not sincere in the same sense as morality. The eccentric's collection of orange-peel may turn to oranges in a Mediterranean festival or to golden apples in a Mediterranean myth. But they are never on the same plane with the difference between giving the orange to a blind beggar and carefully placing the orange-peel so that the beggar may fall and break his leg. Between these two things there is a difference of kind and not of degree. The child does not think it wrong to step on the paving-stone as he thinks it wrong to step on the dog's tail. And it is very certain that whatever jest or sentiment or fancy first set Johnson touching the wooden posts, he never touched wood with any of the feeling with which he stretched out his hands to the timber of that terrible tree, which was the death of God and the life of man.

As already noted, this does not mean that there was no reality or even no religious sentiment in such a mood. As a matter of fact the Catholic Church has taken over with uproarious success the whole of this popular business of giving people local legends and lighter ceremonial movements. In so far as all this sort of paganism was innocent and in touch with nature, there is no reason why it should not be patronised by patron saints as much as by pagan gods. And in any case there are degrees of seriousness in the most natural make-believe. There is all the difference between fancying there are fairies in the wood, which often only means fancying a certain wood as fit for fairies, and really frightening ourselves until we walk a mile rather than pass a house we have told ourselves is haunted. Behind all these things is the fact that beauty and terror are very real things and related to a real spiritual world; and to touch them at all, even in doubt or fancy, is to stir the deep things of the soul. We all understand that and the pagans understood it. The point is that paganism did not really stir the soul except with these doubts and fancies; with the consequence that we to-day can have little beyond doubts and fancies about paganism. All the best critics agree that all the greatest poets, in pagan Hellas for example, had an attitude towards their gods which is quite queer and puzzling to men in the Christian era. There seems to be an admitted conflict between the god and the man; but everybody seems to be doubtful about which is the hero and which is the villain. This doubt does not merely apply to a doubter like Euripides in the Bacchae; it applies to a moderate conservative like Sophocles in the Antigone; or even to a regular Tory and reactionary like Aristophanes in the Frogs. Sometimes it would seem that the Greeks believed above all things in reverence, only they had nobody to revere. But the point of the puzzle is this: that all this vagueness and variation arise from the fact that the whole thing began in fancy and in dreaming; and that there are no rules of architecture for a castle in the clouds.

This is the mighty and branching tree called mythology which ramifies round the whole world, whose remote branches under separate skies bear like coloured birds the costly idols of Asia and the half-baked fetishes of Africa and the fairy kings and princesses of the folk-tales of the forest, and buried amid vines and olives the Lares of the Latins, and carried on the clouds of Olympus the buoyant supremacy of the gods of Greece. These are the myths: and he who has no sympathy with myths has no sympathy with men. But he who has most sympathy with myths will most fully realise that they are not and never were a religion, in the sense that Christianity or even Islam is a religion. They satisfy some of the needs satisfied by a religion; and notably the need for doing certain things at certain dates; the need of the twin ideas of festivity and formality. But though they provide a man with a calendar they do not provide him with a creed. A man did not stand up and say 'I believe in Jupiter and Juno and Neptune,' etc., as he stands up and says 'I believe in God the Father Almighty' and the rest of the Apostles Creed. Many believed in some and not in others, or more in some and less in others, or only in a very vague poetical sense in any. There was no moment when they were all collected into an orthodox order which men would fight and be tortured to keep intact. Still less did anybody ever say in that fashion: 'I believe in Odin and Thor and Freya,' for outside Olympus even the Olympian order grows cloudy and chaotic. It seems clear to me that Thor was not a god at all but a hero. Nothing resembling a religion would picture anybody resembling a god as groping like a pigmy in a great cavern, that turned out to be the glove of a giant. That is the glorious ignorance called adventure. Thor may have been a great adventurer; but to call him a god is like trying to compare Jehovah with Jack and the Beanstalk. Odin seems to have been a real barbarian chief, possibly of the Dark Ages after Christianity. Polytheism fades away at its fringes into fairy-tales or barbaric memories; it is not a thing like monotheism

as held by serious monotheists. Again it does satisfy the need to cry
out on some uplifted name or some noble memory in moments that
are themselves noble and uplifted; such as the birth of a child or the
saving of a city. But the name was so used by many to whom it was
only a name. Finally it did satisfy, or rather it partially satisfied, a
thing very deep in humanity indeed; the idea of surrendering
something as the portion of the unknown powers; of pouring out
wine upon the ground, of throwing a ring into the sea; in a word, of
sacrifice. It is the wise and worthy idea of not taking our advantage
to the full; of putting something in the other balance to ballast our
dubious pride, of paying tithes to nature for our land. This deep
truth of the danger of insolence, or being too big for our boots, runs
through all the great Greek tragedies and makes them great. But it
runs side by side with an almost cryptic agnosticism about the real
nature of the gods to be propitiated. Where that gesture of surrender is most magnificent, as among the great Greeks, there is really
much more idea that the man will be the better for losing the ox
than that the god will be the better for getting it. It is said that in its
grosser forms there are often actions grotesquely suggestive of the
god really eating the sacrifice. But this fact is falsified by the error
that I put first in this note on mythology. It is misunderstanding the
psychology of day-dreams. A child pretending there is a goblin in a
hollow tree will do a crude and material thing, like leaving a piece of
cake for him. A poet might do a more dignified and elegant thing,
like bringing to the god fruits as well as flowers. But the degree of
seriousness in both acts may be the same or it may vary in almost any
degree. The crude fancy is no more a creed than the ideal fancy is a
creed. Certainly the pagan does not disbelieve like an atheist, any
more than he believes like a Christian. He feels the presence of
powers about which he guesses and invents. St. Paul said that the
Greeks had one altar to an unknown god. But in truth all their gods
were unknown gods. And the real break in history did come when
St. Paul declared to them whom they had ignorantly worshipped.

The substance of all such paganism may be summarised thus. It is
an attempt to reach the divine reality through the imagination
alone; in its own field reason does not restrain it at all. It is vital to

the view of all history that reason is something separate from religion even in the most rational of these civilisations. It is only as an afterthought, when such cults are decadent or on the defensive, that a few Neo-Platonists or a few Brahmins are found trying to rationalise them, and even then only by trying to allegorise them. But in reality the rivers of mythology and philosophy run parallel and do not mingle till they meet in the sea of Christendom. Simple secularists still talk as if the Church had introduced a sort of schism between reason and religion. The truth is that the Church was actually the first thing that ever tried to combine reason and religion. There had never before been any such union of the priests and the philosophers. Mythology, then, sought god through the imagination; or sought truth by means of beauty, in the sense in which beauty includes much of the most grotesque ugliness. But the imagination has its own laws and therefore its own triumphs, which neither logicians nor men of science can understand. It remained true to that imaginative instinct through a thousand extravagances, through every crude cosmic pantomime of a pig eating the moon or the world being cut out of a cow, through all the dizzy convolutions and mystic malformations of Asiatic art, through all the stark and staring rigidity of Egyptian and Assyrian portraiture, through every kind of cracked mirror of mad art that seemed to deform the world and displace the sky, it remained true to something about which there can be no argument; something that makes it possible for some artist of some school to stand suddenly still before that particular deformity and say, 'My dream has come true.' Therefore do we all in fact feel that pagan or primitive myths are infinitely suggestive, so long as we are wise enough not to inquire what they suggest. Therefore we all feel what is meant by Prometheus stealing fire from heaven, until some prig of a pessimist or progressive person explains what it means. Therefore we all know the meaning of Jack and the Beanstalk, until we are told. In this sense it is true that it is the ignorant who accept myths, but only because it is the ignorant who appreciate poems. Imagination has its own laws and triumphs; and a tremendous power began to clothe its images, whether images in the mind or in the mud, whether in the bamboo of the South Sea

Islands or the marble of the mountains of Hellas. But there was always a trouble in the triumph, which in these pages I have tried to analyse in vain; but perhaps I might in conclusion state it thus.

The crux and crisis is that man found it natural to worship; even natural to worship unnatural things. The posture of the idol might be stiff and strange; but the gesture of the worshipper was generous and beautiful. He not only felt freer when he bent; he actually felt taller when he bowed. Henceforth anything that took away the gesture of worship would stunt and even maim him for ever. Henceforth being merely secular would be a servitude and an inhibition. If man cannot pray he is gagged; if he cannot kneel he is in irons. We therefore feel throughout the whole of paganism a curious double feeling of trust and distrust. When the man makes the gesture of salutation and of sacrifice, when he pours out the libation or lifts up the sword, he knows he is doing a worthy and a virile thing. He knows he is doing one of the things for which a man was made. His imaginative experiment is therefore justified. But precisely because it began with imagination, there is to the end something of mockery in it, and especially in the object of it. This mockery, in the more intense moments of the intellect, becomes the almost intolerable irony of Greek tragedy. There seems a disproportion between the priest and the altar or between the altar and the god. The priest seems more solemn and almost more sacred than the god. All the order of the temple is solid and sane and satisfactory to certain parts of our nature; except the very centre of it, which seems strangely mutable and dubious, like a dancing flame. It is the first thought round which the whole has been built; and the first thought is still a fancy and almost a frivolity. In that strange place of meeting, the man seems more statuesque than the statue. He himself can stand for ever in the noble and natural attitude of the statue of the Praying Boy. But whatever name be written on the pedestal, whether Zeus or Ammon or Apollo, the god whom he worships is Proteus.

The Praying Boy may be said to express a need rather than to satisfy a need. It is by a normal and necessary action that his hands are lifted; but it is no less a parable that his hands are empty. About the nature of that need there will be more to say; but at this point it

may be said that perhaps after all this true instinct, that prayer and
sacrifice are a liberty and an enlargement, refers back to that vast and
half-forgotten conception of universal fatherhood, which we have
already seen everywhere fading from the morning sky. This is true;
and yet it is not all the truth. There remains an indestructible instinct, in the poet as represented by the pagan, that he is not entirely
wrong in localising his God. It is something in the soul of poetry if
not of piety. And the greatest of poets, when he defined the poet,
did not say that he gave us the universe or the absolute or the infinite; but, in his own larger language, a local habitation and a name.
No poet is merely a pantheist; those who are counted most pantheistic, like Shelley, start with some local and particular image as the
pagans did. After all, Shelley wrote of the skylark because it was a
skylark. You could not issue an imperial or international translation
of it for use in South Africa, in which it was changed to an ostrich.
So the mythological imagination moves as it were in circles, hovering either to find a place or to return to it. In a word, mythology
is a *search*; it is something that combines a recurrent desire with a
recurrent doubt, mixing a most hungry sincerity in the idea of seeking for a place with a most dark and deep and mysterious levity
about all the places found. So far could the lonely imagination lead,
and we must turn later to the lonely reason. Nowhere along this
road did the two ever travel together.

   That is where all these things differed from religion or the reality
in which these different dimensions met in a sort of solid. They differed from the reality not in what they looked like but in what they
were. A picture may look like a landscape; it may look in every
detail exactly like a landscape. The only detail in which it differs is
that it is not a landscape. The difference is only that which divides a
portrait of Queen Elizabeth from Queen Elizabeth. Only in this
mythical and mystical world the portrait could exist before the person; and the portrait was therefore more vague and doubtful. But
anybody who has felt and fed on the atmosphere of these myths will
know what I mean, when I say that in one sense they did not really
profess to be realities. The pagans had dreams about realities; and
they would have been the first to admit, in their own words, that

some came through the gate of ivory and others through the gate of horn. The dreams do indeed tend to be very vivid dreams when they touch on those tender or tragic things, which can really make a sleeper awaken with the sense that his heart has been broken in his sleep. They tend continually to hover over certain passionate themes of meeting and parting, of a life that ends in death or a death that is the beginning of life. Demeter wanders over a stricken world looking for a stolen child; Isis stretches out her arms over the earth in vain to gather the limbs of Osiris; and there is lamentation upon the hills for Atys and through the woods for Adonis. There mingles with all such mourning the mystical and profound sense that death can be a deliverer and an appeasement; that such death gives us a divine blood for a renovating river and that all good is found in gathering the broken body of the god. We may truly call these foreshadowings; so long as we remember that foreshadowings are shadows. And the metaphor of a shadow happens to hit very exactly the truth that is very vital here. For a shadow is a shape; a thing which reproduces shape but not texture. These things were something *like* the real thing; and to say that they were like is to say that they were different. Saying something is like a dog is another way of saying it is not a dog; and it is in this sense of identity that a myth is not a man. Nobody really thought of Isis as a human being; nobody really thought of Demeter as a historical character; nobody thought of Adonis as the founder of a Church. There was no idea that any one of them had changed the world; but rather that their recurrent death and life bore the sad and beautiful burden of the changelessness of the world. Not one of them was a revolution, save in the sense of the revolution of the sun and moon. Their whole meaning is missed if we do not see that they mean the shadows that we are and the shadows that we pursue. In certain sacrificial and communal aspects they naturally suggest what sort of a god might satisfy men; but they do not profess to be satisfied. Anyone who says they do is a bad judge of poetry.

Those who talk about Pagan Christs have less sympathy with Paganism than with Christianity. Those who call these cults 'religions,' and 'compare' them with the certitude and challenge of the Church have much less appreciation than we have of what made heathenism human, or of why classic literature is still something that hangs in the air like a song. It is no very human tenderness for the hungry to prove that hunger is the same as food. It is no very genial understanding of youth to argue that hope destroys the need for happiness. And it is utterly unreal to argue that these images in the mind, admired entirely in the abstract, were even in the same world with a living man and a living polity that were worshipped because they were concrete. We might as well say that a boy playing at robbers is the same as a man in his first day in the trenches; or that boy's first fancies about 'the not impossible she' are the same as the sacrament of marriage. They are fundamentally different exactly where they are superficially similar; we might almost say they are not the same even when they are the same. They are only different because one is real and the other is not. I do not mean merely that I myself believe that one is true and the other is not. I mean that one was never meant to be true in the same sense as the other. The sense in which it was meant to be true I have tried to suggest vaguely here, but it is undoubtedly very subtle and almost indescribable. It is so subtle that the students who profess to put it up as a rival to our religion miss the whole meaning and purport of their own study. We know better than the scholars, even those of us who are no scholars, what was in that hollow cry that went forth over the dead Adonis and why the Great Mother had a daughter wedded to death. We have entered more deeply than they into the Eleusinian Mysteries and have passed a higher grade, where gate within gate guarded the wisdom of Orpheus. We know the meaning of all the myths. We know the last secret revealed to the perfect initiate. And it is not the voice of a priest or a prophet saying 'These things are.' It is the voice of a dreamer and an idealist crying, 'Why cannot these things be?'

VI

THE DEMONS AND THE PHILOSOPHERS

I have dwelt at some little length on this imaginative sort of paganism, which has crowded the world with temples and is everywhere the parent of popular festivity. For the central history of civilisation, as I see it, consists of two further stages before the final stage of Christendom. The first was the struggle between this paganism and something less worthy than itself, and the second the process by which it grew in itself less worthy. In this very varied and often very vague polytheism there was a weakness of original sin. Pagan gods were depicted as tossing men like dice; and indeed they are loaded dice. About sex especially men are born unbalanced; we might almost say men are born mad. They scarcely reach sanity till they reach sanctity. This disproportion dragged down the winged fancies; and filled the end of paganism with a mere filth and litter of spawning gods. But the first point to realise is that this sort of paganism had an early collision with another sort of paganism; and that the issue of that essentially spiritual struggle really determined the history of the world. In order to understand it we must pass to a review of the other kind of paganism. It can be considered much more briefly; indeed there is a very real sense in which the less that is said about it the better. If we have called the first sort of mythology the day-dream, we might very well call the second sort of mythology the nightmare.

Superstition recurs in all ages, and especially in rationalistic ages. I remember defending the religious tradition against a whole luncheon-table of distinguished agnostics; and before the end of our conversation every one of them had procured from his pocket, or exhibited on his watch-chain, some charm or talisman from which he admitted that he was never separated. I was the only person present who had neglected to provide himself with a fetish. Superstition recurs in a rationalist age because it rests on something which, if not identical with rationalism, is not unconnected with scepticism. It is at least very closely connected with agnosticism. It rests on something that is really a very human and intelligible sentiment, like the local invocations of the *numen* in popular paganism. But it is an agnostic sentiment, for it rests on two feelings: first that we do not really know the laws of the universe; and second that they may be very different to all we call reason. Such men realise the real truth that enormous things do often turn upon tiny things. When a whisper comes, from tradition or what not, that one particular tiny thing is the key or clue, something deep and not altogether senseless in human nature tells them that it is not unlikely. This feeling exists in both the forms of paganism here under consideration. But when we come to the second form of it, we find it transformed and filled with another and more terrible spirit.

In dealing with the lighter thing called mythology, I have said little about the most disputable aspect of it; the extent to which such invocation of the spirits of the sea or the elements can indeed call spirits from the vasty deep; or rather, (as the Shakesperean scoffer put it) whether the spirits come when they are called. I believe that I am right in thinking that this problem, practical as it sounds, did not play a dominant part in the poetical business of mythology. But I think it even more obvious, on the evidence, that things of that sort have sometimes appeared, even if they were only appearances. But when we come to the world of superstition, in a more subtle sense, there is a shade of difference; a deepening and a darkening shade. Doubtless most popular superstition is as frivolous as any popular mythology. Men do not believe as a dogma that God would throw a thunderbolt at them for walking under a ladder; more often they amuse themselves with the not very laborious exercise of walking round it. There is no more in it than what I have already adumbrated; a sort of airy agnosticism about the possibilities of so strange a world. But there is another sort of superstition that does definitely look for results; what might be called a realistic superstition. And with that the question of whether spirits do answer or do appear becomes much more serious. As I have said, it seems to me pretty certain that they sometimes do; but about that there is a distinction that has been the beginning of much evil in the world.

Whether it be because the Fall has really brought men nearer to less desirable neighbours in the spiritual world, or whether it is merely that the mood of men eager or greedy finds it easier to imagine evil, I believe that the black magic of witchcraft has been much more practical and much less poetical than the white magic of mythology. I fancy the garden of the witch has been kept much more carefully than the woodland of the nymph. I fancy the evil field has even been more fruitful than the good. To start with, some impulse, perhaps a sort of desperate impulse, drove men to the darker powers when dealing with practical problems. There was a sort of secret and perverse feeling that the darker powers would really do things; that they had no nonsense about them. And indeed that popular phrase exactly expresses the point. The gods of mere mythology had a great deal of nonsense about them. They had a great deal of good nonsense about them; in the happy and hilarious sense in which we talk of the nonsense of Jabberwocky or the Land where Jumblies live. But the man consulting a demon felt as many a man has felt in consulting a detective, especially a private detective; that it was dirty work but the work would really be done. A man did not exactly go into the wood to meet a nymph; he rather went with the hope of meeting a nymph. It was an adventure rather than an assignation. But the devil really kept his appointments and even in one sense kept his promises; even if a man sometimes wished afterwards, like Macbeth, that he had broken them.

In the accounts given us of many rude or savage races we gather that the cult of demons often came after the cult of deities, and even after the cult of one single and supreme deity. It may be suspected that in almost all such places the higher deity is felt to be too far off for appeal in certain petty matters, and men invoke the spirits because they are in a more literal sense familiar spirits. But with the idea of employing the demons who get things done, a new idea appears more worthy of the demons. It may indeed be truly described as the idea of being worthy of the demons; of making oneself fit for their fastidious and exacting society. Superstition of the lighter sort toys with the idea that some trifle, some small gesture such as throwing the salt, may touch the hidden spring that works the mysterious machinery of the world. And there is after all something in the idea of such an Open Sesame. But with the appeal to lower spirits comes the horrible notion that the gesture must not only be very small but very low; that it must be a monkey trick of an utterly ugly and unworthy sort. Sooner or later a man deliberately sets himself to do the most disgusting thing he can think of. It is felt that the extreme of evil will extort a sort of attention or answer from the evil powers under the surface of the world. This is the meaning of most of the cannibalism in the world. For most cannibalism is not a primitive or even a bestial habit. It is artificial and even artistic; a sort of art for art's sake. Men do not do it because they do not think it horrible; but, on the contrary, because they do think it horrible. They wish, in the most literal sense, to sup on horrors. That is why it is often found that rude races like the Australian natives are not cannibals; while much more refined and intelligent races, like the New Zealand Maories, occasionally are. They are refined and intelligent enough to indulge sometimes in a self-conscious diabolism. But if we could understand their minds, or even really understand their language, we should probably find that they were not acting as ignorant, that is as innocent cannibals. They are not doing it because they do not think it wrong, but precisely because they do think it wrong. They are acting like a Parisian decadent at a Black Mass. But the Black Mass has to hide underground from the presence of the real Mass. In other words, the demons have really been in hiding since the coming of Christ on earth. The cannibalism of the higher barbarians is in hiding from the civilisation of the white man. But before Christendom, and especially outside Europe, this was not always so. In the ancient world the demons often wandered abroad like dragons. They could be positively and publicly enthroned as gods. Their enormous images could be set up in public temples in the centre of populous cities. And all over the world the traces can be found of this striking and solid fact, so curiously overlooked by the moderns who speak of all such evil as primitive and early in evolution, that as a matter of fact some of the very highest civilisations of the world were the very places where the horns of Satan were exalted, not only to the stars but in the face of the sun.

Take for example the Aztecs and American Indians of the ancient empires of Mexico and Peru. They were at least as elaborate as Egypt or China and only less lively than that central civilisation which is our own. But those who criticise that central civilisation (which is always their own civilisation) have a curious habit of not merely doing their legitimate duty in condemning its crimes, but of going out of their way to idealise its victims. They always assume that before the advent of Europe there was nothing anywhere but Eden. And Swinburne, in that spirited chorus of the nations in 'Songs Before Sunrise,' used an expression about Spain in her South American conquests which always struck me as very strange. He said something about 'her sins and sons through sinless lands dispersed,' and how they 'made accursed the name of man and thrice accursed the name of God.' It may be reasonable enough that he should say the Spaniards were sinful, but why in the world should he say that the South Americans were sinless? Why should he have supposed that continent to be exclusively populated by archangels or saints perfect in heaven? It would be a strong thing to say of the most respectable neighbourhood; but when we come to think of what we really do know of that society the remark is rather funny. We know that the sinless priests of this sinless people worshipped sinless gods, who accepted as the nectar and ambrosia of their sunny paradise nothing but incessant human sacrifice accompanied by horrible torments. We may note also in the mythology of this American civilisation that element of reversal or violence against instinct of which Dante wrote; which runs backwards everywhere through the unnatural religion of the demons. It is notable not only in ethics but in aesthetics. A South American idol was made as ugly as possible, as a Greek image was made as beautiful as possible. They were seeking the secret of power, by working backwards against their own nature and the nature of things. There was always a sort of yearning to carve at last, in gold or granite or the dark red timber of the forests, a face at which the sky itself would break like a cracked mirror.

In any case it is clear enough that the painted and gilded civilisation of tropical America systematically indulged in human sacrifice. It is by no means clear, so far as I know, that the Eskimos ever indulged in human sacrifice. They were not civilised enough. They were too closely imprisoned by the white winter and the endless dark. Chill penury repressed their noble rage and froze the genial current of the soul. It was in brighter days and broader daylight that the noble rage is found unmistakably raging. It was in richer and more instructed lands that the genial current flowed on the altars, to be drunk by great gods wearing goggling and grinning masks and called on in terror or torment by long cacophonous names that sound like laughter in hell. A warmer climate and a more scientific cultivation were needed to bring forth these blooms; to draw up towards the sun the large leaves and flamboyant blossoms that gave their gold and crimson and purple to that garden, which Swinburne compares to the Hesperides. There was at least no doubt about the dragon.

I do not raise in this connection the special controversy about Spain and Mexico; but I may remark in passing that it resembles exactly the question that must in some sense be raised afterwards about Rome and Carthage. In both cases there has been a queer habit among the English of always siding against the Europeans, and representing the rival civilisation, in Swinburne's phrase, as sinless; when its sins were obviously crying or rather screaming to heaven. For Carthage also was a high civilisation, indeed a much more highly civilised civilisation. And Carthage also founded that civilisation on a religion of fear, sending up everywhere the smoke of human sacrifice. Now it is very right to rebuke our own race or religion for falling short of our own standards and ideals. But it is absurd to pretend that they fell lower than the other races and religions that professed the very opposite standards and ideals. There is a very real sense in which the Christian is worse than the heathen, the Spaniard worse than the Red Indian, or even the Roman potentially worse than the Carthaginian. But there is only one sense in which he is worse; and that is not in being positively worse. The Christian is only worse because it is his business to be better.

This inverted imagination produces things of which it is better not to speak. Some of them indeed might almost be named without being known; for they are of that extreme evil which seems innocent to the innocent. They are too inhuman even to be indecent. But without dwelling much longer in these dark corners, it may be noted as not irrelevant here that certain anti-human antagonisms seem to recur in this tradition of black magic. There may be suspected as running through it everywhere, for instance, a mystical hatred of the idea of childhood. People would understand better the popular fury against the witches, if they remembered that the malice most commonly attributed to them was preventing the birth of children. The Hebrew prophets were perpetually protesting against the Hebrew race relapsing into an idolatry that involved such a war upon children; and it is probable enough that this abominable apostasy from the God of Israel has occasionally appeared in Israel since, in the form of what is called ritual murder; not of course by any representative of the religion of Judaism, but by individual and irresponsible diabolists who did happen to be Jews. This sense that the forces of evil especially threaten childhood is found again in the enormous popularity of the Child Martyr of the Middle Ages. Chaucer did but give another version of a very national English legend, when he conceived the wickedest of all possible witches as the dark alien woman watching behind her high lattice and hearing, like the babble of a brook down the stony street, the singing of little St. Hugh.

Anyhow the part of such speculations that concerns this story centered especially round that eastern end of the Mediterranean, where the nomads had turned gradually into traders and had begun to trade with the whole world. Indeed in the sense of trade and travel and colonial extension, it already had something like an empire of the whole world. Its purple dye, the emblem of its rich pomp and luxury, had steeped the wares which were sold far away amid the last crags of Cornwall and the sails that entered the silence of tropic seas amid all the mystery of Africa. It might be said truly to have painted the map purple. It was already a world-wide success, when the princes of Tyre would hardly have troubled to notice that one of their princesses had condescended to marry the chief of some tribe called Judah; when the merchants of its African outpost would only have curled their bearded and Semitic lips with a slight smile at the mention of a village called Rome. And indeed no two things could have seemed more distant from each other, not only in space but in spirit, than the monotheism of the Palestinian tribe and the very virtues of the small Italian republic. There was but one thing between them; and the thing which divided them has united them. Very various and incompatible were the things that could be loved by the consuls of Rome and the prophets of Israel; but they were at one in what they hated. It is very easy in both cases to represent that hatred as something merely hateful. It is easy enough to make a merely harsh and inhuman figure either of Elijah raving above the slaughter of Carmel or Cato thundering against the amnesty of Africa. These men had their limitations and their local passions; but this criticism of them is unimaginative and therefore unreal. It leaves out something, something immense and intermediate, facing east and west and calling up this passion in its eastern and western enemies; and that something is the first subject of this chapter.

The civilisation that centered in Tyre and Sidon was above all things practical. It has left little in the way of art and nothing in the way of poetry. But it prided itself upon being very efficient; and it followed in its philosophy and religion that strange and sometimes secret train of thought which we have already noted in those who look for immediate effects. There is always in such a mentality an idea that there is a short cut to the secret of all success; something that would shock the world by this sort of shameless thoroughness. They believed, in the appropriate modern phrase, in people who delivered the goods. In their dealings with their god Moloch, they themselves were always careful to deliver the goods. It was an interesting transaction, upon which we shall have to touch more than once in the rest of the narrative; it is enough to say here that it involved the theory I have suggested, about a certain attitude towards children. This was what called up against it in simultaneous fury the servant of one God in Palestine and the guardians of all the household gods in Rome. This is what challenged two things naturally so much divided by every sort of distance and disunion, whose union was to save the world.

I have called the fourth and final division of the spiritual elements into which I should divide heathen humanity by the name of The

Philosophers. I confess that it covers in my mind much that would generally be classified otherwise; and that what are here called philosophies are very often called religions. I believe however that my own description will be found to be much the more realistic and not the less respectful. But we must first take philosophy in its purest and clearest form that we may trace its normal outline; and that is to be found in the world of the purest and clearest outlines, that culture of the Mediterranean of which we have been considering the mythologies and idolatries in the last two chapters.

Polytheism, or that aspect of paganism, was never to the pagan what Catholicism is to the Catholic. It was never a view of the universe satisfying all sides of life; a complete and complex truth with something to say about everything. It was only a satisfaction of one side of the soul of man, even if we call it the religious side; and I think it is truer to call it the imaginative side. But this it did satisfy; in the end it satisfied it to satiety. All that world was a tissue of interwoven tales and cults, and there ran in and out of it, as we have already seen, that black thread among its more blameless colours; the darker paganism that was really diabolism. But we all know that this did not mean that all pagan men thought of nothing but pagan gods. Precisely because mythology only satisfied one mood, they turned in other moods to something totally different. But it is very important to realise that it was totally different. It was too different to be inconsistent. It was so alien that it did not clash. While a mob of people were pouring on a public holiday to the feast of Adonis or the games in honour of Apollo, this or that man would prefer to stop at home and think out a little theory about the nature of things. Sometimes his hobby would even take the form of thinking about the nature of God; or even in that sense about the nature of the gods. But he very seldom thought of pitting his nature of the gods against the gods of nature.

It is necessary to insist on this abstraction in the first student of abstractions. He was not so much antagonistic as absent-minded. His hobby might be the universe; but at first the hobby was as private as if it had been numismatics or playing draughts. And even when his wisdom came to be a public possession, and almost a political institution, it was very seldom on the same plane as the popular and religious institutions. Aristotle, with his colossal commonsense, was perhaps the greatest of all philosophers; certainly the most practical of all philosophers. But Aristotle would no more have set up the Absolute side by side with the Apollo of Delphi, as a similar or rival religion, than Archimedes would have thought of setting up the Lever as a sort of idol or fetish to be substituted for the Palladium of the city. Or we might as well imagine Euclid building an altar to an isosceles triangle, or offering sacrifices to the square of the hypotenuse. The one man meditated on metaphysics as the other man did on mathematics; for the love of truth or for curiosity or for the fun of the thing. But that sort of fun never seems to have interfered very much with the other sort of fun; the fun of dancing or singing to celebrate some rascally romance about Zeus becoming a bull or a swan. It is perhaps the proof of a certain superficiality and even insincerity about the popular polytheism, that men could be philosophers and even sceptics without disturbing it. These thinkers could move the foundations of the world without altering even the outline of that coloured cloud that hung above it in the air.

For the thinkers did move the foundations of the world; even when a curious compromise seemed to prevent them from moving the foundations of the city. The two great philosophers of antiquity do indeed appear to us as defenders of sane and even of sacred ideas; their maxims often read like the answers to sceptical questions too completely answered to be aways recorded. Aristotle annihilated a hundred anarchists and nature-worshipping cranks by the fundamental statement that man is a political animal. Plato in some sense anticipated the Catholic realism, as attacked by the heretical nominalism, by insisting on the equally fundamental fact that ideas are realities; that ideas exist just as men exist. Plato however seemed sometimes almost to fancy that ideas exist as men do not exist; or that the men need hardly be considered where they conflict with the ideas. He had something of the social sentiment that we call Fabian in his ideal of fitting the citizen to the city, like an imaginary head to an ideal hat; and great and glorious as he remains, he has been the father of all faddists. Aristotle anticipated more fully the sacramental sanity that was to combine the body and the soul of things; for he considered the nature of men as well as the nature of morals, and looked to the eyes as well as to the light. But though these great men were in that sense constructive and conservative, they belonged to a world where thought was free to the point of being fanciful. Many other great intellects did indeed follow them, some exalting an abstract vision of virtue, others following more rationalistically the necessity of the human pursuit of happiness. The former had the name of Stoics; and their name has passed into a proverb for what is indeed one of the main moral ideals of mankind: that of strengthening the mind itself until it is of a texture to resist calamity or even pain. But it is admitted that a great number of the philosophers degenerated into what we still call sophists. They became a sort of professional sceptics who went about asking uncomfortable questions, and were handsomely paid for making themselves a nuisance to normal people. It was perhaps an accidental resemblance to such questioning quacks that was responsible for the unpopularity of the great Socrates; whose death might seem to contradict the suggestion of the permanent truce between the philosophers and the gods. But Socrates did not die as a monotheist who denounced polytheism; certainly not as a prophet who denounced idols. It is clear to anyone reading between the lines that there was some notion, right or wrong, of a purely personal influence affecting morals and perhaps politics. The general compromise remained; whether it was that the Greeks thought their myths a joke or that they thought their theories a joke. There was never any collision in which one really destroyed the other, and there was never any combination in which one was really reconciled with the other. They certainly did not work together; if anything the philosopher was a rival of the priest. But both seemed to have accepted a sort of separation of functions and remained parts of the same social system. Another important tradition descends from Pythagoras; who is significant because he stands nearest to the Oriental mystics who must be considered in their turn. He taught a sort of mysticism of mathematics, that number is the ultimate reality; but he also seems to have taught the transmigration of souls like the Brahmins; and to have left to his followers certain traditional tricks of vegetarianism and water-drinking very common among the eastern sages, especially those who figure in fashionable drawing-rooms, like those of the later Roman Empire. But in passing to eastern sages, and the somewhat different atmosphere of the east, we may approach a rather important truth by another path.

One of the great philosophers said that it would be well if philosophers were kings, or kings were philosophers. He spoke as of something too good to be true; but, as a matter of fact, it not unfrequently was true. A certain type, perhaps too little noticed in history, may really be called the royal philosopher. To begin with, apart from actual royalty, it did occasionally become possible for the sage, though he was not what we call a religious founder, to be something like a political founder. And the great example of this, one of the very greatest in the world, will with the very thought of it carry us thousands of miles across the vast spaces of Asia to that very wonderful and in some ways that very wise world of ideas and institutions, which we dismiss somewhat cheaply when we talk of China. Men have served many very strange gods; and trusted themselves loyally to many ideals and even idols. China is a society that has really chosen to believe in intellect. It has taken intellect seriously; and it may be that it stands alone in the world. From a very early age it faced the dilemma of the king and the philosopher by actually appointing a philosopher to advise the king. It made a public institution out of a private individual, who had nothing in the world to do but to be intellectual. It had and has, of course, many other things on the same pattern. It creates all ranks and privileges by public examination; it has nothing that we call an aristocracy; it is a democracy dominated by an intelligensia. But the point here is that it had philosophers to advise kings; and one of those philosophers must have been a great philosopher and a great statesman.

Confucius was not a religious founder or even a religious teacher; possibly not even a religious man. He was not an atheist; he was apparently what we call an agnostic. But the really vital point is that it is utterly irrelevant to talk about his religion at all. It is like talking of theology as the first thing in the story of how Rowland Hill established the postal system or Baden Powell organised the Boy Scouts. Confucius was not there to bring a message from heaven to humanity, but to organise China; and he must have organised it exceedingly well. It follows that he dealt much with morals; but he bound them up strictly with manners. The peculiarity of his scheme, and of his country, in which it contrasts with its great pendant the system of Christendom, is that he insisted on perpetuating an external life with all its forms, that outward continuity might preserve internal peace. Anyone who knows how much habit has to do with health, of mind as well as body, will see the truth in his idea. But he will also see that the ancestor-worship and the reverence for the Sacred Emperor were habits and not creeds. It is unfair to the great Confucius to say he was a religious founder. It is even unfair to him to say he was not a religious founder. It is as unfair as going out of one's way to say that Jeremy Bentham was not a Christian martyr.

But there is a class of most interesting cases in which philosophers were kings, and not merely the friends of kings. The combination is not accidental. It has a great deal to do with this rather elusive question of the function of the philosopher. It contains in it some hint of why philosophy and mythology seldom came to an open rupture. It was not only because there was something a little frivolous about the mythology. It was also because there was something a little supercilious about the philosopher. He despised the myths, but he also despised the mob; and thought they suited each other. The pagan philosopher was seldom a man of the people, at any rate in spirit; he was seldom a democrat and often a bitter critic of democracy. He had about him an air of aristocratic and humane leisure; and his part was most easily played by men who happened to be in such a position. It was very easy and natural for a prince or a prominent person to play at being as philosophical as Hamlet or Theseus in the *Midsummer Night's Dream*. And from very early ages we find ourselves in the presence of these princely intellectuals. In fact, we find one of them in the very first recorded ages of the world; sitting on the primeval throne that looked over ancient Egypt.

The most intense interest of the incident of Akenahten, commonly called the Heretic Pharaoh, lies in the fact that he was the one example, at any rate before Christian times, of one of these royal philosophers who set himself to fight popular mythology in the name of private philosophy. Most of them assumed the attitude of Marcus Aurelius, who is in many ways the model of this sort of monarch and sage. Marcus Aurelius has been blamed for tolerating the pagan amphitheatre or the Christian martyrdoms. But it was characteristic; for this sort of man really thought of popular religion just as he thought of popular circuses. Of him Professor Phillimore has profoundly said 'a great and good man—and he knew it.' The heretic Pharaoh had a philosophy more earnest and perhaps more humble. For there is a corollary to the conception of being too proud to fight. It is that the humble have to do most of the fighting. Anyhow, the Egyptian prince was simple enough to take his own philosophy seriously, and alone among such intellectual princes he affected a sort of *coup d'état*; hurling down the high gods of Egypt with one imperial gesture and lifting up for all men, like a blazing mirror of monotheistic truth, the disc of the universal sun. He had other interesting ideas often to be found in such idealists. In the sense in which we speak of a Little Englander he was a Little Egypter. In art he was a realist because he was an idealist; for realism is more impossible than any other ideal. But after all there falls on him something of the shadow of Marcus Aurelius, stalked by the shadow of Professor Phillimore. What is the matter with this noble sort of prince is that he has nowhere quite escaped being something of a prig. Priggishness is so pungent a smell that it clings amid the faded spices even to an Egyptian mummy. What was the matter with the heretic Pharaoh, as with a good many other heretics, was that he probably never paused to ask himself whether there was *anything* in the popular beliefs and tales of people less educated than himself. And, as already suggested, there was something in them. There was a real human hunger in all that element of feature and locality, that procession of deities like enormous pet animals, in that unwearied watching at certain haunted spots, in all the mazy wanderings of mythology. Nature may not have the name of Isis; Isis may not be really looking for Osiris. But it is true that Nature is really looking for something; Nature is always looking for the supernatural. Something much more definite was to satisfy that need; but a dignified monarch with a disc of the sun did not satisfy it. The royal experiment failed amid a roaring reaction of popular superstitions, in which the priests rose on the shoulders of the people and ascended the throne of the kings.

The next great example I shall take of the princely sage is Gautama, the great Lord Buddha. I know he is not generally classed merely with the philosophers; but I am more and more convinced, from all information that reaches me, that this is the real interpretation of his immense importance. He was by far the greatest and the best of these intellectuals born in the purple. His reaction was perhaps the noblest and most sincere of all the resultant actions of that combination of thinkers and of thrones. For his reaction was renunciation. Marcus Aurelius was content to say, with a refined irony, that even in a palace life could be lived well. The fierier Egyptian king concluded that it could be lived even better after a palace revolution. But the great Gautama was the only one of them who proved he could really do without his palace. One fell back on toleration and the other on revolution. But after all there is something more absolute about abdication. Abdication is perhaps the one really absolute action of an absolute monarch. The Indian prince, reared in Oriental luxury and pomp, deliberately went out and lived the life of a beggar. That is magnificent, but it is not war; that is, it is not necessarily a Crusade in the Christian sense. It does not decide the question of whether the life of a beggar was the life of a saint or the life of a philosopher. It does not decide whether this great man is really to go into the tub of Diogenes or the cave of St. Jerome. Now those who seem to be nearest to the study of Buddha, and certainly those who write most clearly and intelligently about him, convince me for one that he was simply a philosopher who founded a successful school of philosophy, and was turned into a sort of *divus* or sacred being merely by the more mysterious and unscientific atmosphere of all such traditions in Asia. So that it is necessary to say at this point a word about that invisible yet vivid border-line that we cross in passing from the Mediterranean into the mystery of the East.

Perhaps there are no things out of which we get so little of the truth as the truisms; especially when they are really true. We are all in the habit of saying certain things about Asia, which are true enough but which hardly help us because we do not understand their truth; as that Asia is old or looks to the past or is not progressive. Now it is true that Christendom is more progressive, in a sense that has very little to do with the rather provincial notion of an endless fuss of political improvement. Christendom does believe, for Christianity does believe, that man can eventually get somewhere, here or hereafter, or in various ways according to various doctrines. The world's desire can somehow be satisfied as desires are satisfied, whether by a new life or an old love or some form of positive possession and fulfilment. For the rest, we all know there is a rhythm and not a mere progress in things, that things rise and fall; only with us the rhythm is a fairly free and incalculable rhythm. For most of Asia the rhythm has hardened into a recurrence. It is no longer merely a rather topsy-turvy sort of world; it is a wheel. What has happened to all those highly intelligent and highly civilised peoples is that they have been caught up in a sort of cosmic rotation, of which the hollow hub is really nothing. In that sense the worst part of existence is that it may just as well go on like that forever. That is what we really mean when we say that Asia is old or unprogressive or looking backwards. That is why we see even her curved swords as arcs broken from that blinding wheel; why we see her serpentine ornament as returning everywhere, like a snake that is never slain. It has very little to do with the political varnish of progress; all Asiatics might have top-hats on their heads but if they had this spirit still in their hearts, they would only think the hats would vanish and come round again like the planets; not that running after a hat could lead them to heaven or even to home.

Now when the genius of Buddha arose to deal with the matter, this sort of cosmic sentiment was already common to almost everything in the east. There was indeed the jungle of an extraordinarily extravagant and almost asphyxiating mythology. Nevertheless it is possible to have more sympathy with this popular fruitfulness in folk-lore than with some of the higher pessimism that might have withered it. It must always be remembered, however, when all

fair allowances are made, that a great deal of spontaneous eastern imagery really is idolatry; the local and literal worship of an idol. This
is probably not true of the ancient Brahminical system, at least as
seen by Brahmins. But that phrase alone will remind us of a reality of much greater moment. This great reality is the Caste System
of ancient India. It may have had some of the practical advantages of
the Guild System of Medieval Europe. But it contrasts not only with
that Christian democracy, but with every extreme type of Christian aristocracy, in the fact that it does really conceive the social
superiority as a spiritual superiority. This not only divides it fundamentally from the fraternity of Christendom, but leaves it standing   like a mighty and terraced mountain of pride between the
relatively egalitarian levels both of Islam and of China. But the fixity
of this formation through thousands of years is another illustration
of that spirit of repetition that has marked time from time immemorial. Now we may also presume the prevalence of another idea
which we associate with the Buddhists as interpreted by the Theosophists. As a fact, some of the strictest Buddhists repudiate the
idea and still more scornfully repudiate the Theosophists. But
whether the idea is in Buddhism, or only in the birthplace of Buddhism, or only in a tradition or a travesty of Buddhism, it is an idea
entirely proper to this principle of recurrence. I mean of course the
idea of Reincarnation.

But Reincarnation is not really a mystical idea. It is not really a
transcendental idea, or in that sense a religious idea. Mysticism conceives something transcending experience; religion seeks glimpses of
a better good or a worse evil than experience can give. Reincarnation need only extend experiences in the sense of repeating them. It is
no more transcendental for a man to remember what he did in
Babylon before he was born than to remember what he did in Brixton
before he had a knock on the head. His successive lives *need* not be any
more than human lives, under whatever limitations burden human
life. It has nothing to do with seeing God or even conjuring up the
devil. In other words, reincarnation as such does not necessarily escape
from the wheel of destiny; in some sense it is the wheel of destiny.
And whether it was something that Buddha founded, or something

that Buddha found, or something that Buddha entirely renounced when he found, it is certainly something having the general character of that Asiatic atmosphere in which he had to play his part. And the part he played was that of an intellectual philosopher, with a particular theory about the right intellectual attitude towards it.

I can understand that Buddhists might resent the view that Buddhism is merely a philosophy, if we understand by a philosophy merely an intellectual game such as Greek sophists played, tossing up worlds and catching them like balls. Perhaps a more exact statement would be that Buddha was a man who made a metaphysical discipline; which might even be called a psychological discipline. He proposed a way of escaping from all this recurrent sorrow; and that was simply by getting rid of the delusion that is called desire. It was emphatically *not* that we should get what we want better by restraining our impatience for part of it, or that we should get it in a better way or in a better world. It was emphatically that we should leave off wanting it. If once a man realised that there is really no reality, that everything, including his soul, is in dissolution at every instant, he would anticipate disappointment and be intangible to change, existing (in so far as he could be said to exist) in a sort of ecstacy of indifference. The Buddhists call this beatitude and we will not stop our story to argue the point; certainly to us it is indistinguishable from despair. I do not see, for instance, why the disappointment of desire should not apply as much to the most benevolent desires as to the most selfish ones. Indeed the Lord of Compassion seems to pity people for living rather than for dying. For the rest, an intelligent Buddhist wrote 'the explanation of popular Chinese and Japanese Buddhism is that it is not Buddhism.' *That* has doubtless ceased to be a mere philosophy, but only by becoming a mere mythology. One thing is certain; it has never become anything remotely resembling what we call a Church.

It will appear only a jest to say that all religious history has really been a pattern of noughts and crosses. But I do not by noughts mean nothings, but only things that are negative compared with the positive shape or pattern of the other. And though the symbol is of course only a coincidence, it is a coincidence that really does coincide.

The mind of Asia can really be represented by a round O, if not in the sense of a cypher at least of a circle. The great Asiatic symbol of a serpent with its tail in its mouth is really a very perfect image of a certain idea of unity and recurrence that does indeed belong to the Eastern philosophies and religions. It really is a curve that in one sense includes everything, and in another sense comes to nothing. In that sense it does confess, or rather boast, that all argument is an argument in a circle. And though the figure is but a symbol, we can see how sound is the symbolic sense that produces it, the parallel symbol of the Wheel of Buddha generally called the Swastika. The cross is a thing at right angles pointing boldly in opposite directions; but the Swastika is the same thing in the very act of returning to the recurrent curve. That crooked cross is in fact a cross turning into a wheel. Before we dismiss even these symbols as if they were arbitrary symbols, we must remember how intense was the imaginative instinct that produced them or selected them both in the east and the west. The cross has become something more than a historical memory; it does convey, almost as by a mathematical diagram, the truth about the real point at issue; the idea of a conflict stretching outwards into eternity. It is true, and even tautological, to say that the cross is the crux of the whole matter.

In other words the cross, in fact as well as figure, does really stand for the idea of breaking out of the circle that is everything and nothing. It does escape from the circular argument by which everything begins and ends in the mind. Since we are still dealing in symbols, it might be put in a parable in the form of that story about St. Francis, which says that the birds departing with his benediction could wing their way into the infinites of the four winds of heaven, their tracks making a vast cross upon the sky; for compared with the freedom of that flight of birds, the very shape of the Swastika is like a kitten chasing its tail. In a more popular allegory, we might say that when St. George thrust his spear into the monster's jaws, he broke in upon the solitude of the self-devouring serpent and gave it something to bite besides its own tail. But while many fancies might be used as figures of the truth, the truth itself is abstract and absolute; though it is not very easy to sum up except by such figures.

Christianity does appeal to a solid truth outside itself; to something which is in that sense external as well as eternal. It does declare that things are really there; or in other words that things are really things. In this Christianity is at one with common sense; but all religious history shows that this common sense perishes except where there is Christianity to preserve it.

It cannot otherwise exist, or at least endure, because mere thought does not remain sane. In a sense it becomes too simple to be sane. The temptation of the philosophers is simplicity rather than subtlety. They are always attracted by insane simplifications, as men poised above abysses are fascinated by death and nothingness and the empty air. It needed another kind of philosopher to stand poised upon the pinnacle of the Temple and keep his balance without casting himself down. One of these obvious, these too obvious explanations is that everything is a dream and a delusion and there is nothing outside the ego. Another is that all things recur; another, which is said to be Buddhist and is certainly Oriental, is the idea that what is the matter with us is our creation, in the sense of our coloured differentiation and personality, and that nothing will be well till we are again melted into one unity. By this theory, in short, the Creation was the Fall. It is important historically because it was stored up in the dark heart of Asia and went forth at various times in various forms over the dim borders of Europe. Here we can place the mysterious figure of Manes or Manichaeus, the mystic of inversion, whom we should call a pessimist, parent of many sects and heresies; here, in a higher place, the figure of Zoroaster. He has been popularly identified with another of these too simple explanations; the equality of evil and good, balanced and battling in every atom. He also is of the school of sages that may be called mystics; and from the same mysterious Persian garden came upon ponderous wings Mithras, the unknown god, to trouble the last twilight of Rome.

That circle or disc of the sun set up in the morning of the world by the remote Egyptian has been a mirror and a model for all the philosophers. They have made many things out of it, and sometimes gone mad about it, especially when as in these eastern sages the circle became a wheel going round and round in their heads. But the point about them is that they all think that existence can be represented by a diagram instead of a drawing; and the rude drawings of the childish myth-makers are a sort of crude and spirited protest against that view. They cannot believe that religion is really not a pattern but a picture. Still less can they believe that it is a picture of something that really exists outside our minds. Sometimes the philosopher paints the disc all black and calls himself a pessimist; sometimes he paints it all white and calls himself an optimist; sometimes he divides it exactly into halves of black and white and calls himself a dualist, like those Persian mystics to whom I wish there were space to do justice. None of them could understand a thing that began to draw the proportions just as if they were real proportions, disposed in the living fashion which the mathematical draughtsman would call disproportionate. Like the first artist in the cave, it revealed to incredulous eyes the suggestion of a new purpose in what looked like a wildly crooked pattern; he seemed only to be distorting his diagram, when he began for the first time in all the ages to trace the lines of a form—and of a Face.

VII

THE WAR OF THE GODS AND DEMONS

The materialist theory of history, that all politics and ethics are the expression of economics, is a very simple fallacy indeed. It consists simply of confusing the necessary conditions of life with the normal preoccupations of life, that are quite a different thing. It is like saying that because a man can only walk about on two legs, therefore he never walks about except to buy shoes and stockings. Man cannot live without the two props of food and drink, which support him like two legs; but to suggest that they have been the motives of all his movements in history is like saying that the goal of all his military marches or religious pilgrimages must have been the Golden Leg of Miss Kilmansegg or the ideal and perfect leg of Sir Willoughby Patterne. But it is such movements that make up the story of mankind and without them there would practically be no story at all. Cows may be purely economic, in the sense that we cannot see that they do much beyond grazing and seeking better grazing grounds; and that is why a history of cows in twelve volumes would not be very lively reading. Sheep and goats may be pure economists in their external action at least; but that is why the sheep has hardly been a hero of epic wars and empires thought worthy of detailed narration; and even the more active quadruped has not inspired a book for boys called Golden Deeds of Gallant Goats or any similar title. But so far from the movements that make up the story of man being economic, we may say that the story only begins where the motive of the cows and sheep leaves off. It will be hard to maintain that the Crusaders went from their homes into a howling wilderness because cows go from a wilderness to a more comfortable grazing-ground. It will be hard to maintain that the Arctic explorers went north with the same material motive that made the swallows go south. And if you leave things like all the religious wars and all the merely adventurous explorations out of the human story, it will not only cease to be human at all but cease to be a story at all. The outline of history is made of these decisive curves and angles determined by the will of man. Economic history would not even be history.

But there is a deeper fallacy besides this obvious fact; that men need not live for food merely because they cannot live without food. The truth is that the thing most present to the mind of man is not the economic machinery necessary to his existence; but rather that existence itself; the world which he sees when he wakes every morning and the nature of his general position in it. There is something that is nearer to him than livelihood, and that is life. For once that he remembers exactly what work produces his wages and exactly what wages produce his meals, he reflects ten times that it is a fine day or it is a queer world, or wonders whether life is worth living, or wonders whether marriage is a failure, or is pleased and puzzled with his own children, or remembers his own youth, or in any such fashion vaguely reviews the mysterious lot of man. This is true of the majority even of the wage-slaves of our morbid modern industrialism, which by its hideousness and in-humanity has really forced the economic issue to the front. It is immeasurably more true of the multitude of peasants or hunters or fishers who make up the real mass of mankind. Even those dry pedants who think that ethics depend on economics must admit that economics depend on existence. And any number of normal doubts and day-dreams are about existence; not about how we can live, but about why we do. And the proof of it is simple; as simple as suicide. Turn the universe upside down in the mind and you turn all the political economists upside down with it. Suppose that a man wishes to die, and the professor of political economy becomes rather a bore with his elaborate explanations of how he is to live. And all the departures and decisions that make our human past into a story have this character of diverting the direct course of pure economics. As the economist may be excused from calculating the future salary of a suicide, so he may be excused from providing an old age pension for a martyr. As he need not provide for the future of a martyr, so he need not provide for the family of a monk. His plan is modified in lesser and varying degrees by a man being a soldier and dying for his own country, by a

man being a peasant and specially loving his own land, by a man being more or less affected by any religion that forbids or allows him
to do this or that. But all these come back not to an economic calculation about livelihood but to an elemental outlook upon life. They
all come back to what a man fundamentally feels, when he looks
forth from those strange windows which we call the eyes, upon that
strange vision that we call the world.

No wise man will wish to bring more long words into the world.
But it may be allowable to say that we need a new thing; which may
be called psychological history. I mean the consideration of what
things meant in the mind of a man, especially an ordinary man; as
distinct from what is defined or deduced merely from official forms
or political pronouncements. I have already touched on it in such a
case as the totem or indeed any other popular myth. It is not enough
to be told that a tom-cat was called a totem; especially when it was
not called a totem. We want to know what it felt like. Was it like
Whittington's cat or like a witch's cat? Was its real name Pasht[1] or
Puss-In-Boots? That is the sort of thing we need touching the nature of political and social relations. We want to know the real sentiment that was the social bond of many common men, as sane and
as selfish as we are. What did soldiers feel when they saw splendid in
the sky that strange totem that we call the Golden Eagle of the
Legions? What did vassals feel about those other totems the lions or
the leopards upon the shield of their lord? So long as we neglect this
subjective side of history, which may more simply be called the inside of history, there will always be a certain limitation on that
science which can be better transcended by art. So long as the historian cannot do that, fiction will be truer than fact. There will be
more reality in a novel; yes, even in a historical novel.

In nothing is this new history needed so much as in the psychology of war. Our history is stiff with official documents, public
or private, which tell us nothing of the thing itself. At the worst we
only have the official posters, which could not have been spontaneous precisely because they were official. At the best we have only

[1] An Egyptian goddess who was represented as a woman with the head of a lioness
or cat.

the secret diplomacy, which could not have been popular precisely
because it was secret. Upon one or other of these is based the
historical judgment about the real reasons that sustained the struggle. Governments fight for colonies or commercial rights; governments fight about harbours or high tariffs; governments fight for a
gold mine or a pearl fishery. It seems sufficient to answer that governments do not fight at all. Why do the fighters fight? What is the
psychology that sustains the terrible and wonderful thing called a
war? Nobody who knows anything of soldiers believes the silly notion of the dons, that millions of men can be ruled by force. If they
were all to slack, it would be impossible to punish all the slackers.
And the least little touch of slacking would lose a whole campaign
in half a day. What did men really feel about the policy? If it be said
that they accepted the policy from the politician, what did they feel
about the politician? If the vassals warred blindly for their prince,
what did those blind men see in their prince?

There is something we all know which can only be rendered, in
an appropriate language, as *realpolitik*. As a matter of fact, it is an
almost insanely unreal politik. It is always stubbornly and stupidly
repeating that men fight for material ends, without reflecting for a
moment that the material ends are hardly ever material to the men
who fight. In any case no man will die for practical politics, just as
no man will die for pay. Nero could not hire a hundred Christians to
be eaten by lions at a shilling an hour; for men will not be martyred
for money. But the vision called up by real politik, or realistic politics, is beyond example crazy and incredible. Does anybody in the
world believe that a soldier says, 'My leg is nearly dropping off, but I
shall go on till it drops; for after all I shall enjoy all the advantages of
my government obtaining a warm-water port in the Gulf of Fin-
land.' Can anybody suppose that a clerk turned conscript says, 'If I
am gassed I shall probably die in torments; but it is a comfort to
reflect that should I ever decide to become a pearl-diver in the South
Seas, that career is now open to me and my countrymen.' Materialist
history is the most madly incredible of all histories, or even of all romances. Whatever starts wars, the thing that sustains wars is something in the soul; that is something akin to religion. It is what

men feel about life and about death. A man near to death is dealing directly with an absolute; it is nonsense to say he is concerned only with relative and remote complications that death in any case will end. If he is sustained by certain loyalties, they must be loyalties as simple as death. They are generally two ideas, which are only two sides of one idea. The first is the love of something said to be threatened, if it be only vaguely known as home; the second is dislike and defiance of some strange thing that threatens it. The first is far more philosophical than it sounds, though we need not discuss it here. A man does not want his national home destroyed or even changed, because he cannot even remember all the good things that go with it; just as he does not want his house burnt down, because he can hardly count all the things he would miss. Therefore he fights for what sounds like a hazy abstraction, but is really a house. But the negative side of it is quite as noble as well as quite as strong. Men fight hardest when they feel that the foe is at once an old enemy and an eternal stranger, that his atmosphere is alien and antagonistic; as the French feel about the Prussian or the Eastern Christians about the Turk. If we say it is a difference of religion, people will drift into dreary bickerings about sects and dogmas. We will pity them and say it is a difference about death and daylight; a difference that does really come like a dark shadow between our eyes and the day. Men can think of this difference even at the point of death; for it is a difference about the meaning of life.

Men are moved in these things by something far higher and holier than policy; by hatred. When men hung on in the darkest days of the Great War, suffering either in their bodies or in their souls for those they loved, they were long past caring about details of diplomatic objects as motives for their refusal to surrender. Of myself and those I knew best I can answer for the vision that made surrender impossible. It was the vision of the German Emperor's face as he rode into Paris. This is not the sentiment which some of my idealistic friends describe as Love. I am quite content to call it hatred; the hatred of hell and all its works, and to agree that as they do not believe in hell they need not believe in hatred. But in the face of this prevalent prejudice, this long introduction has been unfortunately necessary, to ensure an understanding of what is meant by a religious war. There is a religious war when two worlds meet; that is, when two visions of the world meet; or in more modern language when two moral atmospheres meet. What is the one man's breath is the other man's poison; and it is vain to talk of giving a pestilence a place in the sun. And this is what we must understand, even at the expense of digression, if we would see what really happened in the Mediterranean; when right athwart the rising of the Republic on the Tiber, a thing overtopping and disdaining it, dark with all the riddles of Asia and trailing all the tribes and dependencies of imperialism, came Carthage riding on the sea.

The ancient religion of Italy was on the whole that mixture which we have considered under the head of mythology; save that where the Greeks had a natural turn for the mythology, the Latins seem to have had a real turn for religion. Both multiplied gods, yet they sometimes seem to have multiplied them for almost opposite reasons. It would seem sometimes as if the Greek polytheism branched and blossomed upwards like the boughs of a tree, while the Italian polytheism ramified downward like the roots. Perhaps it would be truer to say that the former branches lifted themselves lightly, bearing flowers; while the latter hung down, being heavy with fruit. I mean that the Latins seem to multiply gods to bring them nearer to men, while the Greek gods rose and radiated outwards into the morning sky. What strikes us in the Italian cults is their local and especially their domestic character. We gain the impression of divinities swarming about the house like flies; of deities clustering and clinging like bats about the pillars or building like birds under the eaves. We have a vision of a god of roofs and a god of gate-posts, of a god of doors and even a god of drains. It has been suggested that all mythology was a sort of fairy-tale; but this was a particular sort of fairy-tale which may truly be called a fireside tale, or a nursery-tale; because it was a tale of the interior of the home; like those which make chairs and tables talk like elves. The old household gods of the Italian peasants seem to have been great, clumsy, wooden images, more featureless than the figure-head which Quilp[2]

[2] A malicious and cunning dwarf in Charles Dickens' *Old Curiosity Shop*.

battered with the poker. This religion of the home was very homely. Of course there were other less human elements in the tangle of Italian mythology. There were Greek deities superimposed on the Roman; there were here and there uglier things underneath, experiments in the cruel kind of paganism, like the Arician rite of the priest slaying the slayer. But these things were always potential in paganism; they are certainly not the peculiar character of Latin paganism. The peculiarity of that may be roughly covered by saying that if mythology personified the forces of nature, this mythology personified nature as transformed by the forces of man. It was the god of the corn and not of the grass, of the cattle and not the wild things of the forest; in short the cult was literally a culture; as when we speak of it as agriculture.

With this there was a paradox which is still for many the puzzle or riddle of the Latins. With religion running through every domestic detail like a climbing plant, there went what seems to many the very opposite spirit; the spirit of revolt. Imperialists and reactionaries often invoke Rome as the very model of order and obedience; but Rome was the very reverse. The real history of ancient Rome is much more like the history of modern Paris. It might be called in modern language a city built out of barricades. It is said that the gate of Janus was never closed because there was an eternal war without; it is almost as true that there was an eternal revolution within. From the first Plebeian riots to the last Servile Wars, the state that imposed peace on the world was never really at peace. The rulers were themselves rebels.

There is a real relation between this religion in private and this revolution in public life. Stories none the less heroic for being hackneyed remind us that the Republic was founded on a tyrannicide that avenged an insult to a wife; that the Tribunes of the people were re-established after another which avenged an insult to a daughter. The truth is that only men to whom the family is sacred will ever have a standard or a status by which to criticise the state. They alone can appeal to something more holy than the gods of the city; the gods of the hearth. That is why men are mystified in seeing that the same nations that are thought rigid in domesticity are also thought restless in politics; for instance the Irish and the French. It is worth while to dwell on this domestic point because it is an exact example of what is meant here by the inside of history, like the inside of houses. Merely political histories of Rome may be right enough in saying that this or that was a cynical or cruel act of the Roman politicians; but the spirit that lifted Rome from beneath was the spirit of all the Romans; and it is not a cant to call it the ideal of Cincinnatus passing from the senate to the plough. Men of that sort had strengthened their village on every side, had extended its victories already over Italians and even over Greeks, when they found themselves confronted with a war that changed the world. I have called it here the war of the gods and demons.

There was established on the opposite coast of the inland sea a city that bore the name of the New Town. It was already much older, more powerful, and more prosperous than the Italian town; but there still remained about it an atmosphere that made the name not inappropriate. It had been called new because it was a colony like New York or New Zealand. It was an outpost or settlement of the energy and expansion of the great commercial cities of Tyre and Sidon. There was a note of the new countries and colonies about it; a confident and commercial outlook. It was fond of saying things that rang with a certain metallic assurance; as that nobody could wash his hands in the sea without the leave of the New Town. For it depended almost entirely on the greatness of its ships, as did the two great ports and markets from which its people came. It brought from Tyre and Sidon a prodigious talent for trade and considerable experience of travel. It brought other things as well.

In a previous chapter I have hinted at something of the psychology that lies behind a certain type of religion. There was a tendency in those hungry for practical results, apart from poetical results, to call upon spirits of terror and compulsion; to move Acheron in despair of bending the gods. There is always a sort of dim idea that these darker powers will really do things, with no nonsense about it. In the interior psychology of the Punic peoples this strange sort of pessimistic practicality had grown to great proportions. In the New Town, which the Romans called Carthage, as in the parent cities of Phoenicia, the god who got things done bore the name of Moloch, who was perhaps identical with the other deity whom we know as Baal, the Lord. The Romans did not at first quite know what to call him or what to make of him; they had to go back to the grossest myth of Greek or Roman origins and compare him to Saturn devouring his children. But the worshippers of Moloch were not gross or primitive. They were members of a mature and polished civilisation, abounding in refinements and luxuries; they were probably far more civilised than the Romans. And Moloch was not a myth; or at any rate his meal was not a myth. These highly civilised people really met together to invoke the blessing of heaven on their empire by throwing hundreds of their infants into a large furnace. We can only realise the combination by imagining a number of Manchester merchants with chimney-pot hats and mutton-chop whiskers, going to church every Sunday at eleven o'clock to see a baby roasted alive.

The first stages of the political or commercial quarrel can be followed in far too much detail, precisely because it is merely political or commercial. The Punic Wars looked at one time as if they would never end; and it is not easy to say when they ever began. The Greeks and the Sicilians had already been fighting vaguely on the European side against the African city. Carthage had defeated Greece and conquered Sicily. Carthage had also planted herself firmly in Spain; and between Spain and Sicily the Latin city was contained and would have been crushed; if the Romans had been of the sort to be easily crushed. Yet the interest of the story really consists in the fact that Rome was crushed. If there had not been certain moral elements as well as the material elements, the story would have ended where Carthage certainly thought it had ended. It is common enough to blame Rome for not making peace. But it was a true popular instinct that there could be no peace with that sort of people. It is common enough to blame the Roman for his *Delenda est Carthago*; Carthage must be destroyed. It is commoner to forget that, to all appearance, Rome itself was destroyed. The sacred savour that hung round Rome for ever, it is too often forgotten, clung to her partly because she had risen suddenly from the dead.

Carthage was an aristocracy, as are most of such mercantile states. The pressure of the rich on the poor was impersonal as well as irresistible. For such aristocracies never permit personal government, which is perhaps why this one was jealous of personal talent. But genius can turn up anywhere, even in a governing class. As if to make the world's supreme test as terrible as possible, it was ordained that one of the great houses of Carthage should produce a man who came out of those gilded palaces with all the energy and originality of Napoleon coming from nowhere. At the worst crisis of the war Rome learned that Italy itself, by a military miracle, was invaded from the north. Hannibal, the Grace of Baal as his name ran in his own tongue, had dragged a ponderous chain of armaments over the starry solitudes of the Alps; and pointed southward to the city which he had been pledged by all his dreadful gods to destroy.

Hannibal marched down the road to Rome, and the Romans who rushed to war with him felt as if they were fighting with a magician. Two great armies sank to right and left of him into the swamps of the Trebia; more and more were sucked into the horrible whirlpool of Cannae; more and more went forth only to fall in ruin at his touch. The supreme sign of all disasters, which is treason, turned tribe after tribe against the falling cause of Rome, and still the unconquerable enemy rolled nearer and nearer to the city; and following their great leader the swelling cosmopolitan army of Carthage passed like a pageant of the whole world; the elephants shaking the earth like marching mountains and the gigantic Gauls with their barbaric panoply and the dark Spaniards girt in gold and the brown Numidians on their unbridled desert horses wheeling and darting like hawks, and whole mobs of deserters and mercenaries and miscellaneous peoples; and the grace of Baal went before them.

The Roman augurs and scribes who said in that hour that it brought forth unearthly prodigies, that a child was born with the head of an elephant or that stars fell down like hailstones, had a far more philosophical grasp of what had really happened than the modern historian who can see nothing in it but a success of strategy concluding a rivalry in commerce. Something far different was felt at the time and on the spot, as it is always felt by those who experience a foreign atmosphere entering their own like a fog or a foul savour. It was no mere military defeat, it was certainly no mere mercantile rivalry, that filled the Roman imagination with such hideous omens of nature herself becoming unnatural. It was Moloch upon the mountain of the Latins, looking with his appalling face across the plain; it was Baal who trampled the vineyards with his feet of stone; it was the voice of Tanit the invisible, behind her trailing veils, whispering of the love that is more horrible than hate. The burning of the Italian cornfields, the ruin of the Italian vines, were something more than actual; they were allegorical. They were the destruction of domestic and fruitful things, the withering of what was human before that inhumanity that is far beyond the human thing called cruelty. The household gods bowed low in darkness under their lowly roofs; and above them went the demons upon a wind from beyond all walls, blowing the trumpet of the Tramontane. The door of the Alps was broken down; and in no vulgar but a very solemn sense, it was Hell let loose. The war of the gods and demons seemed already to have ended; and the gods were dead. The eagles were lost, the legions were broken; and in Rome nothing remained but honour and the cold courage of despair.

In the whole world one thing still threatened Carthage, and that was Carthage. There still remained the inner working of an element strong in all successful commercial states, and the presence of a spirit that we know. There was still the solid sense and shrewdness of the men who manage big enterprises; there was still the advice of the best financial experts; there was still business government; there was still the broad and sane outlook of practical men of affairs; and in these things could the Romans hope. As the war trailed on to what seemed its tragic end, there grew gradually a faint and strange possibility that even now they might not hope in vain. The plain business men of Carthage, thinking as such men do in terms of living and dying races, saw clearly that Rome was not only dying but dead. The war was over; it was obviously hopeless for the Italian city to resist any longer, and inconceivable that anybody should resist when it was hopeless. Under these circumstances, another set of broad, sound business principles remained to be considered. Wars were waged with money, and consequently cost money; perhaps they felt in their hearts, as do so many of their kind, that after all war must be a little wicked because it costs money. The time had now come for peace; and still more for economy. The messages sent by Hannibal from time to time asking for reinforcements were a ridiculous anachronism; there were much more important things to attend to now. It might be true that some consul or other had made a last dash to the Metaurus, had killed Hannibal's brother and flung his head, with Latin fury, into Hannibal's camp; and mad actions of that sort showed how utterly hopeless the Latins felt about their cause. But even excitable Latins could not be so mad as to cling to a lost cause for ever. So argued the best financial experts; and tossed aside more and more letters, full of rather queer alarmist reports. So argued and acted the great Carthaginian Empire. That meaningless prejudice, the curse of commercial states, that stupidity is in some way practical and that genius is in some way futile, led them to starve and abandon that great artist in the school of arms, whom the gods had given them in vain.

Why do men entertain this queer idea that what is sordid must always overthrow what is magnanimous; that there is some dim connection between brains and brutality, or that it does not matter if a man is dull so long as he is also mean? Why do they vaguely think of all chivalry as sentiment and all sentiment as weakness? They do it because they are, like all men, primarily inspired by religion. For them, as for all men, the first fact is their notion of the nature of things; their idea about what world they are living in. And it is their faith that the only ultimate thing is fear and therefore that the very heart of the world is evil. They believe that death is stronger than life, and therefore dead things must be stronger than living things; whether those dead things are gold and iron and machinery or rocks and rivers and forces of nature. It may sound fanciful to say that men we meet at tea-tables or talk to at garden-parties are secretly worshippers of Baal or Moloch. But this sort of commercial mind has its own cosmic vision and it is the vision of Carthage. It has in it the brutal blunder that was the ruin of Carthage. The Punic power fell, because there is in this materialism a mad indifference to real thought. By disbelieving in the soul, it comes to disbelieving in the mind. Being too practical to be moral, it denies what every practical soldier calls the moral of an army. It fancies that money will fight when men will no longer fight. So it was with the Punic merchant princes. Their religion was a religion of despair, even when their practical fortunes were hopeful. How could they understand that the Romans could hope even when their fortunes were hopeless? Their religion was a religion of force and fear; how could they understand that men can still despise fear even when they submit to force? Their philosophy of the world had weariness in its very heart; above all they were weary of warfare; how should they understand those who still wage war even when they are weary of it? In a word, how should they understand the mind of Man, who had so long bowed down before mindless things, money and brute force and gods who had the hearts of beasts? They awoke suddenly to the news that the embers they had disdained too much even to tread out were again breaking everywhere into flames; that Hasdrubal was defeated, that Hannibal was outnumbered, that Scipio had carried the war into Spain; that he had carried it into Africa. Before the very gates of the golden city Hannibal fought his last fight for it and lost; and Carthage fell as nothing has fallen since Satan. The name of the New City remains only as a name. There is no stone of it left upon the sand. Another war was indeed waged before the final destruction: but the destruction was final. Only men digging in its deep foundation centuries after found a heap of hundreds of little skeletons, the holy relics of that religion. For Carthage fell because she was faithful to her own philosophy and had followed out to its logical conclusion her own vision of the universe. Moloch had eaten his children.

The gods had risen again, and the demons had been defeated after all. But they had been defeated by the defeated, and almost defeated by the dead. Nobody understands the romance of Rome, and why she rose afterwards to a representative leadership that seemed almost fated and fundamentally natural who does not keep in mind the agony of horror and humiliation through which she had continued to testify to the sanity that is the soul of Europe. She came to stand alone in the midst of an empire because she had once stood alone

in the midst of a ruin and a waste. After that all men knew in their
hearts that she had been representative of mankind, even when she
was rejected of men. And there fell on her the shadow from a shining and as yet invisible light and the burden of things to be. It is not
for us to guess in what manner or moment the mercy of God might
in any case have rescued the world; but it is certain that the struggle
which established Christendom would have been very different if
there had been an empire of Carthage instead of an empire of Rome.
We have to thank the patience of the Punic wars if, in after ages,
divine things descended at least upon human things and not inhuman. Europe evolved into its own vices and its own impotence, as
will be suggested on another page; but the worst into which it
evolved was not like what it had escaped. Can any man in his senses
compare the great wooden doll, whom the children expected to eat a
little bit of the dinner, with the great idol who would have been expected to eat the children? That is the measure of how far the world
went astray, compared with how far it might have gone astray. If
the Romans were ruthless, it was in a true sense to an enemy, and
certainly not merely a rival. They remembered not trade routes and
regulations, but the faces of sneering men; and hated the hateful soul
of Carthage. And we owe them something if we never needed to cut
down the groves of Venus exactly as men cut down the groves of
Baal. We owe it partly to their harshness that our thoughts of our
human past are not wholly harsh. If the passage from heathenry to
Christianity was a bridge as well as a breach, we owe it to those who
kept that heathenry human. If, after all these ages, we are in some
sense at peace with paganism, and can think more kindly of our fathers, it is well to remember the things that were and the things that
might have been. For this reason alone we can take lightly the load
of antiquity and need not shudder at a nymph on a fountain or a cu-
pid on a valentine. Laughter and sadness link us with things long
past away and remembered without dishonour; and we can see not
altogether without tenderness the twilight sinking around the
Sabine farm and hear the household gods rejoice when Catullus
comes home to Sirmio. *Deleta est Carthago.*

VIII

THE END OF THE WORLD

I was once sitting on a summer day in a meadow in Kent under the shadow of a little village church, with a rather curious companion with whom I had just been walking through the woods. He was one of a group of eccentrics I had come across in my wanderings who had a new religion called Higher Thought; in which I had been so far initiated as to realise a general atmosphere of loftiness or height, and was hoping at some later and more esoteric stage to discover the beginnings of thought. My companion was the most amusing of them, for however he may have stood towards thought, he was at least very much their superior in experience, having travelled beyond the tropics while they were meditating in the suburbs; though he had been charged with excess in telling travellers' tales. In spite of anything said against him, I preferred him to his companions and willingly went with him through the wood; where I could not but feel his sunburnt face and fierce tufted eyebrows and pointed beard gave him something of the look of Pan. Then we sat down in the meadow and gazed idly at the tree-tops and the spire of the village church; while the warm afternoon began to mellow into early evening and the song of a speck of a bird was faint far up in the sky and no more than a whisper of breeze soothed rather than stirred the ancient orchards of the garden of England. Then my companion said to me: 'Do you know why the spire of that church goes up like that?' I expressed a respectable agnosticism, and he answered in an off-hand way, 'Oh, the same as the obelisks; the Phallic Worship of antiquity.' Then I looked across at him suddenly as he lay there leering above his goatlike beard; and for the moment I thought he was not Pan but the Devil. No mortal words can express the immense, the insane incongruity and unnatural perversion of thought involved in saying such a thing at such a moment and in such a place. For one moment I was in the mood in which men burned witches; and then a sense of absurdity equally enormous seemed to open about me like a dawn. 'Why, of course,' I said after a moment's reflection, 'if it hadn't been for phallic worship, they would have built the spire pointing downwards and standing on its own apex.' I could have sat in that field and laughed for an hour. My friend did not seem offended, for indeed he was never thin-skinned about his scientific discoveries. I had only met him by chance and I never met him again, and I believe he is now dead; but though it has nothing to do with the argument, it may be worth while to mention the name of this adherent of Higher Thought and interpreter of primitive religious origins; or at any rate the name by which he was known. It was Louis de Rougemont.

That insane image of the Kentish church standing on the point of its spire, as in some old rustic, topsy-turvy tale, always comes back into my imagination when I hear these things said about pagan origins; and calls to my aid the laughter of the giants. Then I feel as genially and charitably to all other scientific investigators, higher critics, and authorities on ancient and modern religion, as I do to poor Louis de Rougemont. But the memory of that immense absurdity remains as a sort of measure and check by which to keep sane, not only on the subject of Christian churches, but also on the subject of heathen temples. Now a great many people have talked about heathen origins as the distinguished traveller talked about Christian origins. Indeed a great many modern heathens have been very hard on heathenism. A great many modern humanitarians have been very hard on the real religion of humanity. They have represented it as being everywhere and from the first rooted only in these repulsive arcana; and carrying the character of something utterly shameless and anarchical. Now I do not believe this for a moment. I should never dream of thinking about the whole worship of Apollo what De Rougemont could think about the worship of Christ. I would never admit that there was such an atmosphere in a Greek city as that madman was able to smell in a Kentish village. On the contrary, it is the whole point, even of this final chapter upon the final decay of paganism, to insist once more that the worst sort of paganism had already been defeated by the best sort. It was the best sort of paganism that conquered the gold of Carthage. It was the best sort of paganism that wore the laurels of Rome. It was the best thing the world had yet seen, all things considered and on any large scale, that ruled from the wall of the Grampians to the garden of the Euphrates. It was the best that conquered; it was the best that ruled; and it was the best that began to decay.

Unless this broad truth be grasped, the whole story is seen askew. Pessimism is not in being tired of evil but in being tired of good. Despair does not lie in being weary of suffering, but in being weary of joy. It is when for some reason or other the good things in a society no longer work that the society begins to decline; when its food does not feed, when its cures do not cure, when its blessings refuse to bless. We might almost say that in a society without such good things we should hardly have any test by which to register a decline; that is why some of the static commercial oligarchies like Carthage have rather an air in history of standing and staring like mummies, so dried up and swathed and embalmed that no man knows when they are new or old. But Carthage at any rate was dead, and the worst assault ever made by the demons on mortal society had been defeated. But how much would it matter that the worst was dead if the best was dying?

To begin with, it must be noted that the relation of Rome to Carthage was partially repeated and extended in her relation to nations more normal and more nearly akin to her than Carthage. I am not here concerned to controvert the merely political view that Roman statesmen acted unscrupulously towards Corinth or the Greek cities. But I am concerned to contradict the notion that there was nothing but a hypocritical excuse in the ordinary Roman dislike of Greek vices. I am not presenting these pagans as paladins of chivalry, with a sentiment about nationalism never known until Christian times. But I am presenting them as men with the feelings of men; and those feelings were not a pretence. The truth is that one of the weaknesses in nature-worship and mere mythology had already produced a perversion among the Greeks, due to the worst sophistry; the sophistry of simplicity. Just as they became unnatural by worshipping nature, so they actually became unmanly by worshipping man. If Greece led her conqueror, she might have misled her conqueror; but these were things he did originally wish to conquer—even in himself. It is true that in one sense there was less inhumanity even in Sodom and Gomorrah than in Tyre and Sidon. When we consider the war of the demons on the children, we cannot compare even Greek decadence to Punic devil-worship. But it is not true that the sincere revulsion from either need be merely pharisaical. It is not true to human nature or to common sense. Let any lad who has had the luck to grow up sane and simple in his day-dreams of love hear for the first time of the cult of Ganymede; he will not be merely shocked but sickened. And that first impression, as has been said here so often about first impressions, will be right. Our cynical indifference is an illusion; it is the greatest of all illusions; the illusion of familiarity. It is right to conceive the more or less rustic virtues of the ruck of the original Romans as reacting against the very rumour of it, with complete spontaneity and sincerity. It is right to regard them as reacting, if in a lesser degree, exactly as they did against the cruelty of Carthage. Because it was in a less degree they did not destroy Corinth as they destroyed Carthage. But if their attitude and action was rather destructive, in neither case need their indignation have been mere self-righteousness covering mere selfishness. And if anybody insists that nothing could have operated in either case but reasons of state and commercial conspiracies, we can only tell him that there is something which he does not understand; something which possibly he will never understand; something which, until he does understand, he will never understand the Latins. That something is called democracy. He has probably heard the word a good many times and even used it himself; but he has no notion of what it means. All through the revolutionary history of Rome there was an incessant drive towards democracy; the state and the statesman could do nothing without a considerable backing of democracy; the sort of democracy that never has anything to do with diplomacy. It is precisely because of the presence of Roman democracy that we hear so much about Roman oligarchy. For instance, recent historians have tried to explain the valour and victory of Rome in terms of that detestable and detested usury which was practised by some of the Patricians; as if Curius had conquered the men of the Macedonian phalanx by lending them money; or the Consul Nero had negotiated the victory of Metaurus at five per cent. But we realise the usury of the Patricians because of the perpetual revolt of the Plebeians. The rule of the Punic merchant princes had the very soul of usury. But there was never a Punic mob that dared to call them usurers.

Burdened like all mortal things with all mortal sin and weakness, the rise of Rome had really been the rise of normal and especially of popular things; and in nothing more than in the thoroughly normal and profoundly popular hatred of perversion. Now among the Greeks a perversion had become a convention. It is true that it had become so much of a convention, especially a literary convention, that it was sometimes conventionally copied by Roman literary men. But this is one of those complications that always arise out of conventions. It must not obscure our sense of the difference of tone in the two societies as a whole. It is true that Virgil would once in a way take over a theme of Theocritus; but nobody can get the impression that Virgil was particularly fond of that theme. The themes of Virgil were specially and notably the normal themes and nowhere more than in morals; piety and patriotism and the honor of the countryside. And we may well pause upon the name of the poet as we pass into the autumn of antiquity; upon his name who was in so supreme a sense the very voice of autumn, of its maturity and its melancholy; of its fruits of fulfilment and its prospect of decay. Nobody who reads even a few lines of Virgil can doubt that he understood what moral sanity means to mankind. Nobody can doubt his feelings when the demons were driven in flight before the household gods. But there are two particular points about him and his work which are particularly important to the main thesis here. The first is that the whole of his great patriotic epic is in a very peculiar sense founded upon the fall of Troy; that is upon an avowed pride in Troy although she had fallen. In tracing to Trojans the foundation of his beloved race and republic, he began what may be called the great Trojan tradition which runs through medieval and modern history. We have already seen the first hint of it in the pathos of Homer about Hector. But Virgil turned it not merely into a literature but into a legend. And it was a legend of the almost divine dignity that belongs to the defeated. This was one of the traditions that did truly prepare the world for the coming of Christianity and especially of Christian chivalry. This is what did help to sustain civilisation through the incessant defeats of the Dark Ages and the barbarian wars; out of which what we call chivalry was born. It is the moral attitude of the man with his back to the wall; and it was the wall of Troy. All through medieval and modern times this version of the virtues in the Homeric conflict can be traced in a hundred ways co-operating with all that was akin to it in Christian sentiment. Our own countrymen, and the men of other countries, loved to claim like Virgil that their own nation was descended from the heroic Trojans. All sorts of people thought it the most superb sort of heraldry to claim to be descended from Hector. Nobody seems to have wanted to be descended from Achilles. The very fact that the Trojan name has become a Christian name, and been scattered to the last limits of Christendom, to Ireland or the Gaelic Highlands, while the Greek name has remained relatively rare and pedantic, is a tribute to the same truth. Indeed it involves a curiosity of language almost in the nature of a joke. The name has been turned into a verb; and the very phrase about hectoring, in the sense of swaggering, suggests the myriads of soldiers who have taken the fallen Trojan for a model. As a matter of fact, nobody in antiquity was less given to hectoring than Hector. But even the bully pretending to be a conqueror took his title from the conquered. That is why the popularisation of the Trojan origin by Virgil has a vital relation to all those elements that have made men say that Virgil was almost a Christian. It is almost as if two great tools or toys of the same timber, the divine and the human, had been in the hands of Providence; and the only thing comparable to the Wooden Cross of Calvary was the Wooden Horse of Troy. So, in some wild allegory, pious in purpose if almost profane in form, the Holy Child might have fought the Dragon with a wooden sword and a wooden horse.

The other element in Virgil which is essential to the argument is the particular nature of his relation to mythology; or what may here in a special sense be called folklore, the faiths and fancies of the populace. Everybody knows that his poetry at its most perfect is less concerned with the pomposity of Olympus than with the *numina* of natural and agricultural life. Everyone knows where Virgil looked for the causes of things. He speaks of finding them not so much in cosmic allegories of Uranus and Chronos; but rather in Pan and the sisterhood of the nymphs and Sylvanus the old man of the forest. He is perhaps most himself in some passages of the Eclogues, in which he has perpetuated for ever the great legend of Arcadia and the shepherds. Here again it is easy enough to miss the point with petty criticism about all the things that happen to separate his literary convention from ours. There is nothing more artificial than the cry of artificiality as directed against the old pastoral poetry. We have entirely missed all that our fathers meant by looking at the externals of what they wrote. People have been so much amused with the mere fact that the china shepherdess was made of china that they have not even asked why she was made at all. They have been so content to consider the Merry Peasant as a figure in an opera that they have not asked even how he came to go to the opera, or how he strayed on to the stage.

In short, we have only to ask why there is a china shepherdess and not a china shopkeeper. Why were not mantelpieces adorned with figures of city merchants in elegant attitudes; of ironmasters wrought in iron or gold speculators in gold? Why did the opera exhibit a Merry Peasant and not a Merry Politician? Why was there not a ballet of bankers, pirouetting upon pointed toes? Because the ancient instinct and humour of humanity have always told them, under whatever conventions, that the conventions of complex cities were less really healthy and happy than the customs of the countryside. So it is with the eternity of the Eclogues. A modern poet did indeed write things called Fleet Street Eclogues, in which poets took the place of the shepherds. But nobody has yet written anything called Wall Street Eclogues, in which millionaires should take the place of the poets. And the reason is that there is a real if only a recurrent yearning for that sort of simplicity; and there is never that sort of yearning for that sort of complexity. The key to the mystery of the Merry Peasant is that the peasant often is merry. Those who do not believe it are simply those who do not know anything about him, and therefore do not know which are his times for merriment. Those who do not believe in the shepherd's feast or song are merely ignorant of the shepherd's calendar. The real shepherd is indeed very different from the ideal shepherd, but that is no reason for forgetting the reality at the root of the ideal. It needs a truth to make a tradition. It needs a tradition to make a convention. Pastoral poetry is certainly often a convention, especially in a social decline. It was in a social decline that Watteau shepherds and shepherdesses lounged about the gardens of Versailles. It was also in a social decline that shepherds and shepherdesses continued to pipe and dance through the most faded imitations of Virgil. But that is no reason for dismissing the dying paganism without ever understanding its life. It is no reason for forgetting that the very word Pagan is the same as the word Peasant. We may say that this art is only artificiality; but it is not a love of the artificial. On the contrary, it is in its very nature only the failure of nature-worship, or the love of the natural.

For the shepherds were dying because their gods were dying. Paganism lived upon poetry; that poetry already considered under the name of mythology. But everywhere, and especially in Italy, it had been a mythology and a poetry rooted in the countryside; and that rustic religion had been largely responsible for the rustic happiness. Only as the whole society grew in age and experience, there began to appear that weakness in all mythology already noted in the chapter under that name. This religion was not quite a religion. In other words, this religion was not quite a reality. It was the young world's riot with images and ideas like a young man's riot with wine or love-making; it was not so much immoral as irresponsible; it had no foresight of the final test of time. Because it was creative to any extent it was credulous to any extent. It belonged to the artistic side of man, yet even considered artistically it had long become overloaded and entangled. The family trees sprung from the seed of Jupiter were a jungle rather than a forest; the claims of the gods and demigods seemed like things to be settled rather by a lawyer or a professional herald than by a poet. But it is needless to say that it was not only in the artistic sense that these things had grown more anarchic. There had appeared in more and more flagrant fashion that flower of evil that is really implicit in the very seed of nature-worship, however natural it may seem. I have said that I do not believe that natural worship necessarily begins with this particular passion; I am not of the De Rougemont school of scientific folk-lore. I do not believe that mythology must begin with eroticism. But I do believe that mythology must end in it. I am quite certain that mythology did end in it. Moreover, not only did the poetry grow more immoral, but the immorality grew more indefensible. Greek vices, oriental vices, hints of the old horrors of the Semitic demons, began to fill the fancies of decaying Rome, swarming like flies on a dung-heap. The psychology of it is really human enough, to anyone who will try that experiment of seeing history from the inside. There comes an hour in the afternoon when the child is tired of 'pretending'; when he is weary of being a robber or a Red Indian. It is then that he torments the cat. There comes a time in the routine of an ordered civilisation when the man is tired at playing at mythology and pretending that a tree is a maiden or that the moon made love to a man. The effect of this staleness is the same everywhere; it is seen in all drug-taking and dram-drinking and every form of the tendency to increase the dose. Men seek stranger sins or more startling obscenities as stimulants to their jaded sense. They seek after mad oriental religions for the same reason. They try to stab their nerves to life, if it were with the knives of the priests of Baal. They are walking in their sleep and try to wake themselves up with nightmares.

At that stage even of paganism therefore the peasant songs and dances sound fainter and fainter in the forest. For one thing the peasant civilisation was fading, or had already faded from the whole countryside. The Empire at the end was organised more and more on that servile system which generally goes with the boast of organisation; indeed it was almost as servile as the modern schemes for the organisation of industry. It is proverbial that what would once have been a peasantry became a mere populace of the town dependent for bread and circuses; which may again suggest to some a mob dependent upon doles and cinemas. In this as in many other respects, the modern return to heathenism has been a return not even to the heathen youth but rather to the heathen old age. But the causes of it were spiritual in both cases; and especially the spirit of paganism had departed with its familiar spirits. The heart had gone out of it with its household gods, who went along with the gods of the garden and the field and the forest. The Old Man of the Forest was too old; he was already dying. It is said truly in a sense that Pan died because Christ was born. It is almost as true in another sense that men knew that Christ was born because Pan was already dead. A void was made by the vanishing of the whole mythology of mankind, which would have asphyxiated like a vacuum if it had not been filled with theology. But the point for the moment is that the mythology could not have lasted like a theology in any case. Theology is thought, whether we agree with it or not. Mythology was never thought, and nobody could really agree with it or disagree with it. It was a mere mood of glamour and when the mood went it could not be recovered. Men not only ceased to believe in the gods, but they realised that they had never believed in them. They had sung their praises; they had danced round their altars. They had played the flute; they had played the fool.

So came the twilight upon Arcady and the last notes of the pipe sound sadly from the beechen grove. In the great Virgilian poems there is already something of the sadness; but the loves and the household gods linger in lovely lines like that which Mr. Belloc took for a test of understanding; *incipe parve puer risu cognoscere matrem.* But with them as with us, the human family itself began to break down under servile organisation and the herding of the towns. The urban mob became enlightened; that is it lost the mental energy that could create myths. All round the circle of the Mediterranean cities the people mourned for the loss of gods and were consoled with gladiators. And meanwhile something similar was happening to that intellectual aristocracy of antiquity that had been walking about and talking at large ever since Socrates and Pythagoras. They began to betray to the world the fact that they were walking in a circle and saying the same thing over and over again. Philosophy began to be a joke; it also began to be a bore. That unnatural simplification of everything into one system or another, which we have noted as the fault of the philosopher, revealed at once its finality and its futility. Everything was virtue or everything was happiness or everything was fate or everything was good or everything was bad; anyhow, everything was everything and there was no more to be said; so they said it. Everywhere the sages had degenerated into sophists; that is, into hired rhetoricians or askers of riddles. It is one of the symptoms of this that the sage begins to turn not only into a sophist but into a magician. A touch of oriental occultism is very much appreciated in the best houses. As the philosopher is already a society entertainer, he may as well also be a conjurer.

Many moderns have insisted on the smallness of that Mediterranean world; and the wider horizons that might have awaited it with the discovery of the other continents. But this is an illusion; one of the many illusions of materialism. The limits that paganism had reached in Europe were the limits of human existence; at its best it had only reached the same limits anywhere else. The Roman stoics did not need any Chinamen to teach them stoicism. The Pythagoreans did not need any Hindus to teach them about recurrence or the simple life or the beauty of being a vegetarian. In so far as they could get these things from the East, they had already got rather too much of them from the East. The Syncretists were as convinced as Theosophists that all religions are really the same. And how else could they have extended philosophy merely by extending geography? It can hardly be proposed that they should learn a purer religion from the Aztecs or sit at the feet of the Incas of Peru. All the rest of the world was a welter of barbarism. It is essential to recognise that the Roman Empire was recognised as the highest achievement of the human race; and also as the broadest. A dreadful secret seemed to be written as in obscure hieroglyphics across those mighty works of marble and stone, those colossal amphitheatres and aqueducts. Man could do no more.

For it was not the message blazed on the Babylonian wall, that one king was found wanting or his one kingdom given to a stranger. It was no such good news as the news of invasion and conquest.

There was nothing left that could conquer Rome; but there was also nothing left that could improve it. It was the strongest thing that was growing weak. It was the best thing that was going to the bad. It is necessary to insist again and again that many civilisations had met in one civilisation of the Mediterranean sea; that it was already universal with a stale and sterile universality. The peoples had pooled their resources and still there was not enough. The empires had gone into partnership and they were still bankrupt. No philosopher who was really philosophical could think anything except that, in that central sea, the wave of the world had risen to its highest, seeming to touch the stars. But the wave was already stooping; for it was only the wave of the world.

That mythology and that philosophy into which paganism has already been analysed had thus both of them been drained most literally to the dregs. If with the multiplication of magic the third department, which we have called the demons, was even increasingly active, it was never anything but destructive. There remains only the fourth element or rather the first; that which had been in a sense forgotten because it was the first. I mean the primary and overpowering yet impalpable impression that the universe after all has one origin and one aim; and because it has an aim must have an author. What became of this great truth in the background of men's minds, at this time, it is perhaps more difficult to determine. Some of the Stoics undoubtedly saw it more and more clearly as the clouds of mythology cleared and thinned away; and great men among them did much even to the last to lay the foundations of a concept of the moral unity of the world. The Jews still held their secret certainty of it jealously behind high fences of exclusiveness; yet it is intensely characteristic of the society and the situation that some fashionable figures, especially fashionable ladies, actually embraced Judaism. But in the case of many others I fancy there entered at this point a new negation. Atheism became really possible in that abnormal time; for atheism is abnormality. It is not merely the denial of a dogma. It is the reversal of a subconscious assumption in the soul; the sense that there is a meaning and a direction in the world it sees. Lucretius, the first evolutionist who endeavored to substitute Evolution for God, had already dangled before men's eyes his dance of glittering atoms, by which he conceived cosmos as created by chaos. But it was not his strong poetry or his sad philosophy, as I fancy, that made it possible for men to entertain such a vision. It was something in the sense of impotence and despair with which men shook their fists vainly at the stars, as they saw all the best work of humanity sinking slowly and helplessly into a swamp. They could easily believe that even creation itself was not a creation but a perpetual fall, when they saw that the weightiest and worthiest of all human creations was falling by its own weight. They could fancy that all the stars were falling stars; and that the very pillars of their own solemn porticos were bowed under a sort of gradual Deluge. To men in that mood there was a reason for atheism that is in some sense reasonable. Mythology might fade and philosophy might stiffen; but if behind these things there was a reality, surely that reality might have sustained things as they sank. There was no God; if there had been a God, surely this was the very moment when He would have moved and saved the world.

The life of the great civilisation went on with dreary industry and even with dreary festivity. It was the end of the world, and the worst of it was that it need never end. A convenient compromise had been made between all the multitudinous myths and religions of the Empire; that each group should worship freely and merely give a sort of official flourish of thanks to the tolerant Emperor, by tossing a little incense to him under his official title of Divus. Naturally there was no difficulty about that; or rather it was a long time before the world realised that there ever had been even a trivial difficulty anywhere. The members of some Eastern sect or secret society or other seemed to have made a scene somewhere; nobody could imagine why. The incident occurred once or twice again and began to arouse irritation out of proportion to its insignificance. It was not exactly what these provincials said; though of course it sounded queer enough. They seemed to be saying that God was dead and that they themselves had seen him die. This might be one of the many manias produced by the despair of the age; only they did not seem particularly despairing. They seem quite unnaturally joyful about it, and gave the reason that the death of God had allowed them to eat him and drink his blood. According to other accounts God was not exactly dead after all; there trailed through the bewildered imagination some sort of fantastic procession of the funeral of God, at which the sun turned black, but which ended with the dead omnipotence breaking out of the tomb and rising again like the sun. But it was not the strange story to which anybody paid any particular attention; people in that world had seen queer religions enough to fill a madhouse. It was something in the tone of the madmen and their type of formation. They were a scratch company of barbarians and slaves and poor and unimportant people; but their formation was military; they moved together and were very absolute about who and what was really a part of their little system; and about what they said, however mildly, there was a ring like iron. Men used to many mythologies and moralities could make no analysis of the mystery, except the curious conjecture that they meant what they said. All attempts to make them see reason in the perfectly simple matter of the Emperor's statue seemed to be spoken to deaf men. It was as if a new meteoric metal had fallen on the earth; it was a difference of substance to the touch. Those who touched their foundation fancied they had struck a rock.

With a strange rapidity, like the changes of a dream, the proportions of things seemed to change in their presence. Before most men knew what had happened, these few men were palpably present. They were important enough to be ignored. People became suddenly silent about them and walked stiffly past them. We see a new scene, in which the world has drawn its skirts away from these men and women and they stand in the centre of a great space like lepers. The scene changes again and the great space where they stand is overhung on every side with a cloud of witnesses, interminable terraces full of faces looking down towards them intently; for strange things are happening to them. New tortures have been invented for the madmen who have brought good news. That sad and weary society seems almost to find a new energy in establishing its first religious persecution. Nobody yet knows very clearly why that level world has thus lost its balance about the people in its midst; but they stand unnaturally still while the arena and the world seem to revolve round them. And there shone on them in that dark hour a light that has never been darkened; a white fire clinging to that group like an unearthly phosphorescence, blazing its track through the twilights of history and confounding every effort to confound it with the mists of mythology and theory; that shaft of light or lightning by which the world itself has struck and isolated and crowned it; by which its own enemies have made it more illustrious and its own critics have made it more inexplicable; the halo of hatred around the Church of God.

PART II

On The Man Called Christ

I

THE GOD IN THE CAVE

This sketch of the human story began in a cave; the cave which popular science associates with the cave-man and in which practical discovery has really found archaic drawings of animals. The second half of human history, which was like a new creation of the world, also begins in a cave. There is even a shadow of such a fancy in the fact that animals were again present; for it was a cave used as a stable by the mountaineers of the uplands about Bethlehem; who still drive their cattle into such holes and caverns at night. It was here that a homeless couple had crept underground with the cattle when the doors of the crowded caravanserai had been shut in their faces; and it was here beneath the very feet of the passers-by, in a cellar under the very floor of the world, that Jesus Christ was born. But in that second creation there was indeed something symbolical in the roots of the primeval rock or the horns of the prehistoric herd. God also was a Cave-Man, and had also traced strange shapes of creatures, curiously coloured, upon the wall of the world; but the pictures that he made had come to life.

A mass of legend and literature, which increases and will never end, has repeated and rung the changes on that single paradox; that the hands that had made the sun and stars were too small to reach the huge heads of the cattle. Upon this paradox, we might almost say upon this jest, all the literature of our faith is founded. It is at least like a jest in this; that it is something which the scientific critic cannot see. He laboriously explains the difficulty which we have always defiantly and almost derisively exaggerated; and mildly condemns as improbable something that we have almost madly exalted as incredible; as something that would be much too good to be true, except that it is true. When that contrast between the cosmic creation and the little local infancy has been repeated, reiterated, underlined, emphasised, exulted in, sung, shouted, roared, not to say howled, in a hundred thousand hymns, carols, rhymes, rituals, pictures, poems, and popular sermons, it may be suggested that we hardly need a higher critic to draw our attention to something a little odd about it; especially one of the sort that seems to take a long time to see a joke, even his own joke. But about this contrast and combination of ideas one thing may be said here, because it is relevant to the whole thesis of this book. The sort of modern critic of whom I speak is generally much impressed with the importance of education in life and the importance of psychology in education. That sort of man is never tired of telling us that first impressions fix character by the law of causation; and he will become quite nervous if a child's visual sense is poisoned by the wrong colours on a golliwog or his nervous system prematurely shaken by a cacophonous rattle. Yet he will think us very narrow-minded, if we say that this is exactly why there really is a difference between being brought up as a Christian and being brought up as a Jew or a Moslem or an atheist. The difference is that every Catholic child has learned from pictures, and even every Protestant child from stories, this incredible combination of contrasted ideas as one of the very first impressions on his mind. It is not merely a theological difference. It is a psychological difference which can outlast any theologies. It really is, as that sort of scientist loves to say about anything, incurable. Any agnostic or atheist whose childhood has known a real Christmas has ever afterwards, whether he likes it or not, an association in his mind between two ideas that most of mankind must regard as remote from each other; the idea of a baby and the idea of unknown strength that sustains the stars. His instincts and imagination can still connect them, when his reason can no longer see the need of the connection; for him there will always be some savour of religion about the mere picture of a mother and a baby; some hint of mercy and softening about the mere mention of the dreadful name of God. But the two ideas are not naturally or necessarily combined. They would not be necessarily combined for an ancient Greek or a Chinaman, even for Aristotle or Confucius. It is no more inevitable to connect God with an infant than to connect gravitation with a kitten. It has been created in our minds by Christmas because we are Christians; because we are psychological Christians even when we are not theological ones. In other words, this combination of ideas has emphatically, in the much disputed phrase, altered human nature. There is really a difference between the man who knows it and the man who does not. It may not be a difference of moral worth, for the Moslem or the Jew might be worthier according to his lights; but it is a plain fact about the crossing of two particular lights, the conjunction of two stars in our particular horoscope. Omnipotence and impotence, or divinity and infancy, do definitely make a sort of epigram which a million repetitions cannot turn into a platitude. It is not unreasonable to call it unique. Bethlehem is emphatically a place where extremes meet.

Here begins, it is needless to say, another mighty influence for the humanisation of Christendom. If the world wanted what is called a non-controversial aspect of Christianity, it would probably select Christmas. Yet it is obviously bound up with what is supposed to be a controversial aspect (I could never at any stage of my opinions imagine why); the respect paid to the Blessed Virgin. When I was a boy a more Puritan generation objected to a statue upon my parish church representing the Virgin and Child. After much controversy, they compromised by taking away the Child. One would think that this was even more corrupted with Mariolatry, unless the mother was counted less dangerous when deprived of a sort of weapon. But the practical difficulty is also a parable. You cannot chip away the statue of a mother from all round that of a new-born child. You cannot suspend the new-born child in mid-air; indeed you cannot really have a statue of a new-born child at all. Similarly, you cannot suspend the idea of a new-born child in the void or think of him without thinking of his mother. You cannot visit the child without visiting the mother; you cannot in common human life approach the child except through the mother. If we are to think of Christ in this aspect at all, the other idea follows as it is followed in history. We must either leave Christ out of Christmas, or Christmas out of Christ, or we must admit, if only as we admit it in an old picture, that those holy heads are too near together for the haloes not to mingle and cross.

It might be suggested, in a somewhat violent image, that nothing had happened in that fold or crack in the great grey hills except that the whole universe had been turned inside out. I mean that all the eyes of wonder and worship which had been turned outwards to the largest thing were now turned inward to the smallest. The very image will suggest all that multitudinous marvel of converging eyes that makes so much of the coloured Catholic imagery like a peacock's tail. But it is true in a sense that God who had been only a circumference was seen as a centre; and a centre is infinitely small. It is true that the spiritual spiral henceforward works inwards instead of outwards, and in that sense is centripetal and not centrifugal. The faith becomes, in more ways than one, a religion of little things. But its traditions in art and literature and popular fable have quite sufficiently attested, as has been said, this particular paradox of the divine being in the cradle. Perhaps they have not so clearly emphasised the significance of the divine being in the cave. Curiously enough, indeed, tradition has not very clearly emphasised the cave. It is a familiar fact that the Bethlehem scene has been represented in every possible setting of time and country, of landscape and architecture; and it is a wholly happy and admirable fact that men have conceived it as quite different according to their different individual traditions and tastes. But while all have realised that it was a stable, not so many have realised that it was a cave. Some critics have even been so silly as to suppose that there was some contradiction between the stable and the cave; in which case they cannot know much about caves or stables in Palestine. As they see differences that are not there, it is needless to add that they do not see differences that are there. When a well-known critic says, for instance, that Christ being born in a rocky cavern is like Mithras having sprung alive out of a rock, it sounds like a parody upon comparative religion. There is such a thing as the point of a story, even if it is a story in the sense of a lie. And the notion of a hero appearing, like Pallas from the brain of Zeus, mature and without a mother, is obviously the very opposite of the idea of a god being born like an ordinary baby and entirely dependent on a mother. Whichever ideal we might prefer, we should surely see that they are contrary ideals. It is as stupid to connect them because they both contain a substance called stone as to identify the punishment of the Deluge with the baptism in the Jordan because they both contain a substance called water. Whether as a myth or a mystery, Christ was obviously conceived as born in a hole in the rocks primarily because it marked the position of one outcast and homeless. Nevertheless it is true, as I have said, that the cave has not been so commonly or so clearly used as a symbol as the other realities that surrounded the first Christmas.

And the reason for this also refers to the very nature of that new world. It was in a sense the difficulty of a new dimension. Christ was not only born on the level of the world, but even lower than the world. The first act of the divine drama was enacted, not only on no stage set up above the sight-seer, but on a dark and curtained stage sunken out of sight; and that is an idea very difficult to express in most modes of artistic expression. It is the idea of simultaneous happenings on different levels of life. Something like it might have been attempted in the more archaic and decorative medieval art. But the more the artists learned of realism and perspective, the less they could depict at once the angels in the heavens and the shepherds on the hills, and the glory in the darkness that was under the hills. Perhaps it could have been best conveyed by the characteristic expedient of some of the medieval guilds, when they wheeled about the streets a theatre with three stages one above the other, with heaven above the earth and hell under the earth. But in the riddle of Bethlehem it was heaven that was under the earth.

There is in that alone the touch of a revolution, as of the world turned upside down. It would be vain to attempt to say anything adequate, or anything new, about the change which this conception of a deity born like an outcast or even an outlaw had upon the whole conception of law and its duties to the poor and outcast. It is profoundly true to say that after that moment there could be no slaves. There could be and were people bearing that legal title, until the Church was strong enough to weed them out, but there could be no more of the pagan repose in the mere advantage to the state of keeping it a servile state. Individuals became important, in a sense in which no instruments can be important. A man could not be a means to an end, at any rate to any other man's end. All this popular and fraternal element in the story has been rightly attached by tradition to the episode of the Shepherds; the hinds who found themselves talking face to face with the princes of heaven. But there is another aspect of the popular element as represented by the shepherds which has not perhaps been so fully developed; and which is more directly relevant here.

Men of the people, like the shepherds, men of the popular tradition, had everywhere been the makers of the mythologies. It was they who had felt most directly, with least check or chill from philosophy or the corrupt cults of civilisation, the need we have already considered; the images that were adventures of the imagination; the mythology that was a sort of search; the tempting and tantalising hints of something half-human in nature; the dumb significance of seasons and special places. They had best understood that the soul of a landscape is a story and the soul of a story is a personality. But rationalism had already begun to rot away these really irrational though imaginative treasures of the peasant; even as systematic slavery had eaten the peasant out of house and home. Upon all such peasantries everywhere there was descending a dusk and twilight of disappointment, in the hour when these few men discovered what they sought. Everywhere else Arcadia was fading from the forest. Pan was dead and the shepherds were scattered like sheep. And though no man knew it, the hour was near which was to end and to fulfil all things; and though no man heard it, there was one far-off cry in an unknown tongue upon the heaving wilderness of the mountains. The shepherds had found their Shepherd.

And the thing they found was of a kind with the things they sought. The populace had been wrong in many things; but they had not been wrong in believing that holy things could have a habitation and that divinity need not disdain the limits of time and space. And the barbarian who conceived the crudest fancy about the sun being stolen and hidden in a box, or the wildest myth about the god being rescued and his enemy deceived with a stone, was nearer to the secret of the cave and knew more about the crisis of the world, than all those in the circle of cities round the Mediterranean who had become content with cold abstractions or cosmopolitan generalisations;

than all those who were spinning thinner and thinner threads of thought out of the transcendentalism of Plato or the orientalism of Pythagoras. The place that the shepherds found was not an academy or an abstract republic; it was not a place of myths allegorised or dissected or explained or explained away. It was a place of dreams come true. Since that hour no mythologies have been made in the world. Mythology is a search.

We all know that the popular presentation of this popular story, in so many miracle plays and carols, has given to the shepherds the costumes, the language, and the landscape of the separate English and European countrysides. We all know that one shepherd will talk in a Somerset dialect or another talk of driving his sheep from Conway towards Clyde. Most of us know by this time how true is that error, how wise, how artistic, how intensely Christian and Catholic is that anachronism. But some who have seen it in these scenes of medieval rusticity have perhaps not seen it in another sort of poetry, which it is sometimes the fashion to call artificial rather than artistic. I fear that many modern critics will see only a faded classicism in the fact that men like Crashaw[1] and Herrick[2] conceived the shepherds of Bethlehem under the form of the shepherds of Virgil. Yet they were profoundly right; and in turning their Bethlehem play into a Latin Eclogue they took up one of the most important links in human history. Virgil, as we have already seen, does stand for all that saner heathenism that had over-thrown the insane heathenism of human sacrifice; but the very fact that even the Virgilian virtues and the sane heathenism were in incurable decay is the whole problem to which the revelation to the shepherds is the solution. If the world had ever had the chance to grow weary of being demoniac, it might have been healed merely by becoming sane. But if it had grown weary even of being sane, what was to happen, except what did happen? Nor is it false to conceive the Arcadian

[1] Richard Crashaw (1612–1649) was a metaphysical poet who combined mysticism with sensuality. A convert from Puritanism to Catholicism, he is most famous for his religious poems.

[2] Robert Herrick (1591–1674) was the greatest of the Cavalier poets, a disciple of Ben Jonson.

shepherd of the Eclogues as rejoicing in what did happen. One of the Eclogues has even been claimed as a prophecy of what did happen. But it is quite as much in the tone and incidental diction of the great poet that we feel the potential sympathy with the great event; and even in their own human phrases the voices of the Virgilian shepherds might more than once have broken upon more than the tenderness of Italy. . . . *Incipe, parve puer, risu cognoscere matrem.* . . . They might have found in that strange place all that was best in the last traditions of the Latins; and something better than a wooden idol standing up for ever for the pillar of the human family; a household god. But they and all the other mythologists would be justified in rejoicing that the event had fulfilled not merely the mysticism but the materialism of mythology. Mythology had many sins; but it had not been wrong in being as carnal as the Incarnation. With something of the ancient voice that was supposed to have rung through the groves, it could cry again, 'We have seen, he hath seen us, a visible god.' So the ancient shepherds might have danced, and their feet have been beautiful upon the mountains, rejoicing over the philosophers. But the philosophers had also heard.

It is still a strange story, though an old one, how they came out of orient lands, crowned with the majesty of kings and clothed with something of the mystery of magicians. That truth that is tradition has wisely remembered them almost as unknown quantities, as mysterious as their mysterious and melodious names; Melchior, Caspar, Balthazar. But there came with them all that world of wisdom that had watched the stars in Chaldea and the sun in Persia; and we shall not be wrong if we see in them the same curiosity that moves all the sages. They would stand for the same human ideal if their names had really been Confucius or Pythagoras or Plato. They were those who sought not tales but the truth of things; and since their thirst for truth was itself a thirst for God, they also have had their reward. But even in order to understand that reward, we must understand that for philosophy as much as mythology, that reward was the completion of the incomplete.

Such learned men would doubtless have come, as these learned men did come, to find themselves confirmed in much that was true in their own traditions and right in their own reasoning. Confucius would have found a new foundation for the family in the very reversal of the Holy

Family; Buddha would have looked upon a new renunciation, of stars rather than jewels and divinity than royalty. These learned men would still have the right to say, or rather a new right to say, that there was truth in their old teaching. But after all these learned men would have come to learn. They would have come to complete their conceptions with something they had not yet conceived; even to balance their imperfect universe with something they might once have contradicted. Buddha would have come from his impersonal paradise to worship a person. Confucius would have come from his temples of ancestor-worship to worship a child.

We must grasp from the first this character in the new cosmos; that it was larger than the old cosmos. In that sense Christendom is larger than creation; as creation had been before Christ. It included things that had not been there; it also included the things that had been there. The point happens to be well illustrated in this example of Chinese piety, but it would be true of other pagan virtues or pagan beliefs. Nobody can doubt that a reasonable respect for parents is part of a gospel in which God himself was subject in childhood to earthly parents. But the other sense in which the parents were subject to him does introduce an idea that is not Confucian. The infant Christ is not like the infant Confucius; our mysticism conceives him in an immortal infancy. I do not know what Confucius would have done with the Bambino, had it come to life in his arms as it did in the arms of St. Francis. But this is true in relation to all the other religions and philosophies; it is the challenge of the Church. The Church contains what the world does not contain. Life itself does not provide as she does for all sides of life. That every other single system is narrow and insufficient compared to this one; that is not a rhetorical boast; it is a real fact and a real dilemma. Where is the Holy Child amid the Stoics and the ancestor-worshippers? Where is Our Lady of the Moslems, a woman made for no man and set above all angels? Where is St. Michael of the monks of Buddha, rider and master of the trumpets, guarding for every soldier the honour of the sword? What could St. Thomas Aquinas do with the mythology of Brahminism, he who set forth all the science and rationality and even rationalism of Christianity? Yet even if we compare Aquinas with Aristotle, at the other extreme of reason, we shall find the same sense of something added. Aquinas could understand the most logical parts of Aristotle; it is doubtful if Aristotle could have understood the most mystical parts of Aquinas. Even where we can hardly call the Christian greater, we are forced to call him larger. But it is so to whatever philosophy or heresy or modern movement we may turn. How would Francis the Troubadour have fared among the Calvinists, or for that matter among the Utilitarians of the Manchester School? Yet men like Bossuet and Pascal could be as stern and logical as any Calvinist or Utilitarian. How would St. Joan of Arc, a woman waving on men to war with the sword, have fared among the Quakers or the Doukhabors[3] or the Tolstoyan sect of pacifists? Yet any number of Catholic saints have spent their lives in preaching peace and preventing wars. It is the same with all the modern attempts at Syncretism. They are never able to make something larger than the Creed without leaving something out. I do not mean leaving out something divine but something human; the flag or the inn or the boy's tale of battle or the hedge at the end of the field. The Theosophists build a pantheon; but it is only a pantheon for pantheists. They call a Parliament of Religions as a reunion of all the peoples; but it is only a reunion of all the prigs. Yet exactly such a pantheon had been set up two thousand years before by the shores of the Mediterranean; and Christians were invited to set up the image of Jesus side by side with the image of Jupiter, of Mithras, of Osiris, of Atys, or of Ammon. It was the refusal of the Christians that was the turning-point of history. If the Christians had accepted, they and the whole world would have certainly, in a grotesque but exact metaphor, gone to pot. They would all have been boiled down to one lukewarm liquid in that great pot of cosmopolitan corruption in which all the other myths and mysteries were already melting. It was an awful and an appalling escape. Nobody understands the nature of the Church, or the ringing note of the creed descending from antiquity, who does not realise that the whole world once very nearly died of broadmindedness and the brotherhood of all religions.

Here it is the important point that the Magi, who stand for mysticism and philosophy, are truly conceived as seeking something

[3] A Russian sect originating in the eighteenth century emphasizing the supreme authority of inner experience and rejecting all ecclesiastical and civil authority.

new and even as finding something unexpected. That tense sense of crisis which still tingles in the Christmas story and even in every Christmas celebration, accentuates the idea of a search and a discovery. The discovery is, in this case, truly a scientific discovery. For the other mystical figures in the miracle play; for the angel and the mother, the shepherds and the soldiers of Herod, there may be aspects both simpler and more supernatural, more elemental or more emotional. But the wise Men must be seeking wisdom; and for them there must be a light also in the intellect. And this is the light; that the Catholic creed is catholic and that nothing else is catholic. The philosophy of the Church is universal. The philosophy of the philosophers was not universal. Had Plato and Pythagoras and Aristotle stood for an instant in the light that came out of that little cave, they would have known that their own light was not universal. It is far from certain, indeed, that they did not know it already. Philosophy also, like mythology, had very much the air of a search. It is the realisation of this truth that gives its traditional majesty and mystery to the figures of the Three Kings; the discovery that religion is broader than philosophy and that this is the broadest of religions, contained within this narrow space. The Magicians were gazing at the strange pentacle with the human triangle reversed; and they have never come to the end of their calculations about it. For it is the paradox of that group in the cave, that while our emotions about it are of childish simplicity, our thoughts about it can branch with a never-ending complexity. And we can never reach the end even of our own ideas about the child who was a father and the mother who was a child.

We might well be content to say that mythology had come with the shepherds and philosophy with the philosophers; and that it only remained for them to combine in the recognisation of religion. But there was a third element that must not be ignored and one which that religion for ever refuses to ignore, in any revel or reconciliation. There was present in the primary scenes of the drama that Enemy that had rotted the legends with lust and frozen theories into atheism, but which answered the direct challenge with something of that more direct method which we have seen in the conscious cult of the demons. In the description of that demon-worship, of the devouring detestation of innocence shown in the works of its witchcraft and the most inhuman of its human sacrifice, I have said less of its indirect and secret penetration of the saner paganism; the soaking of mythological imagination with sex; the rise of imperial pride into insanity. But both the indirect and the direct influence make themselves felt in the drama of Bethlehem. A ruler under the Roman suzerainty, probably equipped and surrounded with the Roman ornament and order though himself of eastern blood, seems in that hour to have felt stirring within him the spirit of strange things. We all know the story of how Herod, alarmed at some rumour of a mysterious rival, remembered the wild gesture of the capricious despots of Asia and ordered a massacre of suspects of the new generation of the populace. Everyone knows the story; but not everyone has perhaps noted its place in the story of the strange religions of men. Not everybody has seen the significance even of its very contrast with the Corinthian columns and Roman pavement of that conquered and superficially civilised world. Only, as the purpose in his dark spirit began to show and shine in the eyes of the Idumean, a seer might perhaps have seen something like a great grey ghost that looked over his shoulder; have seen behind him filling the dome of night and hovering for the last time over history, that vast and fearful face that was Moloch of the Carthaginians; awaiting his last tribute from a ruler of the races of Shem. The demons also, in that first festival of Christmas, feasted after their own fashion.

Unless we understand the presence of that enemy, we shall not only miss the point of Christianity, but even miss the point of Christmas. Christmas for us in Christendom has become one thing, and in one sense even a simple thing. But like all the truths of that tradition, it is in another sense a very complex thing. Its unique note is the simultaneous striking of many notes; of humility, of gaiety, of gratitude, of mystical fear, but also of vigilance and of drama. It is not only an occasion for the peacemakers any more than for the merry-makers; it is not only a Hindu peace conference any more than it is only a Scandinavian winter feast. There is something defiant in it also; something that makes the abrupt bells at midnight sound like the great guns of a battle that has just been won. All this indescribable thing that we call the Christmas atmosphere only hangs in the air as something like a lingering fragrance or fading vapour from the exultant explosion of that one hour in the Judean hills nearly two thousand years ago. But the savour is still unmistakable, and it is something too subtle or too solitary to be covered by our use of the word peace. By the very nature of the story the rejoicings in the cavern were rejoicings in a fortress or an outlaw's den; properly understood it is not unduly flippant to say they were rejoicings in a dug-out. It is not only true that such a subterranean chamber was a hiding-place from enemies; and that the enemies were already scouring the stony plain that lay above it like a sky. It is not only that the very horse-hoofs of Herod might in that sense have passed like thunder over the sunken head of Christ. It is also that there is in that image a true idea of an outpost, of a piercing through the rock and an entrance into an enemy territory. There is in this buried divinity an idea of *undermining* the world; of shaking the towers and palaces from below; even as Herod the great king felt that earthquake under him and swayed with his swaying palace.

That is perhaps the mightiest of the mysteries of the cave. It is already apparent that though men are said to have looked for hell under the earth, in this case it is rather heaven that is under the earth. And there follows in this strange story the idea of an upheaval of heaven. That is the paradox of the whole position; that henceforth the highest thing can only work from below. Royalty can only return to its own by a sort of rebellion. Indeed the Church from its beginnings, and perhaps especially in its beginnings, was not so much a principality as a revolution against the prince of the world. This sense that the world had been conquered by the great usurper, and was in his possession, has been much deplored or derided by those optimists who identify enlightenment with ease. But it was responsible for all that thrill of defiance and a beautiful danger that made the good news seem to be really both good and new. It was in truth against a huge unconscious usurpation that it raised a revolt, and originally so obscure a revolt. Olympus still occupied the sky like a motionless cloud moulded into many mighty forms; philosophy still sat in the high places and even on the thrones of the kings, when Christ was born in the cave and Christianity in the catacombs. In both cases we may remark the same paradox of revolution; the sense of something despised and of something feared. The cave in one aspect is only a hole or corner into which the outcasts are swept like rubbish; yet in the other aspect it is a hiding-place of something valuable which the tyrants are seeking like treasure. In one sense they are there because the innkeeper would not even remember them, and in another because the king can never forget them. We have already noted that this paradox appeared also in the treatment of the early Church. It was important while it was still insignificant, and certainly while it was still impotent. It was important solely because it was intolerable; and in that sense it is true to say that it was intolerable because it was intolerant. It was resented, because, in its own still and almost secret way, it had declared war. It had risen out of the ground to wreck the heaven and earth of heathenism. It did not try to destroy all that creation of gold and marble; but it contemplated a world without it. It dared to look right through it as though the gold and marble had been glass. Those who charged the Christians with burning down Rome with firebrands were slanderers; but they were at least far nearer to the nature of Christianity than those among the moderns who tell us that the Christians were a sort of ethical society, being martyred in a languid fashion for telling men they had a duty to their neighbors, and only mildly disliked because they were meek and mild.

Herod had his place, therefore, in the miracle play of Bethlehem because he is the menace to the Church Militant and shows it from the first as under persecution and fighting for its life. For those who think this a discord, it is a discord that sounds simultaneously with the Christmas bells. For those who think the idea of the Crusade is one that spoils the idea of the Cross, we can only say that for them the idea of the Cross is spoiled; the idea of the Cross is spoiled quite literally in the cradle. It is not here to the purpose to argue with them on the abstract ethics of fighting; the purpose in this place is merely to sum up the combination of ideas that make up the Christian and Catholic idea, and to note that all of them are already crystallised in the first Christmas story. They are three distinct and commonly contrasted things which are nevertheless one thing; but this is the only thing which can make them one. The first is the human instinct for a heaven that shall be as literal and almost as local as a home. It is the idea pursued by all poets and pagans making myths; that a particular place must be the shrine of the god or the abode of the blest; that fairyland is a land; or that the return of the ghost must be the resurrection of the body. I do not here reason about the refusal of rationalism to satisfy this need. I only say that if the rationalists refuse to satisfy it, the pagans will not be satisfied. This is present in the story of Bethlehem and Jerusalem as it is present in the story of Delos and Delphi; and as it is *not* present in the whole universe of Lucretius or the whole universe of Herbert Spencer. The second element is a philosophy *larger* than other philosophies; larger than that of Lucretius and infinitely larger than that of Herbert Spencer. It looks at the world through a hundred windows where the ancient stoic or the modern agnostic only looks through one. It sees life with thousands of eyes belonging to thousands of different sorts of people, where the other is only the individual standpoint of a stoic or an agnostic. It has something for all moods of man, it finds work for all kinds of men, it understands secrets of psychology, it is aware of depths of evil, it is able to distinguish between real and unreal marvels and miraculous exceptions, it trains itself in tact about hard cases, all with a multiplicity and subtlety and imagination about the varieties of life which is far beyond the bald or breezy platitudes of most ancient or modern moral philosophy. In a word, there is more in it; it finds more in existence to think about; it gets more out of life. Masses of this material about our many-sided life have been added since the time of St. Thomas Aquinas. But St. Thomas Aquinas alone would have found himself limited in the world of Confucius or of Comte. And the third point is this; that while it is local enough for poetry and larger than any other philosophy, it is also a challenge and a fight. While it is deliberately broadened to embrace every aspect of truth, it is still stiffly embattled against every mode of error. It gets every kind of man to fight for it, it gets every kind of weapon to fight with, it widens its knowledge of the things that are fought for and against with every art of curiosity or sympathy; but it never forgets that it is fighting. It proclaims peace on earth and never forgets why there was war in heaven.

This is the trinity of truths symbolised here by the three types in the old Christmas story; the shepherds and the kings and that other king who warred upon the children. It is simply not true to say that other religions and philosophies are in this respect its rivals. It is not true to say that any one of them combines these characters; it is not true to say that any one of them pretends to combine them. Buddhism may profess to be equally mystical; it does not even profess to be equally military. Islam may profess to be equally military; it does not even profess to be equally metaphysical and subtle. Confucianism may profess to satisfy the need of the philosophers for order and reason; it does not even profess to satisfy the need of the mystics for miracle and sacrament and the consecration of concrete things. There are many evidences of this presence of a spirit at once universal and unique. One will serve here which is the symbol of the subject of this chapter; that no other story, no pagan legend or philosophical anecdote or historical event, does in fact affect any of us with that peculiar and even poignant impression produced on us by the word Bethlehem. No other birth of a god or childhood of a sage seems to us to be Christmas or anything like Christmas. It is either too cold or too frivolous, or too formal and classical, or too simple and savage, or too occult and complicated. Not one of us, whatever his opinions, would ever go to such a scene with the sense that he was going home. He might admire it because it was poetical, or because it was philosophical, or any number of other things in separation; but not because it was itself. The truth is that there is a quite peculiar and individual character about the hold of this story on human nature; it is not in its psychological substance at all like a mere legend or the life of a great man. It does not exactly in the ordinary sense turn our minds to greatness; to those extensions and exaggerations of humanity which are turned into gods and heroes, even by the healthiest sort of hero-worship. It does not exactly work outwards, adventurously, to the wonders to be found at the ends of the earth. It is rather something that surprises us from behind, from the hidden and personal part of our being; like that which can sometimes take us off our guard in the pathos of small objects or the blind pieties of the poor. It is rather as if a man had found an inner room in the very heart of his own house, which he had never suspected; and seen a light from within. It is as if he found something at the back of his own heart that betrayed him into good. It is not made of what the world would call strong materials; or rather it is made of materials whose strength is in that winged levity with which they brush us and pass. It is all that is in us but a brief tenderness that is there made eternal; all that means no more than a momentary softening that is in some strange fashion become a strengthening and a repose; it is the broken speech and the lost word that are made positive and suspended unbroken; as the strange kings fade into a far country and the mountains resound no more with the feet of the shepherds; and only the night and the cavern lie in fold upon fold over something more human than humanity.

II

THE RIDDLES OF THE GOSPEL

To understand the nature of this chapter, it is necessary to recur to the nature of this book. The argument which is meant to be the backbone of the book is of the kind called the *reductio ad absurdum*. It suggests that the results of assuming the rationalist thesis are more irrational than ours; but to prove it we must assume that thesis. Thus in the first section I often treated man as merely an animal, to show that the effect was more impossible than if he were treated as an angel. In the sense in which it was necessary to treat man merely as an animal, it is necessary to treat Christ merely as a man. I have to suspend my own beliefs, which are much more positive; and assume this limitation even in order to remove it. I must try to imagine what would happen to a man who did really read the story of Christ as the story of a man; and even of a man of whom he had never heard before. And I wish to point out that a really impartial reading of that kind would lead, if not immediately to belief, at least to a bewilderment of which there is really no solution except in belief. In this chapter, for this reason, I shall bring in nothing of the spirit of my own creed; I shall exclude the very style of diction, and even of lettering, which I should think fitting in speaking in my own person. I am speaking as an imaginary heathen human being, honestly, staring at the Gospel story for the first time.

Now it is not at all easy to regard the New Testament as a New Testament. It is not at all easy to realise the good news as new. Both for good and evil familiarity fills us with assumptions and associations; and no man of our civilisation, whatever he thinks of our religion, can really read the thing as if he had never heard of it before. Of course it is in any case utterly unhistorical to talk as if the New Testament were a neatly bound book that had fallen from heaven. It is simply the selection made by the authority of the Church from a mass of early Christian literature. But apart from any such question, there is a psychological difficulty in feeling the New Testament as new. There is a psychological difficulty in seeing those well-known words simply as they stand and without going beyond what they intrinsically stand for. And this difficulty must indeed be very great; for the result of it is very curious. The result of it is that most modern critics and most current criticism, even popular criticism, makes a comment that is the exact reverse of the truth. It is so completely the reverse of the truth that one could almost suspect that they had never read the New Testament at all.

We have all heard people say a hundred times over, for they seem never to tire of saying it, that the Jesus of the New Testament is indeed a most merciful and humane lover of humanity, but that the Church has hidden this human character in repellant dogmas and stiffened it with ecclesiastical terrors till it has taken on an inhuman character. This is, I venture to repeat, very nearly the reverse of the truth. The truth is that it is the image of Christ in the churches that is almost entirely mild and merciful. It is the image of Christ in the Gospels that is a good many other things as well. The figure in the Gospels does indeed utter in words of almost heart-breaking beauty his pity for our broken hearts. But they are very far from being the only sort of words that he utters. Nevertheless they are almost the only kind of words that the Church in its popular imagery ever represents him as uttering. That popular imagery is inspired by a perfectly sound popular instinct. The mass of the poor are broken, and the mass of the people are poor, and for the mass of mankind the main thing is to carry the conviction of the incredible compassion of God. But nobody with his eyes open can doubt that it is chiefly this idea of compassion that the popular machinery of the Church does seek to carry. The popular imagery carries a great deal to excess the sentiment of 'Gentle Jesus, meek and mild.' It is the first thing that the outsider feels and criticises in a Pieta or a shrine of the Sacred Heart. As I say, while the art may be insufficient, I am not sure that the instinct is unsound. In any case there is something appalling, something that makes the blood run cold, in the idea of having a statue of Christ in wrath. There is something insupportable even to the imagination in the idea of turning the corner of a street or coming out into the spaces of a marketplace, to meet the petrifying petrifaction of *that* figure as it turned upon a generation of vipers, or that face as it looked at the face of a hypocrite. The Church can reasonably be justified therefore if she turns the most merciful face or aspect towards men; but it is certainly the most merciful aspect that she does turn. And the point is here that it is very much more specially and exclusively merciful than any impression that could be formed by a man merely reading the New Testament for the first time. A man simply taking the words of the story as they stand would form quite another impression; an impression full of mystery and possibly of inconsistency; but certainly not merely an impression of mildness. It would be intensely interesting; but part of the interest would consist in its leaving a good deal to be guessed at or explained. It is full of sudden gestures evidently significant except that we hardly know what they signify; of enigmatic silences; of ironical replies. The outbreaks of wrath, like storms above our atmosphere, do not seem to break out exactly where we should expect them, but to follow some higher weather-chart of their own. The Peter whom popular Church teaching presents is very rightly the Peter to whom Christ said in forgiveness, 'Feed my lambs.' He is not the Peter upon whom Christ turned as if he were the devil, crying in that obscure wrath, 'Get thee behind me, Satan.' Christ lamented with nothing but love and pity over Jerusalem which was to murder him. We do not know what strange spiritual atmosphere or spiritual insight led him to sink Bethsaida lower in the pit than Sodom. I am putting aside for the moment all questions of doctrinal inferences or expositions, orthodox or otherwise; I am simply imagining the effect on a man's mind if he did really do what these critics are always talking about doing; if he did really read the New Testament without reference to orthodoxy and even without reference to doctrine. He would find a number of things which fit in far less with the current unorthodoxy than they do with the current orthodoxy. He would find, for instance, that if there are any descriptions that deserved to be called realistic, they are precisely the descriptions of the supernatural. If there is one aspect of the New Testament Jesus in which he may be said to present himself eminently as a practical person, it is in the aspect of an exorcist. There is nothing meek and mild, there is nothing even in the ordinary sense mystical, about the tone of the voice that says 'Hold thy peace and come out of him.' It is much more like the tone of a very business-like lion-tamer or a strong-minded doctor dealing with a homicidal maniac. But this is only a side issue for the sake of illustration; I am not now raising these controversies; but considering the case of the imaginary man from the moon to whom the New Testament is new.

Now the first thing to note is that if we take it merely as a human story, it is in some ways a very strange story. I do not refer here to its tremendous and tragic culmination or to any implications involving triumph in that tragedy. I do not refer to what is commonly called the miraculous element; for on that point philosophies vary and modern philosophies very decidedly waver. Indeed the educated Englishman of to-day may be said to have passed from an old fashion, in which he would not believe in any miracles unless they were ancient, and adopted a new fashion in which he will not believe in any miracles unless they are modern. He used to hold that miraculous cures stopped with the first Christians and is now inclined to suspect that they began with the first Christian Scientists. But I refer here rather specially to unmiraculous and even to unnoticed and inconspicuous parts of the story. There are a great many things about it which nobody would have invented, for they are things that nobody has ever made any particular use of; things which if they were remarked at all have remained rather as puzzles. For instance, there is that long stretch of silence in the life of Christ up to the age of thirty. It is of all silences the most immense and imaginatively impressive. But it is not the sort of thing that anybody is particularly likely to invent in order to prove something; and nobody so far as I know has ever tried to prove anything in particular from it. It is impressive, but it is only impressive as a fact; there is nothing particularly popular or obvious about it as a fable. The ordinary trend of hero-worship and myth-making is much more likely to say the precise opposite. It is much more likely to say (as I believe some of the gospels rejected by the Church do say) that Jesus displayed a divine precocity and began his mission at a miraculously early age. And there is indeed something strange in the thought that he who of all humanity needed least preparation seems to have had most. Whether it was some mode of the divine humility, or some truth of which we see the shadow in the longer domestic tutelage of the higher creatures of the earth, I do not propose to speculate; I mention it simply as an example of the sort of thing that does in any case give rise to speculations, quite apart from recognised religious speculations. Now the whole story is full of these things. It is not by any means, as baldly presented in print, a story that it is easy to get to the bottom of. It is anything but what these people talk of as a simple Gospel. Relatively speaking, it is the Gospel that has the mysticism and the Church that has the rationalism. As I should put it, of course, it is the Gospel that is the riddle and the Church that is the answer. But whatever be the answer, the Gospel as it stands is almost a book of riddles.

First, a man reading the Gospel sayings would not find platitudes. If he had read even in the most respectful spirit the majority of ancient philosophers and of modern moralists, he would appreciate the unique importance of saying that he did not find platitudes. It is more than can be said even of Plato. It is much more than can be said of Epictetus or Seneca or Marcus Aurelius or Apollonius of Tyana. And it is immeasurably more than can be said of most of the agnostic moralists and the preachers of the ethical societies; with their songs of service and their religion of brotherhood. The morality of most moralists ancient and modern, has been one solid and polished cataract of platitudes flowing for ever and ever. That would certainly not be the impression of the imaginary independent outsider studying the New Testament. He would be conscious of nothing so commonplace and in a sense of nothing so continuous as that stream. He would find a number of strange claims that might sound like the claim to be the brother of the sun and moon; a number of very startling pieces of advice; a number of stunning rebukes; a number of strangely beautiful stories. He would see some very gigantesque figures of speech about the impossiblility of threading a needle with a camel or the possibility of throwing a mountain into the sea. He would see a number of very daring simplifications of the difficulties of life; like the advice to shine upon everybody indifferently as does the sunshine or not to worry about the future any more than the birds. He would find on the other hand some passages of almost impenetrable darkness, so far as he is concerned, such as the moral of the parable of the Unjust Steward. Some of these things might strike him as fables and some as truths; but none as truisms. For instance, he would not find the ordinary platitudes in favour of peace. He would find several paradoxes in favour of peace. He would find several ideals of non-resistance, which taken as they stand would be rather too pacific for any pacifist. He would be told in one passage to treat a robber *not* with passive resistance, but rather with positive and enthusiastic encouragement, if the terms be taken literally; heaping up gifts upon the man who had stolen goods. But he would not find a word of all that obvious rhetoric against war which has filled countless books and odes and orations; not a word about the wickedness of war, the wastefulness of war, the appalling scale of the slaughter in war and all the rest of the familiar frenzy; indeed not a word about war at all. There is nothing that throws any particular light on Christ's attitude towards organised warfare, except that he seems to have been rather fond of Roman soldiers. Indeed it is another perplexity, speaking from the same external and human standpoint, that he seems to have got on much better with Romans than he did with Jews. But the question here is a certain tone to be appreciated by merely reading a certain text; and we might give any number of instances of it.

The statement that the meek shall inherit the earth is very far from being a meek statement. I mean it is not meek in the ordinary sense of mild and moderate and inoffensive. To justify it, it would be necessary to go very deep into history and anticipate things undreamed of then and by many unrealised even now; such as the way in which the mystical monks reclaimed the lands which the practical kings had lost. If it was a truth at all, it was because it was a prophecy. But certainly it was not a truth in the sense of a truism. The blessing upon the meek would seem to be a very violent statement; in the sense of doing violence to reason and probability. And with this we come to another important stage in the speculation. As a prophecy it really was fulfilled; but it was only fulfilled long afterwards.

The monasteries were the most practical and prosperous estates and experiments in reconstruction after the barbaric deluge; the meek did really inherit the earth. But nobody could have known anything of the sort at the time—unless indeed there was one who knew. Something of the same thing may be said about the incident of Martha and Mary; which has been interpreted in retrospect and from the inside by the mystics of the Christian contemplative life. But it was not at all an obvious view of it; and most moralists, ancient and modern, could be trusted to make a rush for the obvious. What torrents of effortless eloquence would have flowed from them to swell any slight superiority on the part of Martha; what splendid sermons about the Joy of Service and the Gospel of Work and the World Left Better Than We Found It, and generally all the ten thousand platitudes that can be uttered in favour of taking trouble—by people who need take no trouble to utter them. If in Mary the mystic and child of love Christ was guarding the seed of something more subtle, who was likely to understand it at the time? Nobody else could have seen Clare and Catherine and Teresa shining above the little roof at Bethany. It is so in another way with that magnificent menace about bringing into the world a sword to sunder and divide. Nobody could have guessed then either how it could be fulfilled or how it could be justified. Indeed some freethinkers are still so simple as to fall into the trap and be shocked at a phrase so deliberately defiant. They actually complain of the paradox for not being a platitude.

But the point here is that if we *could* read the Gospel reports as things as new as newspaper reports, they would puzzle us and perhaps terrify us much *more* than the same things as developed by historical Christianity. For instance, Christ after a clear allusion to the eunuchs of eastern courts, said there would be eunuchs of the kingdom of heaven. If this does not mean the voluntary enthusiasm of virginity, it could only be made to mean something much more unnatural or uncouth. It is the historical religion that humanises it for us by experience of Franciscans or of Sisters of Mercy. The mere statement standing by itself might very well suggest a rather dehumanised atmosphere; the sinister and inhuman silence of the Asiatic harem and divan. This is but one instance out of scores; but the moral is that the Christ of the Gospel might actually seem more strange and terrible than the Christ of the Church.

I am dwelling on the dark or dazzling or defiant or mysterious side of the Gospel words, not because they had not obviously a more obvious and popular side, but because this is the answer to a common criticism on a vital point. The freethinker frequently says that Jesus of Nazareth was a man of his time, even if he was in advance of his time; and that we cannot accept his ethics as final for humanity. The freethinker then goes on to criticise his ethics, saying plausibly enough that men cannot turn the other cheek, or that they must take thought for the morrow, or that the self-denial is too ascetic or the monogamy too severe. But the Zealots and the Legionaries did not turn the other cheek any more than we do, if so much. The Jewish traders and Roman tax-gatherers took thought for the morrow as much as we, if not more. We cannot pretend to be abandoning the morality of the past for one more suited to the present. It is certainly not the morality of another age, but it might be of another world.

In short, we can say that these ideals are impossible in themselves. Exactly what we cannot say is that they are impossible for us. They are rather notably marked by a mysticism which, if it be a sort of madness, would always have struck the same sort of people as mad. Take, for instance, the case of marriage and the relations of the sexes. It might very well have been true that a Galilean teacher taught things natural to a Galilean environment; but it is not. It might rationally be expected that a man in the time of Tiberius would have advanced a view conditioned by the time of Tiberius; but he did not. What he advanced was something quite different; something very difficult; but something no more difficult now than it was then. When, for instance, Mahomet made his polygamous compromise we may reasonably say that it was conditioned by a polygamous society. When he allowed a man four wives he was really doing something suited to the circumstances, which might have been less suited to other circumstances. Nobody will pretend that the four wives were like the four winds, something seemingly a part of the order of nature; nobody will say that the figure four was written for ever in stars upon the sky. But neither will anyone say that the figure four is an inconceivable ideal; that it is beyond the power of the mind of man to count up to four; or to count the number of his wives and see whether it amounts to four. It is a practical compromise carrying with it the character of a particular society. If Mahomet had been born in Acton in the nineteenth century, we may well doubt whether he would instantly have filled that suburb with harems of four wives apiece. As he was born in Arabia in the sixth century, he did in his conjugal arrangements suggest the conditions of Arabia in the sixth century. But Christ in his view of marriage does not in the least suggest the conditions of Palestine in the first century. He does not suggest anything at all, except the sacramental view of marriage as developed long afterwards by the Catholic Church. It was quite as difficult for people then as for people now. It was much more puzzling to people then than to people now. Jews and Romans and Greeks did not believe, and did not even understand enough to disbelieve, the mystical idea that the man and the woman had become one sacramental substance. We may think it an incredible or impossible ideal; but we cannot think it any more incredible or impossible than they would have thought it. In other words, whatever else is true, it is not true that the controversy has been altered by time. Whatever else is true, it is emphatically not true that the ideas of Jesus of Nazareth were suitable to his time, but are no longer suitable to our time. Exactly how suitable they were to his time is perhaps suggested in the end of his story.

The same truth might be stated in another way by saying that if the story be regarded as merely human and historical, it is extraordinary how very little there is in the recorded words of Christ that ties him at all to his own time. I do not mean the details of a period, which even a man of the period knows to be passing. I mean the fundamentals which even the wisest man often vaguely assumes to be eternal. For instance, Aristotle was perhaps the wisest and most wide-minded man who ever lived. He founded himself entirely upon fundamentals, which have been generally found to remain rational and solid through all social and historical changes. Still, he lived in a world in which it was thought as natural to have slaves as to have children. And therefore he did permit himself a serious recognition of a difference between slaves and free men. Christ as much as Aristotle lived in a world that took slavery for granted. He did not particularly denounce slavery. He started a movement that could exist in a world with slavery. But he started a movement that could exist in a world without slavery. He never used a phrase that made his philosophy depend even upon the very existence of the social order in which he lived. He spoke as one conscious that everything was ephemeral, including the things that Aristotle thought eternal. By that time the Roman Empire had come to be merely the *orbis terrarum*, another name for the world. But he never made his morality dependent on the existence of the Roman Empire or even on the existence of the world. 'Heaven and earth shall pass away; but my words shall not pass away.'

The truth is that when critics have spoken of the local limitations of the Galilean, it has always been a case of the local limitations of the critics. He did undoubtedly believe in certain things that one particular modern sect of materialists do not believe. But they were not things particularly peculiar to his time. It would be nearer the truth to say that the denial of them is quite peculiar to our time. Doubtless it would be nearer still to the truth to say merely that a certain solemn social importance, in the minority disbelieving them, is peculiar to our time. He believed, for instance, in evil spirits or in the psychic healing of bodily ills; but not because he was a Galilean born under Augustus. It is absurd to say that a man believed things because he was a Galilean under Augustus when he might have believed the same things if he had been an Egyptian under Tutenkamen or an Indian under Gengis Khan. But with this general question of the philosophy of diabolism or of divine miracles I deal elsewhere. It is enough to say that the materialists have to prove the impossibility of miracles against the testimony of all mankind, not against the prejudices of provincials in North Palestine under the first Roman Emperors. What they have to prove, for the present argument, is the presence in the Gospels of those particular prejudices of those particular provincials. And, humanly speaking, it is astonishing how little they can produce even to make a beginning of proving it.

So it is in this case of the sacrament of marriage. We may not believe in sacraments, as we may not believe in spirits, but it is quite clear that Christ believed in this sacrament in his own way and not in any current or contemporary way. He certainly did not get his argument against divorce from the Mosaic law or the Roman law or the habits of the Palestinian people. It would appear to his critics then exactly what it appears to his critics now; an arbitrary and transcendental dogma coming from nowhere save in the sense that it came from him. I am not at all concerned here to defend that dogma; the point here is that it is just as easy to defend it now as it was to defend it then. It is an ideal altogether outside time; difficult at any period; impossible at no period. In other words, if anyone says it is what might be expected of a man walking about in that place at that period, we can quite fairly answer that it is much *more* like what might be the mysterious utterance of a being beyond man, if he walked alive among men.

I maintain therefore that a man reading the New Testament frankly and freshly would *not* get the impression of what is now often meant by a human Christ. The merely human Christ is a made-up figure, a piece of artificial selection, like the merely evolutionary man. Moreover there have been too many of these human Christs found in the same story, just as there have been too many keys to mythology found in the same stories. Three or four separate schools of rationalism have worked over the ground and produced three or four equally rational explanations of his life. The first rational explanation of his life was that he never lived. And this in turn gave an opportunity for three or four different explanations; as that he was a sun-myth or a corn-myth, or any other kind of myth that is also a monomania. Then the idea that he was a divine being who did not exist gave place to the idea that he was a human being who did exist. In my youth it was the fashion to say that he was merely an ethical teacher in the manner of the Essenes, who had apparently nothing very much to say that Hillel or a hundred other Jews might not have said; as that it is a kindly thing to be kind and an assistance to purification to be pure. Then somebody said he was a madman with a Messianic delusion. Then others said he was indeed an original teacher because he cared about nothing but Socialism; or (as others said) about nothing but Pacifism. Then a more grimly scientific character appeared who said that Jesus would never have been heard of at all except for his prophecies of the end of the world. He was important merely as a Millennarian like Dr. Cumming; and created a provincial scare by announcing the exact date of the crack of doom. Among other variants on the same theme was the theory that he was a spiritual healer and nothing else; a view implied by Christian Science, which has really to expound a Christianity without the Crucifixion in order to explain the curing of Peter's wife's mother or the daughter of a centurion. There is another theory that concentrates entirely on the business of diabolism and what it would call the contemporary superstition about demoniacs; as if Christ, like a young deacon taking his first orders, had got as far as exorcism and never got any further. Now each of these explanations in itself seems to me singularly inadequate; but taken together they do suggest something of the very mystery which they miss. There must surely have been something not only mysterious but many-sided about Christ if so many smaller Christs can be carved out of him. If the Christian Scientist is satisfied with him as a spiritual healer and the Christian Socialist is satisfied with him as a social reformer, so satisfied that they do not even expect him to be anything else, it looks as if he really covered rather more ground than they could be expected to expect. And it does seem to suggest that there might be more than they fancy in these other mysterious attributes of casting out devils or prophesying doom.

Above all, would not such a new reader of the New Testament stumble over something that would startle him much more than it startles us? I have here more than once attempted the rather impossible task of reversing time and the historic method; and in fancy looking forward to the facts, instead of backward through the memories. So I have imagined the monster that man might have seemed at first to the mere nature around him. We should have a worse shock if we really imagined the nature of Christ named for the first time. What should we feel at the first whisper of a certain suggestion about a certain man? Certainly it is not for us to blame anybody who should find that first wild whisper merely impious and insane. On the contrary, stumbling on that rock of scandal is the first step. Stark staring incredulity is a far more loyal tribute to that truth than a modernist metaphysic that would make it out merely a matter of degree. It were better to rend our robes with a great cry against blasphemy, like Caiaphas in the judgment, or to lay hold of the man as a maniac possessed of devils like the kinsmen and the crowd, rather than to stand stupidly debating fine shades of pantheism in the presence of so catastrophic a claim. There is more of the wisdom that is one with surprise in any simple person, full of the sensitiveness of simplicity, who should expect the grass to wither and the birds to drop dead out of the air, when a strolling carpenter's apprentice said calmly and almost carelessly, like one looking over his shoulder: 'Before Abraham was, I am.'

III

THE STRANGEST STORY IN THE WORLD

In the last chapter I have deliberately stressed what seems to be nowadays a neglected side of the New Testament story, but nobody will suppose, I imagine, that it is meant to obscure that side that may truly be called human. That Christ was and is the most merciful of judges and the most sympathetic of friends is a fact of considerably more importance in our own private lives than in anybody's historical speculations. But the purpose of this book is to point out that something unique has been swamped in cheap generalisations; and for that purpose it is relevant to insist that even what was most universal was also most original. For instance, we might take a topic which really is sympathetic to the modern mood, as the ascetic vocations recently referred to are not. The exaltation of childhood is something which we do really understand; but it was by no means a thing that was then in that sense understood. If we wanted an example of the originality of the Gospel, we could hardly take a stronger or more startling one. Nearly two thousand years afterwards we happen to find ourselves in a mood that does really feel the mystical charm of the child; we express it in romances and regrets about childhood, in *Peter Pan* or *The Child's Garden of Verses*. And we can say of the words of Christ with so angry an anti-Christian as Swinburne: —

> 'No sign that ever was given
> To faithful or faithless eyes
> Showed ever beyond clouds riven
> So clear a paradise.
>
> Earth's creeds may be seventy times seven
> And blood have defiled each creed
> But if such be the kingdom of heaven
> It must be heaven indeed.'

But that paradise was not clear until Christianity had gradually cleared it. The pagan world, as such, would not have understood any such thing as a serious suggestion that a child is higher or holier than a man. It would have seemed like the suggestion that a tadpole is higher or holier than a frog. To the merely rationalistic mind, it would sound like saying that a bud must be more beautiful than a flower or that an unripe apple must be better than a ripe one. In other words, this modern feeling is an entirely mystical feeling. It is quite as mystical as the cult of virginity; in fact it is the cult of virginity. But pagan antiquity had much more idea of the holiness of the virgin than of the holiness of the child. For various reasons we have come nowadays to venerate children; perhaps partly because we envy children for still doing what men used to do; such as play simple games and enjoy fairy-tales. Over and above this, however, there is a great deal of real and subtle psychology in our appreciation of childhood; but if we turn it into a modern discovery, we must once more admit that the historical Jesus of Nazareth had already discovered it two thousand years too soon. There was certainly nothing in the world around him to help him to the discovery. Here Christ was indeed human; but more human than a human being was then likely to be. Peter Pan does not belong to the world of Pan but the world of Peter.

Even in the matter of mere literary style, if we suppose ourselves thus sufficiently detached to look at it in that light, there is a curious quality to which no critic seems to have done justice. It had among other things a singular air of piling tower upon tower by the use of the *a fortiori*; making a pagoda of degrees like the seven heavens. I have already noted that almost inverted imaginative vision which pictured the impossible penance of the Cities of the Plain. There is perhaps nothing so perfect in all language or literature as the use of these three degrees in the parable of the lilies of the field; in which he seems first to take one small flower in his hand and note its simplicity and even its impotence; then suddenly expands it in flamboyant colours into all the palaces and pavilions full of a great name in national legend and national glory; and then, by yet a third overturn, shrivels it to nothing once more with a gesture as if flinging it away '. . . and if God so clothes the grass that today is and tomorrow is cast into the oven—how much more. . . .' It is like the building of a good Babel tower by white magic in a moment and in the movement of a hand; a tower heaved suddenly up to heaven on the top of which can be seen afar off, higher than we had fancied possible, the figure of man; lifted by three infinities above all other things, on a starry ladder of light logic and swift imagination. Merely in a literary sense it would be more of a masterpiece than most of the masterpieces in the libraries; yet it seems to have been uttered almost at random while a man might pull a flower. But merely in a literary sense also, this use of the comparative in several degrees has about it a quality which seems to me to hint of much higher things than the modern suggestion of the simple teaching of pastoral or communal ethics. There is nothing that really indicates a subtle and in the true sense a superior mind so much as this power of comparing a lower thing with a higher and yet that higher with a higher still; of thinking on three planes at once. There is nothing that wants the rarest sort of wisdom so much as to see, let us say, that the citizen is higher than the slave and yet that the soul is infinitely higher than the citizen or the city. It is not by any means a faculty that commonly belongs to these simplifiers of the Gospel; those who insist on what they call a simple morality and others call a sentimental morality. It is not at all covered by those who are content to tell everybody to remain at peace. On the contrary, there is a very striking example of it in the apparent inconsistency between Christ's sayings about peace and about a sword. It is precisely this power which perceives that while a good peace is better than a good war, even a good war is better than a bad peace. These far-flung comparisons are nowhere so common as in the Gospels; and to me they suggest something very vast. So a thing solitary and solid, with the added dimension of depth or height, might tower over the flat creatures living only on a plane.

This quality of something that can only be called subtle and superior, something that is capable of long views and even of double meanings, is not noted here merely as a counterblast to the commonplace exaggerations of amiability and mild idealism. It is also to be noted in connection with the more tremendous truth touched upon at the end of the last chapter. For this is the very last character that commonly goes with mere megalomania; especially such steep and staggering megalomania as might be involved in that claim. This quality that can only be called intellectual distinction is not, of course, an evidence of divinity. But it is an evidence of a probable distaste for vulgar and vainglorious claims to divinity. A man of that sort, if he were only a man, would be the last man in the world to suffer from that intoxication by one notion from nowhere in particular, which is the mark of the self-deluding sensationalist in religion. Nor is it even avoided by denying that Christ did make this claim. Of no such man as that, of no other prophet or philosopher of the same intellectual order, would it be even possible to pretend that he had made it. Even if the Church had mistaken his meaning, it would still be true that no other historical tradition except the Church had ever even made the same mistake. Mahomedans did not misunderstand Mahomet and suppose he was Allah. Jews did not misinterpret Moses and identify him with Jehovah. Why was this claim alone exaggerated unless this alone was made? Even if Christianity was one vast universal blunder, it is still a blunder as solitary as the Incarnation.

The purpose of these pages is to fix the falsity of certain vague and vulgar assumptions; and we have here one of the most false. There is a sort of notion in the air everywhere that all the religions are equal because all the religious founders were rivals; that they are all fighting for the same starry crown. It is quite false. The claim to that crown, or anything like that crown, is really so rare as to be unique. Mahomet did not make it any more than Micah or Malachi. Confucius did not make it any more than Plato or Marcus Aurelius. Buddha never said he was Bramah. Zoroaster no more claimed to be Ormuz than to be Ahriman. The truth is that, in the common run of cases, it is just as we should expect it to be, in common sense and certainly in Christian philosophy. It is exactly the other way. Normally speaking, the greater a man is, the less likely he is to make the very greatest claim. Outside the unique case we are considering, the only kind of man who ever does make that kind of claim is a very small man; a secretive or self-centered monomaniac. Nobody can imagine Aristotle claiming to be the father of gods and men, come down from the sky; though we might imagine some insane Roman

Emperor like Caligula claiming it for him, or more probably for himself. Nobody can imagine Shakespeare talking as if he were literally divine; though we might imagine some crazy American crank finding it as a cryptogram in Shakespeare's works, or preferably in his own works. It is possible to find here and there human beings who make this supremely superhuman claim. It is possible to find them in lunatic asylums; in padded cells; possibly in strait waistcoats. But what is much more important than their mere materialistic fate in our very materialistic society, under very crude and clumsy laws about lunacy, the type we know as tinged with this, or tending towards it, is a diseased and disproportionate type; narrow yet swollen and morbid to monstrosity. It is by rather an unlucky metaphor that we talk of a madman as cracked; for in a sense he is not cracked enough. He is cramped rather than cracked; there are not enough holes in his head to ventilate it. This impossibility of letting in daylight on a delusion does sometimes cover and conceal a delusion of divinity. It can be found, not among prophets and sages and founders of religions, but only among a low set of lunatics. But this is exactly where the argument becomes intensely interesting; because the argument proves too much. For nobody supposes that Jesus of Nazareth was *that* sort of person. No modern critic in his five wits thinks that the preacher of the Sermon on the Mount was a horrible half-witted imbecile that might be scrawling stars on the walls of a cell. No atheist or blasphemer believes that the author of the Parable of the Prodigal Son was a monster with one mad idea like a cyclops with one eye. Upon any possible historical criticism, he must be put higher in the scale of human beings than that. Yet by all analogy we have really to put him there or else in the highest place of all.

In fact, those who can really take it (as I here hypothetically take it) in a quite dry and detached spirit, have here a most curious and interesting human problem. It is so intensely interesting, considered as a human problem, that it is in a spirit quite disinterested, so to speak, that I wish some of them had turned that intricate human problem into something like an intelligible human portrait. If Christ was simply a human character, he really was a highly complex and contradictory human character. For he combined exactly the two things that lie at the two extremes of human variation. He was exactly what the man with a delusion never is; he was wise; he was a good judge. What he said was always unexpected; but it was always unexpectedly magnanimous and often unexpectedly moderate. Take a thing like the point of the parable of the tares and the wheat. It has the quality that unites sanity and subtlety. It has not the simplicity of a madman. It has not even the simplicity of a fanatic. It might be uttered by a philosopher a hundred years old, at the end of a century of Utopias. Nothing could be less like this quality of seeing beyond and all round obvious things, than the condition of the egomaniac with the one sensitive spot on his brain. I really do not see how these two characters could be convincingly combined, except in the astonishing way in which the creed combines them. For until we reach the full acceptance of the fact as a fact, however marvellous, all mere approximations to it are actually further and further away from it. Divinity is great enough to be divine; it is great enough to call itself divine. But as humanity grows greater, it grows less and less likely to do so. God is God, as the Moslems say; but a great man knows he is not God, and the greater he is the better he knows it. That is the paradox; everything that is merely approaching to that point is merely receding from it. Socrates, the wisest man, knows that he knows nothing. A lunatic may think he is omniscience, and a fool may talk as if he were omniscient. But Christ is in another sense omniscient if he not only knows, but knows that he knows.

Even on the purely human and sympathetic side, therefore, the Jesus of the New Testament seems to me to have in a great many ways the note of something superhuman; that is of something human and more than human. But there is another quality running through all his teachings which seems to me neglected in most modern talk about them as teachings; and that is the persistent suggestion that he has not really come to teach. If there is one incident in the record which affects me personally as grandly and gloriously human, it is the incident of giving wine for the wedding-feast. That is really human in the sense in which a whole crowd of prigs, having the appearance of human beings, can hardly be described as human. It rises superior to all superior persons. It is as human as Herrick and as democratic as Dickens. But even in that story there is something else that has that note of things not fully explained; and in a way here very relevant. I mean the first hesitation, not on any ground touching the nature of the miracle, but on that of the propriety of working any miracles at all, at least at that stage; 'my time is not yet come.' What did that mean? At least it certainly meant a general plan or purpose in the mind, with which certain things did or did not fit in. And if we leave out that solitary strategic plan, we not only leave out the point of the story, but the story.

We often hear of Jesus of Nazareth as a wandering teacher; and there is a vital truth in that view in so far as it emphasises an attitude towards luxury and convention which most respectable people would still regard as that of a vagabond. It is expressed in his own great saying about the holes of the foxes and the nests of the birds, and, like many of his great sayings, it is felt as less powerful than it is, through lack of appreciation of that great paradox by which he spoke of his own humanity as in some way collectively and representatively human; calling himself simply the Son of Man; that is, in effect, calling himself simply Man. It is fitting that the New Man or the Second Adam should repeat in so ringing a voice and with so arresting a gesture the great fact which came first in the original story; that man differs from the brutes by everything, even by deficiency; that he is in a sense less normal and even less native; a stranger upon the earth. It is well to speak of his wanderings in this sense and in the sense that he shared the drifting life of the most homeless and hopeless of the poor. It is assuredly well to remember that he would quite certainly have been moved on by the police and almost certainly arrested by the police, for having no visible means of subsistence. For our law has in it a turn of humour or touch of fancy which Nero and Herod never happened to think of; that of actually punishing homeless people for not sleeping at home.

But in another sense the word 'wandering' as applied to his life is a little misleading. As a matter of fact, a great many of the pagan sages and not a few of the pagan sophists might truly be described as wandering teachers. In some of them their rambling journeys were not altogether without a parallel in their rambling remarks. Apollonius of Tyana, who figured in some fashionable cults as a sort of ideal philosopher, is represented as rambling as far as the Ganges and Ethiopia, more or less talking all the time. There was actually a school of philosophers called the Peripatetics; and most even of the great philosophers give us a vague impression of having very little to do except to walk and talk. The great conversations which give us our glimpses of the great minds of Socrates or Buddha or even Confucius often seem to be parts of a never-ending picnic; and especially, which is the important point, to have neither beginning nor end. Socrates did indeed find the conversation interrupted by the incident of his execution. But it is the whole point, and the whole particular merit, of the position of Socrates that death was only an interruption and an incident. We miss the real moral importance of the great philosopher if we miss that point; that he stares at the executioner with an innocent surprise, and almost an innocent annoyance, at finding anyone so unreasonable as to cut short a little conversation for the elucidation of truth. He is looking for truth and not looking for death. Death is but a stone in the road which can trip him up. His work in life is to wander on the roads of the world and talk about truth for ever. Buddha, on the other hand, did arrest attention by one gesture; it was the gesture of renunciation, and therefore in a sense of denial. But by one dramatic negation he passed into a world of negation that was not dramatic; which he would have been the first to insist was not dramatic. Here again we miss the particular moral importance of the great mystic if we do not see the distinction; that it was his whole point that he had done with drama, which consists of desire and struggle and generally of defeat and disappointment. He passes into peace and lives to instruct others how to pass into it. Henceforth his life is that of the ideal philosopher; certainly a far more really ideal philosopher than Apollonius of Tyana; but still a philosopher in the sense that it is not his business to do anything but rather to explain everything; in his case, we might almost say, mildly and softly to explode everything. For the messages are basically different. Christ said 'Seek first the kingdom, and all these things shall be added unto you.' Buddha said 'Seek first the kingdom, and then you will need none of these things.'

Now compared to these wanderers the life of Jesus went as swift and straight as a thunderbolt. It was above all things dramatic; it did above all things consist in doing something that had to be done. It emphatically would not have been done, if Jesus had walked about the world for ever doing nothing except tell the truth. And even the external movement of it must not be described as a wandering in the sense of forgetting that it was a journey. This is where it was a fulfilment of the myths rather than of the philosophies; it is a journey with a goal and an object, like Jason going to find the Golden Fleece, or Hercules the golden apples of the Hesperides. The gold that he was seeking was death. The primary thing that he was going to do was to die. He was going to do other things equally definite and objective; we might almost say equally external and material. But from first to last the most definite fact is that he is going to die. No two things could possibly be more different than the death of Socrates and the death of Christ. We are meant to feel that the death of Socrates was, from the point of view of his friends at least, a stupid muddle and miscarriage of justice interfering with the flow of a humane and lucid, I had almost said a light philosophy. We are meant to feel that Death was the bride of Christ as Poverty was the bride of St. Francis. We are meant to feel that his life was in that sense a sort of love-affair with death, a romance of the pursuit of the ultimate sacrifice. From the moment when the star goes up like a birthday rocket to the moment when the sun is extinguished like a funeral torch, the whole story moves on wings with the speed and direction of a drama, ending in an act beyond words.

Therefore the story of Christ is the story of a journey, almost in the manner of a military march; certainly in the manner of the quest of a hero moving to his achievement or his doom. It is a story that begins in the paradise of Galilee, a pastoral and peaceful land having really some hint of Eden, and gradually climbs the rising country into the mountains that are nearer to the storm-clouds and the stars, as to a Mountain of Purgatory. He may be met as if straying in strange places, or stopped on the way for discussion or dispute; but his face is set towards the mountain city. That is the meaning of that great culmination when he crested the ridge and stood at the turning of the road and suddenly cried aloud, lamenting over Jerusalem. Some light touch of that lament is in every patriotic poem; or if it is absent, the patriotism stinks with vulgarity. That is the meaning of the stirring and startling incident at the gates of the Temple, when the tables were hurled like lumber down the steps, and the rich merchants driven forth with bodily blows; the incident that must be at least as much of a puzzle to the pacifists as any paradox about non-resistance can be to any of the militarists. I have compared the quest to the journey of Jason, but we must never forget that in a deeper sense it is rather to be compared to the journey of Ulysses. It was not only a romance of travel but a romance of return; and of the end of a usurpation. No healthy boy reading the story regards the rout of the Ithacan suitors as anything but a happy ending. But there are doubtless some who regard the rout of the Jewish merchants and money-changers with that refined repugnance which never fails to move them in the presence of violence, and especially of violence against the well-to-do. The point, here however, is that all these incidents have in them a character of mounting crisis. In other words, these incidents are not incidental. When Apollonius the ideal philosopher is brought before the judgment-seat of Domitian and vanishes by magic, the miracle is entirely incidental. It might have occurred at any time in the wandering life of the Tyanean; indeed, I believe it is doubtful in date as well as in substance. The ideal philosopher merely vanished, and resumed his ideal existence somewhere else for an indefinite period. It is characteristic of the contrast perhaps that Apollonius was supposed to have lived to an almost miraculous old age. Jesus of Nazareth was less prudent in his miracles. When Jesus was brought before the judgment-seat of Pontius Pilate, he did not vanish. It was the crisis and the goal; it was the hour and the power of darkness. It was the supremely supernatural act, of all his miraculous life, that he did not vanish.

Every attempt to amplify that story has diminished it. The task has been attempted by many men of real genius and eloquence as well as by only too many vulgar sentimentalists and self-conscious rhetoricians. The tale has been retold with patronising pathos by elegant sceptics and with fluent enthusiasm by boisterous best-sellers.

It will not be retold here. The grinding power of the plain words of the Gospel story is like the power of mill-stones; and those who can read them simply enough will feel as if rocks had been rolled upon them. Criticism is only words about words; and of what use are words about such words as these? What is the use of word-painting about the dark garden filled suddenly with torchlight and furious faces? 'Are you come out with swords and staves as against a robber? All day I sat in your temple teaching, and you took me not.' Can anything be added to the massive and gathered restraint of that irony; like a great wave lifted to the sky and refusing to fall? 'Daughters of Jerusalem, weep not for me but weep for yourselves and for your children.' As the High Priest asked what further need he had of witnesses, we might well ask what further need we have of words. Peter in a panic repudiated him: 'and immediately the cock crew; and Jesus looked upon Peter, and Peter went out and wept bitterly.' Has anyone any further remarks to offer? Just before the murder he prayed for all the murderous race of men, saying, 'They know not what they do'; is there anything to say to that, except that we know as little what we say? Is there any need to repeat and spin out the story of how the tragedy trailed up the Via Dolorosa and how they threw him in haphazard with two thieves in one of the ordinary batches of execution; and how in all that horror and howling wilderness of desertion one voice spoke in homage, a startling voice from the very last place where it was looked for, the gibbet of the criminal; and he said to that nameless ruffian, 'This night shalt thou be with me in Paradise'? Is there anything to put after that but a full-stop? Or is anyone prepared to answer adequately that farewell gesture to all flesh which created for his Mother a new Son?

It is more within my powers, and here more immediately to my purpose, to point out that in that scene were symbolically gathered all the human forces that have been vaguely sketched in this story. As kings and philosophers and the popular element had been symbolically present at his birth, so they were more practically concerned in his death; and with that we come face to face with the essential fact to be realised. All the great groups that stood about the Cross represent in one way or another the great historical truth of the time; that the world could not save itself. Man could do no more. Rome and Jerusalem and Athens and everything else were going down like a sea turned into a slow cataract. Externally indeed the ancient world was still at its strongest; it is always at that moment that the inmost weakness begins. But in order to understand that weakness we must repeat what has been said more than once; that it was not the weakness of a thing originally weak. It was emphatically the strength of the world that was turned to weakness and the wisdom of the world that was turned to folly.

In this story of Good Friday it is the best things in the world that are at their worst. That is what really shows us the world at its worst. It was, for instance, the priests of a true monotheism and the soldiers of an international civilisation. Rome, the legend, founded upon fallen Troy and triumphant over fallen Carthage, had stood for a heroism which was the nearest that any pagan ever came to chivalry. Rome had defended the household gods and the human decencies against the ogres of Africa and the hermaphrodite monstrosities of Greece. But in the lightning flash of this incident, we see great Rome, the imperial republic, going downward under her Lucretian doom. Scepticism has eaten away even the confident sanity of the conquerors of the world. He who is enthroned to say what is justice can only ask, 'What is truth?' So in that drama which decided the whole fate of antiquity, one of the central figures is fixed in what seems the reverse of his true rôle. Rome was almost another name for responsibility. Yet he stands for ever as a sort of rocking statue of the irresponsible. Man could do no more. Even the practical had become the impracticable. Standing between the pillars of his own judgment-seat, a Roman had washed his hands of the world.

There too were the priests of that pure and original truth that was behind all the mythologies like the sky behind the clouds. It was the most important truth in the world; and even that could not save the world. Perhaps there is something overpowering in pure personal theism; like seeing the sun and moon and sky come together to form one staring face. Perhaps the truth is too tremendous when not broken by some intermediaries divine or human; perhaps it is merely too pure and far away. Anyhow it could not save the world; it could not even convert the world. There were philosophers who held it in its highest and noblest form; but they not only could not convert the world, but they never tried. You could no more fight the jungle of popular mythology with a private opinion than you could clear away a forest with a pocket-knife. The Jewish priests had guarded it jealously in the good and the bad sense. They had kept it as a gigantic secret. As savage heroes might have kept the sun in a box, they kept the Everlasting in the tabernacle. They were proud that they alone could look upon the blinding sun of a single deity; and they did not know that they had themselves gone blind. Since that day their representatives have been like blind men in broad daylight, striking to right and left with their staffs, and cursing the darkness. But there has been that in their monumental monotheism that it has at least remained like a monument, the last thing of its kind, and in a sense motionless in the more restless world which it cannot satisfy. For it is certain that for some reason it cannot satisfy. Since that day it has never been quite enough to say that God is in his heaven and all is right with the world; since the rumour that God had left his heavens to set it right.

And as it was with these powers that were good, or at least had once been good, so it was with the element which was perhaps the best, or which Christ himself seems certainly to have felt as the best. The poor to whom he preached the good news, the common people who heard him gladly, the populace that had made so many popular heroes and demigods in the old pagan world, showed also the weaknesses that were dissolving the world. They suffered the evils often seen in the mob of the city, and especially the mob of the capital, during the decline of a society. The same thing that makes the rural population live on tradition makes the urban population live on rumour. Just as its myths at the best had been irrational, so its likes and dislikes are easily changed by baseless assertion that is arbitrary without being authoritative. Some brigand or other was artificially turned into a picturesque and popular figure and run as a kind of candidate against Christ. In all this we recognise the urban population that we know, with its newspaper scares and scoops. But there was present in this ancient population an evil more peculiar to the ancient world. We have noted it already as the neglect of the individual, even of the individual voting the condemnation and still more of the individual condemned. It was the soul of the hive; a heathen thing. The cry of this spirit also was heard in that hour, 'It is well that one man die for the people.' Yet this spirit in antiquity of devotion to the city and to the state had also been in itself and in its time a noble spirit. It had its poets and its martyrs; men still to be honoured for ever. It was failing through its weakness in not seeing the separate soul of a man, the shrine of all mysticism; but it was only failing as everything else was failing. The mob went along with the Sadducees and the Pharisees, the philosophers and the moralists. It went along with the imperial magistrates and the sacred priests, the scribes and the soldiers, that the one universal human spirit might suffer a universal condemnation; that there might be one deep, unanimous chorus of approval and harmony when Man was rejected of men.

There were solitudes beyond where none shall follow. There were secrets in the inmost and invisible part of that drama that have no symbol in speech; or in any severance of a man from men. Nor is it easy for any words less stark and single-minded than those of the naked narrative even to hint at the horror of exaltation that lifted itself above the hill. Endless expositions have not come to the end of it, or even to the beginning. And if there be any sound that can produce a silence, we may surely be silent about the end and the extremity; when a cry was driven out of that darkness in words dreadfully distinct and dreadfully unintelligible, which man shall never understand in all the eternity they have purchased for him; and for one annihilating instant an abyss that is not for our thoughts had opened even in the unity of the absolute; and God had been forsaken of God.

They took the body down from the cross and one of the few rich men among the first Christians obtained permission to bury it in a rock tomb in his garden; the Romans setting a military guard lest there should be some riot and attempt to recover the body. There was once more a natural symbolism in these natural proceedings; it was well that the tomb should be sealed with all the secrecy of ancient eastern sepulture and guarded by the authority of the Caesars.

For in that second cavern the whole of that great and glorious humanity which we call antiquity was gathered up and covered over; and in that place it was buried. It was the end of a very great thing called human history; the history that was merely human. The mythologies and the philosophies were buried there, the gods and the heroes and the sages. In the great Roman phrase, they had lived. But as they could only live, so they could only die; and they were dead.

On the third day the friends of Christ coming at daybreak to the place found the grave empty and the stone rolled away. In varying ways they realised the new wonder; but even they hardly realised that the world had died in the night. What they were looking at was the first day of a new creation, with a new heaven and a new earth; and in a semblance of the gardener God walked again in the garden, in the cool not of the evening but the dawn.

IV

THE WITNESS OF THE HERETICS

Christ founded the Church with two great figures of speech; in the final words to the Apostles who received authority to found it. The first was the phrase about founding it on Peter as on a rock; the second was the symbol of the keys. About the meaning of the former there is naturally no doubt in my own case; but it does not directly affect the argument here save in two more secondary aspects. It is yet another example of a thing that could only fully expand and explain itself afterwards, and even long afterwards. And it is yet another example of something the very reverse of simple and self-evident even in the language, in so far as it described a man as a rock when he had much more the appearance of a reed.

But the other image of the keys has an exactitude that has hardly been exactly noticed. The keys have been conspicuous enough in the art and heraldry of Christendom; but not everyone has noted the peculiar aptness of the allegory. We have now reached the point in history where something must be said of the first appearance and activities of the Church in the Roman Empire; and for that brief description nothing could be more perfect than that ancient metaphor. The Early Christian was very precisely a person carrying about a key, or what he said was a key. The whole Christian movement consisted in claiming to possess that key. It was not merely a vague forward movement, which might be better represented by a battering-ram. It was not something that swept along with it similar or dissimilar things, as does a modern social movement. As we shall see in a moment, it rather definitely refused to do so. It definitely asserted that there was a key and that it possessed that key and that no other key was like it; in that sense it was as narrow as you please. Only it happened to be the key that could unlock the prison of the whole world; and let in the white daylight of liberty.

The creed was like a key in three respects; which can be most conveniently summed up under this symbol. First, a key is above all things a thing with a shape. It is a thing that depends entirely upon keeping its shape. The Christian creed is above all things the philosophy of shapes and the enemy of shapelessness. That is where it differs from all that formless infinity, Manichean or Buddhist, which makes a sort of pool of night in the dark heart of Asia; the ideal of uncreating all the creatures. That is where it differs also from the analogous vagueness of mere evolutionism; the idea of creatures constantly losing their shape. A man told that his solitary latchkey had been melted down with a million others into a Buddhistic unity would be annoyed. But a man told that his key was gradually growing and sprouting in his pocket, and branching into new wards or complications, would not be more gratified.

Second, the shape of a key is in itself a rather fantastic shape. A savage who did not know it was a key would have the greatest difficulty in guessing what it could possibly be. And it is fantastic because it is in a sense arbitrary. A key is not a matter of abstractions; in that sense a key is not a matter of argument. It either fits the lock or it does not. It is useless for men to stand disputing over it, considered by itself; or reconstructing it on pure principles of geometry or decorative art. It is senseless for a man to say he would like a simpler key; it would be far more sensible to do his best with a crowbar. And thirdly, as the key is necessarily a thing with a pattern, so this was one having in some ways a rather elaborate pattern. When people complain of the religion being so early complicated with theology and things of the kind, they forget that the world had not only got into a hole, but had got into a whole maze of holes and corners. The problem itself was a complicated problem; it did not in the ordinary sense merely involve anything so simple as sin. It was also full of secrets, of unexplored and unfathomable fallacies, of unconscious mental diseases, of dangers in all directions. If the faith had faced the world only with the platitudes about peace and simplicity some moralists would confine it to, it would not have had the faintest effect on that luxurious and labyrinthine lunatic asylum. What it did do we must now roughly describe; it is enough to say here that there was undoubtedly much about the key that seemed complex; indeed there was only one thing about it that was simple. It opened the door.

There are certain recognised and accepted statements in this matter which may for brevity and convenience be described as lies. We have all heard people say that Christianity arose in an age of barbarism. They might just as well say that Christian Science arose in an age of barbarism. They may think Christianity was a symptom of social decay, as I think Christian Science a symptom of mental decay. They may think Christianity a superstition that ultimately destroyed a civilisation, as I think Christian Science a superstition capable (if taken seriously) of destroying any number of civilisations. But to say that a Christian of the fourth or fifth centuries was a barbarian living in a barbarous time is exactly like saying that Mrs. Eddy was a Red Indian. And if I allowed my constitutional impatience with Mrs. Eddy to impel me to call her a Red Indian, I should incidentally be telling a lie. We may like or dislike the imperial civilisation of Rome in the fourth century; we may like or dislike the industrial civilisation of America in the nineteenth century; but that they both were what we commonly mean by a civilisation no person of commonsense could deny if he wanted to. This is a very obvious fact but it is also a very fundamental one; and we must make it the foundation of any further description of constructive Christianity in the past. For good or evil, it was pre-eminently the product of a civilised age, perhaps of an over-civilised age. This is the first fact apart from all praise or blame; indeed I am so unfortunate as not to feel that I praise a thing when I compare it to Christian Science. But it is at least desirable to know something of the savour of a society in which we are condemning or praising anything; and the science that connects Mrs. Eddy with tomahawks or the Mater Dolorosa with totems may for our general convenience be eliminated. The dominant fact, not merely about the Christian religion, but about the whole pagan civilisation, was that which has been more than once repeated in these pages. The Mediterranean was a lake in the real sense of a pool; in which a number of different cults or cultures were, as the phrase goes, pooled. Those cities facing each other round the circle of the lake became more and more one cosmopolitan culture. On its legal and military side it was the Roman Empire; but it was very many-sided. It might be called superstitious in the sense that it contained a great number of varied superstitions; but by no possibility can any part of it be called barbarous.

In this level of cosmopolitan culture arose the Christian religion and the Catholic Church; and everything in the story suggests that it was felt to be something new and strange. Those who have tried to suggest that it evolved out of something much milder or more ordinary have found that in this case their evolutionary method is very difficult to apply. They may suggest that Essenes or Ebionites or such things were the seed; but the seed is invisible; the tree appears very rapidly full-grown; and the tree is something totally different. It is certainly a Christmas tree in the sense that it keeps the kindliness and moral beauty of the story of Bethlehem; but it was as ritualistic as the seven-branched candlestick, and the candles it carried were considerably more than were probably permitted by the first prayer-book of Edward the Sixth. It might well be asked, indeed, why any one accepting the Bethlehem tradition should object to golden or gilded ornament since the Magi themselves brought gold, why he should dislike incense in the church since incense was brought even to the stable. But these are controversies that do not concern me here. I am concerned only with the historical fact, more and more admitted by historians, that very early in its history this thing became visible to the civilisation of antiquity; and that already the Church appeared as a Church; with everything that is implied in a Church and much that is disliked in a Church. We will discuss in a moment how far it was like other ritualistic or magical or ascetical mysteries in its own time. It was certainly not in the least like merely ethical and idealistic movements in our time. It had a doctrine; it had a discipline; it had sacraments; it had degrees of initiation; it admitted people and expelled people; it affirmed one dogma with authority and repudiated another with anathemas. If all these things be the marks of Antichrist, the reign of Antichrist followed very rapidly upon Christ.

Those who maintain that Christianity was not a Church but a moral movement of idealists have been forced to push the period of its perversion or disappearance further and further back. A bishop of Rome writes claiming authority in the very lifetime of St. John the

Evangelist; and it is described as the first papal aggression. A friend
of the Apostles writes of them as men he knew and says they taught
him the doctrine of the Sacrament; and Mr. Wells can only murmur
that the reaction towards barbaric blood-rites may have happened
rather earlier than might be expected. The date of the Fourth
Gospel, which at one time was steadily growing later and later, is
now steadily growing earlier and earlier; until critics are staggered at
the dawning and dreadful possibility that it might be something like
what it professes to be. The last limit of an early date for the extinction of true Christianity has probably been found by the latest German professor whose authority is invoked by Dean Inge. This learned
scholar says that Pentecost was the occasion for the first founding of
an ecclesiastical, dogmatic, and despotic Church utterly alien to the
simple ideals of Jesus of Nazareth. This may be called, in a popular as
well as a learned sense, the limit. What do professors of this kind
imagine that men are made of? Suppose it were a matter of any
merely human movement, let us say that of the conscientious objec-
tors. Some say the early Christians were Pacifists; I do not believe it
for a moment; but I am quite ready to accept the parallel for the sake
of the argument. Tolstoy or some great preacher of peace among
peasants has been shot as a mutineer for defying conscription; and a
little while afterwards his few followers meet together in an upper
room in remembrance of him. They never had any reason for coming together except that common memory; they are men of many
kinds with nothing to bind them, except that the greatest event in
all their lives was this tragedy of the teacher of universal peace. They
are always repeating his words, revolving his problems, trying to
imitate his character. The Pacifists meet at their Pentecost and are
possessed of a sudden ecstacy of enthusiasm and wild rush of the
whirlwind of inspiration, in the course of which they proceed to establish universal Conscription, to increase the Navy Estimates, to insist on everybody going about armed to the teeth and on all the fron-
tiers bristling with artillery; the proceedings concluded with the
singing of 'Boys of the Bulldog Breed' and 'Don't let them scrap the
British Navy.' That is something like a fair parallel to the theory of
these critics; that the transition from their idea of Jesus to their idea of

Catholicism could have been made in the little upper room at Pentecost. Surely anybody's commonsense would tell him that enthusiasts, who only met through their common enthusiasm for a leader whom they loved, would not instantly rush away to establish everything that he hated. No, if the 'ecclesiastical and dogmatic system' is as old as Pentecost it is as old as Christmas. If we trace it back to such very early Christians we must trace it back to Christ.

We may begin then with these two negations. It is nonsense to say that the Christian faith appeared in a simple age; in the sense of an unlettered and gullible age. It is equally nonsense to say that the Christian faith was a simple thing; in the sense of a vague or childish or merely instinctive thing. Perhaps the only point in which we could possibly say that the Church fitted into the pagan world, is the fact that they were both not only highly civilised but rather complicated. They were both emphatically many-sided; but antiquity was then a many-sided hole, like a hexagonal hole waiting for an equally hexagonal stopper. In that sense only the Church was many-sided enough to fit the world. The six sides of the Mediterranean world faced each other across the sea and waited for something that should look all ways at once. The Church had to be both Roman and Greek and Jewish and African and Asiatic. In the very words of the Apostle of the Gentiles, it was indeed all things to all men. Christianity then was not merely crude and simple and was the very reverse of the growth of a barbaric time. But when we come to the contrary charge, we come to a much more plausible charge. It is very much more tenable that the Faith was but the final phase of the decay of civilisation, in the sense of the excess of civilisation; that this superstition was a sign that Rome was dying, and dying of being much too civilised. That is an argument much better worth considering; and we will proceed to consider it.

At the beginning of this book I ventured on a general summary of it, in a parallel between the rise of humanity out of nature and the rise of Christianity out of history. I pointed out that in both cases what had gone before might imply something coming after; but did not in the least imply what did come after. If a detached mind had seen certain apes it might have deduced more anthropoids; it would not have deduced man or anything within a thousand miles of what man has done. In short, it might have seen Pithacanthropus or the Missing Link looming in the future, if possible almost as dimly and doubtfully as we see him looming in the past. But if it foresaw him appearing it would also foresee him disappearing, and leaving a few faint traces just as he has left a few faint traces; if they are traces. To foresee that Missing Link would not be to foresee Man, or anything like Man. Now this earlier explanation must be kept in mind; because it is an exact parallel to the true view of the Church; and the suggestion of it having evolved naturally out of the Empire in decay.

The truth is that in one sense a man might very well have predicted that the imperial decadence would produce something like Christianity. That is, something a little like and gigantically different. A man might very well have said, for instance, 'Pleasure has been pursued so extravagantly that there will be a reaction into pessimism. Perhaps it will take the form of asceticism; men will mutilate themselves instead of merely hanging themselves.' Or a man might very reasonably have said, 'If we weary of our Greek and Latin gods we shall be hankering after some eastern mystery or other; there will be a fashion in Persians or Hindoos.' Or a man of the world might well have been shrewd enough to say, 'Powerful people are picking up these fads; some day the court will adopt one of them and it may become official.' Or yet another and gloomier prophet might be pardoned for saying, 'The world is going down-hill; dark and barbarous superstitions will return, it does not matter much which. They will all be formless and fugitive like dreams of the night.'

Now it is the intense interest of the case that all these prophecies were really fulfilled; but it was not the Church that fulfilled them. It was the Church that escaped from them, confounded them, and rose above them in triumph. In so far as it was probable that the mere nature of hedonism would produce a mere reaction of asceticism, it did produce a mere reaction of asceticism. It was the movement called Manichean and the Church was its mortal enemy. In so far as it would have naturally appeared at that point of history, it did appear; it did also disappear, which was equally natural. The mere pessimist reaction did come with the Manichees and did go with the Manichees.

But the Church did not come with them or go with them; and she had much more to do with their going than with their coming. Or again, in so far as it was probable that even the growth of scepticism would bring in a fashion of eastern religion, it did bring it in; Mithras came from far beyond Palestine out of the heart of Persia, bringing strange mysteries of the blood of bulls. Certainly there was everything to show that some such fashion would have come in any case. But certainly there is nothing in the world to show that it would not have passed away in any case. Certainly an Oriental fad was something eminently fitted to the fourth or fifth century; but that hardly explains it having remained to the twentieth century, and still going strong. In short, in so far as things of the kind might have been expected then, things like Mithraism were experienced then; but it scarcely explains our more recent experiences. And if we were still Mithraists merely because Mithraic head-dresses and other Persian apparatuses might be expected to be all the rage in the days of Domitian, it would almost seem by this time that we must be a little dowdy.

It is the same, as will be suggested in a moment, with the idea of official favouritism. In so far as such favouritism shown towards a fad was something that might have been looked for during the decline and fall of the Roman Empire, it was something that did exist in that Empire and did decline and fall with it. It throws no sort of light on the thing that resolutely refused to decline and fall; that grew steadily while the other was declining and falling; and which even at this moment is going forward with fearless energy, when another aeon has completed its cycle and another civilisation seems almost ready to fall or to decline.

Now the curious fact is this; that the very heresies which the early Church is blamed for crushing testify to the unfairness for which she is blamed. In so far as something deserved the blame, it was precisely the things that she is blamed for blaming. In so far as something was merely a superstition, she herself condemned that superstition. In so far as something was a mere reaction into barbarism, she herself resisted it because it was a reaction into barbarism. In so far as something was a fad of the fading empire, that died and deserved to die, it was the Church alone that killed it. The Church is reproached for being exactly what the heresy was repressed for being. The explanations of the evolutionary historians and higher critics do really explain why Arianism and Gnosticism and Nestorianism were born—and also why they died. They do not explain why the Church was born or why she has refused to die. Above all, they do not explain why she should have made war on the very evils she is supposed to share.

Let us take a few practical examples of the principle; the principle that if there was anything that was really a superstition of the dying empire, it did really die with the dying empire; and certainly was not the same as the very thing that destroyed it. For this purpose we will take in order two or three of the most ordinary explanations of Christian origins among the modern critics of Christianity. Nothing is more common, for instance, than to find such a modern critic writing something like this: 'Christianity was above all a movement of ascetics, a rush into the desert, a refuge in the cloister, a renunciation of all life and happiness; and this was a part of a gloomy and inhuman reaction against nature itself, a hatred of the body, a horror of the material universe, a sort of universal suicide of the senses and even of the self. It came from an eastern fanaticism like that of the fakirs and was ultimately founded on an eastern pessimism, which seems to feel existence itself as an evil.'

Now the most extraordinary thing about this is that it is all quite true; it is true in every detail except that it happens to be attributed entirely to the wrong person. It is not true of the Church; but it is true of the heretics condemned by the Church. It is as if one were to write a most detailed analysis of the mistakes and misgovernment of the ministers of George the Third, merely with the small inaccuracy that the whole story was told about George Washington; or as if somebody made a list of the crimes of the Bolshevists with no variation except that they were all attributed to the Czar. The early Church was indeed very ascetic, in connection with a totally different philosophy; but the philosophy of a war on life and nature as such really did exist in the world, if the critics only knew where to look for it.

What really happened was this. When the Faith first emerged into the world, the very first thing that happened to it was that it was caught in a sort of swarm of mystical and metaphysical sects, mostly out of the East; like one lonely golden bee caught in a swarm of wasps. To the ordinary onlooker, there did not seem to be much difference, or anything beyond a general buzz; indeed in a sense there was not much difference, so far as stinging and being stung were concerned. The difference was that only one golden dot in all that whirring gold-dust had the power of going forth to make hives for all humanity; to give the world honey and wax or (as was so finely said in a context too easily forgotten) 'the two noblest things, which are sweetness and light.' The wasps all died that winter; and half the difficulty is that hardly anyone knows anything about them and most people do not know that they ever existed; so that the whole story of that first phase of our religion is lost. Or, to vary the metaphor, when this movement or some other movement pierced the dyke between the east and west and brought more mystical ideas into Europe, it brought with it a whole flood of other mystical ideas besides its own, most of them ascetical and nearly all of them pessimistic. They very nearly flooded and over-whelmed the purely Christian element. They came mostly from that region that was a sort of dim borderland between the eastern philosophies and the eastern mythologies, and which shared with the wilder philosophers that curious craze for making fantastic patterns of the cosmos in the shape of maps and genealogical trees. Those that are supposed to derive from the mysterious Manes are called Manichean; kindred cults are more generally known as Gnostic; they are mostly of a labyrinthine complexity, but the point to insist on is the pessimism; the fact that nearly all in one form or another regarded the creation of the world as the work of an evil spirit. Some of them had that Asiatic atmosphere that surrounds Buddhism; the suggestion that life is a corruption of the purity of being. Some of them suggested a purely spiritual order which had been betrayed by the coarse and clumsy trick of making such toys as the sun and moon and stars. Anyhow all this dark tide out of the metaphysical sea in the midst of Asia poured through the dykes simultaneously with the creed of

Christ; but it is the whole point of the story that the two were not the same; that they flowed like oil and water. That creed remained in the shape of a miracle; a river still flowing through the sea. And the proof of the miracle was practical once more; it was merely that while all that sea was salt and bitter with the savour of death, of this one stream in the midst of it a man could drink.

Now that purity was preserved by dogmatic definitions and exclusions. It could not possibly have been preserved by anything else. If the Church had not renounced the Manicheans it might have become merely Manichean. If it had not renounced the Gnostics it might have become Gnostic. But by the very fact that it did renounce them it proved that it was not either Gnostic or Manichean. At any rate it proved that something was not either Gnostic or Manichean; and what could it be that condemned them, if it was not the original good news of the runners from Bethlehem and the trumpet of the Resurrection? The early Church was ascetic, but she proved that she was not pessimistic, simply by condemning the pessimists. The creed declared that man was sinful, but it did not declare that life was evil, and it proved it by damning those who did. The condemnation of the early heretics is itself condemned as something crabbed and narrow; but it was in truth the very proof that the Church meant to be brotherly and broad. It proved that the primitive Catholics were specially eager to explain that they did *not* think man utterly vile; that they did *not* think life incurably miserable; that they did *not* think marriage a sin or procreation a tragedy. They were ascetic because asceticism was the only possible purge of the sins of the world; but in the very thunder of their anathemas they affirmed for ever that their asceticism was not to be anti-human or anti-natural; that they did wish to purge the world and not destroy it. And nothing else except those anathemas could possibly have made it clear, amid a confusion which still confuses them with their mortal enemies. Nothing else but dogma could have resisted the riot of imaginative invention with which the pessimists were waging their war against nature; with their Aeons and their Demiurge, their strange Logos and their sinister Sophia. If the Church had not insisted on theology, it would have melted into a mad mythology of the mystics, yet further removed from reason or even from rationalism; and, above all, yet further removed from life and from the love of life. Remember that it would have been an inverted mythology, one contradicting everything natural in paganism; a mythology in which Pluto would be above Jupiter and Hades hang higher than Olympus; in which Brahma and all that has the breath of life would be subject to Seeva, shining with the eye of death.

That the early Church was itself full of an ecstatic enthusiasm for renunciation and virginity makes this distinction much more striking and not less so. It makes all the more important the place where the dogma drew the line. A man might crawl about on all fours like a beast because he was an ascetic. He might stand night and day on the top of a pillar and be adored for being an ascetic. But he could not say that the world was a mistake or the marriage state a sin without being a heretic. What was it that thus deliberately disengaged itself from eastern asceticism by sharp definition and fierce refusal, if it was not something with an individuality of its own; and one that was quite different? If the Catholics are to be confused with the Gnostics, we can only say it was not their fault if they are. And it is rather hard that the Catholics should be blamed by the same critics for persecuting the heretics and also for sympathising with the heresy.

The Church was not a Manichean movement, if only because it was not a movement at all. It was not even merely an ascetical movement, because it was not a movement at all. It would be nearer the truth to call it the tamer of asceticism than the mere leader or loosener of it. It was a thing having its own theory of asceticism, its own type of asceticism, but most conspicuous at the moment as the moderator of other theories and types. This is the only sense that can be made, for instance, of the story of St. Augustine. As long as he was a mere man of the world, a mere man drifting with his time, he actually was a Manichean. It really was quite modern and fashionable to be a Manichean. But when he became a Catholic, the people he instantly turned on and rent in pieces were the Manicheans. The Catholic way of putting it is that he left off being a pessimist to become an ascetic. But as the pessimists interpreted asceticism, it might be said that he left off being an ascetic to become a saint. The war upon life, the denial of nature, were exactly the things he had already found in the heathen world outside the Church, and had to renounce when he entered the Church. The very fact that St. Augustine remains a somewhat sterner or sadder figure than St. Francis or St. Teresa only accentuates the dilemma. Face to face with the gravest or even grimmest of Catholics, we can still ask, 'Why did Catholicism make war on Manichees, if Catholicism was Manichean?'

Take another rationalistic explanation of the rise of Christendom. It is common enough to find another critic saying, 'Christianity did not really rise at all; that is, it did not merely rise from below; it was imposed from above. It is an example of the power of the executive, especially in despotic states. The Empire was really an Empire; that is, it was really ruled by the Emperor. One of the Emperors happened to become a Christian. He might just as well have become a Mithra-ist or a Jew or a Fire-Worshipper; it was common in the decline of the Empire for eminent and educated people to adopt these eccentric eastern cults. But when he adopted it it became the official religion of the Roman Empire; and when it became the official religion of the Roman Empire, it became as strong, as universal and as invinci-ble as the Roman Empire. It has only remained in the world as a relic of that Empire; or, as many have put it, it is but the ghost of Caesar still hovering over Rome.' This also is a very ordinary line taken in the criticism of orthodoxy, to say that it was only officialism that ever made it orthodoxy. And here again we can call on the heretics to refute it.

The whole great history of the Arian heresy might have been in-vented to explode this idea. It is a very interesting history often repeated in this connection; and the upshot of it is in that in so far as there ever was a merely official religion, it actually died because it was merely an official religion; and what destroyed it was the real religion. Arius advanced a version of Christianity which moved, more or less vaguely, in the direction of what we should call Unitarianism; though it was not the same, for it gave to Christ a curious intermediary position between the divine and human. The point is that it seemed to many more reasonable and less fanatical;

and among these were many of the educated class in a sort of reaction against the first romance of conversion. Arians were a sort of moderates and a sort of modernists. And it was felt that after the first squabbles this was the final form of rationalised religion into which civilisation might well settle down. It was accepted by Divus Caesar himself and became the official orthodoxy; the generals and military princes drawn from the new barbarian powers of the north, full of the future, supported it strongly. But the sequel is still more important. Exactly as a modern man might pass through Unitarianism to complete agnosticism, so the greatest of the Arian emperors ultimately shed the last and thinnest pretense of Christianity; he abandoned even Arius and returned to Apollo. He was a Caesar of the Caesars; a soldier, a scholar, a man of large ambitions and ideals; another of the philosopher kings. It seemed to him as if at his signal the sun rose again. The oracles began to speak like birds beginning to sing at dawn; paganism was itself again; the gods returned. It seemed the end of that strange interlude of an alien superstition. And indeed it was the end of it, so far as there was a mere interlude of mere superstition. It was the end of it, in so far as it was the fad of an emperor or the fashion of a generation. If there really was something that began with Constantine, then it ended with Julian.

But there was something that did not end. There had arisen in that hour of history, defiant above the democratic tumult of the Councils of the Church, Athanasius against the world. We may pause upon the point at issue; because it is relevant to the whole of this religious history, and the modern world seems to miss the whole point of it. We might put it this way. If there is one question which the enlightened and liberal have the habit of deriding and holding up as a dreadful example of barren dogma and senseless sectarian strife, it is this Athanasian question of the Co-Eternity of the Divine Son. On the other hand, if there is one thing that the same liberals always offer us as a piece of pure and simple Christianity, untroubled by doctrinal disputes, it is the single sentence, 'God is Love.' Yet the two statements are almost identical; at least one is very nearly nonsense without the other. The barren dogma is only the logical way of stating the beautiful sentiment. For if there be a being without beginning, existing before all things, was He loving when there was nothing to be loved? If through that unthinkable eternity He is lonely, what is the meaning of saying He is love? The only justification of such a mystery is the mystical conception that in His own nature there was something analogous to self-expression; something of what begets and beholds what it has begotten. Without some such idea, it is really illogical to complicate the ultimate essence of deity with an idea like love. If the moderns really want a simple religion of love, they must look for it in the Athanasian Creed. The truth is that the trumpet of true Christianity, the challenge of the charities and simplicities of Bethlehem or Christmas Day, never rang out more arrestingly and unmistakably than in the defiance of Athanasius to the cold compromise of the Arians. It was emphatically he who really was fighting for a God of Love against a God of colourless and remote cosmic control; the God of the stoics and the agnostics. It was emphatically he who was fighting for the Holy Child against the grey deity of the Pharisees and the Sadducees. He was fighting for that very balance of beautiful interdependence and intimacy, in the very Trinity of the Divine Nature, that draws our hearts to the Trinity of the Holy Family. His dogma, if the phrase be not misunderstood, turns even God into a Holy Family.

That this purely Christian dogma actually for a second time rebelled against the Empire, and actually for a second time refounded the Church in spite of the Empire, is itself a proof that there was something positive and personal working in the world, other than whatever official faith the Empire chose to adopt. This power utterly destroyed the official faith that the Empire did adopt. It went on its own way as it is going on its own way still. There are any number of other examples in which is repeated precisely the same process we have reviewed in the case of the Manichean and the Arian. A few centuries afterwards, for instance, the Church had to maintain the same Trinity, which is simply the logical side of love, against another appearance of the isolated and simplified deity in the religion of Islam. Yet there are some who cannot see what the Crusaders were fighting for; and some even who talk as if Christianity had never been anything but a form of what they call Hebraism coming in with the decay of Hellenism. Those people must certainly be very much puzzled by the war between the Crescent and the Cross. If Christianity had never been anything but a simpler morality sweeping away polytheism, there is no reason why Christendom should not have been swept into Islam. The truth is that Islam itself was a barbaric reaction against that very humane complexity that is really a Christian character; that idea of balance in the deity, as of balance in the family, that makes that creed a sort of sanity, and that sanity the soul of civilisation. And that is why the Church is from the first a thing holding its own position and point of view, quite apart from the accidents and anarchies of its age. That is why it deals blows impartially right and left, at the pessimism of the Manichean or the optimism of the Pelagian. It was not a Manichean movement because it was not a movement at all. It was not an official fashion because it was not a fashion at all. It was something that could coincide with movements and fashions, could control them and could survive them.

So might rise from their graves the great heresiarchs to confound their comrades of to-day. There is nothing that the critics now affirm that we cannot call on these great witnesses to deny. The modern critic will say lightly enough that Christianity was but a reaction into asceticism and anti-natural spirituality, a dance of fakirs furious against life and love. But Manes the great mystic will answer them from his secret throne and cry, 'These Christians have no right to be called spiritual; these Christians have no title to be called ascetics; they who compromised with the curse of life and all the filth of the family. Through them the earth is still foul with fruit and harvest and polluted with population. Theirs was no movement against nature, or my children would have carried it to triumph; but these fools renewed the world when I would have ended it with a gesture.' And another critic will write that the Church was but the shadow of the Empire, the fad of a chance Emperor, and that it remains in Europe only as the ghost of the power of Rome. And Arius the deacon will answer out of the darkness of oblivion: 'No, indeed, or the world would have followed my more reasonable religion. For mine went down before demagogues and men defying Caesar; and around my champion was the purple cloak and mine was the glory of the eagles. It was not for lack of these things that I failed.' And yet a third modern will maintain that the creed spread only as a sort of panic of hell-fire; men everywhere attempting impossible things in fleeing from incredible vengence; a nightmare of imaginary remorse; and such an explanation will satisfy many who see something dreadful in the doctrine of orthodoxy. And then there will go up against it the terrible voice of Tertullian, saying, 'And why then was I cast out; and why did soft hearts and heads decide against me when I proclaimed the perdition of all sinners; and what was this power that thwarted me when I threatened all backsliders with hell? For none ever went up that hard road so far as I; and mine was the *Credo Quia Impossibile*.' Then there is the fourth suggestion that there was something of the Semitic secret society in the whole matter; that it was a new invasion of the nomad spirit shaking a kindlier and more comfortable paganism, its cities and its household gods; whereby the jealous monotheistic races could after all establish their jealous God. And Mahomet shall answer out of the whirlwind, the red whirlwind of the desert, 'Who ever served the jealousy of God as I did or left him more lonely in the sky? Who ever paid more honour to Moses and Abraham or won more victories over idols and the images of paganism? And what was this thing that thrust me back with the energy of a thing alive; whose fanaticism could drive me from Sicily and tear up my deep roots out of the rock of Spain? What faith was theirs who thronged in thousands of every class and country crying out that my ruin was the will of God; and what hurled great Godfrey as from a catapult over the wall of Jerusalem; and what brought great Sobieski like a thunderbolt to the gates of Vienna? I think there was more than you fancy in the religion that has so matched itself with mine.'

Those who would suggest that the faith was a fanaticism are doomed to an eternal perplexity. In their account it is bound to appear as fanatical for nothing, and fanatical against everything. It is ascetical and at war with ascetics, Roman and in revolt against Rome, monotheistic and fighting furiously against monotheism; harsh in its condemnation of harshness; a riddle not to be explained even as unreason. And what sort of unreason is it that seems reasonable to millions of educated Europeans through all the revolutions of some sixteen hundred years? People are not amused with a puzzle or a paradox or a mere muddle in the mind for all that time. I know of no explanation except that such a thing is not unreason but reason; that if it is fanatical it is fanatical for reason and fanatical against all the unreasonable things. That is the only explanation I can find of a thing from the first so detached and so confident, condemning things that looked so like itself, refusing help from powers that seemed so essential to its existence, sharing on its human side all the passions of the age, yet always at the supreme moment suddenly rising superior to them, never saying exactly what it was expected to say and never needing to unsay what it had said; I can find no explanation except that, like Pallas from the brain of Jove, it had indeed come forth out of the mind of God, mature and mighty and armed for judgment and for war.

V

THE ESCAPE FROM PAGANISM

The modern missionary, with his palm-leaf hat and his umbrella, has become rather a figure of fun. He is chaffed among men of the world for the ease with which he can be eaten by cannibals and the narrow bigotry which makes him regard the cannibal culture as lower than his own. Perhaps the best part of the joke is that the men of the world do not see that the joke is against themselves. It is rather ridiculous to ask a man just about to be boiled in a pot and eaten, at a purely religious feast, why he does not regard all religions as equally friendly and fraternal. But there is a more subtle criticism uttered against the more old-fashioned missionary; to the effect that he generalises too broadly about the heathen and pays too little attention to the difference between Mahomet and Mumbo-Jumbo. There was probably truth in this complaint, especially in the past; but it is my main contention here that the exaggeration is all the other way at present. It is the temptation of the professors to treat mythologies too much as theologies; as things thoroughly thought out and seriously held. It is the temptation of the intellectuals to take much too seriously the fine shades of various schools in the rather irresponsible metaphysics of Asia. Above all it is their temptation to miss the real truth implied in the idea of Aquinas contra Gentiles or Athanasius contra mundum.

If the missionary says, in fact, that he is exceptional in being a Christian, and that the rest of the races and religions can be collectively classified as heathen, he is perfectly right. He may say it in quite the wrong spirit, in which case he is spiritually wrong. But in the cold light of philosophy and history, he is intellectually right. He may not be right-minded, but he is right. He may not even have a right to be right, but he is right. The outer world to which he brings his creed really is something subject to certain generalisations covering all its varieties, and is not merely a variety of similar creeds. Perhaps it is in any case too much of a temptation to pride or hypocrisy to call it heathenry. Perhaps it would be better simply to call it humanity. But there are certain broad characteristics of what we call humanity while it remains in what we call heathenry. They are not necessarily bad characteristics; some of them are worthy of the respect of Christendom; some of them have been absorbed and transfigured in the substance of Christendom. But they existed before Christendom and they still exist outside Christendom, as certainly as the sea existed before a boat and all round a boat; and they have as strong and as universal and as unmistakable a savour as the sea.

For instance, all real scholars who have studied the Greek and Roman culture say one thing about it. They agree that in the ancient world religion was one thing and philosophy quite another. There was very little effort to rationalise and at the same time to realise a real belief in the gods. There was very little pretense of any such real belief among the philosophers. But neither had the passion or perhaps the power to persecute the other, save in particular and peculiar cases; and neither the philosopher in his school nor the priest in his temple seems ever to have seriously contemplated his own concept as covering the world. A priest sacrificing to Artemis in Calydon did not seem to think that people would some day sacrifice to her instead of to Isis beyond the sea; a sage following the vegetarian rule of the Neo-Pythagoreans did not seem to think it would universally prevail and exclude the methods of Epictetus or Epicurus. We may call this liberality if we like; I am not dealing with an argument but describing an atmosphere. All this, I say, is admitted by all scholars; but what neither the learned nor the unlearned have fully realised, perhaps, is that this description is really an exact description of all non-Christian civilisation to-day; and especially of the great civilisations of the East. Eastern paganism really is much more all of a piece, just as ancient paganism was much more all of a piece, than the modern critics admit. It is a many-coloured Persian Carpet as the other was a varied and tesselated Roman pavement; but the one real crack right across that pavement came from the earthquake of the Crucifixion.

The modern European seeking his religion in Asia is reading his religion into Asia. Religion there is something different; it is both more and less. He is like a man mapping out the sea as land; marking waves as mountains; not understanding the nature of its peculiar permanence. It is perfectly true that Asia has its own dignity and poetry and high civilisation. But it is not in the least true that Asia has its own definite dominions of moral government, where all loyalty is conceived in terms of morality; as when we say that Ireland is Catholic or that New England was Puritan. The map is not marked out in religions, in our sense of churches. The state of mind is far more subtle, more relative, more secretive, more varied and changing, like the colours of the snake. The Moslem is the nearest approach to a militant Christian; and that is precisely because he is a much nearer approach to an envoy from western civilisation. The Moslem in the heart of Asia almost stands for the soul of Europe. And as he stands between them and Europe in the matter of space, so he stands between them and Christianity in the matter of time. In that sense the Moslems in Asia are merely like the Nestorians in Asia. Islam, historically speaking, is the greatest of the Eastern heresies. It owed something to the quite isolated and unique individuality of Israel; but it owed more to Byzantium and the theological enthusiasm of Christendom. It owed something even to the Crusades. It owed nothing whatever to Asia. It owed nothing to the atmosphere of the ancient and traditional world of Asia, with its immemorial etiquette and its bottomless or bewildering philosophies. All that ancient and actual Asia felt the entrance of Islam as something foreign and western and warlike, piercing it like a spear.

Even where we might trace in dotted lines the domains of Asiatic religions, we should probably be reading into them something dogmatic and ethical belonging to our own religion. It is as if a European ignorant of the American atmosphere were to suppose that each 'state' was a separate sovereign state as patriotic as France or Poland; or that when a Yankee referred fondly to his 'home town' he meant he had no other nation, like a citizen of ancient Athens or Rome. As he would be reading a particular sort of loyalty into America, so we are reading a particular sort of loyalty into Asia. There are loyalties of other kinds; but not what men in the west mean by being a believer, by trying to be a Christian, by being a good Protestant or a practising Catholic. In the intellectual world it means something far more vague and varied by doubts and speculations. In the moral world it means something far more loose and drifting. A professor of Persian at one of our great universities, so passionate a partisan of the East as practically to profess a contempt for the West, said to a friend of mine: 'You will never understand oriental religions, because you always conceive religion as connected with ethics. This kind has really nothing to do with ethics.' We have most of us known some Masters of the Higher Wisdom, some Pilgrims upon the Path to Power, some eastern esoteric saints and seers, who had really nothing to do with ethics. Something different, something detached and irresponsible, tinges the moral atmosphere of Asia and touches even that of Islam. It was very realistically caught in the atmosphere of *Hassan*[1]; and a very horrible atmosphere too. It is even more vivid in such glimpses as we get of the genuine and ancient cults of Asia. Deeper than the depths of metaphysics, far down in the abysses of mystical meditations, under all that solemn universe of spiritual things, is a secret, an intangible and a terrible levity. It does not really very much matter what one does. Either because they do not believe in a devil, or because they do believe in a destiny, or because experience here is everything and eternal life something totally different, but for some reason they are totally different. I have read somewhere that there were three great friends famous in medieval Persia for their unity of mind. One became the responsible and respected Vizier of the Great King; the second was the poet Omar, pessimist and epicurean, drinking wine in mockery of Mahomet; the third was the Old Man of the Mountain who maddened his people with hashish that they might murder other people with daggers. It does not really much matter what one does.

The Sultan in *Hassan* would have understood all those three men; indeed he was all those three men. But this sort of universalist cannot have what we call a character; it is what we call a chaos. He cannot choose; he cannot fight; he cannot repent; he cannot hope. He is

[1] A Persian mystery-play of the Shiites. Performed in a highly emotional manner which necessitates making provision for the safety of those of the hated Sunnite sect. The heroes of the play are Shiite martyrs.

not in the same sense creating something; for creation means rejection. He is not, in our religious phrase, making his soul. For our doctrine of salvation does really mean a labour like that of a man trying to make a statue beautiful; a victory with wings. For that there must be a final choice; for a man cannot make statues without rejecting stone. And there really is this ultimate unmorality behind the metaphysics of Asia. And the reason is that there has been nothing through all those unthinkable ages to bring the human mind sharply to the point; to tell it that the time has come to choose. The mind has lived too much in eternity. The soul has been too immortal; in the special sense that it ignores the idea of mortal sin. It has had too much of eternity, in the sense that it has not had enough of the hour of death and the day of judgment. It is not crucial enough; in the literal sense that it has not had enough of the cross. That is what we mean when we say that Asia is very old. But strictly speaking Europe is quite as old as Asia; indeed in a sense any place is as old as any other place. What we mean is that Europe has not merely gone on growing older. It has been born again.

Asia is all humanity; as it has worked out its human doom. Asia, in its vast territory, in its varied populations, in its heights of past achievement and its depths of dark speculation, is itself a world; and represents something of what we mean when we speak of the world. It is a cosmos rather than a continent. It is the world as man has made it; and contains many of the most wonderful things that man has made. Therefore Asia stands as the one representative of paganism and the one rival to Christendom. But everywhere else where we get glimpses of that mortal destiny, they suggest stages in the same story. Where Asia trails away into the southern archipelagoes of the savages, or where a darkness full of nameless shapes dwells in the heart of Africa, or where the last survivors of lost races linger in the cold volcano of prehistoric America, it is all the same story; sometimes perhaps later chapters of the same story. It is men entangled in the forest of their own mythology; it is men drowned in the sea of their own metaphysics. Polytheists have grown weary of the wildest of fictions. Monotheists have grown weary of the most wonderful of truths. Diabolists here and there have such a hatred of heaven and earth that they have tried to take refuge in hell. It is the Fall of Man; and it is exactly that fall that was being felt by our own fathers at the first moment of the Roman decline. We also were going down that wide road; down that easy slope; following the magnificent procession of the high civilisations of the world.

If the Church had not entered the world then, it seems probable that Europe would be now very much what Asia is now. Something may be allowed for a real difference of race and environment, visible in the ancient as in the modern world. But after all we talk about the changeless East very largely because it has not suffered the great change. Paganism in its last phase showed considerable signs of becoming equally changeless. This would not mean that new schools or sects of philosophy would not arise; as new schools did arise in Antiquity and do arise in Asia. It does not mean that there would be no real mystics or visionaries; as there were mystics in Antiquity and are mystics in Asia. It does not mean that there would be no social codes, as there were codes in Antiquity and are codes in Asia. It does not mean that there could not be good men or happy lives, for God has given all men a conscience and conscience can give all men a kind of peace. But it does mean that the tone and proportion of all these things, and especially the proportion of good and evil things, would be in the unchanged West what they are in the changeless East. And nobody who looks at that changeless East honestly, and with a real sympathy, can believe that there is anything there remotely resembling the challenge and revolution of the Faith.

In short, if classic paganism had lingered until now, a number of things might well have lingered with it; and they would look very like what we call the religions of the East. There would still be Pythagoreans teaching reincarnation, as there are still Hindus teaching reincarnation. There would still be Stoics making a religion out of reason and virtue, as there are still Confucians making a religion out of reason and virtue. There would still be Neo-Platonists studying transcendental truths, the meaning of which was mysterious to other people and disputed even amongst themselves; as the Buddhists still study a transcendentalism mysterious to others and disputed among themselves. There would still be intelligent

Apollonians apparently worshipping the sun-god but explaining that they were worshipping the divine principle; just as there are still intelligent Parsees apparently worshipping the sun but explaining that they are worshipping the deity. There would still be wild Dionysians dancing on the mountain as there are still wild Dervishes dancing in the desert. There would still be crowds of people attending the popular feasts of the gods, in pagan Europe as in pagan Asia. There would still be crowds of gods, local and other, for them to worship. And there would still be a great many more people who worshipped them than people who believed in them. Finally there would still be a very large number of people who did worship gods and did believe in gods; and who believed in gods and worshipped gods simply because they were demons. There would still be Levantines secretly sacrificing to Moloch as there are still Thugs[2] secretly sacrificing to Kalee.[3] There would still be a great deal of magic; and a great deal of it would be black magic. There would still be a considerable admiration of Seneca and a considerable imitation of Nero; just as the exalted epigrams of Confucius could coexist with the tortures of China. And over all that tangled forest of traditions growing wild or withering would brood the broad silence of a singular and even nameless mood; but the nearest name of it is nothing. All these things, good and bad, would have an indescribable air of being too old to die.

None of these things occupying Europe in the absence of Christendom would bear the least likeness to Christendom. Since the Pythagorean Metempsychosis would still be there, we might call it the Pythagorean religion as we talk about the Buddhist religion. As the noble maxims of Socrates would still be there, we might call it the Socratic religion as we talk about the Confucian religion. As the

---

[2] Thugs were members of a former confederacy or fraternity of northern India, worshippers of Kalee, in whose honor murder, usually by strangling, was made a profession; the members of the fraternity derived their main support from plunder thus secured. They were suppressed by the British, 1830–1840.

[3] Kalee is a malignant form of Hindu female deity, means "the black". Portrayed as dripping with blood, encircled with snakes and adorned with skulls. Worshipped with obscene and bloody rites, formerly with human sacrifice.

popular holiday was still marked by a mythological hymn to Adonis, we might call it the religion of Adonis as we talk about the religion of Juggernaut. As literature would still be based on the Greek mythology, we might call that mythology a religion, as we call the Hindu mythology a religion. We might say that there were so many thousands or millions of people belonging to that religion, in the sense of frequenting such temples or merely living in a land full of such temples. But if we called the last tradition of Pythagoras or the lingering legend of Adonis by the name of a religion, then we must find some other name for the Church of Christ.

If anybody says that philosophic maxims preserved through many ages, or mythological temples frequented by many people, are things of the same class and category as the Church, it is enough to answer quite simply that they are not. Nobody thinks they are the same when he sees them in the old civilisation of Greece and Rome; nobody would think they were the same if that civilisation had lasted two thousand years longer and existed at the present day; nobody can in reason think they are the same in the parallel pagan civilisation in the East, as it is at the present day. None of these philosophies or mythologies are anything like a Church; certainly nothing like a Church Militant. And, as I have shown elsewhere, even if this rule were not already proved, the exception would prove the rule. The rule is that pre-Christian or pagan history does not produce a Church Militant; and the exception, or what some would call the exception, is that Islam is at least militant if it is not Church. And that is precisely because Islam is the one religious rival that is *not* pre-Christian and therefore not in that sense pagan. Islam was a product of Christianity; even if it was a by-product; even if it was a bad product. It was a heresy or parody emulating and therefore imitating the Church. It is no more surprising that Mahomedanism had something of her fighting spirit than that Quakerism had something of her peaceful spirit. After Christianity there are any number of such emulations or extensions. Before it there are none.

The Church Militant is thus unique because it is an army marching to effect a universal deliverance. The bondage from which the world is thus to be delivered is something that is very well symbolised by the state of Asia as by the state of pagan Europe. I do not mean merely their moral or immoral state. The missionary, as a matter of fact, has much more to say for himself than the enlightened imagine, even when he says that the heathen are idolatrous and immoral. A touch or two of realistic experience about Eastern religion, even about Moslem religion, will reveal some startling insensibilities in ethics; such as the practical indifference to the line between passion and perversion. It is not prejudice but practical experience which says that Asia is full of demons as well as gods. But the evil I mean is in the mind. And it is in the mind wherever the mind has worked for a long time alone. It is what happens when all dreaming and thinking have come to an end in an emptiness that is at once negation and necessity. It sounds like an anarchy, but it is also a slavery. It is what has been called already the wheel of Asia; all those recurrent arguments about cause and effect or things beginning and ending in the mind, which make it impossible for the soul really to strike out and go anywhere or do anything. And the point is that it is not necessarily peculiar to Asiatics; it would have been true in the end of Europeans — if something had not happened. If the Church Militant had not been a thing marching, all men would have been marking time. If the Church Militant had not endured a discipline, all men would have endured a slavery.

What that universal yet fighting faith brought into the world was hope. Perhaps the one thing common to mythology and philosophy was that both were really sad; in the sense that they had not this hope even if they had touches of faith or charity. We may call Buddhism a faith; though to us it seems more like a doubt. We may call the Lord of Compassion a Lord of Charity, though it seems to us a very pessimist sort of pity. But those who insist most on the antiquity and size of such cults must agree that in all their ages they have not covered all their areas with that sort of practical and pugnacious hope. In Christendom hope has never been absent; rather it has been errant, extravagant, excessively fixed upon fugitive chances. Its perpetual revolution and reconstruction has at least been an evidence of people being in better spirits. Europe did very truly renew its youth like the eagles; just as the eagles of Rome rose again over the legions of Napoleon, or we have seen soaring but yesterday the silver eagle of Poland. But in the Polish case even revolution always went with religion. Napoleon himself sought a reconciliation with religion. Religion could never be finally separated even from the most hostile of the hopes; simply because it was the real source of the hopefulness. And the cause of this is to be found simply in the religion itself. Those who quarrel about it seldom even consider it in itself. There is neither space nor place for such a full consideration here; but a word may be said to explain a reconciliation that always recurs and still seems to require explanation.

There will be no end to the weary debates about liberalising theology, until people face the fact that the only liberal part of it is really the dogmatic part. If dogma is incredible, it is because it is incredibly liberal. If it is irrational, it can only be in giving us more assurance of freedom than is justified by reason. The obvious example is that essential form of freedom which we call free-will. It is absurd to say that a man shows his liberality in denying his liberty. But it is tenable that he has to affirm a transcendental doctrine in order to affirm his liberty. There is a sense in which we might reasonably say that if man has a primary power of choice, he has in that fact a supernatural power of creation, as if he could raise the dead or give birth to the unbegotten. Possibly in that case a man must be a miracle; and certainly in that case he must be a miracle in order to be a man; and most certainly in order to be a free man. But it is absurd to forbid him to be a free man and do it in the name of a more free religion.

But it is true in twenty other matters. Anybody who believes at all in God must believe in the absolute supremacy of God. But in so far as that supremacy does allow of any degrees that can be called liberal or illiberal, it is self-evident that the illiberal power is the deity of the rationalists and the liberal power is the deity of the dogmatists. Exactly in proportion as you turn monotheism into monism you turn it into despotism. It is precisely the unknown God of the scientist, with his impenetrable purpose and his inevitable and unalterable law, that reminds us of a Prussian autocrat making rigid plans in a remote tent and moving mankind like machinery. It is precisely the God of miracles and of answered prayers who reminds us of a liberal and popular prince, receiving petitions, listening to parliaments and considering the cases of a whole people. I am not now arguing the rationality of this conception in other respects; as a matter of fact it is not, as some suppose, irrational; for there is nothing irrational in the wisest and most well-informed king acting differently according to the action of those he wishes to save. But I am here only noting the general nature of liberality, or of free or enlarged atmosphere of action. And in this respect it is certain that the king can only be what we call magnanimous if he is what some call capricious. It is the Catholic, who has the feeling that his prayers do make a difference, when offered for the living and the dead, who also has the feeling of living like a free citizen in something almost like a constitutional commonwealth. It is the monist who lives under a single iron law who must have the feeling of living like a slave under a sultan. Indeed I believe that the original use of the word *suffragium*, which we now use in politics for a vote, was that employed in theology about a prayer. The dead in Purgatory were said to have the suffrages of the living. And in this sense, of a sort of right of petition to the supreme ruler, we may truly say that the whole of the Communion of Saints, as well as the whole of the Church Militant, is founded on universal suffrage.

But above all, it is true of the most tremendous issue; of that tragedy which has created the divine comedy of our creed. Nothing short of the extreme and strong and startling doctrine of the divinity of Christ will give that particular effect that can truly stir the popular sense like a trumpet; the idea of the king himself serving in the ranks like a common soldier. By making that figure merely human we make that story much less human. We take away the point of the story which actually pierces humanity; the point of the story which was quite literally the point of a spear. It does not especially humanise the universe to say that good and wise men can die for their opinions; any more than it would be any sort of uproariously popular news in an army that good soldiers may easily get killed. It is no news that King Leonidas is dead any more than that Queen Anne is dead; and men did not wait for Christianity to be men, in the full sense of being heroes. But if we are describing, for the moment, the atmosphere of what is generous and popular and even picturesque, any knowledge of human nature will tell us that no sufferings of the sons of men, or even of the servants of God, strike the same note as the notion of the master suffering instead of his servants. And this is given by the theological and emphatically not by the scientific deity. No mysterious monarch, hidden in his starry pavilion at the base of the cosmic campaign, is in the least like that celestial chivalry of the Captain who carries his five wounds in the front of battle.

What the denouncer of dogma really means is not that dogma is bad; but rather that dogma is too good to be true. That is, he means that dogma is too liberal to be likely. Dogma gives man too much freedom when it permits him to fall. Dogma gives even God too much freedom when it permits him to die. That is what the intelligent sceptics ought to say; and it is not in the least my intention to deny that there is something to be said for it. They mean that the universe is itself a universal prison; that existence itself is a limitation and a control; and it is not for nothing that they call causation a chain. In a word, they mean quite simply that they cannot believe these things; not in the least that they are unworthy of belief. We say, not lightly but very literally, that the truth has made us free. They say that it makes us so free that it cannot be the truth. To them it is like believing in fairyland to believe in such freedom as we enjoy. It is like believing in men with wings to entertain the fancy of men with wills. It is like accepting a fable about a squirrel in conversation with a mountain to believe in a man who is free to ask or a God who is free to answer. This is a manly and a rational negation for which I for one shall always show respect. But I decline to show any respect for those who first of all clip the wings and cage the squirrel, rivet the chains and refuse the freedom, close all the doors of the cosmic prison on us with a clang of eternal iron, tell us that our emancipation is a dream and our dungeon a necessity; and then calmly turn round and tell us they have a freer thought and a more liberal theology.

The moral of all this is an old one; that religion is revelation. In other words, it is a vision, and a vision received by faith; but it is a vision of reality. The faith consists in a conviction of its reality. That, for example, is the difference between a vision and a day-dream. And that is the difference between religion and mythology. That is the difference between faith and all that fancy-work, quite human and more or less healthy, which we considered under the head of mythology. There is something in the reasonable use of the very word vision that implies two things about it; first that it comes very rarely, possibly that it comes only once; and secondly that it probably comes once and for all. A day-dream may come every day. A day-dream may be different every day. It is something more than the difference between telling ghost-stories and meeting a ghost.

But if it is not a mythology neither is it a philosophy. It is not a philosophy because, being a vision, it is not a pattern but a picture. It is not one of those simplifications which resolve everything into an abstract explanation; as that everything is recurrent; or everything is relative; or everything is inevitable; or everything is illusive. It is not a process but a story. It has proportions, of the sort seen in a picture or a story; it has not the regular repetitions of a pattern or a process; but it replaces them by being convincing as a picture or a story is convincing. In other words, it is exactly, as the phrase goes, like life. For indeed it is life. An example of what is meant here might well be found in the treatment of the problem of evil. It is easy enough to make a plan of life of which the background is black, as the pessimists do; and then admit a speck or two of star-dust more or less accidental, or at least in the literal sense insignificant. And it is easy enough to make another plan on white paper, as the Christian Scientists do, and explain or explain away somehow such dots or smudges as may be difficult to deny. Lastly it is easiest of all, perhaps, to say as the dualists do, that life is like a chess-board in which the two are equal; and can as truly be said to consist of white squares on a black board or of black squares on a white board. But every man feels in his heart that none of these three paper plans is like life; that none of these worlds is one in which he can live. Something tells him that the ultimate idea of a world is not bad or even neutral; staring at the sky or the grass or the truths of mathematics or even a new-laid egg, he has a vague feeling like the shadow of that saying of the great Christian philosopher, St. Thomas Aquinas, 'Every existence, as such, is good.' On the other hand, something else tells him that it is unmanly and debased and even diseased to minimise evil to a dot or even a blot. He realises that optimism is morbid. It is if possible even more morbid than pessimism. These vague but healthy feelings, if he followed them out, would result in the idea that evil is in some way an exception but an enormous exception; and ultimately that evil is an invasion or yet more truly a rebellion. He does not think that everything is right or that everything is wrong, or that everything is equally right and wrong. But he does think that right has a right to be right and therefore a right to be there; and wrong has no right to be wrong and therefore no right to be there. It is the prince of the world; but it is also a usurper. So he will apprehend vaguely what the vision will give to him vividly; no less than all that strange story of treason in heaven and the great desertion by which evil damaged and tried to destroy a cosmos that it could not create. It is a very strange story and its proportions and its lines and colours are as arbitrary and absolute as the artistic composition of a picture. It is a vision which we do in fact symbolise in pictures by titanic limbs and passionate tints of plumage; all that abysmal vision of falling stars and the peacock panoplies of the night. But that strange story has one small advantage over the diagrams. It is like life.

Another example might be found, not in the problem of evil, but in what is called the problem of progress. One of the ablest agnostics of the age once asked me whether I thought mankind grew better or grew worse or remained the same. He was confident that the alternative covered all possibilities. He did not see that it only covered patterns and not pictures; processes and not stories. I asked him whether he thought that Mr. Smith of Golder's Green got better or worse or remained exactly the same between the age of thirty and forty. It then seemed to dawn on him that it would rather depend on Mr. Smith; and how he chose to go on. It had never occurred to him that it might depend on how mankind chose to go on; and that its course was not a straight line or an upward or downward curve, but a track like that of a man across a valley, going where he liked and stopping where he chose, going into a church or falling drunk in a ditch. The life of man is a story; an adventure story; and in our vision the same is true even of the story of God.

The Catholic faith is the reconciliation because it is the realisation both of mythology and philosophy. It is a story and in that sense one of a hundred stories; only it is a true story. It is a philosophy and in that sense one of a hundred philosophies; only it is a philosophy that is like life. But above all, it is a reconciliation because it is something that can only be called the philosophy of stories. That normal narrative instinct which produced all the fairy tales is something that is neglected by all the philosophies—except one. The Faith is the justification of that popular instinct; the finding of a philosophy for it or the analysis of the philosophy in it. Exactly as a man in an adventure story has to pass various tests to save his life, so the man in this philosophy has to pass several tests and save his soul. In both there is an idea of free will operating under conditions of design; in other words, there is an aim and it is the business of a man to aim at it; we therefore watch to see whether he will hit it. Now this deep and democratic and dramatic instinct is derided and dismissed in all the other philosophies. For all the other philosophies avowedly end where they begin; and it is the definition of a story that it ends differently; that it begins in one place and ends in another. From Buddha and his wheel to Akhen Aten and his disc, from Pythagoras with his abstraction of number to Confucius with his religion of routine, there is not one of them that does not in some way sin against the soul of a story. There is none of them that really grasps this human notion of the tale, the test, the adventure; the ordeal of the free man. Each of them starves the story-telling instinct, so to speak, and does something to spoil human life considered as a romance; either by fatalism (pessimist or optimist) and that destiny that is the death of adventure; or by indifference and that detachment that is the death of drama; or by a fundamental scepticism that dissolves the actors into atoms; or by a materialistic limitation blocking the vista of moral consequences; or a mechanical recurrence making even moral tests monotonous; or a bottomless relativity making even practical tests insecure. There is such a thing as a human story; and there is such a thing as the divine story which is also a human story; but there is no such thing as a Hegelian story or a Monist story or a relativist story or a determinist story; for every story, yes, even a penny dreadful or a cheap novelette, has something in it that belongs to our universe and not theirs. Every short story does truly begin with creation and end with a last judgment.

And *that* is the reason why the myths and the philosophers were at war until Christ came. That is why the Athenian democracy killed Socrates out of respect for the gods; and why every strolling sophist gave himself the airs of a Socrates whenever he could talk in a superior fashion of the gods; and why the heretic Pharaoh wrecked his huge idols and temples for an abstraction and why the priests could return in triumph and trample his dynasty under foot; and why Buddhism had to divide itself from Brahminism, and why in every age and country outside Christendom there has been a feud for ever between the philosopher and the priest. It is easy enough to say that the philosopher is generally the more rational; it is easier still to forget that the priest is always the more popular. For the priest told the people stories; and the philosopher did not understand the philosophy of stories. It came into the world with the story of Christ.

And this is why it had to be a revelation or vision given from above. Any one who will think of the theory of stories or pictures will easily see the point. The true story of the world must be told by somebody to somebody else. By the very nature of a story it cannot be left to occur to anybody. A story has proportions, variations, surprises, particular dispositions, which cannot be worked out by rule in the abstract, like a sum. We could not deduce whether or no Achilles would give back the body of Hector from a Pythagorean theory of number or recurrence; and we could not infer for ourselves in what way the world would get back the body of Christ, merely from being told that all things go round and round upon the wheel of Buddha. A man might perhaps work out a proposition of Euclid without having heard of Euclid; but he would not work out the precise legend of Eurydice without having heard of Eurydice. At any rate he would not be certain how the story would end and whether Orpheus was ultimately defeated. Still less could he guess the end of our story; or the legend of our Orpheus rising, not defeated, from the dead.

To sum up; the sanity of the world was restored and the soul of man offered salvation by something which did indeed satisfy the two warring tendencies of the past; which had never been satisfied in full and most certainly never satisfied together. It met the mythological search for romance by being a story and the philosophical search for truth by being a true story. That is why the ideal figure had to be a historical character, as nobody had ever felt Adonis or Pan to be a historical character. But that is also why the historical character had to be the ideal figure; and even fulfil many of the functions given to these other ideal figures; why he was at once the sacrifice and the feast, why he could be shown under the emblems of the growing vine or the rising sun. The more deeply we think of the matter the more we shall conclude that, if there be indeed a God, his creation could hardly have reached any other culmination than this granting of a real romance to the world. Otherwise the two sides of the human mind could never have touched at all; and the brain of man would have remained cloven and double; one lobe of it dreaming impossible dreams and the other repeating invariable calculations. The picture-makers would have remained forever painting the portrait of nobody. The sages would have remained for ever adding up numerals that came to nothing. It was that abyss that nothing but an incarnation could cover; a divine embodiment of our dreams; and he stands above that chasm whose name is more than priest and older even than Christendom; Pontifex Maximus, the mightiest maker of a bridge.

But even with that we return to the more specially Christian symbol in the same tradition; the perfect pattern of the keys. This is a historical and not a theological outline, and it is not my duty here to defend in detail that theology, but merely to point out that it could not even be justified in design without being justified in detail—like a key. Beyond the broad suggestion of this chapter I attempt no apologetic about why the creed should be accepted. But in answer to the historical query of why it was accepted, and is accepted, I answer for millions of others in my reply; because it fits the lock; because it is like life. It is one among many stories; only it happens to be a true story. It is one among many philosophies; only it happens to be the truth. We accept it; and the ground is solid under our feet and the road is open before us. It does not imprison us in a dream of destiny or a consciousness of the universal delusion. It opens to us not only incredible heavens, but what seems to some an equally incredible earth, and makes it credible. This is the sort of truth that is hard to explain because it is a fact; but it is a fact to which we can call witnesses. We are Christians and Catholics not because we worship a key, but because we have passed a door; and felt the wind that is the trumpet of liberty blow over the land of the living.

VI

THE FIVE DEATHS OF THE FAITH

It is not the purpose of this book to trace the subsequent history of Christianity, especially the later history of Christianity; which involves controversies of which I hope to write more fully elsewhere. It is devoted only to the suggestion that Christianity, appearing amid heathen humanity, had all the character of a unique thing and even of a supernatural thing. It was not like any of the other things; and the more we study it the less it looks like any of them. But there is a certain rather peculiar character which marked it henceforward even down to the present moment, with a note on which this book may well conclude.

I have said that Asia and the ancient world had an air of being too old to die. Christendom has had the very opposite fate. Christendom has had a series of revolutions and in each one of them Christianity has died. Christianity has died many times and risen again; for it had a God who knew the way out of the grave. But the first extraordinary fact which marks this history is this: that Europe has been turned upside down over and over again; and that at the end of each of these revolutions the same religion has again been found on top. The Faith is always converting the age, not as an old religion but as a new religion. This truth is hidden from many by a convention that is too little noticed. Curiously enough, it is a convention of the sort which those who ignore it claim especially to detect and denounce. They are always telling us that priests and ceremonies are not religion and that religious organisation can be a hollow sham; but they hardly realise how true it is. It is so true that three or four times at least in the history of Christendom the whole soul seemed to have gone out of Christianity; and almost every man in his heart expected its end. This fact is only masked in medieval and other times by that very official religion which such critics pride themselves on seeing through. Christianity remained the official religion of a Renaissance prince or the official religion of an eighteenth-century bishop, just as an ancient mythology remained the official religion of Julius Ceasar or the Arian creed long remained the official religion of Julian the Apostate. But there was a difference between the cases of Julius and of Julian; because the Church had begun its strange career. There was no reason why men like Julius should not worship gods like Jupiter for ever in public and laugh at them for ever in private. But when Julian treated Christianity as dead, he found it had come to life again. He also found, incidentally, that there was not the faintest sign of Jupiter ever coming to life again. This case of Julian and the episode of Arianism is but the first of a series of examples that can only be roughly indicated here. Arianism, as has been said, had every human appearance of being the natural way in which that particular superstition of Constantine might be expected to peter out. All the ordinary stages had been passed through; the creed had become a respectable thing, had become a ritual thing, had then been modified into a rational thing; and the rationalists were ready to dissipate the last remains of it, just as they do to-day. When Christianity rose again suddenly and threw them, it was almost as unexpected as Christ rising from the dead. But there are many other examples of the same thing, even about the same time. The rush of missionaries from Ireland, for instance, has all the air of an unexpected onslaught of young men on an old world, and even on a Church that showed signs of growing old. Some of them were martyred on the coast of Cornwall; and the chief authority on Cornish antiquities told me that he did not believe for a moment that they were martyred by heathens but (as he expressed it with some humour) 'by rather slack Christians.'

Now if we were to dip below the surface of history, as it is not in the scope of this argument to do, I suspect that we should find several occasions when Christendom was thus to all appearance hollowed out from within by doubt and indifference, so that only the old Christian shell stood as the pagan shell had stood so long. But the difference is that in every such case, the sons were fanatical for the faith where the fathers had been slack about it. This is obvious in the case of the transition from the Renaissance to the Counter-Reformation. It is obvious in the case of a transition from the eighteenth century to the many Catholic revivals of our own time. But I suspect many other examples which would be worthy of separate studies.

The Faith is not a survival. It is not as if the Druids had managed somehow to survive somewhere for two thousand years. That is what might have happened in Asia or ancient Europe, in that indifference or tolerance in which mythologies and philosophies could live for ever side by side. It has not survived; it has returned again and again in this western world of rapid change and institutions perpetually perishing. Europe, in the tradition of Rome, was always trying revolution and reconstruction; rebuilding a universal republic. And it always began by rejecting this old stone and ended by making it the head of the corner; by bringing it back from the rubbish-heap to make it the crown of the capitol. Some stones of Stonehenge are standing and some are fallen; and as the stone falleth so shall it lie. There has not been a Druidic renaissance every century or two, with the young Druids crowned with fresh mistletoe, dancing in the sun on Salisbury Plain. Stonehenge has not been rebuilt in every style of architecture from the rude round Norman to the last rococo of the Baroque. The sacred place of the Druids is safe from the vandalism of restoration.

But the Church in the West was not in a world where things were too old to die; but in one in which they were always young enough to get killed. The consequence was that superficially and externally it often did get killed; nay, it sometimes wore out even without getting killed. And there follows a fact I find it somewhat difficult to describe, yet which I believe to be very real and rather important. As a ghost is the shadow of a man, and in that sense the shadow of life, so at intervals there passed across this endless life a sort of shadow of death. It came at the moment when it would have perished had it been perishable. It withered away everything that was perishable. If such animal parallels were worthy of the occasion, we might say that the snake shuddered and shed a skin and went on, or even that the cat went into convulsions as it lost only one of its nine-hundred-and-ninety-nine lives. It is truer to say, in a more dignified image, that a clock struck and nothing happened; or that a bell tolled for an execution that was everlastingly postponed.

What was the meaning of all that dim but vast unrest of the twelfth century; when, as it has been so finely said, Julian stirred in his sleep? Why did there appear so strangely early, in the twilight of dawn after the Dark Ages, so deep a scepticism as that involved in urging nominalism[1] against realism? For realism against nominalism was really realism against rationalism, or something more destructive than what we call rationalism. The answer is that just as some might have thought the Church simply a part of the Roman Empire, so others later might have thought the Church only a part of the Dark Ages. The Dark Ages ended as the Empire had ended; and the Church should have departed with them, if she had been also one of the shades of night. It was another of those spectral deaths or simulations of death. I mean that if nominalism had succeeded, it would have been as if Arianism had succeeded, it would have been the beginning of a confession that Christianity had failed. For nominalism is a far more fundamental scepticism than mere atheism. Such was the question that was openly asked as the Dark Ages broadened into that daylight that we call the modern world. But what was the answer? The answer was Aquinas in the chair of Aristotle, taking all knowledge for his province; and tens of thousands of lads down to the lowest ranks of peasant and serf, living in rags and on crusts about the great colleges, to listen to the scholastic philosophy.

What was the meaning of all that whisper of fear that ran round the west under the shadow of Islam, and fills every old romance with incongruous images of Saracen knights swaggering in Norway or the Hebrides? Why were men in the extreme west, such as King John if I remember rightly, accused of being secretly Moslems, as men are accused of being secretly atheists? Why was there that fierce alarm among some of the authorities about the rationalistic Arab version to Aristotle? Authorities are seldom alarmed like that except when it is too late. The answer is that hundreds of people probably

[1] Nominalism denies that universals (represented by such common nouns as cow, dog, etc.) exist in the mind or in things. A universal is thus only a word (a nomen). Realism, on the other hand, insists on the existence of universals in both the mind and reality.

believed in their hearts that Islam would conquer Christendom; that Averroes was more rational than Anselm; that the Saracen culture was really, as it was superficially, a superior culture. Here again we should probably find a whole generation, the older generation, very doubtful and depressed and weary. The coming of Islam would only have been the coming of Unitarianism a thousand years before its time. To many it may have seemed quite reasonable and quite probable and quite likely to happen. If so, they would have been surprised at what did happen. What did happen was a roar like thunder from thousands and thousands of young men, throwing all their youth into one exultant counter-charge; the Crusades. It was the sons of St. Francis, the Jugglers of God, wandering singing over all the roads of the world; it was the Gothic going up like a flight of arrows; it was the waking of the world. In considering the war of the Albigensians, we come to the breach in the heart of Europe and the landslide of a new philosophy that nearly ended Christendom for ever. In that case the new philosophy was also a very old philosophy; it was pessimism. It was none the less like modern ideas because it was as old as Asia; most modern ideas are. It was the Gnostics returning; but why did the Gnostics return? Because it was the end of an epoch, like the end of the Empire; and should have been the end of the Church. It was Schopenhauer hovering over the future; but it was also Manichaeus rising from the dead; that men might have death and that they might have it more abundantly.

It is rather more obvious in the case of the Renaissance, simply because the period is so much nearer to us and people know so much more about it. But there is more even in that example than most people know. Apart from the particular controversies which I wish to reserve for a separate study, the period was far more chaotic than those controversies commonly imply. When Protestants call Latimer a martyr to Protestantism, and Catholics reply that Campion was a martyr to Catholicism, it is often forgotten that many who perished in such persecutions could only be described as martyrs to atheism or anarchism or even diabolism. That world was almost as wild as our own; the men wandering about in it included the sort of man who says there is no God, the sort of man who says he is himself

God, the sort of man who says something that nobody can make head or tail of. If we could have the *conversation* of the age following the Renaissance, we should probably be shocked by its shameless negations. The remarks attributed to Marlowe are probably pretty typical of the talk in many intellectual taverns. The transition from Pre-Reformation to Post-Reformation Europe was through a void of very yawning questions; yet again in the long run the answer was the same. It was one of those moments when, as Christ walked on the water, so was Christianity walking in the air.

But all these cases are remote in date and could only be proved in detail. We can see the fact much more clearly in the case when the paganism of the Renaissance ended Christianity and Christianity unaccountably began all over again. But we can see it most clearly of all in the case which is close to us and full of manifest and minute evidence; the case of the great decline of religion that began about the time of Voltaire. For indeed it is our own case; and we ourselves have seen the decline of that decline. The two hundred years since Voltaire do not flash past us at a glance like the fourth and fifth centuries or the twelfth and thirteenth centuries. In our own case we can see this oft-repeated process close at hand; we know how completely a society can lose its fundamental religion without abolishing its official religion; we know how men can all become agnostics long before they abolish bishops. And we know that also in this last ending, which really did look to us like the final ending, the incredible thing has happened again; the Faith has a better following among the young men than among the old. When Ibsen spoke of the new generation knocking at the door, he certainly never expected that it would be the church-door.

At least five times, therefore, with the Arian and the Albigensian, with the Humanist sceptic, after Voltaire and after Darwin, the Faith has to all appearance gone to the dogs. In each of these five cases it was the dog that died. How complete was the collapse and how strange the reversal, we can only see in detail in the case nearest to our own time.

A thousand things have been said about the Oxford Movement and the parallel French Catholic revival; but few have made us feel the simplest fact about it; that it was a surprise. It was a puzzle as well as a surprise; because it seemed to most people like a river turning backwards from the sea and trying to climb back into the mountains. To have read the literature of the eighteenth and nineteenth centuries is to know that nearly everybody had come to take it for granted that religion was a thing that would continually broaden like a river, till it reached an infinite sea. Some of them expected it to go down in a cataract of catastrophe, most of them expected it to widen into an estuary of equality and moderation; but all of them thought its returning on itself a prodigy as incredible as witchcraft. In other words, most moderate people thought that faith like freedom would be slowly broadened down; and some advanced people thought that it would be very rapidly broadened down, not to say flattened out. All that world of Guizot and Macaulay and the commercial and scientific liberality was perhaps more certain than any men before or since about the direction in which the world is going. People were so certain about the direction that they only differed about the pace. Many anticipated with alarm, and a few with sympathy, a Jacobin revolt that should guillotine the Archbishop of Canterbury or a Chartist riot that should hang the parsons on the lamposts. But it seemed like a convulsion in nature that the Archbishop instead of losing his head should be looking for his mitre; and that instead of diminishing the respect due to parsons we should strengthen it to the respect due to priests. It revolutionised their very vision of revolution; and turned their very topsyturveydom topsyturvey.

In short, the whole world being divided about whether the stream was going slower or faster, became conscious of something vague but vast that was going against the stream. Both in fact and figure there is something deeply disturbing about this, and that for an essential reason. A dead thing can go with the stream, but only a living thing can go against it. A dead dog can be lifted on the leaping water with all the swiftness of a leaping hound; but only a live dog can swim backwards. A paper boat can ride the rising deluge with all the airy arrogance of a fairy ship; but if the fairy ship sails upstream it is really rowed by the fairies. And among the things that merely went with the tide of apparent progress and enlargement, there was many a demagogue or sophist whose wild gestures were in truth as lifeless as the movement of a dead dog's limbs wavering in the eddying water; and many a philosophy uncommonly like a paper boat, of the sort that it is not difficult to knock into a cocked hat. But even the truly living and even life-giving things that went with that stream did not thereby prove that they were living or life-giving. It was this other force that was unquestionably and unaccountably alive; the mysterious and unmeasured energy that was thrusting back the river. That was felt to be like the movement of some great monster; and it was none the less clearly a living monster because most people thought it a prehistoric monster. It was none the less an unnatural, an incongruous, and to some a comic upheaval; as if the Great Sea Serpent had suddenly risen out of the Round Pond—unless we consider the Sea Serpent as more likely to live in the Serpentine. This flippant element in the fantasy must not be missed, for it was one of the clearest testimonies to the unexpected nature of the reversal. That age did really feel that a preposterous quality in prehistoric animals belonged also to historic rituals; that mitres and tiaras were like the horns or crests of antediluvian creatures; and that appealing to a Primitive Church was like dressing up as a Primitive Man.

The world is still puzzled by that movement; but most of all because it still moves. I have said something elsewhere of the rather random sort of reproaches that are still directed against it and its much greater consequences; it is enough to say here that the more such critics reproach it the less they explain it. In a sense it is my concern here, if not to explain it, at least to suggest the direction of the explanation; but above all, it is my concern to point out one particular thing about it. And that is that it had all happened before; and even many times before.

To sum up, in so far as it is true that recent centuries have seen an attenuation of Christian doctrine, recent centuries have only seen what the most remote centuries have seen. And even the modern example has only ended as the medieval and pre-medieval examples ended. It is already clear, and grows clearer every day, that it is not going to end in the disappearance of the diminished creed; but rather in the return of those parts of it that had really disappeared. It is going to end as the Arian compromise ended, as the attempts at a compromise with Nominalism and even with Albigensianism ended. But the point to seize in the modern case, as in all the other cases, is that what returns is not in that sense a simplified theology; not according to that view a purified theology; it is simply theology. It is that enthusiasm for theological studies that marked the most doctrinal ages; it is the divine science. An old Don with D. D. after his name may have become the typical figure of a bore; but that was because he was himself bored with his theology, not because he was excited about it. It was precisely because he was admittedly more interested in the Latin of Plautus than in the Latin of Augustine, in the Greek of Xenophon than in the Greek of Chrysostom. It was precisely because he was more interested in a dead tradition than in a decidedly living tradition. In short, it was precisely because he was himself a type of the time in which Christian faith was weak. It was not because men would not hail, if they could, the wonderful and almost wild vision of a Doctor of Divinity.

There are people who say they wish Christianity to remain as a spirit. They mean, very literally, that they wish it to remain as a ghost. But it is not going to remain as a ghost. What follows this process of apparent death is not the lingering of the shade; it is the resurrection of the body. These people are quite prepared to shed pious and reverential tears over the Sepulchre of the Son of Man; what they are not prepared for is the Son of God walking once more upon the hills of morning. These people, and indeed most people, were indeed by this time quite accustomed to the idea that the old Christian candle-light would fade into the light of common day. To many of them it did quite honestly appear like that pale yellow flame of a candle when it is left burning in daylight. It was all the more unexpected, and therefore all the more unmistakable, that the seven-branched candle-stick suddenly towered to heaven like a miraculous tree and flamed until the sun turned pale. But other ages have seen the day conquer the candle-light and then the candle-light conquer the day. Again and again, before our time, men have grown content with a diluted doctrine. And again and again there has followed on that dilution, coming as out of the darkness in a crimson cataract, the strength of the red original wine. And we only say once more to-day as has been said many times by our fathers: 'Long years and centuries ago our fathers or the founders of our people drank, as they dreamed, of the blood of God. Long years and centuries have passed since the strength of that giant vintage has been anything but a legend of the age of giants. Centuries ago already is the dark time of the second fermentation, when the wine of Catholicism turned into the vinegar of Calvinism. Long since that bitter drink has been itself diluted; rinsed out and washed away by the waters of oblivion and the wave of the world. Never did we think to taste again even that bitter tang of sincerity and the spirit, still less the richer and the sweeter strength of the purple vineyards in our dreams of the age of gold. Day by day and year by year we have lowered our hopes and lessened our convictions; we have grown more and more used to seeing those vats and vineyards overwhelmed in the water-floods and the last savour and suggestion of that special element fading like a stain of purple upon a sea of grey. We have grown used to dilution, to dissolution, to a watering down that went on for ever. But 'Thou hast kept the good wine until now.'

This is the final fact, and it is the most extraordinary of all. The faith has not only often died but it has often died of old age. It has not only been often killed but it has often died a natural death; in the sense of coming to a natural and necessary end. It is obvious that it has survived the most savage and the most universal persecutions from the shock of the Diocletian fury to the shock of the French Revolution. But it has a more strange and even a more weird tenacity; it has survived not only war but peace. It has not only died often but degenerated often and decayed often; it has survived its own weakness and even its own surrender. We need not repeat what is so obvious about the beauty of the end of Christ in its wedding of youth and death. But this is almost as if Christ had lived to the last possible span, had been a white-haired sage of a hundred and died of natural decay, and then had risen again rejuvenated, with trumpets and the rending of the sky. It was said truly enough that human Christianity in its recurrent weakness was sometimes too much wedded to the powers of the world; but if it was wedded it has very often been widowed. It is a strangely immortal sort of widow. An enemy may have said at one moment that it was but an aspect of the power of the Caesars; and it sounds as strange to-day as to call it an aspect of the power of the Pharaohs. An enemy might say that it was the official faith of feudalism; and it sounds as convincing now as to say that it was bound to perish with the ancient Roman villa. All these things did indeed run their course to its normal end; and there seemed no course for the religion but to end with them. It ended and it began again.

'Heaven and earth shall pass away, but my words shall not pass away.' The civilisation of antiquity was the whole world: and men no more dreamed of its ending than of the ending of daylight. They could not imagine another order unless it were in another world. The civilisation of the world has passed away and those words have not passed away. In the long night of the Dark Ages feudalism was so familiar a thing that no man could imagine himself without a lord: and religion was so woven into that network that no man would have believed they could be torn asunder. Feudalism itself was torn to rags and rotted away in the popular life of the true Middle Ages; and the first and freshest power in that new freedom was the old religion. Feudalism had passed away, and the words did not pass away. The whole medieval order, in many ways so complete and almost cosmic a home for man, wore out gradually in its turn: and here at least it was thought that the words would die. They went forth across the radiant abyss of the Renaissance and in fifty years were using all its light and learning for new religious foundations, new apologetics, new saints. It was supposed to have been withered up at last in the dry light of the Age of Reason; it was supposed to have disappeared ultimately in the earthquake of the Age of Revolution. Science explained it away; and it was still there. History disinterred it in the past; and it appeared suddenly in the future. To-day it stands once more in our path; and even as we watch it, it grows.

If our social relations and records retain their continuity, if men really learn to apply reason to the accumulating facts of so crushing a story, it would seem that sooner or later even its enemies, will learn from their incessant and interminable disappointments not to look for anything so simple as its death. They may continue to war with it, but it will be as they war with nature; as they war with the landscape, as they war with the skies.'Heaven and earth shall pass away, but my words shall not pass away.' They will watch for it to stumble; they will watch for it to err; they will no longer watch for it to end. Insensibly, even unconsciously, they will in their own silent anticipations fulfil the relative terms of that astounding prophecy; they will forget to watch for the mere extinction of what has so often been vainly extinguished; and will learn instinctively to look first for the coming of the comet or the freezing of the star.

CONCLUSION

THE SUMMARY OF THIS BOOK

I have taken the liberty once or twice of borrowing the excellent phrase about an Outline of History; though this study of a special truth and a special error can of course claim no sort of comparison with the rich and many-sided encyclopedia of history, for which that name was chosen. And yet there is a certain reason in the reference; and a sense in which the one thing touches and even cuts across the other. For the story of the world as told by Mr. Wells could here only be criticised as an outline. And, strangely enough, it seems to me that it is only wrong as an outline. It is admirable as an accumulation of history; it is splendid as a store-house or treasury of history; it is a fascinating disquisition on history; it is most attractive as an amplification of history; but it is quite false as an outline of history. The one thing that seems to me quite wrong about it is the outline; the sort of outline that can really be a single line, like that which makes all the difference between a caricature of the profile of Mr. Winston Churchill and of Sir Alfred Mond. In simple and homely language, I mean the things that stick out; the things that make the simplicity of a silhouette. I think the proportions are wrong; the proportions of what is certain as compared with what is uncertain, of what played a great part as compared with what played a smaller part, of what is ordinary and what is extraordinary, of what really lies level with an average and what stands out as an exception.

I do not say it as a small criticism of a great writer, and I have no reason to do so; for in my own much smaller task I feel I have failed in very much the same way. I am very doubtful whether I have conveyed to the reader the main point I meant about the proportions of history, and why I have dwelt so much more on some things than others. I doubt whether I have clearly fulfilled the plan that I set out in the introductory chapter; and for that reason I add these lines as a sort of summary in a concluding chapter. I do believe that the things on which I have insisted are more essential to an outline of history than the things which I have subordinated or dismissed. I do not believe that the past is most truly pictured as a thing in which humanity merely fades away into nature, or civilisation merely fades away into barbarism, or religion fades away into mythology, or our own religion fades away into the religions of the world. In short I do not believe that the best way to produce an outline of history is to rub out the lines. I believe that, of the two, it would be far nearer the truth to tell the tale very simply, like a primitive myth about a man who made the sun and stars or a god who entered the body of a sacred monkey. I will therefore sum up all that has gone before in what seems to me a realistic and reasonably proportioned statement; the short story of mankind.

In the land lit by that neighbouring star, whose blaze is the broad daylight, there are many and very various things, motionless and moving. There moves among them a race that is in its relation to others a race of gods. The fact is not lessened but emphasised because it can behave like a race of demons. Its distinction is not an individual illusion, like one bird pluming itself on its own plumes; it is a solid and a many-sided thing. It is demonstrated in the very speculations that have led to its being denied. That men, the gods of this lower world, are linked with it in various ways is true; but it is another aspect of the same truth. That they grow as the grass grows and walk as the beasts walk is a secondary necessity that sharpens the primary distinction. It is like saying that a magician must after all have the appearance of a man; or that even the fairies could not dance without feet. It has lately been the fashion to focus the mind entirely on these mild and subordinate resemblances and to forget the main fact altogether. It is customary to insist that man resembles the other creatures. Yes; and that very resemblance he alone can see. The fish does not trace the fish-bone pattern in the fowls of the air; or the elephant and the emu compare skeletons. Even in the sense in which man is at one with the universe it is an utterly lonely universality. The very sense that he is united with all things is enough to sunder him from all.

Looking around him by this unique light, as lonely as the literal flame that he alone has kindled, this demigod or demon of the visible world makes that world visible. He sees around him a world of a certain style or type. It seems to proceed by certain rules or at least repetitions. He sees a green architecture that builds itself without visible hands; but which builds itself into a very exact plan or pattern, like a design already drawn in the air by an invisible finger. It is not, as is now vaguely suggested, a vague thing. It is not a growth or a groping of blind life. Each seeks an end; a glorious and radiant end, even for every daisy or dandelion we see in looking across the level of a common field. In the very shape of things there is more than green growth; there is the finality of the flower. It is a world of crowns. This impression, whether or no it be an illusion, has so profoundly influenced this race of thinkers and masters of the material world, that the vast majority have been moved to take a certain view of that world. They have concluded, rightly or wrongly, that the world had a plan as the tree seemed to have a plan; and an end and crown like the flower. But so long as the race of thinkers was able to think, it was obvious that the admission of this idea of a plan brought with it another thought more thrilling and even terrible. There was someone else, some strange and unseen being, who had designed these things, if indeed they were designed. There was a stranger who was also a friend; a mysterious benefactor who had been before them and built up the woods and hills for their coming, and had kindled the sunrise aganst their rising, as a servant kindles a fire. Now this idea of a mind that gives a meaning to the universe has received more and more confirmation within the minds of men, by meditations and experiences much more subtle and searching than any such argument about the external plan of the world. But I am concerned here with keeping the story in its most simple and even concrete terms; and it is enough to say here that most men, including the wisest men, have come to the conclusion that the world has such a final purpose and therefore such a first cause. But most men in some sense separated themselves from the wisest men, when it came to the treatment of that idea. There came into existence two ways of treating that idea; which between them made up most of the religious history of the world.

The majority, like the minority, had this strong sense of a second meaning in things; of a strange master who knew the secret of the world. But the majority, the mob or mass of men, naturally tended to treat it rather in the spirit of gossip. The gossip, like all gossip, contained a great deal of truth and falsehood. The world began to tell itself tales about the unknown being or his sons or servants or messengers. Some of the tales may truly be called old wives' tales; as professing only to be very remote memories of the morning of the world; myths about the baby moon or the half-baked mountains. Some of them might more truly be called travellers' tales; as being curious but contemporary tales brought from certain borderlands of experience; such as miraculous cures or those that bring whispers of what has happened to the dead. Many of them are probably true tales; enough of them are probably true to keep a person of real commonsense more or less conscious that there really is something rather marvellous behind the cosmic curtain. But in a sense it is only going by appearances; even if the appearances are called apparitions. It is a matter of appearances—and disappearances. At the most these gods are ghosts; that is, they are glimpses. For most of us they are rather gossip about glimpses. And for the rest, the whole world is full of rumours, most of which are almost avowedly romances. The great majority of the tales about gods and ghosts and the invisible king are told, if not for the sake of the tale, at least for the sake of the topic. They are evidence of the eternal interest of the theme; they are not evidence of anything else, and they are not meant to be. They are mythology or the poetry that is not bound in books—or bound in any other way.

Meanwhile the minority, the sages or thinkers, had withdrawn apart and had taken up an equally congenial trade. They were drawing up plans of the world; of the world which all believed to have a plan. They were trying to set forth the plan seriously and to scale. They were setting their minds directly to the mind that had made the mysterious world; considering what sort of a mind it might be and what its ultimate purpose might be. Some of them made that mind much more impersonal than mankind has generally made it; some simplified it almost to a blank; a few, a very few, doubted it altogether. One or two of the more morbid fancied that it might be evil and an enemy; just one or two of the more degraded in the other class worshipped demons instead of gods. But most of these theorists were theists: and they not only saw a moral plan in nature, but they generally laid down a moral plan for humanity. Most of them were good men who did good work: and they were remembered and reverenced in various ways. They were scribes; and their scriptures became more or less holy scriptures. They were law-givers; and their tradition became not only legal but ceremonial. We may say that they received divine honours, in the sense in which kings and great captains in certain countries often received divine honours. In a word, wherever the other popular spirit, the spirit of legend and gossip could come into play, it surrounded them with the more mystical atmosphere of the myths. Popular poetry turned the sages into saints. But that was all it did. They remained themselves; men never really forgot that they were men, only made into gods in the sense that they were made into heroes. Divine Plato, like Divus Ceasar, was a title and not a dogma. In Asia, where the atmosphere was more mythological, the man was made to look more like a myth, but he remained a man. He remained a man of a certain special class or school of men, receiving and deserving great honour from mankind. It is the order or school of the philosophers; the men who have set themselves seriously to trace the order across any apparent chaos in the vision of life. Instead of living on imaginative rumours and remote traditions and the tail-end of exceptional experiences about the mind and meaning behind the world, they have tried in a sense to project the primary purpose of that mind *a priori*. They have tried to put on paper a possible plan of the world; almost as if the world were not yet made.

Right in the middle of all these things stands up an enormous exception. It is quite unlike anything else. It is a thing final like the trump of doom,though it is also a piece of good news; or news that seems too good to be true. It is nothing less than the loud assertion that this mysterious maker of the world has visited his world in person. It declares that really and even recently, or right in the middle of historic times, there did walk into the world this original invisible being; about whom the thinkers make theories and the mythologists hand down myths; the Man Who Made the World. That such a higher personality exists behind all things had indeed always been implied by all the best thinkers, as well as by all the most beautiful legends. But nothing of this sort had ever been implied in any of them. It is simply false to say that the other sages and heroes had claimed to be that mysterious master and maker, of whom the world had dreamed and disputed. Not one of them had ever claimed to be anything of the sort. Not one of their sects or schools had ever claimed that they had claimed to be anything of the sort. The most that any religious prophet had said was that he was the true servant of such a being. The most that any visionary had ever said was that men might catch glimpses of the glory of that spiritual being; or much more often of lesser spiritual beings. The most that any primitive myth had ever suggested was that the Creator was present at the Creation. But that the Creator was present at scenes a little subsequent to the supper-parties of Horace, and talked with tax-collectors and government officials in the detailed daily life of the Roman Empire, and that this fact continued to be firmly asserted by the whole of that great civilisation for more than a thousand years—that is something utterly unlike anything else in nature. It is the one great startling statement that man has made since he spoke his first articulate word, instead of barking like a dog. Its unique character can be used as an argument against it as well as for it. It would be easy to concentrate on it as a case of isolated insanity; but it makes nothing but dust and nonsense of comparative religion.

It came on the world with a wind and rush of running messengers proclaiming that apocalyptic portent; and it is not unduly fanciful to say that they are running still. What puzzles the world, and its wise philosophers and fanciful pagan poets, about the priests and people of the Catholic Church is that they still behave as if they were messengers. A messenger does not dream about what his message might be, or argue about what it probably would be; he delivers it as it is. It is not a theory or a fancy but a fact. It is not relevant to this intentionally rudimentary outline to prove in detail that it is a fact; but merely to point out that these messengers do deal with it as men deal with a fact. All that is condemned in Catholic tradition, authority, and dogmatism and the refusal to retract and modify, are but the natural human attributes of a man with a message relating to a fact. I desire to avoid in this last summary all the controversial complexities that may once more cloud the simple lines of that strange story; which I have already called, in words that are much too weak, the strangest story in the world. I desire merely to mark those main lines and specially to mark where the great line is really to be drawn. The religion of the world, in its right proportions, is not divided into fine shades of mysticism or more or less rational forms of mythology. It is divided by the line between the men who are bringing that message and the men who have not yet heard it, or cannot yet believe it.

But when we translate the terms of that strange tale back into the more concrete and complicated terminology of our time, we find it covered by names and memories of which the very familiarity is a falsification. For instance, when we say that a country contains so many Moslems, we really mean that it contains so many monotheists; and we really mean, by that, that it contains so many men; men with the old average assumption of men — that the invisible ruler remains invisible. They hold it along with the customs of a certain culture and under the simpler laws of a certain law-giver; but so they would if their law-giver were Lycurgus or Solon. They testify to something which is a necessary and noble truth; but was never a new truth. Their creed is not a new colour; it is the neutral and normal tint that is the background of the many-coloured life of man. Mahomet did not, like the Magi, find a new star; he saw through his own particular window a glimpse of the great grey field of the ancient starlight. So when we say that the country contains so many Confucians or Buddhists, we mean it contains so many pagans whose prophets have given them another and rather vaguer version of the invisible power; making it not only invisible but almost impersonal. When we say that they also have temples and idols and priests and periodical festivals, we simply mean that this sort of heathen is enough of a human being to admit the popular element of pomp and pictures and feasts and fairy-tales. We only mean that Pagans have more sense than Puritans. But what the gods are supposed to *be*, what the priests are commissioned to *say*, is not a sensational secret like what those running messengers of the Gospel had to say. Nobody else except those mesengers has any Gospel; nobody else has any good news; for the simple reason that nobody else has any news.

Those runners gather impetus as they run. Ages afterwards they still speak as if something had just happened. They have not lost the speed and momentum of messengers; they have hardly lost, as it were, the wild eyes of witnesses. In the Catholic Church, which is the cohort of the message, there are still those headlong acts of holiness that speak of something rapid and recent; a self-sacrifice that startles the world like a suicide. But it is not a suicide; it is not pessimistic; it is still as optimistic as St. Francis of the flowers and birds. It is newer in spirit than the newest schools of thought; and it is almost certainly on the eve of new triumphs. For these men serve a mother who seems to grow more beautiful as new generations rise up and call her blessed. We might sometimes fancy that the Church grows younger as the world grows old.

For this is the last proof of the miracle; that something so supernatural should have become so natural. I mean that anything so unique when seen from the outside should only seem universal when seen from the inside. I have not minimised the scale of the miracle, as some of our milder theologians think it wise to do. Rather have I deliberately dwelt on that incredible interruption, as a blow that broke the very backbone of history. I have great sympathy with the monotheists, the Moslems, or the Jews, to whom it seems a blasphemy; a blasphemy that might shake the world. But it did not shake the world; it steadied the world. That fact, the more we consider it, will seem more solid and more strange. I think it a piece of plain justice to all the unbelievers to insist upon the audacity of the act of faith that is demanded of them. I willingly and warmly agree that it is, in itself, a suggestion at which we might expect even the brain of the believer to reel, when he realised his own belief. But the brain of the believer does not reel; it is the brains of the unbelievers that reel. We can see their brains reeling on every side and into every extravagance of ethics and psychology; into pessimism and the denial of life; into pragmatism and the denial of logic; seeking their omens in nightmares and their canons in contradictions; shrieking for fear at the far-off sight of things beyond good and evil, or whispering of strange stars where two and two make five. Meanwhile this solitary thing that seems at first so outrageous in outline remains solid and sane in substance. It remains the moderator of all these manias; rescuing reason from the Pragmatists exactly as it rescued laughter from the Puritans. I repeat that I have deliberately emphasised its intrinsically defiant and dogmatic character. The mystery is how anything so startling should have remained defiant and dogmatic and yet become perfectly normal and natural. I have admitted freely that, considering the incident in itself, a man who says he is God may be classed with a man who says he is glass. But the man who says he is glass is not a glazier making windows for all the world. He does not remain for after ages as a shining and crystalline figure, in whose light everything is as clear as crystal.

But this madness has remained sane. The madness has remained sane when everything else went mad. The madhouse has been a house to which, age after age, men are continually coming back as to a home. That is the riddle that remains; that anything so abrupt and abnormal should still be found a habitable and hospitable thing. I care not if the sceptic says it is a tall story; I cannot see how so toppling a tower could stand so long without foundation. Still less can I see how it could become, as it has become, the home of man. Had it merely appeared and disappeared, it might possibly have been remembered or explained as the last leap of the rage of illusion, the ultimate myth of the ultimate mood, in which the mind struck the sky and broke. But the mind did not break. It is the one mind that remains unbroken in the break-up of the world. If it were an error, it seems as if the error could hardly have lasted a day. If it were a mere ecstasy, it would seem that such an ecstasy could not endure for an hour. It has endured for nearly two thousand years; and the world within it has been more lucid, more level-headed, more reasonable in its hopes, more healthy in its instincts, more humorous and cheerful in the face of fate and death, than all the world outside. For it was the soul of Christendom that came forth from the incredible Christ; and the soul of it was common sense. Though we dared not look on His face we could look on His fruits; and by His fruits we should know Him. The fruits are solid and the fruitfulness is much more than a metaphor; and nowhere in this sad world are boys happier in apple-trees, or men in more equal chorus singing as they tread the vine, than under the fixed flash of this instant and intolerant enlightenment; the lightning made eternal as the light.

APPENDIX I

ON PREHISTORIC MAN

On re-reading these pages I feel that I have tried in many places and with many words, to say something that might be said in one word. In a sense this study is meant to be superficial. That is, it is not meant as a study of the things that need to be studied. It is rather a reminder of the things that are seen so quickly that they are forgotten almost as quickly. Its moral, in a manner of speaking, is that first thoughts are best; so a flash might reveal a landscape; with the Eiffel Tower or the Matterhorn standing up in it as they would never stand up again in the light of common day. I ended the book with an image of everlasting lightning; in a very different sense, alas, this little flash has lasted only too long. But the method has also certain practical disadvantages upon which I think it well to add these two notes. It may seem to simplify too much and to ignore out of ignorance. I feel this especially in the passage about the prehistoric pictures; which is not concerned with all that the learned may learn from prehistoric pictures, but with the single point of what anybody could learn from there being any prehistoric pictures at all. I am conscious that this attempt to express it in terms of innocence may exaggerate even my own ignorance. Without any pretence of scientific research or information, I should be sorry to have it thought that I knew no more than what was needed, in that passage, of the stages into which primitive humanity has been divided. I am aware, of course, that the story is elaborately stratified; and that there were many such stages before the Cro-Magnon or any peoples with whom we associate such pictures. Indeed recent studies about the Neanderthal and other races rather tend to repeat the moral that is here most relevant. The notion noted in these pages of something necessarily slow or late in the development of religion, will gain little indeed from these later revelations about the precursors of the reindeer picture-maker. The learned appear to hold that, whether the reindeer picture could be religious or not, the people that lived before it were religious already; burying their dead with the significant signs of mystery and hope. This obviously brings us back to the same argument; an argument that is not approached by any measurement of the earlier man's skull. It is little use here to compare the head of the man with the head of the monkey, if it certainly never came into the head of the monkey to bury another monkey with nuts in his grave to help him towards a heavenly monkeyhouse. Talking of skulls, I am also aware of the story of the Cro-Magnon skull that was much larger and finer than a modern skull. It is a very funny story; because an eminent evolutionist, awakening to a somewhat belated caution, protested against anything being inferred from one specimen. It is the duty of a solitary skull to prove that our fathers were our inferiors. Any solitary skull presuming to prove that they were superior is felt to be suffering from swelled head.

APPENDIX II

ON AUTHORITY AND ACCURACY

In this book which is merely meant as a popular criticism of popular fallacies, often indeed of very vulgar errors, I feel that I have sometimes given an impression of scoffing at serious scientific work. It was however the very reverse of my intentions. I am not arguing with the scientist who explains the elephant, but only with the sophist who explains it away. And as a matter of fact the sophist plays to the gallery, as he did in ancient Greece. He appeals to the ignorant, especially when he appeals to the learned. But I never meant my own criticism to be an impertinence to the truly learned. We all owe an infinite debt to the researches, especially the recent researches, of single minded students in these matters; and I have only professed to pick up things here and there from them. I have not loaded my abstract argument with quotations and references, which only make a man look more learned than he is; but in some cases I find that my own loose fashion of allusion is rather misleading about my own meaning. The passage about Chaucer and the Child Martyr is badly expressed; I only mean that the English poet probably had in mind the English saint; of whose story he gives a sort of foreign version. In the same way two statements in the chapter on Mythology follow each other in such a way that it may seem to be suggested that the second story about Monotheism refers to the Southern Seas. I may explain that Atahocan belongs not to Australasian but to American savages. So in the chapter called "The Antiquity of Civilisation," which I feel to be the most unsatisfactory, I have given my own impression of the meaning of the development of Egyptian monarchy too much, perhaps, as if it were identical with the facts on which it was formed as given in works like those of Professor J. L. Myres. But the confusion was not intentional; still less was there any intention to imply, in the remainder of the chapter, that the anthropological speculations about races are less valuable than they

undoubtedly are. My criticism is strictly relative; I may say that the
Pyramids are plainer than the tracks of the desert; without denying
that wiser men than I may see tracks in what is to me the trackless
sand.

ST. THOMAS AQUINAS

1933

TO
DOROTHY COLLINS

WITHOUT WHOSE HELP THE AUTHOR
WOULD HAVE BEEN MORE
THAN NORMALLY HELPLESS

INTRODUCTION

By Raymond Dennehy

There is praise and there is praise. It is one thing for a book to be widely praised by laymen, quite another thing for it to be praised by experts in the field and quite another thing yet for it to be praised by the members of both groups. Chesterton's book on Aquinas has not only earned the praise of layman and expert alike but has also earned the praise of the expert's expert, the late Etienne Gilson, the greatest of all historians of mediaeval thought. His studies on Thomas Aquinas are the benchmark for all subsequent Thomistic scholarship. After reading Chesterton's *St. Thomas Aquinas*, Gilson remarked: "For many years I have studied St. Thomas and written on him and now a journalist writes a better book about him than I have!"

The key word in this high praise is "journalist". To be sure, Chesterton was more than a journalist; he was a brilliant observer of modern manners and morals, a perceptive literary critic and formidable Catholic polemicist. Nevertheless, if you had to come up with one word that characterizes the man and his work better than any other, you could not do better than to call him a "journalist", but in the best sense of the word. Chesterton was always aware of the state of cultural rupture in the modern world. The condition is hardly new to history, but it is always devastating. On the one hand, we have journalism that seeks not to inform or enrich but to titilate; on the other hand, we have intellectuals, who could and should write for the public, writing instead for other intellectuals. But Chesterton had the ability, and he exercised it, to reach the reading public on any number of substantial matters, the philosophical and theological included. What he has accomplished in his book on Thomas Aquinas is the preeminent case in point.

Like all great works, simplicity, penetration and relevance are its hallmarks. It is a masterpiece of simplicity in the sense in which Michaelangelo's painting on the ceiling of the Sistine Chapel is a masterpiece of simplicity. Consider that much reproduced segment

413

of it, "God the Father creating Adam". How do you represent God, if you have never seen him? How do you represent Adam, not simply as man but as the creature made in the Creator's image and likeness, if, again, you have never seen the Creator? Michaelangelo's solution was so simple and in this very simplicity absolutely brilliant. The solution is all in the hands. By representing God the Father in human form, he gets across the idea of man as His image; and by painting God's hand deliberately touching Adam's limp, receptive hand, he gets across the truth that the all-important difference between God and man is that God, as Creator, is the source of all being and life, while man, as creature, is the recipient of being and life, totally dependent on God. From these truths spring all theological and philosophical understanding of God, His creation, and man's relationship to them both.

This, in analogous fashion, is the sense in which Chesterton's book is a masterpiece. With simplicity and lucidity, he has penetrated the very heart of Thomas Aquinas' thought. You will not find him tarrying over the complexities and subtleties of the Thomistic texts or attempting to furnish the reader with a representative sampling of the many topics on which Aquinas wrote. Instead he confines himself to the exposition of three points: 1) St. Thomas' affirmation of the goodness of creation against the Manichean doctrine of its evilness, 2) his philosophical realism and consequent defense of common sense, 3) the primacy of the doctrine of being in Thomistic philosophy. When you understand these three points, you have grasped the essence of St. Thomas's thought.

It was noted at the outset that, besides simplicity and penetration, Chesterton's book is characterized by relevance. For what he has accomplished by his masterful exposition of Aquinas goes beyond the exposition itself. Explaining the glories of St. Thomas to the layman is, to be sure, justification enough for the book. But in accomplishing that he brings a message to modern man who lives in a world "turned upside down". His message is that St. Thomas has the intellectual view of things that will set it right side up. And the aforementioned three points of Chesterton's focus constitute the Archimedes' lever needed for the task.

I. St. Thomas' affirmation of the goodness of creation against the Manichean doctrine of its evilness: "Now nobody will begin to understand the Thomist philosophy, or indeed the Catholic philosophy, who does not realise that the primary and fundamental part of it is entirely the praise of life, the praise of Being, the praise of God as the Creator of the world." In these words we have a stellar illustration of Chesterton's penetrative powers, powers which also enable him to put his finger on one of the most disruptive forces of present-day society—the heritage of Manicheanism. The glorification of the body and sexual license prevalent today cannot rightfully be understood if they are not seen as, in large part, a reaction to the denigration of creation. Like the former, the latter is an aberration. To get to the source of the aberration and its correction, Chesterton calls our attention to the departure St. Thomas makes from the doctrine of St. Augustine, which is tainted with the very Manicheanism against which the Bishop of Hippo so brilliantly argued. The roots of Manicheanism are in the writings of Plato, and Augustinianism is not insignificantly influenced by Platonism. As Chesterton puts it, "After a thousand years of extension, the miscalculation of Platonism had come very near to Manicheanism."

The exact problem is that the Manichees identified purity with sterility, in contrast to Thomas Aquinas who always identified purity with fruitfulness. The insinuation of Manicheanism in Platonism and the insinuation of Platonism in Augustinianism produced a heritage of deformed Christianity which was in turn transmitted to the modern world by Calvin and other figures of the Reformation. Writers such as D. H. Lawrence accordingly assume that Christianity is life-denying and body-hating. Thus the "nonesense" of Lawrence's writings on human sexuality might have been avoided had he realized that the Catholic view of marriage was very similar to his.

Chesterton alerts his readers to the importance of this context for an understanding of Aquinas' departure from Augustine on the view of creation. Aquinas understood, as does Chesterton, that there are dangers inside the Church as well as outside and that those inside are often more dangerous than those outside. Just as in the seventeenth century when Calvinism was the outside danger and Jansenism the inside danger, so in the thirteenth century, where the outside danger was the Albigensian revolution, the inside danger was the traditionalism of Augustianism. Thus Aquinas' defense of the goodness of creation at once furnishes the unsurpassed, hard-headed intellectual defense of the Catholic doctrine and a light to enable modern man to see the aberration of his assumed view of human sexuality.

2. St Thomas' philosophical realism and defense of common sense: ". . . Aquinas is almost always on the side of simplicity, and supports the ordinary man's acceptance of ordinary truisms. . . . [I]t is his purpose to justify common sense." The man in the street has no doubt that things are real and that the knowledge he derives from seeing, touching, hearing, tasting and smelling them is knowledge about them. The disputes of modern philosophers over whether things really exist or are simply ideas in our minds might cause enough perplexity in him to make an inquisitive furrow in his brow, but they would only weaken his confidence in modern philosophers; his confidence in things and in his knowledge of them would remain unshaken. If you want to get reason back into daily life, you have to show that philosophy is reasonable. And it will seem anything but reasonable if it outrages common sense, which it surely will do, and surely has done, if it denies, or even casts doubt on, what common sense knows very well; namely, that things are not mere ideas or illusions of the mind.

Chesterton the journalist proclaims the glories of the *philosophia perennis* to the reading public. There can be a perennial philosophy only if philosophy harmonizes with our common sense experiences; only if it can be shown that, far from being at odds with that experience, the philosophy of St. Thomas grows organically from the soil of the ordinary man's daily experiences; only if it can be shown that its theories and conclusions are the flowering of the mind's reflections on experience. Thus does Chesterton see fit to emphasize, both by eloquence and repetition, the humility of Aquinas before nature and the concrete, sensible things which comprise it; for it is from these that all our knowledge is derived.

3. The primacy of the doctrine of being in Thomistic philosophy: Chesterton's elucidation of St. Thomas' doctrine of being furnishes

another brilliant example of his ability to simplify without distorting. In response to those moderns who deny that we see a reality called "green" when we perceive green grass and assert instead that green is only an image in the retina, thereby raising the question, "Do we see grass?", Aquinas answers that we are aware of *Ens*: "Long before . . . [a child] knows that grass is grass, or self is self, he knows that something is something." And from this idea of affirmation he gets the idea of contradiction. From the apprehension of being there immediately follows the fundamental principle, known as the principle of contradiction, that a thing cannot be and not be at the same time and in the same way. "Henceforth", writes Chesterton, "in common or popular language, there is a false and a true." The irony of understatement can be so powerful!

Yes, Chesterton was a journalist and it is therefore not surprising that he could demonstrate the journalist's knack of putting things in simple terms. But his genius lay in this, that his simplifications are not oversimplifications. Instead they are direct appeals to the good sense of both literati and common men. He grabs both by their lapels to get their attention and then says, at times wryly, at other times thunderously and, yet at other times, straightforwardly, "Look, I know that I'm trying to say in very simple terms things that St. Thomas felt obliged to say in terms that were often subtle and complex. But, don't you see? The truths he was getting at—the basic principles of reality and reason—are in themselves really quite simple. Your basic intuitions were right all along; it is the modern philosophers who are wrong; the world's really not turned upside down; they only made it seem that way."

INTRODUCTORY NOTE

This book makes no pretence to be anything but a popular sketch of a great historical character who ought to be more popular. Its aim will be achieved, if it leads those who have hardly even heard of St. Thomas Aquinas to read about him in better books. But from this necessary limitation certain consequences follow, which should perhaps be allowed for from the start.

First, it follows that the tale is told very largely to those who are not of the communion of St. Thomas; and who may be interested in him as I might be in Confucius or Mahomet. Yet, on the other hand, the very need of presenting a clean-cut outline involved its cutting into other outlines of thought, among those who may think differently. If I write a sketch of Nelson mainly for foreigners, I may have to explain elaborately many things that all Englishmen know, and possibly cut out, for brevity, many details that many Englishmen would like to know. But, on the other side, it would be difficult to write a very vivid and moving narrative of Nelson, while entirely concealing the fact that he fought with the French. It would be futile to make a sketch of St. Thomas and conceal the fact that he fought with heretics; and yet the fact itself may embarrass the very purpose for which it is employed. I can only express the hope, and indeed the confidence, that those who regard me as the heretic will hardly blame me for expressing my own convictions, and certainly not for expressing my hero's convictions. There is only one point upon which such a question concerns this very simple narrative. It is the conviction, which I have expressed once or twice in the course of it, that the sixteenth-century schism was really a belated revolt of the thirteenth-century pessimists. It was a back-wash of the old Augustinian Puritanism against the Aristotelian liberality. Without that, I could not place my historical figure in history. But the whole is meant only for a rough sketch of a figure in a landscape; and not of a landscape with figures.

Second, it follows that in any such simplification I can hardly say much of the philosopher beyond showing that he had a philosophy.

I have only, so to speak, given samples of that philosophy. Lastly, it follows that it is practically impossible to deal adequately with the theology. A lady I know picked up a book of selections from St. Thomas, with a commentary; and began hopefully to read a section with the innocent heading, "The Simplicity of God." She then laid down the book with a sigh and said, "Well, if that's His simplicity, I wonder what His complexity is like." With all respect to that excellent Thomistic commentary, I have no desire to have this book laid down, at the very first glance, with a similar sigh. I have taken the view that the biography is an introduction to the philosophy, and that the philosophy is an introduction to the theology; and that I can only carry the reader just beyond the first stage of the story.

Third, I have not thought it necessary to notice those critics who, from time to time, desperately play to the gallery by reprinting paragraphs of medieval demonology in the hope of horrifying the modern public merely by an unfamiliar language. I have taken it for granted that educated men know that Aquinas and all his contemporaries, and all his opponents for centuries after, did believe in demons, and similar facts, but I have not thought them worth mentioning here, for the simple reason that they do not help to detach or distinguish the portrait. In all that, there was no disagreement between Protestant or Catholic theologians, for all the hundreds of years during which there was any theology; and St. Thomas is not notable as holding such views, except in holding them rather mildly. I have not discussed such matters, not because I have any reason to conceal them, but because they do not in any way personally concern the one person whom it is here my business to reveal. There is hardly room, even as it is, for such a figure in such a frame.

I

ON TWO FRIARS

Let me at once anticipate comment by answering to the name of that notorious character, who rushes in where even the Angels of the Angelic Doctor might fear to tread. Some time ago I wrote a little book of this type and shape on St. Francis of Assisi; and some time after (I know not when or how, as the song says, and certainly not why) I promised to write a book of the same size, or the same smallness on St. Thomas Aquinas. The promise was Franciscan only in its rashness; and the parallel was very far from being Thomistic in its logic. You can make a sketch of St. Francis: you could only make a plan of St. Thomas, like the plan of a labyrinthine city. And yet in a sense he would fit into a much larger or a much smaller book. What we really know of his life might be pretty fairly dealt with in a few pages; for he did not, like St. Francis, disappear in a shower of personal anecdotes and popular legends. What we know, or could know, or may eventually have the luck to learn, of his work, will probably fill even more libraries in the future than it has filled in the past. It was allowable to sketch St. Francis in an outline; but with St. Thomas everything depends on the filling up of the outline. It was even medieval in a manner to illuminate a miniature of the Poverello, whose very title is a diminutive. But to make a digest, in the tabloid manner, of the Dumb Ox of Sicily passes all digestive experiments in the matter of an ox in a tea-cup. But we must hope it is possible to make an outline of biography, now that anybody seems capable of writing an outline of history or an outline of anything. Only in the present case the outline is rather an outsize. The gown that could contain the colossal friar is not kept in stock.

I have said that these can only be portraits in outline. But the concrete contrast is here so striking, that even if we actually saw the two human figures in outline, coming over the hill in their friar's gowns, we should find that contrast even comic. It would be like seeing, even afar off, the silhouettes of Don Quixote and Sancho Panza, or of Falstaff and Master Slender. St. Francis was a lean and lively little man; thin as a thread and vibrant as a bowstring; and in his motions like an arrow from the bow. All his life was a series of plunges and scampers; darting after the beggar, dashing naked into the woods, tossing himself into the strange ship, hurling himself into the Sultan's tent and offering to hurl himself into the fire. In appearance he must have been like a thin brown skeleton autumn leaf dancing eternally before the wind; but in truth it was he that was the wind.

St. Thomas was a huge heavy bull of a man, fat and slow and quiet; very mild and magnanimous but not very sociable; shy, even apart from the humility of holiness; and abstracted, even apart from his occasional and carefully concealed experiences of trance or ecstasy. St. Francis was so fiery and even fidgety that the ecclesiastics, before whom he appeared quite suddenly, thought he was a madman. St. Thomas was so stolid that the scholars, in the schools which he attended regularly, thought he was a dunce. Indeed, he was the sort of schoolboy, not unknown, who would much rather be thought a dunce than have his own dreams invaded, by more active or animated dunces. This external contrast extends to almost every point in the two personalities. It was the paradox of St. Francis that while he was passionately fond of poems, he was rather distrustful of books. It was the outstanding fact about St. Thomas that he loved books and lived on books; that he lived the very life of the clerk or scholar in *The Canterbury Tales*, who would rather have a hundred books of Aristotle and his philosophy than any wealth the world could give him. When asked for what he thanked God most, he answered simply, "I have understood every page I ever read." St. Francis was very vivid in his poems and rather vague in his documents; St. Thomas devoted his whole life to documenting whole systems of Pagan and Christian literature; and occasionally wrote a hymn like a man taking a holiday. They saw the same problem from different angles, of simplicity and subtlety; St. Francis thought it would be enough to pour out his heart to the Mohammedans, to persuade them not to worship Mahound. St. Thomas bothered his head with every hair-splitting distinction and deduction, about the Absolute or the Accident, merely to prevent them from misunderstanding Aristotle. St. Francis was the son of a shopkeeper, or middle class trader; and while his whole life was a revolt against the mercantile life of his father, he retained none the less, something of the quickness and social adaptability which makes the market hum like a hive. In the common phrase, fond as he was of green fields, he did not let the grass grow under his feet. He was what American millionaires and gangsters call a live wire. It is typical of the mechanistic moderns that, even when they try to imagine a live thing, they can only think of a mechanical metaphor from a dead thing. There is such a thing as a live worm; but there is no such thing as a live wire. St. Francis would have heartily agreed that he was a worm; but he was a very live worm. Greatest of all foes to the go-getting ideal, he had certainly abandoned getting, but he was still going. St. Thomas, on the other hand, came out of a world where he might have enjoyed leisure, and he remained one of those men whose labour has something of the placidity of leisure. He was a hard worker, but nobody could possibly mistake him for a hustler. He had something indefinable about him, which marks those who work when they need not work. For he was by birth a gentleman of a great house, and such repose can remain as a habit, when it is no longer a motive. But in him it was expressed only in its most amiable elements; for instance, there was possibly something of it in his effortless courtesy and patience. Every saint is a man before he is a saint; and a saint may be made of every sort or kind of man; and most of us will choose between these different types according to our different tastes. But I will confess that, while the romantic glory of St. Francis has lost nothing of its glamour for me, I have in later years grown to feel almost as much affection, or in some aspects even more, for this man who unconsciously inhabited a large heart and a large head, like one inheriting a large house, and exercised there an equally generous if rather more absent-minded hospitality. There are moments when St. Francis, the most unworldly man who ever walked the world, is almost too efficient for me.

St. Thomas Aquinas has recently reappeared, in the current culture of the colleges and the salons, in a way that would have been quite startling even ten years ago. And the mood that has concentrated on him is doubtless very different from that which popularised St. Francis quite twenty years ago.

The Saint is a medicine because he is an antidote. Indeed that is why the saint is often a martyr; he is mistaken for a poison because he is an antidote. He will generally be found restoring the world to sanity by exaggerating whatever the world neglects, which is by no means always the same element in every age. Yet each generation seeks its saint by instinct; and he is not what the people want, but rather what the people need. This is surely the very much mistaken meaning of those words to the first saints, "Ye are the salt of the earth," which caused the Ex-Kaiser to remark with all solemnity that his beefy Germans were the salt of the earth; meaning thereby merely that they were the earth's beefiest and therefore best. But salt seasons and preserves beef, not because it is like beef; but because it is very unlike it. Christ did not tell his apostles that they were only the excellent people, or the only excellent people, but that they were the exceptional people; the permanently incongruous and incompatible people; and the text about the salt of the earth is really as sharp and shrewd and tart as the taste of salt. It is because they were the exceptional people, that they must not lose their exceptional quality. "If salt lose its savour, wherewith shall it be salted?" is a much more pointed question than any mere lament over the price of the best beef. If the world grows too worldly, it can be rebuked by the Church; but if the Church grows too worldly, it cannot be adequately rebuked for worldliness by the world.

Therefore it is the paradox of history that each generation is converted by the saint who contradicts it most. St. Francis had a curious and almost uncanny attraction for the Victorians; for the nineteenth century English who seemed superficially to be most complacent about their commerce and their comon sense. Not only a rather complacent Englishman like Matthew Arnold, but even the English Liberals whom he criticised for their complacency, began slowly to discover the mystery of the Middle Ages through the strange story told in feathers and flames in the hagiographical pictures of Giotto. There was something in the story of St. Francis that pierced through all those English qualities which are most famous and fatuous, to all those English qualities which are most hidden and human: the secret softness of heart; the poetical vagueness of mind; the love of landscape and of animals. St. Francis of Assisi was the only medieval Catholic who really became popular in England on his own merits. It was largely because of a subconscious feeling that the modern world had neglected those particular merits. The English middle classes found their only missionary in the figure, which of all types in the world they most despised; an Italian beggar.

So, as the nineteenth century clutched at the Franciscan romance, precisely because it had neglected romance, so the twentieth century is already clutching at the Thomist rational theology, because it has neglected reason. In a world that was too stolid, Christianity returned in the form of a vagabond; in a world that has grown a great deal too wild, Christianity has returned in the form of a teacher of logic. In the world of Herbert Spencer men wanted a cure for indigestion; in the world of Einstein they want a cure for vertigo. In the first case, they dimly perceived the fact that it was after a long fast that St. Francis sang the Song of the Sun and the praise of the fruitful earth. In the second case, they already dimly perceived that, even if they only want to understand Einstein, it is necessary first to understand the use of the understanding. They begin to see that, as the eighteenth century thought itself the age of reason, and the nineteenth century thought itself the age of common sense, the twentieth century cannot as yet even manage to think itself anything but the age of uncommon nonsense. In those conditions the world needs a saint; but above all, it needs a philosopher. And these two cases do show that the world, to do it justice, has an instinct for what it needs. The earth was really very flat, for those Victorians who most vigorously repeated that it was round, and Alverno of the Stigmata stood up as a single mountain in the plain. But the earth is an earthquake, a ceaseless and apparently endless earthquake, for the moderns for whom Newton has been scrapped along with Ptolemy. And for them there is something more steep and even incredible than a mountain; a piece of really solid ground; the level of the level-headed man. Thus in our time the two saints have appealed to two generations, an age of romantics and an age of sceptics; yet in their own age they were doing the same work; a work that has changed the world.

Again, it may be said truly that the comparison is idle, and does not fit in well even as a fancy; since the men were not properly even of the same generation or the same historic moment. If two friars are to be presented as a pair of Heavenly Twins, the obvious comparison is between St. Francis and St. Dominic. The relations of St. Francis and St. Thomas were, at nearest, those of uncle and nephew; and my fanciful excursus may appear only a highly profane version of "Tommy make room for your uncle"[1]. For if St. Francis and St. Dominic were the great twin brethren, Thomas was obviously the first great son of St. Dominic, as was his friend Bonaventure of St. Francis. Nevertheless, I have a reason (indeed two reasons) for taking as a text the accident of two title-pages; and putting St. Thomas beside St. Francis, instead of pairing him off with Bonaventure the Franciscan. It is because the comparison, remote and perverse as it may seem, is really a sort of short cut to the heart of history; and brings us by the most rapid route to the real question of the life and work of St.Thomas Aquinas. For most people now have a rough but picturesque picture in their minds of the life and work of St. Francis of Assisi. And the shortest way of telling the other story is to say that, while the two men were thus a contrast in almost every feature, they were really doing the same thing. One of them was doing it in the world of the mind and the other in the world of the worldly. But it was the same great medieval movement; still but little understood. In a constructive sense, it was more important than the Reformation. Nay, in a constructive sense, it was the Reformation.

About this medieval movement there are two facts that must first be emphasised. They are not, of course, contrary facts, but they are perhaps answers to contrary fallacies. First, in spite of all that was once said about superstition, the Dark Ages and the sterility of Scholasticism, it was in every sense a movement of enlargement, always moving towards greater light and even greater liberty. Second, in spite of all that was said later on about progress and the Renaissance and forerunners of modern thought, it was almost entirely a movement of orthodox theological enthusiasm, unfolded from within. It was *not* a compromise with the world, or a surrender to heathens or

[1] "Tommy Make Room for Your Uncle" is a song written by T. S. Lansdale in 1875.

heretics, or even a mere borrowing of external aids, even when it did borrow them. In so far as it did reach out to the light of common day, it was like the action of a plant which by its own force thrusts out its leaves into the sun; not like the action of one who merely lets daylight into a prison.

In short, it was what is technically called a Development in doctrine. But there seems to be a queer ignorance, not only about the technical, but the natural meaning of the word Development. The critics of Catholic theology seem to suppose that it is not so much an evolution as an evasion; that it is at best an adaptation. They fancy that its very success is the success of surrender. But that is not the natural meaning of the word Development. When we talk of a child being well-developed, we mean that he has grown bigger and stronger with his own strength; not that he is padded with borrowed pillows or walks on stilts to make him look taller. When we say that a puppy develops into a dog, we do not mean that his growth is a gradual compromise with a cat; we mean that he becomes more doggy and not less. Development is the expansion of all the possibilites and implications of a doctrine, as there is time to distinguish them and draw them out; and the point here is that the enlargement of medieval theology was simply the full comprehension of that theology. And it is of primary importance to realise this fact first, about the time of the great Dominican and the first Franciscan, because their tendency, humanistic and naturalistic in a hundred ways, was truly the development of the supreme doctrine, which was also the dogma of all dogmas. It is in this that the popular poetry of St. Francis and the almost rationalistic prose of St. Thomas appear most vividly as part of the same movement. There are both great growths of Catholic development, depending upon external things only as every living and growing thing depends on them; that is, it digests and transforms them, but continues in its own image and not in theirs. A Buddhist or a Communist might dream of two things which simultaneously eat each other, as the perfect form of unification. But it is not so with living things. St. Francis was content to call himself the Troubadour of God; but not content with the God of the Troubadours. St. Thomas did not reconcile Christ to Aristotle; he reconciled Aristotle to Christ.

Yes; in spite of the contrasts that are as conspicuous and even comic as the comparison between the fat man and the thin man, the tall man and the short; in spite of the contrast between the vagabond and the student, between the apprentice and the aristocrat, between the book-hater and the book-lover, between the wildest of all missionaries and the mildest of all professors, the great fact of medieval history is that these two great men were doing the same great work; one in the study and the other in the street. They were not bringing something new into Christianity, in the sense of something heathen or heretical into Christianity; on the contrary, they were bringing Christianity into Christendom. But they were bringing it back against the pressure of certain historic tendencies, which had hardened into habits in many great schools and authorites in the Christian Church; and they were using tools and weapons which seemed to many people to be associated with heresy or heathenry. St. Francis used Nature much as St. Thomas used Aristotle; and to some they seemed to be using a Pagan goddess and a Pagan sage. What they were really doing, and especially what St. Thomas was really doing, will form the main matter of these pages; but it is convenient to be able to compare him from the first with a more popular saint; because we may thus sum up the substance of it in the most popular way. Perhaps it would sound too paradoxical to say that these two saints saved us from Spirituality; a dreadful doom. Perhaps it may be misunderstood if I say that St. Francis, for all his love of animals, saved us from being Buddhists; and that St. Thomas, for all his love of Greek philosophy, saved us from being Platonists. But it is best to say the truth in its simplest form; that they both reaffirmed the Incarnation, by bringing God back to earth.

This analogy, which may seem rather remote, is really perhaps the best practical preface to the philosophy of St. Thomas. As we shall have to consider more closely later on, the purely spiritual or mystical side of Catholicism had very much got the upper hand in the first Catholic centuries; through the genius of Augustine, who had been a Platonist, and perhaps never ceased to be a Platonist; through the transcendentalism of the supposed work of the Areopagite; through the Oriental trend of the later Empire and something Asiatic about the almost pontifical kinghood of Byzantium; all these things weighed down what we should now roughly call the Western element; though it has as good a right to be called the Christian element; since its common sense is but the holy familiarity of the word made flesh. Anyhow, it must suffice for the moment to say that theologians had somewhat stiffened into a sort of Platonic pride in the possession of intangible and untranslatable truths within; as if no part of their wisdom had any root anywhere in the real world. Now the first thing that Aquinas did, though by no means the last, was to say to these pure trancendentalists something substantially like this.

"Far be it from a poor friar to deny that you have these dazzling diamonds in your head, all designed in the most perfect mathematical shapes and shining with a purely celestial light; all there, almost before you begin to think, let alone to see or hear or feel. But I am not ashamed to say that I find my reason fed by my senses; that I owe a great deal of what I think to what I see and smell and taste and handle; and that so far as my reason is concerned, I feel obliged to treat all this reality as real. To be brief, in all humility, I do not believe that God meant Man to exercise only that peculiar, uplifted and abstracted sort of intellect which you are so fortunate as to possess: but I believe that there is a middle field of facts which are given by the senses to be the subject matter of the reason; and that in that field the reason has a right to rule, as the representative of God in Man. It is true that all this is lower than the angels; but it is higher than the animals, and all the actual material objects Man finds around him. True, man also can be an object; and even a deplorable object. But what man has done man may do; and if an antiquated old heathen called Aristotle can help me to do it I will thank him in all humility."

Thus began what is commonly called the appeal to Aquinas and Aristotle. It might be called the appeal to Reason and the Authority of the Senses. And it will be obvious that there is a sort of popular parallel to it in the fact that St. Francis did not only listen for the angels, but also listened to the birds. And before we come to those aspects of St. Thomas that were very severely intellectual, we may note that in him as in St. Francis there is a preliminary practical element which is rather moral; a sort of good and straightforward humility; and a readiness in the man to regard even himself in some ways as an animal; as St. Francis compared his body to a donkey. It may be said that the contrast holds everywhere, even in zoological metaphor, and that if St. Francis was like that common or garden donkey who carried Christ into Jerusalem, St. Thomas, who was actually compared to an ox, rather resembled that Apocalyptic monster of almost Assyrian mystery; the winged bull. But again, we must not let all that can be contrasted eclipse what was common; or forget that neither of them would have been too proud to wait as patiently as the ox and ass in the stable of Bethlehem.

There were of course, as we shall soon see, many other much more curious and complicated ideas in the philosophy of St. Thomas; besides this primary idea of a central common sense that is nourished by the five senses. But at this stage, the point of the story is not only that this was a Thomist doctrine, but that it is a truly and eminently Christian doctrine. For upon this point modern writers write a great deal of nonsense; and show more than their normal ingenuity in missing the point. Having assumed without argument, at the start, that all emancipation must lead men away from religion and towards irreligion, they have just blankly and blindly forgotten what is the outstanding feature of the religion itself.

It will not be possible to conceal much longer from anybody the fact that St. Thomas Aquinas was one of the great liberators of the human intellect. The sectarians of the seventeenth and eighteenth centuries were essentially obscurantists, and they guarded an obscurantist legend that the Schoolman was an obscurantist. This was wearing thin even in the nineteenth century; it will be impossible in the twentieth. It has nothing to do with the truth of their theology or his; but only with the truth of historical proportion, which begins to reappear as quarrels begin to die down. Simply as one of the facts that bulk big in history, it is true to say that Thomas was a very great man who reconciled religion with reason, who expanded it towards experimental science, who insisted that the senses were the windows of the soul and that the reason had a divine right to feed upon facts, and that it was the business of the Faith to digest the strong meat of the toughest and most practical of pagan philosophies. It is a fact, like the military strategy of Napoleon, that Aquinas was thus fighting for all that is liberal and enlightened, as compared with his rivals, or for that matter his successors and supplanters. Those who, for other reasons, honestly accept the final effect of the Reformation will none the less face the fact, that it was the Schoolman who was the Reformer; and that the later Reformers were by comparison reactionaries. I use the word not as a reproach from my own stand-point, but as a fact from the ordinary modern progressive standpoint. For instance, they riveted the mind back to the literal sufficiency of the Hebrew Scriptures; when St. Thomas had already spoken of the Spirit giving grace to the Greek philosophies. He insisted on the social duty of works; they only on the spiritual duty of faith. It was the very life of the Thomist teaching that Reason can be trusted: it was the very life of Lutheran teaching that Reason is utterly untrustworthy.

Now when this fact is found to be a fact, the danger is that all the unstable opposition will suddenly slide to the opposite extreme. Those who up to that moment have been abusing the Schoolman as a dogmatist will begin to admire the Schoolman as a Modernist who diluted dogma. They will hastily begin to adorn his statue with all the faded garlands of progress, to present him as a man in advance of his age, which is always supposed to mean in agreement with our age; and to load him with the unprovoked imputation of having produced the modern mind. They will discover his attraction, and somewhat hastily assume that he was like themselves, because he was attractive. Up to a point this is pardonable enough; up to a point it has already happened in the case of St. Francis. But it would not go beyond a certain point in the case of St. Francis. Nobody, not even a Freethinker like Renan or Matthew Arnold, would pretend that St. Francis was anything but a devout Christian, or had any other original motive except the imitation of Christ. Yet St. Francis also had that liberating and humanising effect upon religion; though perhaps rather on the imagination than the intellect. But nobody says that St. Francis was loosening the Christian code, when he was obviously tightening it; like the rope round his friar's frock. Nobody says he merely opened the gates to sceptical science, or sold the pass to heathen humanism, or looked forward only to the Renaissance or met the Rationalists half way. No biographer pretends that St. Francis, when he is reported to have opened the Gospels at random and read the great texts about Poverty, really only opened the *Aeneid* and practised the *Sors Virgiliana* out of respect for heathen letters and learning. No historian will pretend that St. Francis wrote *The Canticle of the Sun* in close imitation of a Homeric Hymn to Apollo or loved birds because he had carefully learned all the tricks of the Roman Augurs.

In short, most people, Christian or heathen, would now agree that the Franciscan sentiment was primarily a Christian sentiment, unfolded from within, out of an innocent (or, if you will, ignorant) faith in the Christian religion itself. Nobody, as I have said, says that St. Francis drew his primary inspiration from Ovid. It would be every bit as false to say that Aquinas drew his primary inspiration from Aristotle. The whole lesson of his life, especially of his early life, the whole story of his childhood and choice of a career, shows that he was supremely and directly devotional; and that he passionately loved the Catholic worship long before he found he had to fight for it. But there is also a special and clinching instance of this, which once more connects St. Thomas with St. Francis. It seems to be strangely forgotten that both these saints were in actual fact imitating a Master, who was not Aristotle let alone Ovid, when they sanctified the senses or the simple things of nature; when St. Francis walked humbly among the beasts or St. Thomas debated courteously among the Gentiles.

Those who miss this, miss the point of the religion, even if it be a superstition; nay, they miss the very point they would call most superstitious. I mean the whole staggering story of the God-Man in the Gospels. A few even miss it touching St. Francis and his unmixed and unlearned appeal to the Gospels. They will talk of the readiness of St. Francis to learn from the flowers or the birds as something that can only point onward to the Pagan Renaissance. Whereas the fact stares them in the face; first, that it points backwards to the New Testament, and second that it points forward, if it points to anything, to the Aristotelian realism of the *Summa* of St.

Thomas Aquinas. They vaguely imagine that anybody who is humanising divinity must be paganising divinity; without seeing that the humanising of divinity is actually the strongest and starkest and most incredible dogma in the Creed. St. Francis was becoming more like Christ, and not merely more like Buddha, when he considered the lilies of the field or the fowls of the air; and St. Thomas was becoming more of a Christian, and not merely more of an Aristotelian, when he insisted that God and the image of God had come in contact through matter with a material world. These saints were, in the most exact sense of the term, Humanists; because they were insisting on the immense importance of the human being in the theological scheme of things. But they were not Humanists marching along a path of progress that leads to Modernism and general scepticism; for in their very Humanism they were affirming a dogma now often regarded as the most superstitious Superhumanism. They were strengthening that staggering doctrine of Incarnation, which the sceptics find it hardest to believe. There cannot be a stiffer piece of Christian divinity than the divinity of Christ.

This is a point that is here very much to the point; that these men became more orthodox, when they became more rational or natural. Only by being thus orthodox could they be thus rational and natural. In other words, what may really be called a liberal theology was unfolded from within, from out of the original mysteries of Catholicism. But that liberality had nothing to do with liberalism; in fact it cannot even now coexist with liberalism.[2] The matter is so cogent, that I will take one or two special ideas of St. Thomas to illustrate what I mean. Without anticipating the elementary sketch of Thomism that must be made later, the following points may be noted here.

For instance, it was a very special idea of St. Thomas that Man is to be studied in his whole manhood; that a man is not a man without his body, just as he is not a man without his soul. A corpse is not a man; but also a ghost is not a man. The earlier school of Augustine

[2] I use the world liberalism here in the strictly limited theological sense, in which Newman and other theologians use it. In its popular political sense, as I point out later, St. Thomas rather tended to be a Liberal, especially for his time.

and even of Anselm had rather neglected this, treating the soul as the only necessary treasure, wrapped for a time in a negligible napkin. Even here they were less orthodox in being more spiritual. They sometimes hovered on the edge of those Eastern deserts that stretch away to the land of transmigration; where the essential soul may pass through a hundred unessential bodies; reincarnated even in the bodies of beasts or birds. St. Thomas stood up stoutly for the fact that a man's body is his body as his mind is his mind; and that *he* can only be a balance and union of the two. Now this is in some ways a naturalistic notion, very near to the modern respect for material things; a praise of the body that might be sung by Walt Whitman or justified by D. H. Lawrence: a thing that might be called Humanism or even claimed by Modernism. In fact, it may be Materialism; but it is the flat contrary of Modernism. It is bound up, in the modern view, with the most monstrous, the most material, and therefore the most miraculous of miracles. It is specially connected with the most startling sort of dogma, which the Modernist can least accept; the Resurrection of the Body.

Or again, his argument for Revelation is quite rationalistic; and on the other side, decidedly democratic and popular. His argument for Revelation is not in the least an argument against Reason. On the contrary, he seems inclined to admit that truth could be reached by a rational process, if only it were rational enough; and also long enough. Indeed, something in his character, which I have called elsewhere optimism, and for which I know no other approximate term, led him rather to exaggerate the extent to which all men would ultimately listen to reason. In his controversies, he always assumes that they will listen to reason. That is, he does emphatically believe that men can be convinced by argument; when they reach the end of the argument. Only his common sense also told him that the argument never ends. I might convince a man that matter as the origin of Mind is quite meaningless, if he and I were very fond of each other and fought each other every night for forty years. But long before he was convinced on his deathbed, a thousand other materialists would have been born, and nobody can explain everything to everybody. St. Thomas takes the view that the souls of all the ordinary hard-working and simple-minded people are quite as important as the souls of thinkers and truth-seekers; and he asks how all these people are possibly to find time for the amount of reasoning that is needed to find truth. The whole tone of the passage shows both a respect for scientific enquiry and a strong sympathy with the average man. His argument for Revelation is not an argument against Reason; but it is an argument for Revelation. The *conclusion* he draws from it is that men must receive the highest moral truths in a miraculous manner; or most men would not receive them at all. His arguments are rational and natural; but his own deduction is all for the supernatural; and, as is common in the case of his argument, it is not easy to find any deduction except his own deduction. And when we come to that, we find it is something as simple as St. Francis himself could desire; the message from heaven; the story that is told out of the sky; the fairytale that is really true.

It is plainer still in more popular problems like Free Will. If St. Thomas stands for one thing more than another, it is what may be called subordinate sovereignties or autonomies. He was, if the flippancy may be used, a strong Home Ruler. We might even say he was always defending the independence of dependent things. He insisted that such a thing could have its own rights in its own region. It was his attitude to the Home Rule of the reason and even the senses; "Daughter am I in my father's house; but mistress in my own." And in exactly this sense he emphasised a certain dignity in Man, which was sometimes rather swallowed up in the purely theistic generalisations about God. Nobody would say he wanted to divide Man from God; but he did want to distinguish Man from God. In this strong sense of human dignity and liberty there is much that can be and is appreciated now as a noble humanistic liberality. But let us not forget that its upshot was that very Free Will, or moral responsibility of Man, which so many modern liberals would deny. Upon this sublime and perilous liberty hang heaven and hell, and all the mysterious drama of the soul. It is distinction and not division; but a man *can* divide himself from God, which, in a certain aspect, is the greatest distinction of all.

Again, though it is a more metaphysical matter, which must be mentioned later, and then only too slightly, it is the same with the old philosophical dispute about the Many and the One. Are things so different that they can never be classified; or so unified that they can never be distinguished? Without pretending to answer such questions here, we may say broadly that St. Thomas comes down definitely on the side of Variety, as a thing that is real as well as Unity. In this, and questions akin to this, he often departs from the great Greek philosophers who were sometimes his models; and entirely departs from the great Oriental philosophers who are in some sense his rivals. He seems fairly certain that the difference between chalk and cheese, or pigs and pelicans, is not a mere illusion, or dazzle of our bewildered mind blinded by a single light; but is pretty much what we all feel it to be. It may be said that this is mere common sense; the common sense that pigs are pigs; to that extent related to the earthbound Aristotelian common sense; to a human and even a heathen common sense. But note that here again the extremes of earth and heaven meet. It is also connected with the dogmatic Christian idea of the Creation; of a Creator who created pigs, as distinct from a Cosmos that merely evolved them.

In all these cases we see repeated the point stated at the start. The Thomist movement in metaphysics, like the Franciscan movement in morals and manners, was an enlargement and a liberation, it was emphatically a growth of Christian theology from within; it was emphatically *not* a shrinking of Christian theology under heathen or even human influences. The Franciscan was free to be a friar, instead of being bound to be a monk. But he was more of a Christian, more of a Catholic, even more of an ascetic. So the Thomist was free to be an Aristotelian, instead of being bound to be an Augustinian. But he was even more of a theologian; more of an orthodox theologian; more of a dogmatist, in having recovered through Aristotle the most defiant of all dogmas, the wedding of God with Man and therefore with Matter. Nobody can understand the greatness of the thirteenth century, who does not realise that it was a great growth of new things produced by a living thing. In that sense it was really bolder and freer than what we call the Renaissance, which was a resurrection of old things discovered in a dead thing. In that sense medievalism was not a Renascence, but rather a Nascence. It did not model its temples upon the tombs, or call up dead gods from Hades. It made an architecture as new as modern engineering: indeed it still remains the most modern architecture. Only it was followed at the Renaissance by a more antiquated architecture. In that sense the Renaissance might be called the Relapse. Whatever may be said of the Gothic and the Gospel according to St. Thomas, they were not a Relapse. It was a new thrust like the titanic thrust of Gothic engineering; and its strength was in a God who makes all things new.

In a word, St. Thomas was making Christendom more Christian in making it more Aristotelian. This is not a paradox but a plain truism, which can only be missed by those who may know what is meant by an Aristotelian, but have simply forgotten what is meant by a Christian. As compared with a Jew, a Moslem, a Buddhist, a Deist, or most obvious alternatives, a Christian *means* a man who believes that deity or sanctity has attached to matter or entered the world of the senses. Some modern writers, missing this simple point, have even talked as if the acceptance of Aristotle was a sort of concession to the Arabs; like a Modernist vicar making a concession to the Agnostics. They might as well say that the Crusades were a concession to the Arabs as say that Aquinas rescuing Aristotle from Averrhoes was a concessions to the Arabs. The Crusaders wanted to recover the place where the body of Christ had been, because they believed, rightly or wrongly, that it was a Christian place. St. Thomas wanted to recover what was in essence the body of Christ itself; the sanctified body of the Son of Man which had become a miraculous medium between heaven and earth. And he wanted the body, and all its senses, because he believed, rightly or wrongly, that it was a Christian thing. It might be a humbler or homelier thing than the Platonic mind; that is why it was Christian. St. Thomas was, if you will, taking the lower road when he walked in the steps of Aristotle. So was God, when He worked in the workshop of Joseph.

Lastly, these two great men were not only united to each other but separated from most of their comrades and contemporaries by the very revolutionary character of their own revolution. In 1215, Dominic Guzman, the Castilian, founded an Order very similar to that of Francis; and, by a most curious coincidence of history, at almost exactly the same moment as Francis. It was directed primarily to preaching the Catholic philosophy to the Albigensian heretics; whose own philosophy was one of the many forms of that Manicheanism with which this story is much concerned. It had its roots in the remote mysticism and moral detachment of the East; and it was therefore inevitable that the Dominicans should be rather more a brotherhood of philosophers, where the Franciscans were by comparison a brotherhood of poets. For this and other reasons, St. Dominic and his followers are little known or understood in modern England; they were involved eventually in a religious war, which followed on a theological argument; and there was something in the atmosphere of our country, during the last century or so, which made the theological argument even more incomprehensible than the religious war. The ultimate effect is in some ways curious; because St. Dominic, even more than St. Francis, was marked by that intellectual independence, and strict standard of virtue and veracity, which Protestant cultures are wont to regard as specially Protestant. It was of him that the tale was told, and would certainly have been told more widely among us if it had been told of a Puritan, that the Pope pointed to his gorgeous Papal Palace and said, "Peter can no longer say 'Silver and gold have I none' "; and the Spanish friar answered, "No, and neither can he now say, 'Rise and walk.' "

Thus there is another way in which the popular story of St. Francis can be a sort of bridge between the modern and medieval world. And it is based on that very fact already mentioned: that St. Francis and St. Dominic stand together in history as having done the same work, and yet are divided in English popular tradition in the most strange and startling way. In their own lands they are like Heavenly Twins, irradiating the same light from heaven, seeming sometimes to be two saints in one halo, as another order depicted Holy Poverty as two knights on one horse. In the legends of our own land, they are about as much united as St. George and the Dragon. Dominic is still conceived as an Inquisitor devising thumbscrews; while Francis is already accepted as a humanitarian deploring mousetraps. It seems, for instance, quite natural to us, and full of the same associations of flowers and starry fancies, that the name of Francis should belong to Francis Thompson. But I fancy it would seem less natural to call him Dominic Thompson; or find that a man, with a long record of popular sympathies and practical tenderness to the poor, could bear such a name as Dominic Plater.[3] It would sound as if he had been called Torquemada Thompson.

Now there must be something wrong behind this contradiction; turning those who were allies at home into antagonists abroad. On any other question, the fact would be apparent to common sense. Suppose English Liberals or Free-Traders found that, in remote parts of China, it was generally held that Cobden[4] was a cruel monster but Bright[5] a stainless saint. They would think there was a mistake somewhere. Suppose that American Evangelicals learned that in France or Italy, or other civilizations impenetrable by Moody[6] and Sankey, there was a popular belief that Moody was an angel but Sankey a devil; they would guess that there must be a muddle somewhere. Some other later accidental distinction must have cut across the main course of a historical tendency. These parallels are not so fantastic as they may sound. Cobden and Bright have actually been called 'child-torturers', in anger at their alleged callousness about the evils amended by the Factory Acts; and some would call the Moody and Sankey sermon on Hell a hellish exhibition. All that is a matter of opinion; but both men held the same sort of opinion, and there must be a blunder in an opinion that separates them so completely. And of course there is a complete blunder in the legend about St. Dominic. Those who know anything about St. Dominc know that he was a missionary and not a militant persecutor; that his contribution to religion was the Rosary and not the Rack; that

[3] Charles Dominic Plater, S. J. (1875–1921) was a leader in the British Catholic social movement during the early twentieth century. Best known for his role in founding and directing the work of the Catholic Social Guild.

[4] Richard Cobden (1804–1854) was a British politician of the Anti-Corn Law League.

[5] John Bright (1811–1889), an orator and British statesman, was the co-founder of that League. Both Cobden and Bright were leading spokesmen for the Manchester School of Economics.

[6] Dwight Lyman Moody (1837–1899) was an American evangelist who met Ira Sankey in 1870 and joined him in evangelistic campaigns.

his whole career is meaningless, unless we understand that his famous victories were victories of persuasion and not persecution. He did believe in the justification of persecution; in the sense that the secular arm could repress religious disorders. So did everybody else believe in persecution; and none more than the elegant blasphemer, Frederick II who believed in nothing else. Some say he was the first to burn heretics; but anyhow, he thought it was one of his imperial privileges and duties to persecute heretics. But to talk as if Dominic did nothing but persecute heretics, is like blaming Father Matthew,[7] who persuaded millions of drunkards to take a temperance pledge, because the accepted law sometimes allowed a drunkard to be arrested by a policeman. It is to miss the whole point; which is that this particular man had a genius for conversion, quite apart from compulsion. The real difference between Francis and Dominic, which is no discredit to either of them, is that Dominic did happen to be confronted with a huge campaign for the conversion of heretics, while Francis had only the more subtle task of the conversion of human beings. It is an old story that, while we may need somebody like Dominic to convert the heathen to Christianity, we are in even greater need of somebody like Francis, to convert the Christians to Christianity. Still, we must not lose sight of St. Dominic's special problem, which was that of dealing with a whole population, kingdoms and cities and countrysides, that had drifted from the Faith and solidified into strange and abnormal new religions. That he did win back masses of men so deceived, merely by talking and preaching, remains an enormous triumph worthy of a colossal trophy. St. Francis is called humane because he tried to convert Saracens and failed; St. Dominic is called bigoted and besotted because he tried to convert Albigensians and suceeded. But we happen to be in a curious nook or corner of the hills of history, from which we can see Assisi and the Umbrian hills, but are out of sight of the vast battle-field of the Southern Crusade; the miracle of Muret and the greater miracle of Dominic, when the roots of the Pyrenees and the shores of the Mediterranean saw defeated the Asiatic despair.

[7] Theobald Matthew (1796–1856) was an Irish priest better known as the Apostle of Temperance. He was remarkably successful in the promotion of total abstinence.

But there is an earlier and more essential link between Dominic and Francis, which is more to the immediate purpose of this book. They were in later times bracketed in glory, because they were in their own time bracketed in infamy; or at least in unpopularity. For they did the most unpopular thing that men can do; they started a popular movement. A man who dares to make a direct appeal to the populace always makes a long series of enemies — beginning with the populace. In proportion as the poor begin to understand that he means to help and not hurt them, the solid classes above begin to close in, resolved to hinder and not help. The rich, and even the learned, sometimes feel not unreasonably that the thing will change the world, not only in its worldliness or its wordly wisdom, but to some extent perhaps in its real wisdom. Such a feeling was not unnatural in this case; when we consider, for instance, St. Francis's really reckless attitude about rejecting books and scholarship; or the tendency that the Friars afterwards showed to appeal to the Pope in contempt of local bishops and ecclesiastical officers. In short, St. Dominic and St. Francis created a Revolution, quite as popular and unpopular as the French Revolution. But it is very hard today to feel that even the French Revolution was as fresh as it really was. The Marseillaise once sounded like the human voice of the volcano or the dance-tune of the earthquake, and the kings of the earth trembled, some fearing that the heavens might fall; some fearing far more that justice might be done. The Marseillaise is played today at diplomatic dinner-parties, where smiling monarchs meet beaming millionaires, and is rather less revolutionary than "Home Sweet Home". Also, it is highly pertinent to recall, the modern revolutionists would now call the revolt of the French Jacobins insufficient, just as they would call the revolt of the Friars insufficient. They would say that neither went far enough; but many, in their own day, thought they went very much too far. In the case of the Friars, the higher orders of the State, and to some extent even of the Church, were profoundly shocked at such a loosening of wild popular preachers among the people. It is not at all easy for us to feel that distant events were thus disconcerting and even disreputable. Revolutions turn into institutions; revolts that renew the youth of old societies in their turn grow old; and the past, which was full of new things, of splits and innovations and insurrections, seems to us a single texture of tradition.

But if we wish for one fact that will make vivid this shock of change and challenge, and show how raw and ragged, how almost rowdy in its reckless novelty, how much of the gutter and how remote from refined life, this experiment of the Friars did really seem to many in its own day, there is here a very relevant fact to reveal it. It shows how much a settled and already ancient Christendom did feel it as something like the end of an age; and how the very roads of the earth seem to shake under the feet of the new and nameless army; the march of the Beggars. A mystic nursery rhyme suggests the atmosphere of such a crisis; "Hark, hark, the dogs do bark; the Beggars are coming to town". There were many towns that almost fortified themselves against them and many watchdogs of property and rank did really bark, and bark loudly, when those Beggars went by; but louder was the singing of the Beggars who sang their Canticle to the Sun, and louder the baying of the Hounds of Heaven; the *Domini canes* of the medieval pun; the Dogs of God. And if we would measure how real and rending seemed that revolution, what a break with the past, we can see it in the first and most extraordinary event in the life of St. Thomas Aquinas.

II

THE RUNAWAY ABBOT

Thomas Aquinas, in a strange and rather symbolic manner, sprang out of the very centre of the civilised world of his time; the central knot or coil of the powers then controlling Christendom. He was closely connected with all of them; even with some of them that might well be described as destroying Christendom. The whole religious quarrel, the whole international quarrel, was for him, a family quarrel. He was born in the purple; almost literally on the hem of the imperial purple; for his own cousin was the Holy Roman Emperor. He could have quartered half the kingdoms of Europe on his shield — if he had not thrown away the shield. He was Italian and French and German and in every way European. On one side, he inherited from the energy that made the episode of the Normans, whose strange organising raids rang and rattled like flights of arrows in the corners of Europe and the ends of the earth; one flight of them following Duke William far northward through the blinding snows to Chester; another treading in Greek and Punic footsteps through the island of Sicily to the gates of Syracuse. Another bond of blood bound him to the great Emperors of the Rhine and Danube who claimed to wear the crown of Charlemagne; Red Barbarossa, who sleeps under the rushing river, was his great uncle, and Frederick II, the Wonder of the World, his second cousin, and yet he held by a hundred more intimate ties to the lively inner life, the local vivacity, the little walled nations and the thousand shrines of Italy. While inheriting this physical kinship with the Emperor, he maintained far more firmly his spiritual kinship with the Pope. He understood the meaning of Rome, and in what sense it was still ruling the world; and was not likely to think that the German Emperors of his time, any more than the Greek Emperors of a previous time, would be able to be really Roman in defiance of Rome. To this cosmopolitan comprehensiveness in his inherited position, he afterwards added many things of his own, that made for mutual understanding among the peoples, and gave him something of the character of an ambassador and interpreter. He travelled a great deal; he was not only well known in Paris and the German universities, but he almost certainly visited England; probably he went to Oxford and London; and it has been said that we may be treading in the footsteps of him and his Dominican companions, whenever we go down by the river to the railway-station that still bears the name of Black-friars. But the truth applies to the travels of his mind as well as his body. He studied the literature even of the opponents of Christianity much more carefully and impartially than was then the fashion; he really tried to understand the Arabian Aristotelianism of the Moslems; and wrote a highly humane and reasonable treatise on the problem of the treatment of the Jews. He always attempted to look at everything from the inside; but he was certainly lucky in having been born in the inside of the state system and the high politics of his day. What he thought of them may perhaps be inferred from the next passage in his history.

St. Thomas might thus stand very well for the International Man, to borrow the title of a modern book. But it is only fair to remember that he lived in the International Age; in a world that was international in a sense not to be suggested in any modern book, or by any modern man. If I remember right, the modern candidate for the post of International Man was Cobden, who was an almost abnormally national man; a narrowly national man; a very fine type, but one which can hardly be imagined except as moving between Midhurst and Manchester. He had an international policy and he indulged in international travel; but if he always remained a national person, it was because he remained a normal person; that is normal to the nineteenth century. But it was not so in the thirteenth century. There a man of international influence, like Cobden, could be also almost a man of international nationality. The names of nations and cities and places of origin did not connote that deep division that is the mark of the modern world. Aquinas as a student was nicknamed the ox of Sicily, though his birthplace was near Naples; but this did not prevent the city of Paris regarding him as simply and solidly as a Parisian, because he had been a glory of the Sorbonne, that it proposed to bury his bones when he was dead. Or take a more obvious contrast with modern times. Consider what is meant in most modern talk by a German Professor. And then realise that the greatest of all German Professors, Albertus Magnus, was himself one of the glories of the University of Paris; and it was in Paris that Aquinas supported him. Think of the modern German Professor being famous throughout Europe for his popularity when lecturing in Paris.

Thus, if there was war in Christendom, it was international war in the special sense in which we speak of international peace. It was not the war of two nations; but the war of two internationalisms: of two World States: the Catholic Church and the Holy Roman Empire. The political crisis in Christendom affected the life of Aquinas at the start in one sharp disaster, and afterwords in many indirect ways. It had many elements; the Crusades; the embers of the Albigensian pessimism, over which St. Dominic had triumphed in argument and Simon de Montfort in arms; the dubious experiment of an Inquisition which started from it; and many other things. But, broadly speaking, it is the period of the great duel between the Popes and the Emperors, that is the German Emperors who called themselves Holy Roman Emperors, the House of Hohenstaufen. The particular period of the life of Aquinas, however, is entirely overshadowed by the particular Emperor who was himself more an Italian than a German; the brilliant Frederick II who was called the Wonder of the World. It may be remarked, in passing, that Latin was the most living of languages at this time, and we often feel a certain weakness in the necessary translation. For I seem to have read somewhere that the word used was stronger than the Wonder of the World; that his medieval title was *Stupor Mundi*, which is more exactly the Stupefaction of the World. Something of the sort may be noted later of philosophical language, and the weakness of translating a word like *Ens* by a word like Being. But for the moment the parenthesis has another application; for it might well be said that Frederick did indeed stupefy the world; that there was something stunning and blinding about the blows he struck at religion, as in that blow which almost begins the biography of Thomas Aquinas. He may also be called stupefying in another sense; in that his very brilliancy has made some of his modern admirers very stupid.

For Frederick II is the first figure, and that a rather fierce and ominous figure, who rides across the scene of his cousin's birth and boyhood:

a scene of wild fighting and of fire. And it may be allowable to pause for a parenthesis upon his name, for two particular reasons: first that his romantic reputation, even among modern historians, covers and partly conceals the true background of the time; and second that the tradition in question directly involves the whole status of St. Thomas Aquinas. The nineteenth century view, still so strangely called the modern view by many moderns, touching such a man as Frederick II was well summed up by some solid Victorian, I think by Macaulay; Frederick was "a statesman in an age of Crusaders; a philosopher in an age of monks." It may be noted that the antithesis involves the assumption that a Crusader cannot easily be a states-man; and that a monk cannot easily be a philosopher. Yet, to take only that special instance, it would be easy to point out that the cases of two famous men in the age of Frederick II would alone be strong enough to upset both the assumption and the antithesis. St. Louis, though a Crusader and even an unsuccessful Crusader, was really a far more successful statesman than Frederick II. By the test of prac-tical politics, he popularised, solidified and sanctified the most pow-erful government in Europe, the order and concentration of the French Monarchy; the single dynasty that steadily increased in strength for five hundred years up to the glories of the Grand Siècle whereas Frederick went down in ruin before the Papacy and the Re-publics and a vast combination of priests and peoples. The Holy Ro-man Empire he wished to found was an ideal rather in the sense of a dream; it was certainly never a fact like the square and solid State which the French statesman did found. Or, to take another example from the next generation one of the most strictly practical statesmen in history, our own Edward I, was also a Crusader.

The other half of the antithesis is even more false and here even more relevant. Frederick II was not a philosopher in the age of monks. He was a gentleman dabbling in philosophy in the age of the monk Thomas Aquinas. He was doubtless an intelligent and even bril-liant gentleman; but if he did leave any notes on the nature of Being and Becoming, or the precise sense in which realities can be relative to Reality, I do not imagine those notes are now exciting under-graduates at Oxford or literary men in Paris, let alone the little groups of Thomists who have already sprung up even in New York and Chicago. It is no disrespect to the Emperor to say that he certainly was not a philosopher in the sense in which Thomas Aquinas was a philosopher, let alone so great or so universal or so permanent a philosopher. And Thomas Aquinas lived in that very age of monks, and in that very world of monks, which Macaulay talks of as if it were incapable of producing philosophy.

We need not dwell on the causes of this Victorian prejudice, which some still think so very advanced. It arose mainly from one narrow or insular notion; that no man could possibly be building up the best of the modern world, if he went with the main movement of the medieval world. These Victorians thought that only the heretic had ever helped humanity; only the man who nearly wrecked medieval civilisation could be of any use in constructing modern civilisation. Hence came a score of comic fables; as that the cathedrals must have been built by a secret society of Freemasons; or that the epic of Dante must be a cryptogram referring to the political hopes of Garibaldi. But the generalisation is not in its nature probable and it is not in fact true. This medieval period was rather specially the period of communal or corporate thinking, and in some matters it was really rather larger than the individualistic modern thinking. This could be proved in a flash from the mere fact of the use of the word 'statesman'. To a man of Macaulay's period, a statesman *always* meant a man who maintained the more narrow national interests of his own state against other states, as Richelieu maintained those of France, or Chatham of England, or Bismarck of Prussia. But if a man actually wanted to defend all these states, to combine all these states, to make a living brotherhood of all these states, to resist some outer peril as from the Mongolian millions— then that poor devil, of course, could not really be called a statesman. He was only a Crusader.

In this way it is but fair to Frederick II to say that he was a Crusader; if he was also rather like an Anti-Crusader. Certainly he was an international statesman. Indeed he was a particular type, which may be called an international soldier. The international soldier is always very much disliked by internationalists. They dislike

Charlemagne and Charles V and Napoleon; and everybody who tried to create the World State for which they cry aloud day and night. But Frederick is more dubious and less doubted; he was supposed to be the head of the Holy Roman Empire; and accused of wanting to be the head of a very Unholy Roman Empire. But even if he were Antichrist, he would still be a witness to the unity of Christendom.

Nevertheless, there is a queer quality in that time; which, while it was international was also internal and intimate. War, in the wide modern sense, is possible, not because more men disagree, but because more men agree. Under the peculiarly modern coercions, such as Compulsory Education and Conscription, there are such very large *peaceful* areas, that they can all agree upon War. In that age men disagreed even about war; and peace might break out anywhere. Peace was interrupted by feuds and feuds by pardons. Individuality wound in and out of a maze; spiritual extremes were walled up with one another in one little walled town; and we see the great soul of Dante divided, a cloven flame; loving and hating his own city. This individual complexity is intensely vivid in the particular story we have here to tell, in a very rough outline. If anyone wishes to know what is meant by saying that action was more individual, and indeed incalculable, he may well note some of the stages in the story of the great feudal house of Aquino, which had its castle not far from Naples. In the mere hasty anecdote we have now to tell, we shall note in succession five or six stages of this sort. Landulf of Aquino, a heavy feudal fighter typical of the time, rode in armour behind the imperial banners, and attacked a monastery, because the Emperor regarded the monastery as a fortress held for his enemy the Pope. Later, we shall see, the same feudal lord sent his own son to the same monastery; probably on the friendly advice of the same Pope. Later still, another of his sons, entirely on his own, rebelled against the Emperor, and went over to the armies of the Pope. For this he was executed by the Emperor, with promptitude and despatch. I wish we knew more about that brother of Thomas Aquinas who risked and lost his life to support the cause of the Pope; which was in all human essentials the cause of the People. He may not have been a saint; but he must have had some qualitites of a martyr. Meanwhile, two other brothers, still ardent and active apparently, in the service of the Emperor who killed the third brother, themselves proceeded to kidnap another brother, because they did not approve of his sympathy with the new social movements in religion. That is the sort of tangle in which this one distinguished medieval family found itself. It was not a war of nations; but it was a rather widespread family quarrel.

The reason for dwelling here, however, upon the position of the Emperor Frederick, as a type of his time, in his culture and his violence, in his concern for philosophy and his quarrel with religion, is not merely concerned with these things. He may here be the first figure that crosses the stage, because one of his very typical actions precipitated the first action, or obstinate inaction, which began the personal adventures of Thomas Aquinas in this world. The story also illustrates the extraordinary tangle in which a family like that of the Count of Aquino found itself; being at once so close to the Church and so much at odds with it. For Frederick II, in the course of these remarkable manoeuvres, military and political, which ranged from burning heretics to allying himself with Saracens, made a swoop as of a predatory eagle (and the Imperial eagle was rather predatory) upon a very large and wealthy monastery; the Benedictine Abbey of Monte Cassino; and stormed and sacked the place.

Some miles from the monastery of Monte Cassino stood a great crag or cliff, standing up like a pillar of the Apennines. It was crowned with a castle that bore the name of The Dry Rock, and was the eyrie in which the eaglets of the Aquino branch of the Imperial family were nursed to fly. Here lived Count Landulf of Aquino, who was the father of Thomas Aquinas and some seven other sons. In military affairs he doubtless rode with his family, in the feudal manner; and apparently had something to do with the destruction of the monastery. But it was typical of the tangle of the time, that Count Landulf seems afterwards to have thought that it would be a tactful and delicate act to put in his son Thomas as Abbot of the monastery. This would be of the nature of a graceful apology to the Church, and also, it would appear, the solution of a family difficulty.

For it had been long apparent to Count Landulf that nothing could be done with his seventh son Thomas, except to make him an Abbot or something of that kind. Born in 1226, he had from childhood a mysterious objection to becoming a predatory eagle, or even to taking an ordinary interest in falconry or tilting or any other gentlemanly pursuits. He was a large and heavy and quiet boy, and phenomenally silent, scarcely opening his mouth except to say suddenly to his schoolmaster in an explosive manner, "What is God?" The answer is not recorded but it is probable that the asker went on worrying out answers for himself. The only place for a person of this kind was the Church and presumably the cloister; and so far as that went, there was no particular difficulty. It was easy enough for a man in Count Landulf's position to arrange with some monastery for his son to be recieved there; and in this particular case he thought it would be a good idea if he were received in some official capacity, that would be worthy of his wordly rank. So everything was smoothly arranged for Thomas Aquinas becoming a monk, which would seem to be what he himself wanted; and sooner or later becoming Abbot of Monte Cassino. And then the curious thing happened.

In so far as we may follow rather dim and disputed events, it would seem that the young Thomas Aquinas walked into his father's castle one day and calmly announced that he had become one of the Begging Friars, of the new order founded by Dominic the Spaniard; much as the eldest son of the squire might go home and airily inform the family that he had married a gypsy; or the heir of a Tory Duke state that he was walking tomorrow with the Hunger Marchers organised by alleged Communists. By this, as has been noted already, we may pretty well measure the abyss between the old monasticism and the new, and the earthquake of the Dominican and Franciscan revolution. Thomas had appeared to wish to be a Monk; and the gates were silently opened to him and the long avenues of the abbey, the very carpet, so to speak, laid for him up to the throne of the mitred abbot. He said he wished to be a Friar, and his family flew at him like wild beasts; his brothers pursued him along the public roads, half-rent his friar's frock from his back and finally locked him up in a tower like a lunatic.

It is not very easy to trace the course of this furious family quarrel, and how it eventually spent itself against the tenacity of the young Friar; according to some stories, his mother's disapproval was short-lived and she went over to his side; but it was not only his relatives that were embroiled. We might say that the central governing class of Europe, which partly consisted of his family, were in a turmoil over the deplorable youth; even the Pope was asked for tactful intervention, and it was at one time proposed that Thomas should be allowed to wear the Dominican habit while acting as Abbot in the Benedictine Abbey. To many this would seem a tactful compromise; but it did not commend itself to the narrow medieval mind of Thomas Aquinas. He indicated sharply that he wished to be a Dominican in the Dominican Order, and not at a fancy-dress ball; and the diplomatic proposal appears to have been dropped.

Thomas of Aquino wanted to be a Friar. It was a staggering fact to his contemporaries; and it is rather an intriguing fact even to us; for this desire, limited literally and strictly to this statement, was the one practical thing to which his will was clamped with adamantine obstinacy till his death. He would not be an Abbot; he would not be a Monk; he would not even be a Prior or ruler in his own fraternity; he would not be a prominent or important Friar; he would be a Friar. It is as if Napoleon had insisted on remaining a private soldier all his life. Something in this heavy, quiet, cultivated, rather academic gentleman would not be satisfied till he was, by fixed authoritative proclamation and official pronouncement, established and appointed to be a Beggar. It is all the more interesting because, while he did more than his duty a thousand times over, he was not at all like a Beggar; nor at all likely to be a good Beggar. He had nothing of the native vagabond about him, as had his great precursors; he was not born with something of the wandering minstrel, like St. Francis; or something of the tramping missionary, like St. Dominic. But he insisted upon putting himself under military orders, to do these things at the will of another, if required. He may be compared with some of the more magnanimous aristocrats who have enrolled themselves in revolutionary armies; or some of the best of the poets and scholars who volunteered as private soldiers in the Great War. Something in the courage and consistency of Dominic and Francis had challenged his deep sense of justice; and while remaining a very reasonable person, and even a diplomatic one, he never let anything shake the iron immobility of this one decision of his youth; nor was he to be turned from his tall and towering ambition to take the lowest place.

The first effect of his decision, as we have seen, was much more stimulating and even startling. The General of the Dominicans, under whom Thomas had enrolled himself, was probably well aware of the diplomatic attempts to dislodge him and the worldly difficulties of resisting them. His expedient was to take his young follower out of Italy altogether; bidding him proceed with a few other friars to Paris. There was something prophetic even about this first progress of the travelling teacher of the nations; for Paris was indeed destined to be in some sense the goal of his spiritual journey; since it was there that he was to deliver both his great defence of the Friars and his great defiance to the antagonists of Aristotle. But this his first journey to Paris was destined to be broken off very short indeed. The friars had reached a turn of the road by a wayside fountain, a little way north of Rome, when they were overtaken by a wild cavalcade of captors, who seized on Thomas like brigands, but who were in fact only rather needlessly agitated brothers. He had a large number of brothers: perhaps only two were here involved. Indeed he was the seventh; and friends of Birth Control may lament that this philosopher was needlessly added to the noble line of ruffians who kidnapped him. It was an odd affair altogether. There is something quaint and picturesque in the idea of kidnapping a begging friar, who might in a sense be called a runaway abbot. There is a comic and tragic tangle in the motives and purposes of such a trio of strange kinsmen. There is a sort of Christian cross-purposes in the contrast between the feverish illusion of the importance of things, always marking men who are called practical; and the much more practical pertinacity of the man who is called theoretical.

Thus at least did those three strange brethren stagger or trail along their tragic road, tied together, as it were, like criminal and constable; only that the criminals were making the arrest. So their figures are seen for an instant against the horizon of history; brothers as sinister as any since Cain and Abel. For this queer outrage in the great family of Aquino does really stand out symbolically, as representing something that will forever make the Middle Ages a mystery and a bewilderment; capable of sharply contrasted interpretations like darkness and light. For in two of those men there raged, we might say screamed, a savage pride of blood and blazonry of arms, though they were princes of the most refined world of their time, which would seem more suitable to a tribe dancing round a totem. For the moment they had forgotten everything except the name of a family, that is narrower than a tribe, and far narrower than a nation. And the third figure of that trio, born of the same mother and perhaps visibly one with the others in face or form, had a conception of brotherhood broader than most modern democracy, for it was not national but international; a faith in mercy and modesty far deeper than any mere mildness of manners in the modern world; and a drastic oath of poverty, which would now be counted quite a mad exaggeration of the revolt against plutocracy and pride. Out of the same Italian castle came two savages and one sage; or one saint more pacific than most modern sages. That is the double aspect confusing a hundred controversies. That is what makes the riddle of the mediaeval age; that it was not one age but two ages. We look into the moods of some men, and it might be the Stone Age; we look into the minds of other men, and they might be living in the Golden Age; in the most modern sort of Utopia. There were always good men and bad men; but in this time good men who were subtle lived with bad men who were simple. They lived in the same family; they were brought up in the same nursery; and they came out to struggle, as the brothers of Aquino struggled by the way-side, when they dragged the new friar along the road and shut him up in the castle on the hill.

When his relations tried to despoil him of his friar's frock he seems to have laid about them in the fighting manner of his fathers, and it would seem successfully, since this attempt was abandoned. He accepted the imprisonment itself with his customary composure, and probably did not mind very much whether he was left to philosophise in a dungeon or in a cell. Indeed there is something in the way the whole tale is told, which suggests that through a great part of that strange abduction, he had been carried about like a lumbering stone statue. Only one tale told of his captivity shows him merely in anger; and that shows him angrier than he ever was before or after. It struck the imagination of his own time for more important reasons; but it has an interest that is psychological as well as moral. For once in his life, for the first time and the last, Thomas of Aquino was really *hors de lui*; riding a storm outside that tower of intellect and contemplation in which he commonly lived. And that was when his brothers introduced into his room some specially gorgeous and painted courtesan, with the idea of surprising him by a sudden temptation, or at least involving him in a scandal. His anger was justified, even by less strict moral standards than his own; for the meanness was even worse than the foulness of the expedient. Even on the lowest grounds, he knew his brothers knew, and they knew that he knew, that it was an insult to him as a gentleman to suppose that he would break his pledge upon so base a provocation; and he had behind him a far more terrible sensibility; all that huge ambition of humility which was to him the voice of God out of heaven. In this one flash alone we see that huge unwieldy figure in an attitude of activity, or even animation; and he was very animated indeed. He sprang from his seat and snatched a brand out of the fire, and stood brandishing it like a flaming sword. The woman not unnaturally shrieked and fled, which was all that he wanted; but it is quaint to think of what she must have thought of that madman of monstrous stature juggling with flames and apparently threatening to burn down the house. All he did, however, was to stride after her to the door and bang and bar it behind her; and then, with a sort of impulse of violent ritual, he rammed the burning brand into the door, blackening and blistering it with one big black sign of the cross. Then he returned, and dropped it again into the fire; and sat down on that seat of sedentary scholarship, that chair of philosophy, that secret throne of contemplation, from which he never rose again.

III

THE ARISTOTELIAN REVOLUTION

Albert, the Swabian, rightly called the Great, was the founder of modern science. He did more than any other man to prepare that process, which has turned the alchemist into the chemist, and the astrologer into the astronomer. It is odd that, having been in his time, in this sense almost the first astronomer, he now lingers in legend almost as the last astrologer. Serious historians are abandoning the absurd notion that the mediaeval Chruch persecuted all scientists as wizards. It is very nearly the opposite of the truth. The world sometimes persecuted them as wizards, and sometimes ran after them as wizards; the sort of pursuing that is the reverse of persecuting. The Church alone regarded them really and solely as scientists. Many an enquiring cleric was charged with mere magic in making his lenses and mirrors; he was charged by his rude and rustic neighbours; and would probably have been charged in exactly the same way if they had been Pagan neighbours or Puritan neighbours or Seventh-Day Adventist neighbours. But even then he stood a better chance when judged by the Papacy, than if he had been merely lynched by the laity. The Catholic Pontiff did not denounce Albertus Magnus as a magician. It was the half-heathen tribes of the north who admired him as a magician. It is the half-heathen tribes of the industrial towns today, the readers of cheap dream-books, and quack pamphlets, and newspaper prophets, who still admire him as an astrologer. It is admitted that the range of his recorded knowledge, of strictly material and mechanical facts, was amazing in a man of his time. It is true that, in most other cases, there was a certain limitation to the data of medieval science; but this certainly had nothing to do with medieval religion. For the data of Aristotle, and the great Greek civilisation, were in many ways more limited still. But it is not really so much a question of access to the facts, as of attitude to the facts. Most of the Schoolmen, if informed by the only informants they had that a unicorn has one horn or a salamander lives in the fire, still used it more as an illustration of logic than an incident of life. What they really said was, "If a unicorn has one horn, two unicorns have as many horns as one cow." And that is not one inch the less a fact because the unicorn is a fable. But with Albertus in medieval times, as with Aristotle in ancient times, there did begin something like the idea of emphasising the question: "But *does* the unicorn only have one horn or the salamander a fire instead of a fireside?" Doubtless when the social and geographical limits of medieval life began to allow them to search the fire for salamanders or the desert for unicorns, they had to modify many of their scientific ideas. A fact which will expose them to the very proper scorn of a generation of scientists which has just discovered that Newton is nonsense, that space is limited, and that there is no such thing as an atom.

This great German, known in his most famous period as a professor in Paris, was previously for some time professor at Cologne. In that beautiful Roman city, there gathered round him in thousands the lovers of that extraordinary life; the student life of the Middle Ages. They came together in great groups called Nations; and the fact illustrates very well the difference between medieval nationalism and modern nationalism. For although there might any morning be a brawl between the Spanish students and the Scottish students, or between the Flemish and the French, and swords flash or stones fly on the most purely patriotic principles, the fact remains that they had all come to the same school to learn the same philosophy. And though that might not prevent the starting of a quarrel, it might have a great deal to do with the ending of it. Before these motley groups of men from the ends of the earth, the father of science unrolled his scroll of strange wisdom; of sun and comet, of fish and bird. He was an Aristotelian developing, as it were, the one experimental hint of Aristotle; and in this he was entirely original. He cared less to be original about the deeper matters of men and morals; about which he was content to hand on a decent and Christianised Aristotelianism; he was even in a sense ready to compromise upon the merely metaphysical issue of the Nominalists[1] and the

[1] See note I, p. 385.

Realists. He would never have maintained alone the great war that was coming, for a balanced and humanised Christianity; but when it came, he was entirely on its side. He was called the Universal Doctor, because of the range of his scientific studies; yet he was in truth a specialist. The popular legend is never quite wrong; if a man of science is a magician, he was a magician. And the man of science has always been much *more* of a magician than the priest; since he would "control the elements" rather than submit to the Spirit who is more elementary than the elements.

Among the students thronging into the lecture-rooms there was one student, conspicuous by his tall and bulky figure, and completely failing or refusing to be conspicuous for anything else. He was so dumb in the debates that his fellows began to assume an American significance in the word dumbness; for in that land it is a synonym for dullness. It is clear that, before long, even his imposing stature began to have only the ignominious immensity of the big boy left behind in the lowest form. He was called the Dumb Ox. He was the object, not merely of mockery, but of pity. One good-natured student pitied him so much as to try to help him with his lessons, going over the elements of logic like an alphabet in a horn-book. The dunce thanked him with pathetic politeness; and the philanthropist went on swimmingly, till he came to a passage about which he was himself a little doubtful; about which, in point of fact, he was wrong. Whereupon the dunce, with every appearance of embarrassment and disturbance, pointed out a possible solution which happened to be right. The benevolent student was left staring, as at a monster, at this mysterious lump of ignorance and intelligence; and strange whispers began to run round the schools.

A regular religious biographer of Thomas Aquinas (who, needless to say, was the dunce in question) has said that by the end of this interview "his love of truth overcame his humility"; which, properly understood, is precisely true. But it does not, in the secondary psychological and social sense, describe all the welter of elements that went on within that massive head. All the relatively few anecdotes about Aquinas have a very peculiar vividness if we visualise the type of man; and this is an excellent example. Amid those elements was something of the difficulty which the generalising intellect has in adapting itself suddenly to a tiny detail of daily life; there was something of the shyness of really well-bred people about showing off; there was something even, perhaps, of that queer paralysis, and temptation to prefer even misunderstandings to long explanations, which led Sir James Barrie,[2] in his amusing sketch, to allow himself to be saddled with a Brother Henry he never possessed, rather than exert himself to put in a word of warning. These other elements doubtless worked with the very extraordinary humility of this very extraordinary man; but another element worked with his equally unquestionable 'love of truth' in bringing the misunderstanding to an end. It is an element that must never be left out of the make-up of St. Thomas. However dreamy or distracted or immersed in theories he might be, he had any amount of Common Sense; and by the time it came, not only to being taught, but to being taught wrong, there was something in him that said sharply, 'Oh, this has got to stop!'

It seems probable that it was Albertus Magnus himself, the lecturer and learned teacher of all these youths, who first suspected something of the kind. He gave Thomas small jobs to do, of annotation or exposition; he persuaded him to banish his bashfulness so as to take part in at least one debate. He was a very shrewd old man and had studied the habits of other animals besides the salamander and the unicorn. He had studied many specimens of the most monstrous of all monstrosities; that is called Man. He knew the signs and marks of the sort of man, who is in an innocent way something of a monster among men. He was too good a schoolmaster not to know that the dunce is not always a dunce. He learned with amusement that this dunce had been nicknamed the Dumb Ox by his schoolfellows. All that is natural enough; but it does not take away the savour of something rather strange and symbolic, about the extraordinary emphasis with which he spoke at last. For Aquinas was still generally known only as one obscure and obstinately unresponsive pupil, among many more brilliant and promising pupils, when the great Albert broke silence with his famous cry and prophecy; "You

---

[2] Sir James Barrie (1860–1937) was a novelist and a playwright.

call him a Dumb Ox; I tell you this Dumb Ox shall bellow so loud
that his bellowings will fill the world".

To Albertus Magnus, as to Aristotle or Augustine or any number
of other and older teachers, St. Thomas was always ready, with the
hearty sort of humility, to give thanks for all his thinking. None the
less, his own thinking was an advance on Albertus and the other
Aristotelians, just as it was an advance on Augustine and the Augustinians. Albert had drawn attention to the direct study of natural
facts, if only through fables like the unicorn and the salamander but
the monster called Man awaited a much more subtle and flexible
vivi-section. The two men, however, became close friends and their
friendship counts for a great deal in this central fight of the Middle
Ages. For, as we shall see, the rehabilitation of Aristotle was a
revolution almost as revolutionary as the exaltation of Dominic and
Francis; and St. Thomas was destined to play a striking part in both.

It will be realised that the Aquino family had ultimately abandoned
its avenging pursuit of its ugly duckling; who, as a black friar,
should perhaps be called its black sheep. Of that escape some picturesque stories are told. The black sheep generally profits at last by
quarrels among the white sheep of a family. They begin by quarrelling with him, but they end by quarrelling with each other. There is
a rather confusing account concerning which members of his family
came over to his side, while he was still imprisoned in the tower.
But it is a fact that he was very fond of his sisters, and therefore
probably not a fable that it was they who engineered his escape.
According to the story, they rigged up a rope to the top of the
tower, attached to a big basket, and it must have been rather a big
basket if he was indeed lowered in this fashion from his prison, and
escaped into the world. Anyhow, he did escape by energy, external
or internal. But it was only an individual energy. The world was
still pursuing and persecuting the Friars, quite as much as when they
fled along the road to Rome. Thomas Aquinas had the good fortune
to gather under the shadow of the one great outstanding Friar,
whose respectability it was difficult to dispute, the learned and orthodox Albertus; but even he and his were soon troubled by the
growing storm that threatened the new popular movements in the

Church. Albertus was summoned to Paris, to receive the degree of a
Doctor; but everyone knew that every move in that game had the
character of a challenge. He made only the request, which probably
looked like an eccentric request, that he should take his Dumb Ox
along with him. They set out, like ordinary Friars or religious vaga-
bonds; they slept in such monasteries as they could find; and finally
in the monastery of St. James in Paris, where Thomas met another
Friar who was also another friend.

Perhaps under the shadow of the storm that menaced all Friars,
Bonaventure, the Franciscan, grew into so great a friendship with
Thomas the Dominican, that their contemporaries compared them
to David and Jonathan. The point is of some interest; because it
would be quite easy to represent the Franciscan and the Dominican
as flatly contradicting each other. The Franciscan may be represented as the Father of all the Mystics; and the Mystics can be represented as men who maintain that the final fruition or joy of the
soul is rather a sensation than a thought. The motto of the Mystics
has always been, "Taste and see". Now St. Thomas also began by
saying, "Taste and see"; but he said it of the first rudimentary impressions of the human animal. It might well be maintained that the
Franciscan puts Taste last and the Dominican puts it first. It might
be said that the Thomist begins with something solid like the taste
of an apple, and afterwards deduces a divine life for the intellect;
while the Mystic exhausts the intellect first, and says finally that the
sense of God is something like the taste of an apple. A common
enemy might claim that St. Thomas begins with the taste of fruit
and St. Bonaventure ends with the taste of fruit. But they are both
right; if I may say so, it is a privilege of people who contradict each
other in their cosmos to be both right. The Mystic is right in saying
that the relation of God and Man is essentially a love-story; the pattern and type of all love-stories. The Dominican rationalist is equally
right in saying that the intellect is at home in the topmost heavens;
and that the appetite for truth may outlast and even devour all the
duller appetites of man.

At the moment Aquinas and Bonaventure were encouraged in the
possibility that they were both right; by the almost universal agreement

that they were both wrong. It was in any case a time of wild disturbance, and, as is common in such times, those who were trying to put things right were most vigorously accused of putting things wrong. Nobody knew who would win in that welter; Islam, or the Manichees of the Midi; or the two-faced and mocking Emperor; or the Crusades; or the old Orders of Christendom. But some men had a very vivid feeling that everything was breaking up; and that all the recent experiments or excesses were part of the same social dissolution; and there were two things that such men regarded as signs of ruin; one was the awful apparition of Aristotle out of the East, a sort of Greek god supported by Arabian worshippers; and the other was the new freedom of the Friars. It was the opening of the monastery and the scattering of the monks to wander over the world. The general feeling that they wandered like sparks from a furnace hitherto contained; the furnace of the abnormal love of God: the sense that they would utterly unbalance the common people with the counsels of perfection; that they would drift into being demagogues; all this finally burst out in a famous book called *The Perils of the Latter Times*, by a furious reactionary, William de St. Amour. It challenged the French King and the Pope, so that they established an enquiry. And Aquinas and Bonaventure, the two incongruous friends, with their respectively topsy-turvy universes, went up to Rome together, to defend the freedom of the Friars.

Thomas Aquinas defended the great vow of his youth, for freedom and for the poor; and it was probably the topmost moment of his generally triumphant career; for he turned back the whole backward movement of his time. Responsible authorities have said that, but for him, the whole great popular movement of the Friars might have been destroyed. With this popular victory the shy and awkward student finally becomes a historical character and a public man. After that, he was identified with the Mendicant Orders. But while St. Thomas may be said to have made his name in the defence of the Mendicant Orders against the reactionaries, who took the same view of them as his own family had taken, there is generally a difference between a man making his name and a man really doing his work. The work of Thomas Aquinas was yet to come; but less shrewd observers than he could already see that it was coming. Broadly speaking, the danger was the danger of the orthodox, or those who too easily identify the old order with the orthodox, forcing a final and conclusive condemnation of Aristotle. There had already been rash and random condemnations to that effect, issued here and there, and the pressure of the narrower Augustinians upon the Pope and the principal judges became daily more pressing. The peril had appeared, not unnaturally, because of the historical and geographical accident of the Moslem proximity to the culture of Byzantium. The Arabs had got hold of the Greek manuscripts before the Latins who were the true heirs of the Greeks. And Moslems, though not very orthodox Moslems, were turning Aristotle into a pantheist philosophy still less acceptable to orthodox Christians. This second controversy, however, requires more explanation than the first. As is remarked on an introductory page, most modern people do know that St. Francis at least was a liberator of large sympathies; that, whatever their positive view of medievalism, the Friars were in a relative sense a popular movement, pointing to greater fraternity and freedom; and a very little further information would inform them that this was every bit as true of the Dominican as of the Franciscan Friars. Nobody now is particularly likely to start up in defence of feudal abbots or fixed and stationary monks, against such impudent innovators as St. Francis and St. Thomas. We may therefore be allowed to summarise briefly the great debate about the Friars, though it shook all Christendom in its day. But the greater debate about Aristotle presents a greater difficulty; because there are modern misconceptions about it which can only be approached with a little more elaboration.

Perhaps there is really no such thing as a Revolution recorded in history. What happened was always a Counter-Revolution. Men were always rebelling against the last rebels; or even repenting of the last rebellion. This could be seen in the most casual contemporary fashions, if the fashionable mind had not fallen into the habit of seeing the very latest rebel as rebelling against all ages at once. The Modern Girl with the lipstick and the cocktail is as much a rebel against the Woman's Rights Woman of the '80's, with her stiff stick-up collars and strict teetotalism, as the latter was a rebel against the Early Victorian lady of the languid waltz tunes and the album full of quotations from Byron; or as the last, again, was a rebel against a Puritan mother to whom the waltz was a wild orgy and Byron the Bolshevist of his age. Trace even the Puritan mother back through history and she represents a rebellion against the Cavalier laxity of the English Church, which was at first a rebel against the Catholic civilisation, which had been a rebel against the Pagan civilisation. Nobody but a lunatic could pretend that these things were a progress; for they obviously go first one way and then the other. But whichever is right, one thing is certainly wrong; and that is the modern habit of looking at them only from the modern end. For that is only to see the end of the tale; they rebel against they know not what, because it arose they know not when; intent only on its ending, they are ignorant of its beginning; and therefore of its very being. The difference between the smaller cases and the larger, is that in the latter there is really so huge a human upheaval that men start from it like men in a new world; and that very novelty enables them to go on very long; and generally to go on too long. It is *because* these things start with a vigorous revolt that the intellectual impetus lasts long enought to make them seem like a survival. An excellent example of this is the real story of the revival and the neglect of Aristotle. By the end of the medieval time, Aristotelianism did eventually grow stale. Only a very fresh and successful novelty ever gets quite so stale as that.

When the moderns, drawing the blackest curtain of obscurantism that ever obscured history, decided that nothing mattered much before the Renaissance and the Reformation, they instantly began their modern career by falling into a big blunder. It was the blunder about Platonism. They found, hanging about the courts of the swaggering princes of the sixteenth century (which was as far back in history as they were allowed to go) certain anti-clerical artists and scholars who said they were bored with Aristotle and were supposed to be secretly indulging in Plato. The moderns, utterly ignorant of the whole story of the medievals, instantly fell into the trap. They assumed that Aristotle was some crabbed antiquity and tyranny

from the black back of the Dark Ages, and that Plato was an entirely
new Pagan pleasure never yet tasted by Christian men. Father Knox
has shown in what a startling state of innocence is the mind of Mr.
H. L. Mencken, for instance, upon this point. In fact, of course, the
story is exactly the other way round. If anything, it was Platonism
that was the old orthodoxy. It was Aristotelianism that was the very
modern revolution. And the leader of that modern revolution was
the man who is the subject of this book.

The truth is that the historical Catholic Church began by being
Platonist; by being rather too Platonist. Platonism was in that very
golden Greek air that was breathed by the first great Greek theologians. The Christian Fathers were much more like the Neo-
Platonists than were the scholars of the Renaissance; who were only
Neo-Neo-Platonists. For Chrysostom or Basil it was as ordinary and
normal to think in terms of the Logos, or the Wisdom which is the
aim of philosophers, as it is to any men of any religion today to talk
about social problems or progress or the economic crisis throughout
the world. St. Augustine followed a natural mental evolution when
he was a Platonist before he was a Manichean, and a Manichean before he was a Christian. And it was exactly in that last association that
the first faint hint, of the danger of being *too* Platonist, may be seen.

From the Renaissance to the nineteenth century, the Moderns
have had an almost monstrous love of the Ancients. In considering
medieval life, they could never regard the Christians as anything but
the pupils of the Pagans; of Plato in ideas, or Aristotle in reason and
science. It was not so. On some points, even from the most monot-
onously modern standpoint, Catholicism was centuries ahead of
Platonism or Aristotelianism. We can see it still, for instance, in the
tiresome tenacity of Astrology. On that matter the philosophers
were all in favour of superstition; and the saints and all such superstitious people were against superstition. But even the great saints
found it difficult to get disentangled from this superstition. Two
points were always put by those suspicious of the Aristotelianism of
Aquinas; and they sound to us now very quaint and comic, taken together. One was the view that the stars are personal beings, governing our lives; the other the great general theory that men have

one mind between them; a view obviously opposed to immortality; that is, to individuality. Both linger among the Moderns; so strong is still the tyranny of the Ancients. Astrology sprawls over the Sunday papers, and the other doctrine has its hundredth form in what is called Communism; or the Soul of the Hive.

For on one preliminary point, this position must not be misunderstood. When we praise the practical value of the Aristotelian Revolution, and the originality of Aquinas in leading it, we do not mean that the Scholastic philosophers before him had not been philosophers, or had not been highly philosophical, or had not been in touch with ancient philosophy. In so far as there was ever a bad break in philosophical history, it was not before St. Thomas, or at the beginning of medieval history; it was after St. Thomas and at the beginning of modern history. The great intellectual tradition that comes down to us from Pythagoras and Plato was never interrupted or lost through such trifles as the sack of Rome, the triumph of Attila or all the barbarian invasions of the Dark Ages. It was only lost after the introduction of printing, the discovery of America, the founding of the Royal Society and all the enlightenment of the Renaissance and the modern world. It was there, if anywhere, that there was lost or impatiently snapped the long thin delicate thread that had descended from distant antiquity; the thread of that unusual human hobby; the habit of thinking. This is proved by the fact that the printed books of this later period largely had to wait for the eighteenth century, or the end of the seventeenth century, to find even the names of the new philosophers; who were at the best a new kind of philosophers. But the decline of the Empire, the Dark Ages and the early Middle Ages, though too much tempted to neglect what was opposed to Platonic philosophy, had never neglected philosophy. In that sense St. Thomas, like most other very original men, has a long and clear pedigree. He himself is constantly referring back to the authorities from St. Augustine to St. Anselm, and from St. Anselm to St. Albert, and even when he differs, he also defers.

A very learned Anglican once said to me, not perhaps without a touch of tartness, "I can't understand why everybody talks as if

Thomas Aquinas were the beginning of the Scholastic philosophy. I could understand their saying he was the end of it." Whether or no the comment was meant to be tart, we may be sure that the reply of St. Thomas would have been perfectly urbane. And indeed it would be easy to answer, with a certain placidity, that in his Thomist language, the end of a thing does not mean its destruction, but its fulfilment. No Thomist will complain, if Thomism is the end of our philosophy, in the sense in which God is the end of our existence. For that does not mean that we cease to exist, but that we become as perennial as the *philosophia perennis*. Putting this claim on one side, however, it is important to remember that my distinguished interlocutor was perfectly right, in that there had been whole dynasties of doctrinal philosophers before Aquinas, leading up to the day of the great revolt of the Aristotelians. Nor was even that revolt a thing entirely abrupt and unforeseen. An able writer in the *Dublin Review* not long ago pointed out that in some respects the whole nature of metaphysics had advanced a long way since Aristotle, by the time it came to Aquinas. And that it is no disrespect to the primitive and gigantic genius of the Stagirite to say that in some respects he was really but a rude and rough founder of philosophy, compared with some of the subsequent subtleties of medievalism; that the Greek gave a few grand hints which the Scholastics developed into the most delicate fine shades. This may be an overstatement, but there is a truth in it. Anyhow, it is certain that even in Aristotelian philosophy, let alone Platonic philosophy, there was already a tradition of highly intelligent interpretation. If that delicacy afterwards degenerated into hair-splitting, it was none the less delicate hair-splitting; and work requiring very scientific tools.

What made the Aristotelian Revolution really revolutionary was the fact that it was really religious. It is the fact, so fundamental that I thought it well to lay it down in the first few pages of this book; that the revolt was largely a revolt of the most Christian elements in Christendom. St. Thomas, every bit as much as St. Francis, felt subconsciously that the hold of his people was slipping on the solid Catholic doctrine and discipline, worn smooth by more than a thousand years of routine; and that the Faith needed to be shown under a new light and dealt with from another angle. But he had no motive except the desire to make it popular for the salvation of the people. It was true, broadly speaking, that for some time past it had been too Platonist to be popular. It needed something like the shrewd and homely touch of Aristotle to turn it again into a religion of common sense. Both the motive and the method are illustrated in the war of Aquinas against the Augustinians.

First, it must be remembered that the Greek influence continued to flow from the Greek Empire; or at least from the centre of the Roman Empire which was in the Greek city of Byzantium, and no longer in Rome. That influence was Byzantine in every good and bad sense; like Byzantine art, it was severe and mathematical and a little terrible; like Byzantine etiquette, it was Oriental and faintly decadent. We owe to the learning of Mr. Christopher Dawson much enlightenment upon the way in which Byzantium slowly stiffened into a sort of Asiatic theocracy, more like that which served the Sacred Emperor in China. But even the unlearned can see the difference, in the way in which Eastern Christianity flattened everything, as it flattened the faces of the images into icons. It became a thing of patterns rather than pictures; and it made definite and destructive war upon statues. Thus we see, strangely enough, that the East was the land of the Cross and the West was the land of the Crucifix. The Greeks were being dehumanised by a radiant symbol, while the Goths were being humanised by an instrument of torture. Only the West made realistic pictures of the greatest of all the tales out of the East. Hence the Greek element in Christian theology tended more and more to be a sort of dried up Platonism; a thing of diagrams and abstractions; to the last indeed noble abstractions, but not sufficiently touched by that great thing that is by definition almost the opposite of abstraction: Incarnation. Their Logos was the Word; but not the Word made Flesh. In a thousand very subtle ways, often escaping doctrinal definition, this spirit spread over the world of Christendom from the place where the Sacred Emperor sat under his golden mosaics; and the flat pavement of the Roman Empire was at last a sort of smooth pathway for Mahomet. For Islam was the ultimate fulfilment of the Iconoclasts. Long before that, however, there was this tendency to make the Cross merely decorative like the Crescent; to make it a pattern like the Greek key or the Wheel of Buddha. But there is something passive about such a world of patterns, and the Greek Key does not open any door, while the Wheel of Buddha always moves round and never moves on.

Partly through these negative influences, partly through a necessary and noble asceticism which sought to emulate the awful standard of the martyrs, the earlier Christian ages had been excessively anti-corporeal and too near the danger-line of Manichean mysticism. But there was far less danger in the fact that the saints macerated the body than in the fact that the sages neglected it. Granted all the grandeur of Augustine's contribution to Christianity, there was in a sense a more subtle danger in Augustine the Platonist than even in Augustine the Manichee. There came from it a mood which unconsciously committed the heresy of dividing the substance of the Trinity. It thought of God too exclusively as a Spirit who purifies or a Saviour who redeems; and too little as a Creator who creates. That is why men like Aquinas thought it right to correct Plato by an appeal to Aristotle; Aristotle who took things as he found them, just as Aquinas accepted things as God created them. In all the work of St. Thomas the world of positive creation is perpetually present. Humanly speaking, it was he who saved the human element in Christian theology, if he used for convenience certain elements in heathen philosophy. Only, as has already been urged, the human element is also the Christian one.

The panic upon the Aristotelian peril, that had passed across the high places of the Church, was probably a dry wind from the desert. It was really filled rather with fear of Mahomet than fear of Aristotle. And this was ironic, because there was really much more difficulty in reconciling Aristotle with Mahomet than in reconciling him with Christ. Islam is essentially a simple creed for simple men; and nobody can ever really turn pantheism into a simple creed. It is at once too abstract and too complicated. There are simple believers in a personal God; and there are atheists more simple-minded than any believers in a personal God. But few can, in mere simplicity, accept a godless universe as a god. And while the Moslem, as compared with the Christian, had perhaps a less human God, he had if possible a more personal God. The will of Allah was very much of a will, and could not be turned into a stream of tendency. On all that cosmic and abstract side the Catholic was more accommodating than the Moslem — up to a point. The Catholic could admit at least that Aristotle was right about the impersonal elements of a personal God. Hence, we may say broadly of the Moslem philosophers, that those who became good philosophers became bad Moslems. It is not altogether unnatural that many bishops and doctors feared that the Thomists might become good philosophers and bad Christians. But there were also many, of the strict school of Plato and Augustine, who stoutly denied that they were even good philosophers. Between those rather incongruous passions, the love of Plato and the fear of Mahomet, there was a moment when the prospects of any Aristotelian culture in Christendom looked very dark indeed. Anathema after anathema was thundered from high places; and under the shadow of the persecution, as so often happens, it seemed for a moment that barely one or two figures stood alone in the storm-swept area. They were both in the black and white of the Dominicans; for Albertus and Aquinas stood firm.

In that sort of combat there is always confusion; and majorities change into minorities and back again, as if by magic. It is always difficult to date the turn of the tide, which seems to be a welter of eddies; the very dates seeming to overlap and confuse the crisis. But the change, from the moment when the two Dominicans stood alone to the moment when the whole Church at last wheeled into line with them, may perhaps be found at about the moment when they were practically brought before a hostile but a not unjust judge. Stephen Tempier, the Bishop of Paris, was apparently a rather fine specimen of the old fanatical Churchman, who thought that admiring Aristotle was a weakness likely to be followed by adoring Apollo. He was also, by a piece of bad luck, one of the old social conservatives, who had intensely resented the popular revolution of the Preaching Friars. But he was an honest man; and Thomas Aquinas never asked for anything but permission to address honest men. All around him there were other Aristotelian revolutionaries of a much more dubious sort. There was Siger, the sophist from Brabant, who learned all his Aristotelianism from the Arabs; and had an ingenious theory about how an Arabian agnostic could also be a Christian. There were a thousand young men of the sort that had shouted for Abelard; full of the youth of the thirteenth century and drunken with the Greek wine of Stagira. Over against them, lowering and implacable, was the old Puritan party of the Augustinians; only too delighted to class the rationalistic Albert and Thomas with the equivocal Moslem meta-physicians.

It would seem that the triumph of Thomas was really a personal triumph. He withdrew not a single one of his propositions; though it is said that the reactionary Bishop did condemn some of them after his death. On the whole, however, Aquinas convinced most of his critics that he was quite as good a Catholic as they were. There was a sequel of squabbles between the Religious Orders, following upon this controversial crisis. But it is probably true to say that the fact, that a man like Aquinas had managed even partially to satisfy a man like Tempier, was the end of the essential quarrel. What was already familiar to the few became familiar to the many; that an Aristotelian could really be a Christian. Another fact assisted in the common conversion. It rather curiously resembles the story of the translation of the Bible; and the alleged Catholic suppression of the Bible. Behind the scenes, where the Pope was much more tolerant than the Paris Bishop, the friends of Aquinas had been hard at work producing a new translation of Aristotle. It demonstrated that in many ways the heretical translation had been a very heretical translation. With the final consummation of this work, we may say that the great Greek philosophy entered finally into the system of Christendom. The process has been half humourously described as the Baptism of Aristotle.

We have all heard of the humility of the man of science; of many who were very genuinely humble; and of some who were very proud of their humility. It will be the somewhat too recurrent burden of this brief study that Thomas Aquinas really did have the humility of the man of science; as a special variant of the humility of the saint. It is true that he did not himself contribute anything concrete in the experiment or detail of physical science; in this, it may be said, he even lagged behind the last generation, and was far less of an experimental scientist than his tutor Albertus Magnus. But for all that, he was historically a great friend to the freedom of science. The principles he laid down, properly understood, are perhaps the best that can be produced for protecting science from mere obscurantist persecution. For instance, in the matter of the inspiration of Scripture, he fixed first on the obvious fact, which was forgotten by four furious centuries of sectarian battle, that the meaning of Scripture is very far from self-evident; and that we must often interpret it in the light of other truths. If a literal interpretation is really and flatly contradicted by an obvious fact, why then we can only say that the literal interpretation must be a false interpretation. But the fact must really be an obvious fact. And unfortunately, nineteenth-century scientists were just as ready to jump to the conclusion that any guess about nature was an obvious fact, as were seventeenth-century sectarians to jump to the conclusion that any guess about Scripture was the obvious explanation. Thus, private theories about what the Bible ought to mean, and premature theories about what the world ought to mean, have met in loud and widely advertised controversy, especially in the Victorian time; and this clumsy collision of two very impatient forms of ignorance was known as the quarrel of Science and Religion.

But St. Thomas had the scientific humility in this very vivid and special sense; that he was ready to take the lowest place; for the examination of the lowest things. He did not, like a modern specialist, study the worm as if it were the world; but he was willing to begin to study the reality of the world in the reality of the worm. His Aristotelianism simply meant that the study of the humblest fact will lead to the study of the highest truth. That for him the process was logical and not biological, was concerned with philosophy rather than science, does not alter the essential idea that he believed in beginning at the bottom of the ladder. But he also gave, by his view of Scripture and Science, and other questions, a sort of charter for pioneers more purely practical than himself. He practically said that if they could really prove their practical discoveries, the traditional interpretation of Scripture must give way before those discoveries. He could hardly, as the common phrase goes, say fairer than that. If the matter had been left to him, and men like him, there never would have been any quarrel between Science and Religion. He did his very best to map out two provinces for them, and to trace a just frontier between them.

It is often cheerfully remarked that Christianity has failed, by which is meant that it has never had that sweeping, imperial and imposed supremacy, which has belonged to each of the great revolutions, every one of which has subsequently failed. There was never a moment when men could say that every man was a Christian; as they might say for several months that every man was a Royalist or a Republican or a Communist. But if sane historians want to understand the sense in which the Christian character has succeeded, they could not find a better case than the massive moral pressure of a man like St. Thomas, in support of the buried rationalism of the heathens, which had as yet only been dug up for the amusement of the heretics. It was, quite strictly and exactly, because a new kind of man was conducting rational enquiry in a new kind of way, that men forgot the curse that had fallen on the temples of the dead demons and the palaces of the dead despots; forgot even the new fury out of Arabia against which they were fighting for their lives; because the man who was asking them to return to sense, or to return to their senses, was not a sophist but a saint. Aristotle had described the magnanimous man, who is great and knows that he is great. But Aristotle would never have recovered his own greatness, but for the miracle that created the more magnanimous man; who is great and knows that he is small.

There is a certain historical importance in what some would call the heaviness of the style employed. It carries a curious impression of candour, which really did have, I think, a considerable effect upon contemporaries. The saint has sometimes been called a sceptic. The truth is that he was very largely tolerated as a sceptic because he was obviously a saint. When he seemed to stand up as a stubborn Aristotelian, hardly distinguishable from the Arabian heretics, I do seriously believe that what protected him was very largely the prodigious power of his simplicity and his obvious goodness and love of truth. Those who went out against the haughty confidence of the heretics were stopped and brought up all standing, against a sort of huge humility which was like a mountain; or perhaps like that immense valley that is the mould of a mountain. Allowing for all medieval conventions, we can feel that with the other innovators, this was not always so. The others, from Abelard down to Siger of Brabant, have never quite lost, in the long process of history, a faint air of showing off. Nobody could feel for a moment that Thomas Aquinas was showing off. The very dullness of diction, of which some complain, was enormously convincing. He could have given wit as well as wisdom; but he was so prodigiously in earnest that he gave his wisdom without his wit.

After the hour of triumph came the moment of peril. It is always so with alliances, and especially because Aquinas was fighting on two fronts. His main business was to defend the Faith against the abuse of Aristotle; and he boldly did it by supporting the use of Aristotle. He knew perfectly well that armies of atheists and anarchists were roaring applause in the background at his Aristotelian victory over all he held most dear. Nevertheless, it was never the existence of atheists, any more than Arabs or Aristotelian pagans, that disturbed the extraordinary controversial composure of Thomas Aquinas. The real peril that followed on the victory he had won for Aristotle was vividly presented in the curious case of Siger of Brabant; and it is well worth study, for anyone who would begin to comprehend the strange history of Christendom. It is marked by one rather queer quality; which has always been the unique note of the Faith, though it is not noticed by its modern enemies, and rarely by its modern friends. It is the fact symbolised in the legend of Antichrist, who was the double of Christ; in the profound proverb that the Devil is the ape of God. It is the fact that falsehood is never so false as when it is very nearly true. It is when the stab comes near the nerve of truth, that the Christian conscience cries out in pain. And Siger of Brabant, following on some of the Arabian Aristotelians, advanced a theory which most modern newspaper readers would instantly have declared to be the same as the theory of St. Thomas. That was what finally roused St. Thomas to his last and most emphatic protest. He had won his battle for a wider scope of philosophy and science; he had cleared the ground for a general understanding about faith and enquiry; an understanding that has generally been observed among Catholics, and certainly never deserted without disaster. It was the idea that the scientist should go on exploring and experimenting freely, so long as he did not claim an infallibility and finality which it was against his own principles to claim. Meanwhile the Church should go on developing and defining, about supernatural things, so long as she did not claim a right to alter the deposit of faith, which it was against her own principles to claim. And when he had said this, Siger of Brabant got up and said something so horribly like it, and so horribly unlike, that (like Antichrist) he might have deceived the very elect.

Siger of Brabant said this: the Church must be right theologically, but she can be wrong scientifically. There are two truths; the truth of the supernatural world, and the truth of the natural world, which contradicts the supernatural world. While we are being naturalists, we can suppose that Christianity is all nonsense; but then, when we remember that we are Christians, we must admit that Christianity is true even if it is nonsense. In other words, Siger of Brabant split the human head in two, like the blow in an old legend of battle; and declared that a man has two minds, with one of which he must entirely believe and with the other may utterly disbelieve. To many this would at least seem like a parody of Thomism. As a fact, it was the assassination of Thomism. It was not two ways of finding the same truth; it was an untruthful way of pretending that there are two truths. And it is extraordinarily interesting to note that this is the one occasion when the Dumb Ox really came out like a wild bull. When he stood up to answer Siger of Brabant, he was altogether transfigured, and the very style of his sentences, which is a thing like the tone of a man's voice, is suddenly altered. He had never been angry with any of the enemies who disagreed with him. But these enemies had attempted the worst treachery: they had made him agree with them.

Those who complain that theologians draw fine distinctions could hardly find a better example of their own folly. In fact, a fine distinction can be a flat contradiction. It was notably so in this case. St. Thomas was willing to allow the one truth to be approached by two paths, precisely *because* he was sure there was only one truth.

Because the Faith was the one truth, nothing discovered in nature could ultimately contradict the Faith. Because the Faith was the one truth, nothing really deduced from the Faith could ultimately contradict the facts. It was in truth a curiously daring confidence in the reality of his religion; and though some may linger to dispute it, it has been justified. The scientific facts, which were supposed to contradict the Faith in the nineteenth century, are nearly all of them regarded as unscientific fictions in the twentieth century. Even the materialists have fled from materialism; and those who lectured us about determinism in psychology are already talking about indeterminism in matter. But whether his confidence was right or wrong, it was specially and supremely a confidence that there is one truth which cannot contradict itself. And this last group of enemies suddenly sprang up, to tell him they entirely agreed with him in saying that there are two contradictory truths. Truth, in the medieval phrase, carried two faces under one hood; and these double-faced sophists practically dared to suggest that it was the Dominican hood.

So, in his last battle and for the first time, he fought as with a battle-axe. There is a ring in the words altogether beyond the almost impersonal patience he maintained in debate with so many enemies. "Behold our refutation of the error. It is not based on documents of faith, but on the reasons and statements of the philosophers themselves. If then anyone there be who, boastfully taking pride in his supposed wisdom, wishes to challenge what we have written, let him not do it in some corner nor before children who are powerless to decide on such difficult matters. Let him reply openly if he dare. He shall find me then confronting him, and not only my negligible self, but many another whose study is truth. We shall do battle with his errors or bring a cure to his ignorance."

The Dumb Ox is bellowing now; like one at bay and yet terrible and towering over all the baying pack. We have already noted why, in this one quarrel with Siger of Brabant, Thomas Aquinas let loose such thunders of purely moral passion; it was because the whole work of his life was being betrayed behind his back, by those who had used his victories over the reactionaries. The point at the moment is that this is perhaps his one moment of personal passion, save for a single flash in the troubles of his youth; and he is once more fighting his enemies with a firebrand. And yet, even in this isolated apocalypse of anger, there is one phrase that may be commended for all time to men who are angry with much less cause. If there is one sentence that could be carved in marble, as representing the calmest and most enduring rationality of his unique intelligence, it is a sentence which came pouring out with all the rest of this molten lava. If there is one phrase that stands before history as typical of Thomas Aquinas, it is that phrase about his own argument: "It is not based on documents of faith, but on the reasons and statements of the philosophers themselves." Would that all Orthodox doctors in deliberation were as reasonable as Aquinas in anger! Would that all Christian apologists would remember that maxim; and write it up in large letters on the wall, before they nail any theses there. At the top of his fury, Thomas Aquinas understands, what so many defenders of orthodoxy will not understand. It is no good to tell an atheist that he is an atheist; or to charge a denier of immortality with the infamy of denying it; or to imagine that one can force an opponent to admit he is wrong, by proving that he is wrong on somebody else's principles, but not on his own. After the great example of St. Thomas, the principle stands, or ought always to have stood established; that we must either not argue with a man at all, or we must argue on his grounds and not ours. We may do other things *instead* of arguing, according to our views of what actions are morally permissible; but if we argue we must argue 'on the reasons and statements of the philosophers themselves.' This is the common sense in a saying attributed to a friend of St. Thomas, the great St. Louis, King of France, which shallow people quote as a sample of fanaticism; the sense of which is, that I must either argue with an infidel as a real philosopher can argue, or else 'thrust a sword through his body as far as it will go.' A real philosopher (even of the opposite school) will be the first to agree that St. Louis was entirely philosophical.

So, in the last great controversial crisis of his theological campaign, Thomas Aquinas contrived to give his friends and enemies not only a lesson in theology, but a lesson in controversy. But it was in fact his last controversy. He had been a man with a huge controversial appetite, a thing that exists in some men and not others, in saints and in sinners. But after this great and victorious duel with Siger of Brabant, he was suddenly overwhelmed with a desire for silence and repose. He said one strange thing about this mood of his to a friend, which will fall into its more appropriate place elsewhere. He fell back on the extreme simplicities of his monastic round and seemed to desire nothing but a sort of permanent retreat. A request came to him from the Pope that he should set out upon some further mission of diplomacy or disputation; and he made ready to obey. But before he had gone many miles on the journey, he was dead.

IV

A MEDITATION ON THE MANICHEES

There is one casual anecdote about St. Thomas Aquinas which illuminates him like a lightning-flash, not only without but within. For it not only shows him as a character, and even as a comedy character, and shows the colours of his period and social background; but also, as if for an instant, makes a transparency of his mind. It is a trivial incident which occurred one day, when he was reluctantly dragged from his work, and we might almost say from his play. For both were for him found in the unusual hobby of thinking, which is for some men a thing much more intoxicating than mere drinking. He had declined any number of society invitations, to the courts of kings and princes, not because he was unfriendly, for he was not; but because he was always glowing within with the really gigantic plans of exposition and argument which filled his life. On one occasion, however, he was invited to the court of King Louis IX of France, more famous as the great St. Louis; and for some reason or other, the Dominican authorities of his Order told him to accept; so he immediately did so, being an obedient friar even in his sleep; or rather in his permanent trance of reflection.

It is a real case against conventional hagiography that it sometimes tends to make all saints seem to be the same. Whereas in fact no men are more different than saints; not even murderers. And there could hardly be a more complete contrast, given the essentials of holiness, than between St. Thomas and St. Louis. St. Louis was born a knight and a king; but he was one of those men in whom a certain simplicity, combined with courage and activity, makes it natural, and in a sense easy, to fulfil directly and promptly any duty or office, however official. He was a man in whom holiness and healthiness had no quarrel; and their issue was in action. He did not go in for thinking much, in the sense of theorising much. But, even in theory, he had that sort of presence of mind, which belongs to the rare and really practical man when he has to think. He never said the

wrong thing; and he was orthodox by instinct. In the old pagan
proverb about kings being philosophers or philosophers kings, there
was a certain miscalculation, connected with a mystery that only
Christianity could reveal. For while it is possible for a king to wish
very much to be a saint, it is not possible for a saint to wish very
much to be a king. A good man will hardly be always dreaming of
being a great monarch; but, such is the liberality of the Church, that
she cannot forbid even a great monarch to dream of being a good
man. But Louis was a straight-forward soldierly sort of person who
did not particularly mind being a king, any more than he would
have minded being a captain or a sergeant or any other rank in his
army. Now a man like St. Thomas would definitely dislike being a
king, or being entangled with the pomp and politics of kings; not
only his humility, but a sort of subconscious fastidiousness and fine
dislike of futility, often found in leisurely and learned men with
large minds, would really have prevented him making contact with
the complexity of court life. Also, he was anxious all his life to keep
out of politics; and there was no political symbol more striking, or
in a sense more challenging, at that moment, than the power of the
King in Paris.

Paris was truly at that time an *aurora borealis*; a Sunrise in the
North. We must realise that lands much nearer to Rome had rotted
with paganism and pessimism and Oriental influences of which the
most respectable was that of Mahound. Provence and all the South
had been full of a fever of nihilism or negative mysticism, and from
Northern France had come the spears and swords that swept away
the unchristian thing. In Northern France also sprang up that splendour of building that shine like swords and spears: the first spires of
the Gothic. We talk now of grey Gothic buildings; but they must
have been very different when they went up white and gleaming into the northern skies, partly picked out with gold and bright colours; a new flight of architecture, as startling as flying-ships. The
new Paris ultimately left behind by St. Louis must have been a thing
white like lilies and splendid as the oriflamme. It was the beginning
of the great new thing: the nation of France, which was to pierce
and overpower the old quarrel of Pope and Emperor in the lands

from which Thomas came. But Thomas came very unwillingly, and, if we may say it of so kindly a man, rather sulkily. As he entered Paris, they showed him from the hill that splendour of new spires beginning, and somebody said something like, "How grand it must be to own all this." And Thomas Aquinas only muttered, "I would rather have that Chrysostom MS. I can't get hold of."

Somehow they steered that reluctant bulk of reflection to a seat in the royal banquet hall; and all that we know of Thomas tells us that he was perfectly courteous to those who spoke to him, but spoke little, and was soon forgotten in the most brilliant and noisy clatter in the world: the noise of French talking. What the Frenchmen were talking about we do not know; but they forgot all about the large fat Italian in their midst, and it seems only too possible that he forgot all about them. Sudden silences will occur even in French conversation; and in one of these the interruption came. There had long been no word or motion in that huge heap of black and white weeds, like motley in mourning, which marked him as a mendicant friar out of the streets, and contrasted with all the colours and patterns and quarterings of that first and freshest dawn of chivalry and heraldry. The triangular shields and pennons and pointed spears, the triangular swords of the Crusade, the pointed windows and the conical hoods, repeated everywhere that fresh French medieval spirit that did, in every sense, come to the point. But the colours of the coats were gay and varied, with little to rebuke their richness; for St. Louis, who had himself a special quality of coming to the point, had said to his courtiers, "Vanity should be avoided; but every man should dress well, in the manner of his rank, that his wife may the more easily love him."

And then suddenly the goblets leapt and rattled on the board and the great table shook, for the friar had brought down his huge fist like a club of stone, with a crash that startled everyone like an explosion; and had cried out in a strong voice, but like a man in the grip of a dream, "And *that* will settle the Manichees!"

The palace of a king, even when it is the palace of a saint, has it conventions. A shock thrilled through the court, and every one felt as if the fat friar from Italy had thrown a plate at King Louis, or knocked his crown sideways. They all looked timidly at the terrible seat, that was for a thousand years the throne of the Capets; and many there were presumably prepared to pitch the big black-robed beggarman out of the window. But St. Louis, simple as he seemed, was no mere medieval fountain of honour or even fountain of mercy; but also the fountain of two eternal rivers; the irony and the courtesy of France. And he turned to his secretaries, asking them in a low voice to take their tablets round to the seat of the absent-minded controversialist, and take a note of the argument that had just occurred to him; because it must be a very good one and he might forget it. I have paused upon this anecdote, first, as has been said, because it is the one which gives us the most vivid snapshot of a great medieval character; indeed of two great medieval characters. But it also specially fitted to be taken as a type or a turning-point, because of the glimpse it gives of the man's main preoccupation; and the sort of thing that might have been found in his thoughts, if they had been thus surprised at any moment by a philosophical eaves-dropper or through a psychological keyhole. It was not for nothing that he was still brooding, even in the white court of St. Louis, upon the dark cloud of the Manichees.

This book is meant only to be the sketch of a man; but it must at least lightly touch, later on, upon a method and a meaning; or what our journalism has an annoying way of calling a message. A few very inadequate pages must be given to the man in relation to his theology and his philosophy; but the thing of which I mean to speak here is something at once more general and more personal even than his philosophy. I have therefore introduced it here, before we come to anything like technical talk about his philosophy. It was some-thing that might alternatively be called his moral attitude, or his temperamental predisposition, or the purpose of his life so far as social and human effects were concerned: for he knew better than most of us that there is but one purpose in this life, and it is one that is beyond this life. But if we wanted to put in a picturesque and simplified form what he wanted for the world, and what was his work in history, apart from theoretical and theological definitions, we might well say that it really was to strike a blow and settle the Manichees.

The full meaning of this may not be apparent to those who do not study theological history; and perhaps even less apparent to those who do. Indeed it may seem equally irrelevant to the history and the theology. In history St. Dominic and Simon de Montfort between them had already pretty well settled the Manichees. And in theology, of course, an encyclopaedic doctor like Aquinas dealt with a thousand other heresies besides the Manichean heresy. Nevertheless, it does represent his main position and the turn he gave to the whole history of Christendom.

I think it well to interpose this chapter, though its scope may seem more vague than the rest; because there is a sort of big blunder about St. Thomas and his creed, which is an obstacle for most modern people in even beginning to understand them. It arises roughly thus. St. Thomas, like other monks, and especially other saints, lived a life of renunciation and austerity; his fasts, for instance, being in marked contrast to the luxury in which he might have lived if he chose. This element stands high in his religion, as a manner of asserting the will against the power of nature, of thanking the Redeemer by partially sharing his sufferings, of making a man ready for anything as a missionary or martyr, and similar ideals. These happen to be rare in the modern industrial society of the West, outside his communion; and it is therefore assumed that they are the whole meaning of that communion. Because it is uncommon for an alderman to fast for forty days, or a politician to take a Trappist vow of silence, or a man about town to live a life of strict celibacy, the average outsider is convinced, not only that Catholicism is nothing except asceticism, but that asceticism is nothing except pessimism. He is so obliging as to explain to Catholics why they hold this heroic virtue in respect; and is ever ready to point out that the philosophy behind it is an Oriental hatred of anything connected with Nature, and a purely Schopenhauerian disgust with the Will to Live. I read in a "high-class" review of Miss Rebecca West's book on St. Augustine, the astounding statement that the Catholic Church regards sex as having the nature of sin. How marriage can be a sacrament if sex is a sin, or why it is the Catholics who are in favour of birth and their foes who are in favour of birth-control, I will leave the critic to worry out for himself. My concern is not with that part of the argument; but with another.

The ordinary modern critic, seeing this ascetic ideal in an authoritative Church, and not seeing it in most other inhabitants of Brixton or Brighton, is apt to say, "This is the result of Authority; it would be better to have Religion without Authority." But in truth, a wider experience outside Brixton or Brighton would reveal the mistake. It is rare to find a fasting alderman or a Trappist politician, but it is still more rare to see nuns supended in the air on hooks or spikes; it is unusual for a Catholic Evidence Guild orator in Hyde Park to begin his speech by gashing himself all over with knives; a stranger calling at an ordinary presbytery will seldom find the parish priest lying on the floor with a fire lighted on his chest and scorching him while he utters spiritual ejaculations. Yet all these things are done all over Asia, for instance, by voluntary enthusiasts acting solely on the great impulse of Religion; of Religion, in their case, not commonly imposed by any immediate Authority; and certainly not imposed by this particular Authority. In short, a real knowledge of mankind will tell anybody that Religion is a very terrible thing; that it is truly a raging fire, and that Authority is often quite as much needed to restrain it as to impose it. Asceticism, or the war with the appetites, is itself an appetite. It can never be eliminated from among the strange ambitions of Man. But it can be kept in some reasonable control; and it is indulged in much saner proportion under Catholic Authority than in Pagan or Puritan anarchy. Meanwhile, the whole of this ideal, though an essential part of Catholic idealism when it is understood, is in some ways entirely a side issue. It is not the primary principle of Catholic philosophy; it is only a particular deduction from Catholic ethics. And when we begin to talk about primary philosophy, we realise the full and flat contradiction between the monk fasting and the fakir hanging himself on hooks.

Now nobody will begin to understand the Thomist philosophy, or indeed the Catholic philosophy, who does not realise that the primary and fundamental part of it is entirely the praise of Life, the praise of Being, the praise of God as the Creator of the World.

Everything else follows a long way after that, being conditioned by
various complications like the Fall or the vocation of heroes. The
trouble occurs because the Catholic mind moves upon two planes;
that of the Creation and that of the Fall. The nearest parallel is, for
instance, that of England invaded; there might be strict martial law
in Kent because the enemy had landed in Kent, and relative liberty
in Hereford; but this would not affect the affection of an English pa-
triot for Hereford or Kent, and strategic caution in Kent would not
affect the love of Kent. For the love of England would remain, both
of the parts to be redeemed by discipline and the parts to be enjoyed
in liberty. Any extreme of Catholic asceticism is a wise, or unwise,
precaution against the evil of the Fall; it is *never* a doubt about the
good of the Creation. And *that* is where it really does differ, not only
from the rather excessive eccentricity of the gentleman who hangs
himself on hooks, but from the whole cosmic theory which is the
hook on which he hangs. In the case of many Oriental religions, it
really is true that the asceticism is pessimism; that the ascetic tortues
himself to death out of an abstract hatred of life; that he does not
merely mean to control Nature as he should, but to contradict Nature as much as he can. And though it takes a milder form than
hooks in millions of the religious populations of Asia, it is a fact far
too little realised, that the dogma of the denial of life does really rule as
a first principal on so vast a scale. One historic form it took was that
great enemy of Christianity from its beginnings: the Manichees.

What is called the Manichean philosophy has had many forms; indeed it has attacked what is immortal and immutable with a very
curious kind of immortal mutability. It is like the legend of the
magician who turns himself into a snake or a cloud; and the whole
has that nameless note of irresponsibility, which belongs to much of
the metaphysics and morals of Asia, from which the Manichean
mystery came. But it is always in one way or another a notion that
nature is evil; or that evil is at least rooted in nature. The essential point is that as evil has roots in nature, so it has rights in nature. Wrong has as much right to exist as right. As already stated
this notion took many forms. Sometimes it was a dualism, which
made evil an equal partner with good; so that neither could be called

an usurper. More often it was a general idea that demons had made the material world, and if there were any good spirits, they were concerned only with the spiritual world. Later, again, it took the form of Calvinism, which held that God had indeed made the world, but in a special sense, made the evil as well as the good: had made an evil will as well as an evil world. On this view, if a man chooses to damn his soul alive, he is not thwarting God's will but rather fulfilling it. In these two forms, of the early Gnosticism and the later Calvinism, we see the superficial variety and fundamental unity of Manicheanism. The old Manicheans taught that Satan originated the whole work of creation commonly attributed to God. The new Calvinists taught that God originates the whole work of damnation commonly attributed to Satan. One looked back to the first day when a devil acted like a god, the other looked forward to a last day when a god acted like a devil. But both had the idea that the creator of the earth was primarily the creator of the evil, whether we call him a devil or a god.

Since there are a good many Manicheans among the Moderns, as we may remark in a moment, some may agree with this view, some may be puzzled about it, some may only be puzzled about why we should object to it. To understand the medieval controversy, a word must be said of the Catholic doctrine, which is as modern as it is medieval. That 'God looked on all things and saw that they were good' contains a subtlety which the popular pessimist cannot follow, or is too hasty to notice. It is the thesis that there are no bad things, but only bad uses of things. If you will, there are no bad things but only bad thoughts; and especially bad intentions. Only Calvinists can really believe that hell is paved with good intentions. That is exactly the one thing it cannot be paved with. But it is possible to have bad intentions about good things; and good things, like the world and the flesh have been twisted by a bad intention called the devil. But he cannot make *things* bad; they remain as on the first day of creation. The work of heaven alone was material; the making of a material world. The work of hell is entirely spiritual.

This error then had many forms; but especially, like nearly every error, it had two forms, a fiercer one which was outside the Church and attacking the Church, and a subtler one, which was inside the Church and corrupting the Church. There has never been a time when the Church was not torn between that invasion and that treason. It was so, for instance, in the Victorian time. Darwinian "competition," in commerce or race conflict, was every bit as brazen an atheist assault, in the nineteenth century, as the Bolshevist No-God movement in the twentieth century. To brag of brute prosperity, to admire the most muddly millionaires who had cornered wheat by a trick, to talk about the 'unfit' (in imitation of the scientific thinker who would finish them off because he cannot even finish his own sentence — unfit for what?) — all that is as simply and openly Anti-Christian as the Black Mass. Yet some weak and wordly Catholics did use this cant in defence of Capitalism, in their first rather feeble resistance to Socialism. At least they did until the great Encyclical of the Pope on the Rights of Labour put a stop to all their nonsense. The evil is always both within and without the Church; but in a wilder form outside and a milder form inside. So it was, again, in the seventeenth century, when there was Calvinism outside and Jansenism inside. And so it was in the thirteenth century, when the obvious danger outside was in the revolution of the Albigensians; but the potential danger inside was in the very traditionalism of the Augustinians. For the Augustinians derived only from Augustine, and Augustine derived partly from Plato, and Plato was right, but not quite right. It is a mathematical fact that if a line be not perfectly directed towards a point, it will actually go further away from it as it comes nearer to it. After a thousand years of extension, the miscalculation of Platonism had come very near to Manicheanism.

Popular errors are nearly always right. They nearly always refer to some ultimate reality, about which those who correct them are themselves incorrect. It is a very queer thing that "Platonic Love" has come to mean for the un-lettered something rather purer and cleaner than it means for the learned. Yet even those who realise the great Greek evil may well realise that perversity often comes out of the wrong sort of purity. Now it was the inmost lie of the Manichees that they identified purity with sterility. It is singularly contrasted with the language of St. Thomas, which always connects purity with fruitfulness; whether it be natural or supernatural. And, queerly enough, as I have said, there does remain a sort of reality in the vulgar colloquialism that the affair between Sam and Susan is "quite Platonic." It is true that, quite apart from the local perversion, there was in Plato a sort of idea that people would be better without their bodies; that their heads might fly off and meet in the sky in merely intellectual marriage, like cherubs in a picture. The ultimate phase of this "Platonic" philosophy was what inflamed poor D. H. Lawrence into talking nonsense, and he was probably unaware that the Catholic doctrine of marriage would say much of what he said, without talking nonsense. Anyhow, it is historically important to see that Platonic love did somewhat distort both human and divine love, in the theory of the early theologians. Many medieval men, who would indignantly deny the Albigensian doctrine of sterility, were yet in an emotional mood to abandon the body in despair; and some of them to abandon everything in despair.

In truth, this vividly illuminates the provincial stupidity of those who object to what they call "creeds and dogmas." It was precisely the creed and dogma that saved the sanity of the world. These people generally propose an alternative religion of intuition and feeling. If, in the really Dark Ages, there had been a religion of feeling, it would have been a religion of black and suicidal feeling. It was the rigid creed that resisted the rush of suicidal feeling. The critics of asceticism are probably right in supposing that many a Western hermit did *feel* rather like an Eastern fakir. But he could not really *think* like an Eastern fakir; because he was an orthodox Catholic. And what kept his thought in touch with healthier and more humanistic thought was simply and solely the Dogma. He could not deny that a good God had created the normal and natural world; he could not say that the devil had made the world; because he was not a Manichee. A thousand enthusiasts for celibacy, in the day of the great rush to the desert or the cloister, might have called marriage a sin, if they had only considered their individiual ideals, in the modern manner, and their own immediate feelings about marriage. Fortunately, they had to accept the Authority of the Church, which had definitely said that marriage was not a sin. A modern emotional religion might at any moment have turned Catholicism into Manichaeism. But when Religion would have maddened men, Theology kept them sane.

In this sense St. Thomas stands up simply as the great orthodox theologian, who reminded men of the creed of Creation, when many of them were still in the mood of mere destruction. It is futile for the critics of medievalism to quote a hundred medieval phrases that may be supposed to sound like mere pessimism, if they will not understand the central fact; that medieval men did not care about being medieval and did not accept the authority of a mood, because it was melancholy, but did care very much about orthodoxy, which is not a mood. It was because St. Thomas could *prove* that his glorification of the Creator and His creative joy was more orthodox than any atmospheric pessimism, that he dominated the Church and the world, which accepted that truth as a test. But when this immense and impersonal importance is allowed for, we may agree that there was a personal element as well. Like most of the great religious teachers, he was fitted individually for the task that God had given him to do. We can if we like call that talent instinctive; we can even descend to calling it temperamental.

Anybody trying to popularise a medieval philosopher must use language that is very modern and very unphilosophical. Nor is this a sneer at modernity; it arises from the moderns having dealt so much in moods and emotions, especially in the arts, that they have developed a large but loose vocabulary, which deals more with atmosphere than with actual attitude or position. As noted elsewhere, even the modern philosophers are more like the modern poets; in giving an individual tinge even to truth, and often looking at all life through different coloured spectacles. To say that Schopenhauer had the blues, or that William James had a rather rosier outlook, would often convey more than calling the one a Pessimist or the other a Pragmatist. This modern moodiness has its value, though the moderns overrate it; just as medieval logic had its value, though it was overrated in the later Middle Ages. But the point is that to explain the medievals to the moderns, we must often use this modern language of mood. Otherwise the character will be missed, through certain prejudices and ignorances about all such medieval characters. Now there is something that lies all over the work of St. Thomas Aquinas like a great light; which is something quite primary and perhaps unconscious with him, which he would perhaps have passed over as an irrelevant personal quality; and which can now only be expressed by a rather cheap journalistic term, which he would probably have thought quite senseless.

Nevertheless, the only working word for that atmosphere is Optimism. I know that the word is now even more degraded in the twentieth century than it was in the nineteenth century. Men talked lately of being Optimists about the issue of War; they talk now of being Optimists about the revival of Trade; they may talk tomorrow of being Optimists about the International Ping-pong Tournament. But men in the Victorian time did mean a little more than that, when they used the word Optimist of Browning or Stevenson or Walt Whitman. And in a rather larger and more luminous sense than in the case of these men, the term was basically true of Thomas Aquinas. He did, with a most solid and colossal conviction, believe in Life; and in something like what Stevenson called the great theorem of the livableness of life. It breathes somehow in his very first phrases about the reality of Being. If the morbid Renaissance intellectual is supposed to say, "To be or not to be — that is the question," then the massive medieval doctor does most certainly reply in a voice of thunder, "To be — that is the answer." The point is important; many not unnaturally talk of the Renaissance as the time when certain men began to believe in Life. The truth is that it was the time when a few men, for the first time, began to disbelieve in Life. The medievals had put many restrictions, and some excessive restrictions, upon the universal human hunger and even fury for Life. Those restrictions had often been expressed in fanatical and rabid terms; the terms of those resisting a great natural force; the force of men who desired to live. Never until modern thought began, did they really have to fight with men who desired to die. That horror had threatened them in Asiatic Albigensianism, but it never became normal to them — until now.

But this fact becomes very vivid indeed, when we compare the greatest of Christian philosophers with the only men who were anything like his equals, or capable of being his rivals. They were people with whom he did not directly dispute; most of them he had never seen; some of them he had never heard of. Plato and Augustine were the only two with whom he could confer as he did with Bonaventure or even Averrhoes. But we must look elsewhere for his real rivals, and the only real rivals of the Catholic theory. They are the heads of great heathen systems; some of them very ancient, some very modern, like Buddha on the one hand or Nietzsche on the other. It is when we see his gigantic figure against this vast and cosmic background, that we realise, first, that he was the only optimist theologian, and second, that Catholicism is the only optimist theology. Something milder and more amiable may be made out of the deliquescence of theology, and the mixture of the creed with everything that contradicts it; but among consistent cosmic creeds, this is the only one that is entirely on the side of Life.

Comparative religion has indeed allowed us to compare religions — and to contrast them. Fifty years ago, it set out to prove that all religions were much the same; generally proving, alternately, that they were all equally worthy and that they were all equally worthless. Since then this scientific process has suddenly begun to be scientific, and discovered the depths of the chasms as well as the heights of the hills. It is indeed an excellent improvement that sincerely religious people should respect each other. But respect has discovered difference, where contempt knew only indifference. The more we really appreciate the noble revulsion and renunciation of Buddha, the more we see that intellectually it was the converse and almost the contrary of the salvation of the world by Christ. The Christian would escape from the world into the universe: the Buddhist wishes to escape from the universe even more than from the world. One would uncreate himself; the other would return to his Creation: to his Creator. Indeed it was so genuinely the converse of the idea of the Cross as the Tree of Life, that there is some excuse for setting up the two things side by side, as if they were of equal significance. They are in one sense parallel and equal; as a mound and a hollow, as a valley and a hill. There is a sense in which that sublime despair is the only alternative to that divine audacity. It is even true that the truly spiritual and intellectual man sees it as a sort of dilemma; a very hard and terrible choice. There is little else on earth that can compare with these for completeness. And he who will not climb the mountain of Christ does indeed fall into the abyss of Buddha.

The same is true, in a less lucid and dignified fashion, of most other alternatives of heathen humanity; nearly all are sucked back into that whirlpool of recurrence which all the ancients knew. Nearly all return to the one idea of returning. That is what Buddha described so darkly as the Sorrowful Wheel. It is true that the sort of recurrence which Buddha described as the Sorrowful Wheel, poor Nietzsche actually managed to describe as the Joyful Wisdom. I can only say that if bare repetition was his idea of Joyful Wisdom, I should be curious to know what was his idea of Sorrowful Wisdom. But as a fact, in the case of Nietzsche, this did not belong to the moment of his breaking out, but to the moment of his breaking down. It came at the end of his life, when he was near to mental collapse; and it is really quite contrary to his earlier and finer inspirations of wild freedom or fresh and creative innovation. Once at least he had tried to break out; but he also was only broken — on the wheel.

Alone upon the earth, and lifted and liberated from all the wheels and whirlpools of the earth, stands up the faith of St. Thomas; weighted and balanced indeed with more than Oriental metaphysics and more than Pagan pomp and pageantry; but vitally and vividly alone in declaring that life is a living story, with a great beginning and a great close; rooted in the primeval joy of God and finding its fruition in the final happiness of humanity; opening with the colossal chorus in which the sons of God shouted for joy, and ending in that mystical comradeship, shown in a shadowy fashion in those ancient words that move like an archaic dance; "For His delight is with the sons of men."

It is the fate of this sketch to be sketchy about philosophy, scanty or rather empty about theology, and to achieve little more than a decent silence on the subject of sanctity. And yet it must none the less be the recurrent burden of this little book, to which it must return with some monotony, that in this story the philosophy did depend on the theology, and the theology did depend on the sanctity. In other words, it must repeat the first fact, which was emphasised in the first chapter: that this great intellectual creation was a Christian and Catholic creation and cannot be understood as anything else. It was Aquinas who baptised Aristotle, when Aristotle could not have baptised Aquinas; it was a purely Christian miracle which raised the great Pagan from the dead. And this is proved in three ways (as St. Thomas himself might say), which it will be well to summarise as a sort of summary of this book.

First, in the life of St. Thomas, it is proved in the fact that only his huge and solid orthodoxy could have supported so many things which then seemed to be unorthodox. Charity covers a multitude of sins; and in that sense orthodoxy covers a multitude of heresies; or things which are hastily mistaken for heresies. It was precisely because his personal Catholicism was so convincing, that his impersonal Aristotelianism was given the benefit of the doubt. He did not smell of the faggot because he did smell of the firebrand; of the firebrand he had so instantly and instinctively snatched up, under a real assault on essential Catholic ethics. A typically cynical modern phrase refers to the man who is so good that he is good for nothing. St. Thomas was so good that he was good for everything; that his warrant held good for what others considered the most wild and daring speculations, ending in the worship of nothing. Whether or no he baptised Aristotle, he was truly the godfather of Aristotle, he was his sponsor; he swore that the old Greek would do no harm; and the whole world trusted his word.

Second, in the philosophy of St. Thomas, it is proved by the fact that everything depended on the new Christian *motive* for the study of facts, as distinct from truths. The Thomist philosophy began with the lowest roots of thought, the senses and the truisms of the reason; and a Pagan sage might have scorned such things, as he scorned the servile arts. But the materialism, which is merely cynicism in a Pagan, can be Christian humility in a Christian. St. Thomas was willing to begin by recording the facts and sensations of the material world, just as he would have been willing to begin by washing up the plates and dishes in the monastery. The point of his

Aristotelianism was that even if common sense about concrete things really was a sort of servile labour, he must not be ashamed to be *servus servorum Dei*. Among heathens the mere sceptic might become the mere cynic; Diogenes in his tub had always a touch of the tub-thumper; but even the dirt of the cynics was dignified into dust and ashes among the saints. If we miss that, we miss the whole meaning of the greatest revolution in history. There was a new *motive* for beginning with the most material, and even with the meanest things.

Third, in the theology of St. Thomas, it is proved by the tremendous truth that supports all that theology; or any other Christian theology. There really was a new reason for regarding the senses, and the sensations of the body, and the experiences of the common man, with a reverence at which great Aristotle would have stared, and no man in the ancient world could have begun to understand. The Body was no longer what it was when Plato and Porphyry and the old mystics had left it for dead. It had hung upon a gibbet. It had risen from a tomb. It was no longer possible for the soul to despise the senses, which had been the organs of something that was more than man. Plato might despise the flesh; but God had not despised it. The senses had truly become sanctified; as they are blessed one by one at a Catholic baptism. "Seeing is believing" was no longer the platitude of a mere idiot, or common individual, as in Plato's world; it was mixed up with real conditions of real belief. Those revolving mirrors that send messages to the brain of man, that light that breaks upon the brain, these had truly revealed to God himself the path to Bethany or the light on the high rock of Jerusalem. These ears that resound with common noises had reported also to the secret knowlege of God the noise of the crowd that strewed palms and the crowd that cried for Crucifixion. After the Incarnation had become the idea that is central in our civilisation, it was inevitable that there should be a return to materialism, in the sense of the serious value of matter and the making of the body. When once Christ had risen, it was inevitable that Aristotle should rise again.

Those are three real reasons, and very sufficient reasons, for the general support given by the saint to a solid and objective philosophy.

And yet there was something else, very vast and vague, to which I have tried to give a faint expression by the interposition of this chapter. It is difficult to express it fully, without the awful peril of being popular, or what the Modernists quite wrongly imagine to be popular; in short, passing from religion to religiosity. But there is a general tone and temper of Aquinas, which it is as difficult to avoid as daylight in a great house of windows. It is that *positive* position of his mind, which is filled and soaked as with sunshine with the warmth of the wonder of created things. There is a certain private audacity, in his communion, by which men add to their private names the tremendous titles of the Trinity and the Redemption; so that some nun may be called "of the Holy Ghost"; or a man bear such a burden as the title of St. John of the Cross. In this sense, the man we study may specially be called St. Thomas of the Creator. The Arabs have a phrase about the hundred names of God; but they also inherit the tradition of a tremendous name unspeakable because it expresses Being itself, dumb and yet dreadful as an instant inaudible shout; the proclamation of the Absolute. And perhaps no other man ever came so near to calling the Creator by His own name, which can only be written I Am.

V

THE REAL LIFE OF ST. THOMAS

At this point, even so crude and external a sketch of a great saint involves the necessity of writing something that cannot fit in with the rest; the one thing which it is important to write and impossible to write. A saint may be any kind of man, with an additional quality that is at once unique and universal. We might even say that the one thing which separates a saint from ordinary men is his readiness to be one with ordinary men. In this sense the word ordinary must be understood in its native and noble meaning; which is connected with the word order. A saint is long past any desire for distinction; he is the only sort of superior man who has never been a superior person. But all this arises from a great central fact, which he does not condescend to call a privilege, but which is in its very nature a sort of privacy; and in that sense almost a form of private property. As with all sound private property, it is enough for him that he has it, he does not desire to limit the number of people who have it. He is always trying to hide it, out of a sort of celestial good manners; and Thomas Aquinas tried to hide it more than most. To reach it, in so far as we can reach it, it will be best to begin with the upper strata; and reach what was in the inside from what was most conspicuous on the outside.

The appearance or bodily presence of St. Thomas Aquinas is really easier to resurrect than that of many who lived before the age of portrait painting. It has been said that in his bodily being or bearing there was little of the Italian; but this is at the best, I fancy an unconscious comparison between St. Thomas and St. Francis; and at worst, only a comparison between him and the hasty legend of vivacious organ-grinders and incendiary ice-cream men. Not all Italians are vivacious organ-grinders, and very few Italians are like St. Francis. A nation is never a type, but it is nearly always a tangle of two or three roughly recognizable types. St. Thomas was of a certain type, which is not so much common in Italy, as common to uncommon Italians.

His bulk made it easy to regard him humorously as the sort of walking wine-barrel, common in the comedies of many nations; he joked about it himself. It may be that he, and not some irritated partisan of the Augustinian or Arabian parties, was responsible for the sublime exaggeration that a crescent was cut out of the dinner-table to allow him to sit down. It is quite certain that it was an exaggeration; and that his stature was more remarked than his stoutness; but, above all, that his head was quite powerful enough to dominate his body. And his head was of a very real and recognisable type, to judge by the traditional portraits and the personal descriptions. It was that sort of head with the heavy chin and jaws, the Roman nose and the big rather bald brow, which, in spite of its fullness, gives also a curious concave impression of hollows here and there, like caverns of thought. Napoleon carried that head upon a short body. Mussolini carries it today, upon a rather taller but equally active one. It can be seen in the busts of several Roman Emperors, and occasionally above the shabby shirt-front of an Italian waiter; but he is generally a head waiter. So unmistakable is the type, that I cannot but think that the most vivid villain of light fiction, in the Victorian shocker called *The Woman in White*, was really sketched by Wilkie Collins from an actual Italian Count; he is so complete a contrast to the conventional skinny, swarthy and gesticulating villain whom the Victorians commonly presented as an Italian Count. Count Fosco,[1] it may be remembered (I hope) by some, was a calm, corpulent, colossal gentleman, whose head was exactly like a bust of Napoleon of heroic size. He may have been a melodramatic villain; but he was a tolerably convincing Italian—of that kind. If we recall his tranquil manner, and the excellent common sense of his everyday external words and actions, we shall probably have a merely material image of the type of Thomas Aquinas; given only the slight effort of faith required to imagine Count Fosco turned suddenly into a saint.

The pictures of St. Thomas, though many of them painted long after his death, are all obviously pictures of the same man. He rears himself defiantly, with the Napoleonic head and the dark bulk of

[1] Count Fosco—the first fat villain in English literature. He appears in Wilke Collins' novel *The Woman in White* (1860).

body, in Raphael's 'Dispute About the Sacrament.' A portrait by Ghirlandajo emphasises a point which specially reveals what may be called the neglected Italian quality in the man. It also emphasises points that are very important in the mystic and the philosopher. It is universally attested that Aquinas was what is commonly called an absent-minded man. That type has often been rendered in painting, humorous or serious; but almost always in one of two or three conventional ways. Sometimes the expression of the eyes is merely vacant, as if absent-mindedness did really mean a permanent absence of mind. Sometimes it is rendered more respectfully as a wistful expression, as of one yearning for something afar off, that he cannot see and can only faintly desire. Look at the eyes in Ghirlandajo's portrait of St. Thomas; and you will see a sharp difference. While the eyes are indeed completely torn away from the immediate surroundings, so that the pot of flowers above the philosopher's head might fall on it without attracting his attention, they are not in the least wistful, let alone vacant. There is kindled in them a fire of instant inner excitement; they are vivid and very Italian eyes. The man is thinking about something; and something that has reached a crisis; not about nothing or about anything; or, what is almost worse, about everything. There must have been that smouldering vigilance in his eyes, the moment before he smote the table and startled the banquet hall of the King.

Of the personal habits that go with the personal physique, we have also a few convincing and confirming impressions. When he was not sitting still, reading a book, he walked round and round the cloisters and walked fast and even furiously, a very characteristic action of men who fight their battles in the mind. Whenever he was interrupted, he was very polite and more apologetic than the apologizer. But there was that about him, which suggested that he was rather happier when he was not interrupted. He was ready to stop his truly Peripatetic tramp: but we feel that when he resumed it, he walked all the faster.

All this suggests that his superficial abstraction, that which the world saw, was of a certain kind. It will be well to understand the quality, for there are several kinds of absence of mind, including that of some pretentious poets and intellectuals, in whom the mind has never been noticeably present. There is the abstraction of the contemplative, whether he is the true sort of Christian contemplative, who is contemplating Something, or the wrong sort of Oriental contemplative, who is contemplating Nothing. Obviously St. Thomas was not a Buddhist mystic; but I do not think his fits of abstraction were even those of a Christian mystic. If he had trances of true Christian mysticism, he took jolly good care that *they* should not occur at other people's dinner-tables. I think he had the sort of bemused fit, which really belongs to the practical man rather than the entirely mystical man. He uses the recognised distinction between the active life and the contemplative life, but in the cases concerned here, I think even his contemplative life was an active life. It had nothing to do with his higher life, in the sense of ultimate sanctity. It rather reminds us that Napoleon would fall into a fit of apparent boredom at the Opera, and afterwards confess that he was thinking how he could get three army corps at Frankfurt to combine with two army corps at Cologne. So, in the case of Aquinas, if his daydreams were dreams, they were dreams of the day; and dreams of the day of battle. If he talked to himself, it was because he was arguing with somebody else. We can put it another way, by saying that his daydreams, like the dreams of a dog, were dreams of hunting; of pursuing the error as well as pursuing the truth; of following all the twists and turns of evasive falsehood, and tracking it at last to its lair in hell. He would have been the first to admit that the erroneous thinker would probably be more surprised to learn where his thought came from, than anybody else to discover where it went to. But this notion of *pursuing* he certainly had, and it was the beginning of a thousand mistakes and misunderstandings that pursuing is called in Latin Persecution. Nobody had less than he had of what is commonly called the temper of a persecutor; but he had the quality which in desperate times is often driven to persecute; and that is simply the sense that everything lives somewhere, and nothing dies unless it dies in its own home. That he did sometimes, in this sense, "urge in dreams the shadowy chase" even in broad daylight, is quite true. But he was an active dreamer, if not what is commonly called a man of action; and in that chase he was truly to be counted among the *domini canes*; and surely the mightiest and most magnanimous of the Hounds of Heaven.

There may be many who do not understand the nature even of this sort of abstraction. But then, unfortunately, there are many who do not understand the nature of any sort of argument. Indeed, I think there are fewer people now alive who understand argument than there were twenty or thirty years ago; and St. Thomas might have preferred the society of the atheists of the early nineteenth century, to that of the blank sceptics of the early twentieth. Anyhow, one of the real disadvantages of the great and glorious sport, that is called argument, is its inordinate length. If you argue honestly, as St. Thomas always did, you will find that the subject sometimes seems as if it would never end. He was strongly conscious of ths fact, as appears in many places; for instance his argument that most men must have a revealed religion, because they have not time to argue. No time, that is, to argue fairly. There is always time to argue unfairly; not least in a time like ours. Being himself resolved to argue, to argue honestly, to answer everybody, to deal with everything, he produced books enough to sink a ship or stock a library; though he died in comparatively early middle age. Probably he could not have done it at all, if he had not been thinking even when he was not writing; but above all thinking *combatively*. This, in his case, certainly did not mean bitterly or spitefully or uncharitably; but it did mean combatively. As a matter of fact, it is generally the man who is not ready to argue, who is ready to sneer. That is why, in recent literature, there has been so little argument and so much sneering.

We have noted that there are barely one or two occasions on which St. Thomas indulged in a denunciation. There is not a single occasion on which he indulged in a sneer. His curiously simple character, his lucid but laborious intellect, could not be better summed up than by saying that he did not know how to sneer. He was in a double sense an intellectual aristocrat: but he was never an intellectual snob. He never troubled at all whether those to whom he talked were more or less of the sort whom the world thinks worth talking to; and it was apparent by the impression of his contemporaries that those who received the ordinary scraps of his wit or wisdom were quite as likely to be nobodies as somebodies, or even quite as likely to be noodles as clever people. He was interested in the souls of all his fellow creatures, but not in classifying the minds of any of them; in a sense it was too personal and in another sense too arrogant for his particular mind and temper. He was very much interested in the subject he was talking about; and may sometimes have talked for a long time, though he was probably silent for a much longer time. But he had all the unconscious contempt which the really intelligent have for an intelligentsia.

Like most men concerned with the common problems of men, he seems to have had a considerable correspondence; considering that correspondence was so much more difficult in his time. We have records of a great many cases in which complete strangers wrote to ask him questions, and sometimes rather ridiculous questions. To all of these he replied with a characteristic mixture of patience and that sort of rationality, which in some rational people tends to be impatience. Somebody, for instance, asked him whether the names of all the blessed were written on a scroll exhibited in heaven. He wrote back with untiring calm; "So far as I can see, this is not the case; but there is no harm in saying so."

I have remarked on the portrait of St. Thomas by an Italian painter, which shows him alert even in abstraction; and only silent as if about to speak. Pictures in that great tradition are generally full of small touches that show a very large imagination. I mean the sort of imagination on which Ruskin remarked, when he saw that in Tintoretto's sunlit scene of the Crucifixion the face of Christ is dark and undecipherable; but the halo round his head unexpectedly faint and grey like the colour of ashes. It would be hard to put more powerfully the idea of Divinity itself in eclipse. There is a touch, which it may be fanciful to find equally significant, in the portrait of Thomas Aquinas. The artist, having given so much vividness and vigilance to the eyes, may have felt that he stressed too much the merely combative concentration of the saint; but anyhow for some reason he has blazoned upon his breast a rather curious emblem, as if it were some third symbolic and cyclopean eye. At least it is no normal Christian sign; but something more like the disk of the sun such as held the face of a heathen god; but the face itself is dark and occult, and only the rays breaking from it are a ring of fire. I do not know whether any traditional meaning has been attached to this; but its imaginative meaning is strangely apt. That secret sun, dark with excess of light, or not showing its light save in the enlightenment of others, might well be the exact emblem of that inner and ideal life of the saint, which was not only hidden by his external words and actions, but even hidden by his merely outward and automatic silences and fits of reflection. In short, this spiritual detachment is not to be confused with his common habit of brooding or falling into a brown study. He was a man entirely careless of all casual criticism of his casual demeanour; as are many men built on a big masculine model and unconsciously inheriting a certain social splendour and largesse. But about his real life of sanctity he was intensely secretive. Such secrecy has indeed generally gone with sanctity; for the saint has an unfathomable horror of playing the Pharisee. But in Thomas Aquinas it was even more sensitive, and what many in the world would call morbid. He did not mind being caught wool-gathering over the wine-cups of the King's banquet; for that was merely upon a point of controversy. But when there was some question of his having seen St. Paul in a vision, he was in an agony of alarm lest it should be discussed; and the story remains somewhat uncertain in consequence. Needless to say, his followers and admirers were as eager to collect these strictly miraculous stories as he was eager to conceal them; and one or two seem to be preserved with a fairly solid setting of evidence. But there are certainly fewer of them, known to the world, than in the case of many saints equally sincere and even equally modest, but more preoccupied with zeal and less sensitive about publicity.

The truth is that about all such things, in life and death, there is a sort of enormous quiet hanging about St. Thomas. He was one of those large things who take up little room. There was naturally a certain stir about his miracles after his death; and about his burial at the time when the University of Paris wished to bury him. I do not know in detail the long history of the other plans of sepulture, which have ultimately ended with his sacred bones lying in the church of St. Sernin in Toulouse; at the very base of the battle-fields where his Dominicans had warred down the pestilence of pessimism from the East. But somehow, it is not easy to think of his shrine as the scene of the more jolly, rowdy and vulgar devotion either in its medieval or modern form. He was very far from being a Puritan, in the true sense; he made a provision for a holiday and banquet for his young friends, which has quite a convivial sound. The trend of his writing, especially for his time, is reasonable in its recognition of physical life; and he goes out of his way to say that men must vary their lives with jokes and even with pranks. But for all that, we cannot somehow see his personality as a sort of magnet for mobs; or the road to the tomb of St. Thomas at Toulouse having always been a long street of taverns, like that to the tomb of St. Thomas at Canterbury. I think he rather disliked noise; there is a legend that he disliked thunderstorms; but it is contradicted by the fact that in an actual shipwreck he was supremely calm. However that may be, and it probably concerned his health, in some ways sensitive, he certainly was very calm. We have a feeling that we should gradually grow conscious of his presence; as of an immense background.

Here, if this slight sketch could be worthy of its subject, there should stand forth something of that stupendous certitude, in the presence of which all his libraries of philosophy, and even theology, were but a litter of pamphlets. It is certain that this thing was in him from the first, in the form of conviction, long before it could possibly have even begun to take the form of controversy. It was very vivid in his childhood; and his were exactly the circumstances in which the anecdotes of the nursery and the playground are likely enough to have been really preserved. He had from the first that full and final test of truly orthodox Catholicity; the impetuous, impatient, intolerant passion for the poor; and even that readiness to be rather a nuisance to the rich, out of a hunger to feed the hungry. This can have had nothing to do with the intellectualism of which he was afterwards accused; still less with any habit of dialectic. It would seem unlikely that at the age of six he had any ambition to answer Averrhoes, or that he knew what Effective Causality is; or even that he had worked out, as he did in later life, the whole theory by which a man's love of himself is Sincere and Constant and Indulgent; and that this should be transferred intact (if possible) to his love of his neighbour. At this early age he did not understand all this. He only did it. But all the atmosphere of his actions carries a sort of conviction with it. It is beautifully typical, for instance, of that sort of aristocratic *ménage*, that his parents seem to have objected mildly, if at all, to his handing out things to beggars and tramps; but it was intensely disliked by the upper servants.

Still, if we take the thing as seriously as all childish things should be taken, we may learn something from that mysterious state of innocence, which is the first and best spring of all our later indignations. We may begin to understand why it was that there grew steadily with his growing mind, a great and very solitary mind, an ambition that was the inversion of all the things about him. We shall guess what had continuously swelled within him, whether in protest or prophecy or prayer for deliverance, before he startled his family by flinging away not only the trappings of nobility, but all forms of ambition, even ecclesiastical ambition. His childhood may contain the hint of that first stride of his manhood, from the house onto the highway; and his proclamation that he also would be a Beggar.

There is another case of a sort of second glimpse or sequel, in which an incident well known in the external sense gives us also a glimpse of the internal. After the affair of the firebrand, and the woman who tempted him in the tower, it is said that he had a dream; in which two angels girded him with a cord of fire, a thing of terrible pain and yet giving a terrible strength; and he awoke with a great cry in the darkness. This also has something very vivid about it, under the circumstances; and probably contains truths that will be some day better understood, when priests and doctors have learned to talk to each other without the stale etiquette of nineteenth-century negations. It would be easy to analyse the dream, as the very nineteenth-century doctor did in *Armadale*[2], resolving it into the details of the past days; the cord from his struggle

[2] A novel written by Wilke Collins. In the novel, Allan Armadale has a mysterious dream, the interpretation of which is an important element in the plot. Dr. Hawbury offers a rational analysis of the dream and explains its events as mere reproductions during sleep of images and impressions experienced by Armadale while awake. Armadale's friend Midwinter, however, is convinced that the dream is supernatural in origin and is in fact a premonition of danger for Armadale. It is Midwinter's interpretation which proves accurate in the end.

against being stripped of his Friar's frock; the thread of fire running through the tapestries of the night, from the firebrand he had snatched from the fireside. But even in *Armadale* the dream was fulfilled mystically as well, and the dream of St. Thomas was fulfilled very mystically indeed. For he did in fact remain remarkably untroubled on that side of his human nature after the incident; though it is likely enough that the incident had caused an upheaval of his normal humanity, which produced a dream stronger than a nightmare. This is no place to analyse the psychological fact, which puzzles Non-Catholics so much: of the way in which priests do manage to be celibate without ceasing to be virile. Anyhow, it seems probable that in this matter he was less troubled than most. This has nothing to do with true virtue, which is of the will; saints as holy as he have rolled themselves in brambles to distract the pressure of passion; but he never needed much in the way of a counter-irritant; for the simple reason that in this way, as in most ways, he was not very often irritated. Much must remain unexplained, as part of the mysteries of grace; but there is probably some truth in the psychological idea of "sublimation"; that is the lifting of a lower energy to higher ends; so that appetite almost faded in the furnace of his intellectual energy. Between supernatural and natural causes, it is probable that he never knew or suffered greatly on this side of his mind.

There are moments when the most orthodox reader is tempted to hate the hagiographer as much as he loves the holy man. The holy man always conceals his holiness; that is the one invariable rule. And the hagiographer sometimes seems like a persecutor trying to frustrate the holy man; a spy or eavesdropper hardly more respectful than an American interviewer. I admit that these sentiments are fastidious and one-sided, and I will now proceed to prove my penitence by mentioning one or two of the incidents that could only have come to common knowledge in this deplorable way.

It seems certain that he did live a sort of secondary and mysterious life; the divine double of what is called a double life. Somebody seems to have caught a glimpse of the sort of solitary miracle which modern psychic people call Levitation; and he must surely have either been a liar or a literal witness, for there could have been no doubts or degrees about such a prodigy happening to such a person; it must have been like seeing one of the huge pillars of the church suspended like a cloud. Nobody knows, I imagine, what spiritual storm of exaltation or agony produces this convulsion in matter or space; but the thing does almost certainly occur. Even in the case of ordinary Spiritualist mediums, for whatever reason, the evidence is very difficult to refute. But probably the most representative revelation of this side of his life may be found in the celebrated story of the miracle of the crucifix; when in the stillness of the church of St. Dominic in Naples, a voice spoke from the carven Christ, and told the kneeling Friar that he had written rightly, and offered him the choice of a reward among all the things of the world.

Not all, I think, have appreciated the point of this particular story as applied to this particular saint. It is an old story, in so far as it is simply the offer made to a devotee of solitude or simplicity, of the pick of all the prizes of life. The hermit, true or false, the fakir, the fanatic or the cynic, Stylites on his column or Diogenes in his tub, can all be pictured as tempted by the powers of the earth, of the air or of the heavens, with the offer of the best of everything; and replying that they want nothing. In the Greek cynic or stoic it really meant the mere negative; that he wanted nothing. In the Oriental mystic or fanatic, it sometimes meant a sort of positive negative; that he wanted Nothing; that Nothing was really what he wanted. Sometimes it expressed a noble independence, and the twin virtues of antiquity, the love of liberty and the hatred of luxury. Sometimes it only expressed a self-sufficiency that is the very opposite of sanctity. But even the stories of real saints, of this sort, do not quite cover the case of St. Thomas. He was not a person who wanted nothing; and he was a person who was enormously interested in everything. His answer is not so inevitable or simple as some may suppose. As compared with many other saints, and many other philosophers, he was avid in his acceptance of Things; in his hunger and thirst for Things. It was his special spiritual thesis that there really are things; and not only the Thing; that the Many existed as well as the One. I do not mean things to eat or drink or wear, though he never denied to these their place in the noble hierarchy of Being; but rather things to think about, and especially things to prove, to experience and to know. Nobody supposes that Thomas Aquinas, when offered by God his choice among all the gifts of God, would ask for a thousand pounds, or the Crown of Sicily, or a present of rare Greek wine. But he might have asked for things that he really wanted; and he was a man who could want things; as he wanted the lost manuscript of St. Chrysostom. He might have asked for the solution of an old difficulty; or the secret of a new science; or a flash of the inconceivable intuitive mind of the angels; or any one of a thousand things that would really have satisfied his broad and virile appetite for the very vastness and variety of the universe. The point is that for him, when the voice spoke from between the outstretched arms of the Crucified, those arms were truly opened wide, and opening most gloriously the gates of all the worlds; they were arms pointing to the east and to the west, to the ends of the earth and the very extremes of existence. They were truly spread out with a gesture of omnipotent generosity; the Creator himself offering Creation itself; with all its millionfold mystery of separate beings, and the triumphal chorus of the creatures. That is the blazing background of multitudinous Being that gives the particular strength, and even a sort of surprise, to the answer of St. Thomas, when he lifted at last his head and spoke with, and for, that almost blasphemous audacity which is one with the humility of his religion; "I will have Thyself."

Or, to add the crowning and crushing irony to this story, so uniquely Christian for those who can really understand it, there are some who feel that the audacity is softened by insisting that he said, "*Only* Thyself."

Of these miracles, in the strictly miraculous sense, there are not so many as in the lives of less immediately influential saints; but they are probably pretty well authenticated; for he was a well-known public man in a prominent position, and, what is even more convenient for him, he had any number of highly incensed enemies, who could be trusted to sift his claims. There is at least one miracle of healing; that of a woman who touched his gown; and several incidents that may be variants of the story of the crucifix at Naples. One of these stories, however, has a further importance as bringing us to another section of his more private, personal or even emotional religious life; the section that expressed itself in poetry. When he was stationed at Paris, the other Doctors of the Sorbonne put before him a problem about the nature of the mystical change in the elements of the Blessed Sacrament, and he proceeded to write, in his customary manner, a very careful and elaborately lucid statement of his own solution. Needless to say, he felt with hearty simplicity the heavy responsibility and gravity of such a judicial decision; and not unnaturally seems to have worried about it more than he commonly did over his work. He sought for guidance in more than usually prolonged prayer and intercession; and finally, with one of those few but striking bodily gestures that mark the turning points of his life, he threw down his thesis at the foot of the crucifix on the altar, and left it lying there; as if awaiting judgment. Then he turned and came down the altar steps and buried himself once more in prayer; but the other Friars, it is said, were watching; and well they might be. For they declared afterwards that the figure of Christ had come down from the cross before their mortal eyes; and stood upon the scroll, saying "Thomas, thou hast written well concerning the Sacrament of My Body." It was after this vision that the incident is said to have happened, of his being born up miraculously in mid-air.

An acute observer said of Thomas Aquinas in his own time, "He could alone restore all philosophy, if it had been burnt by fire." That is what is meant by saying that he was an original man, a creative mind; that he could have made his own cosmos out of stones and straws, even without the manuscripts of Aristotle or Augustine. But there is here a not uncommon confusion, between the thing in which a man is most original and that in which he is most interested; or between the thing that he does best and the thing that he loves most. Because St. Thomas was a unique and striking philosopher, it is almost unavoidable that this book should be merely, or mainly, a sketch of his philosophy. It cannot be, and does not pretend to be, a sketch of his theology. But this is because the theology of a saint is simply the theism of a saint; or rather the theism of all saints. It is less individual, but it is much more intense. It is concerned with the common origin; but it is hardly an occasion for originality. Thus we are forced to think first of Thomas as the maker of the Thomist philosophy; as we think first of Christopher Columbus as the discoverer of America, though he may have been quite sincere in his pious hope to convert the Khan of

Tartary; or of James Watt as the discoverer of the steam-engine, though he may have been a devout fire-worshipper, or a sincere Scottish Calvinist, or all kinds of curious things. Anyhow, it is but natural that Augustine and Aquinas, Bonaventure and Duns Scotus, all the doctors and the saints, should draw nearer to each other as they approach the divine unity in things; and that there should in that sense be less difference between them in theology than in philosophy. It is true that, in some matters, the critics of Aquinas thought his philosophy had unduly affected his theology. This is especially so, touching the charge that he made the state of Beatitude too intellectual, conceiving it as the satisfaction of the love of truth; rather than specially as the truth of love. It is true that the mystics and the men of the Franciscan school, dwelt more lovingly on the admitted supremacy of love. But it was mostly a matter of emphasis; perhaps tinged faintly by temperament; possibly (to suggest something which is easier to feel than to explain), in the case of St. Thomas, a shadowy influence of a sort of shyness. Whether the supreme ecstasy is more affectional than intellectual is no very deadly matter of quarrel among men who believe it is both, but do not profess even to imagine the actual experience of either. But I have a sort of feeling that, even if St. Thomas had thought it was as emotional as St. Bonaventure did, he would never have been so emotional about it. It would always have embarrassed him to write about love at such length.

The one exception permitted to him was the rare but remarkable output of his poetry. All sanctity is secrecy; and his sacred poetry was really a secretion; like the pearl in a very tightly closed oyster. He may have written more of it than we know; but part of it came into public use through the particular circumstance of his being asked to compose the office for the Feast of Corpus Christi: a festival first established after the controversy to which he had contributed, in the scroll that he laid on the altar. It does certainly reveal an entirely different side of his genius; and it certainly was genius. As a rule, he was an eminently practical prose writer; some would say a very prosaic prose writer. He maintained controversy with an eye on only two qualities; clarity and courtesy. And he maintained these because they were entirely practical qualities; affecting the probabilities of conversion. But the composer of the Corpus Christi service was not merely what even the wild and woolly would call a poet; he was what the most fastidious would call an artist. His double function rather recalls the double activity of some great Renaissance craftsman, like Michelangelo or Leonardo da Vinci, who would work on the outer wall, planning and building the fortifications of the city; and then retire into the inner chamber to carve or model some cup or casket for a reliquary. The Corpus Christi Office is like some old musical instrument, quaintly and carefully inlaid with many coloured stones and metals; the author has gathered remote texts about pasture and fruition like rare herbs; there is a notable lack of the loud and obvious in the harmony; and the whole is strung with two strong Latin lyrics. Father John O'Connor has translated them with an almost miraculous aptitude; but a good translator will be the first to agree that no translation is good; or, at any rate, good enough. How are we to find eight short English words which actually stand for "*Sumit unus, sumunt mille; quantum isti, tantum ille*"?[3] How is anybody really to render the sound of the "*Pange Lingua*", when the very first syllable has a clang like the clash of cymbals?

There was one other channel, besides that of poetry, and it was that of private affections, by which this large and shy man could show that he had really as much *Caritas* as St. Francis; and certainly as much as any Franciscan theologian. Bonaventure was not likely to think that Thomas was lacking in the love of God, and certainly he was never lacking in the love of Bonaventure. He felt for his whole family a steady, we might say a stubborn tenderness; and, considering how his family had treated him, this would seem to call not only for charity, but for his characteristic virtue of patience. Towards the end of his life, he seems to have leaned especially on his love of one of the brethren, a Friar named Reginald, who received from him some strange and rather startling confidences, of the kind that he very seldom gave even to his friends. It was to Reginald that he gave that last and rather extraordinary hint, which was the end of his controversial career, and practically of his earthly life; a hint that history has never been able to explain.

[3] This may be translated as "one receives, a thousand receive; however many they, that much is he".

He had returned victorious from his last combat with Siger of Brabant; returned and retired. This particular quarrel was the one point, as we may say, in which his outer and his inner life had crossed and coincided; he realised how he had longed from childhood to call up all allies in the battle for Christ; how he had only long afterwards called up Aristotle as an ally; and now in that last nightmare of sophistry, he had for the first time truly realised that some might really wish Christ to go down before Aristotle. He never recovered from the shock. He won his battle, because he was the best brain of his time, but he could not forget such an inversion of the whole idea and purpose of his life. He was the sort of man who hates hating people. He had not been used to hating even their hateful ideas, beyond a certain point. But in the abyss of anarchy opened by Siger's sophistry of the Double Mind of Man, he had seen the possibility of the perishing of all idea of religion, and even of all idea of truth. Brief and fragmentary as are the phrases that record it, we can gather that he came back with a sort of horror of that outer world, in which there blew such wild winds of doctrine, and a longing for the inner world which any Catholic can share, and in which the saint is not cut off from simple men. He resumed the strict routine of religion, and for some time said nothing to anybody. And then something happened (it is said while he was celebrating Mass) the nature of which will never be known among mortal men.

His friend Reginald asked him to return also to his equally regular habits of reading and writing, and following the controversies of the hour. He said with a singular emphasis, "I can write no more." There seems to have been a silence; after which Reginald again ventured to approach the subject; and Thomas answered him with even greater vigour, "I can write no more. I have seen things which make all my writings like straw."

In 1274, when Aquinas was nearly fifty, the Pope, rejoicing in the recent victory over the Arabian sophists, sent word to him, asking him to come to a Council on these controversial matters, to be held at Lyons. He rose in automatic obedience, as a soldier rises; but we may fancy that there was something in his eyes that told those around him that obedience to the outer command would not in fact frustrate obedience to some more mysterious inner command; a signal that only he had seen. He set out with his friend on the journey, proposing to rest for the night with his sister, to whom he was deeply devoted; and when he came into her house he was stricken down with some unnamed malady. We need not discuss the doubtful medical problems. It is true that he had always been one of those men, healthy in the main, who are overthrown by small illnesses; it is equally true that there is no very clear account of this particular illness. He was eventually taken to a monastery at Fossanuova; and his strange end came upon him with great strides. It may be worth remarking, for those who think that he thought too little of the emotional or romantic side of religious truth, that he asked to have The Song of Solomon read through to him from beginning to end. The feelings of the men about him must have been mingled and rather indescribable; and certainly quite different from his own. He confessed his sins and he received his God; and we may be sure that the great philosopher had entirely forgotten philosophy. But it was not entirely so with those who had loved him, or even those who merely lived in his time. The elements of the narrative are so few, yet so essential, that we have a strong sense in reading the story of the two emotional sides of the event. Those men must have known that a great mind was still labouring like a great mill in the midst of them. They must have felt that, for that moment, the inside of the monastery was larger than the outside. It must have resembled the case of some mighty modern engine, shaking the ramshackle building in which it is for the moment enclosed. For truly that machine was made of the wheels of all the worlds; and revolved like that cosmos of concentric spheres which, whatever its fate in the face of changing science, must always be something of a symbol for philosophy; the depth of double and triple transparencies more mysterious than darkness; the sevenfold, the terrible crystal. In the world of that mind there was a wheel of angels, and a wheel of planets, and a wheel of plants or of animals; but there was also a just and intelligible order of all earthly things, a sane authority and a self-respecting liberty, and a hundred answers to a hundred questions in the complexity of ethics or economics. But there must have been a moment, when men knew that the thunderous mill of thought had stopped suddenly; and that after the shock of stillness that wheel would shake the world no more; that there was nothing now within that hollow house but a great hill of clay; and the confessor, who had been with him in the inner chamber, ran forth as if in fear, and whispered that his confession had been that of a child of five.

VI

THE APPROACH TO THOMISM

The fact that Thomism is the philosophy of common sense is itself a matter of common sense. Yet it wants a word of explanation, because we have so long taken such matters in a very uncommon sense. For good or evil, Europe since the Reformation, and most especially England since the Reformation, has been in a peculiar sense the home of paradox. I mean in the very peculiar sense that paradox was at home, and that men were at home with it. The most familiar example is the English boasting that they are practical *because* they are not logical. To an ancient Greek or a Chinaman this would seem exactly like saying that London clerks excel in adding up their ledgers, because they are not accurate in their arithmetic. But the point is not that it is a paradox; it is that parodoxy has become orthodoxy; that men repose in a paradox as placidly as in a platitude. It is not that the practical man stands on his head, which may sometimes be a stimulating if startling gymnastic; it is that he *rests* on his head; and even sleeps on his head. This is an important point, because the use of paradox is to awaken the mind. Take a good paradox, like that of Oliver Wendell Holmes: "Give us the luxuries of life and we will dispense with the necessities." It is amusing and therefore arresting; it has a fine air of defiance; it contains a real if romantic truth. It is all part of the fun that it is stated almost in the form of a contradiction in terms. But most people would agree that there would be considerable danger in basing the whole social system on the notion that necessaries are not necessary; as some have based the whole British Constitution on the notion that nonsense will always work out as common sense. Yet even here, it might be said that the invidious example has spread, and that the modern industrial system does really say, "Give us luxuries like coal-tar soap, and we will dispense with necessities like corn."

So much is familiar; but what is not even now realised is that not only the practical politics, but the abstract philosophies of the modern world have had this queer twist. Since the modern world began in the sixteenth century, nobody's system of philosophy has really corresponded to everybody's sense of reality; to what, if left to themselves, common men would call common sense. Each started with a paradox; a peculiar point of view demanding the sacrifice of what they would call a sane point of view. That is the one thing common to Hobbes and Hegel, to Kant and Bergson, to Berkeley and William James. A man had to believe something that no normal man would believe, if it were suddenly propounded to his simplicity; as that law is above right, or right is outside reason, or things are only as we think them, or everything is relative to a reality that is not there. The modern philosopher claims, like a sort of confidence man, that if once we will grant him this, the rest will be easy; he will straighten out the world, if once he is allowed to give this one twist to the mind.

It will be understood that in these matters I speak as a fool; or, as our democratic cousins would say, a moron; anyhow as a man in the street; and the only object of this chapter is to show that the Thomist philosophy is nearer than most philosophies to the mind of the man in the street. I am not, like Father D'Arcy, whose admirable book on St. Thomas has illuminated many problems for me, a trained philosopher, acquainted with the technique of the trade. But I hope Father D'Arcy will forgive me if I take one example from his book, which exactly illustrates what I mean. He, being a trained philosopher, is naturally trained to put up with philosophers. Also, being a trained priest, he is naturally accustomed, not only to suffer fools gladly, but (what is sometimes even harder) to suffer clever people gladly. Above all, his wide reading in metaphysics has made him patient with clever people when they indulge in folly. The consequence is that he can write calmly and even blandly sentences like these. "A certain likeness can be detected between the aim and method of St. Thomas and those of Hegel. There are, however, also remarkable differences. For St. Thomas it is impossible that contradictories should exist together, and again reality and intelligibility correspond, but a thing must first be, to be intelligible."

Let the man in the street be forgiven, if he adds that the "remarkable difference" seems to him to be that St. Thomas was sane and Hegel was mad. The moron refuses to admit that Hegel can both exist and not exist; or that it can be possible to understand Hegel, if there is no Hegel to understand. Yet Father D'Arcy mentions this Hegelian paradox as if it were all in the day's work; and of course it is, if the work is reading all the modern philosophers as searchingly and sympathetically as he has done. And this is what I mean by saying that a modern philosophy starts with a stumbling-block. It is surely not too much to say that there *seems* to be a twist, in saying that contraries are not incompatible; or that a thing can "be" intelligible and not as yet "be" at all.

Against all this the philosophy of St. Thomas stands founded on the universal common conviction that eggs are eggs. The Hegelian may say that an egg is really a hen, because it is a part of an endless process of Becoming; the Berkeleian may hold that poached eggs only exist as a dream exists; since it is quite as easy to call the dream the cause of the eggs as the eggs the cause of the dream; the Pragmatist may believe that we get the best out of scrambled eggs by forgetting that they ever were eggs, and only remembering the scramble. But no pupil of St. Thomas needs to addle his brains in order adequately to addle his eggs; to put his head at any peculiar angle in looking at eggs, or squinting at eggs, or winking the other eye in order to see a new simplification of eggs. The Thomist stands in the broad daylight of the brotherhood of men, in their common consciousness that eggs are not hens or dreams or mere practical assumptions; but things attested by the Authority of the Senses, which is from God.

Thus, even those who appreciate the metaphysical depth of Thomism in other matters have expressed surprise that he does not deal at all with what many now think the main metaphysical question; whether we can prove that the primary act of recognition of any reality is real. The answer is that St. Thomas recognised instantly, what so many modern sceptics have begun to suspect rather laboriously; that a man must either answer that question in the affirmative, or else never answer any question, never ask any question, never even exist intellectually, to answer or to ask. I suppose it is true in a sense that a man can be a fundamental sceptic, but he cannot be anything else; certainly not even a defender of fundamental scepticism. If a man feels that all the movements of his own mind are meaningless, then his mind is meaningless, and he is meaningless; and it does not mean anything to attempt to discover his meaning. Most fundamental sceptics appear to survive, because they are not consistently sceptical and not at all fundamental. They will first deny everything and then admit something, if for the sake of argument — or often rather of attack without argument. I saw an almost startling example of this essential frivolity in the professor of final scepticism, in a paper the other day. A man wrote to say that he accepted nothing but Solipsism, and added that he had often wondered it was not a more common philosophy. Now Solipsism simply means that a man believes in his own existence, but not in anybody or anything else. And it never struck this simple sophist, that if his philosophy was true, there obviously were no other philosophers to profess it.

To this question "Is there anything?" St. Thomas begins by answering "Yes"; if he began by answering "No", it would not be the beginning, but the end. That is what some of us call common sense. Either there is no philosophy, no philosophers, no thinkers, no thought, no anything; or else there is a real bridge between the mind and reality. But he is actually less exacting than many thinkers, much less so than most rationalist and materialist thinkers, as to what that first step involves; he is content, as we shall see, to say that it involves the recognition of Ens or Being as something definitely beyond ourselves. Ens is Ens: Eggs are eggs, and it is not tenable that all eggs were found in a mare's nest.

Needless to say, I am not so silly as to suggest that all the writings of St. Thomas are simple and straightforward; in the sense of being easy to understand. There are passages I do not in the least understand myself; there are passages that puzzle much more learned and logical philosophers than I am; there are passages about which the greatest Thomists still differ and dispute. But that is a question of a thing being hard to read or understand: not hard to accept when understood. That is a mere matter of "The Cat sat on the Mat" being written in Chinese characters; or "Mary had a Little Lamb" in Egyptian hieroglyphics. The only point I am stressing here is that Aquinas is almost always on the side of simplicity, and supports the ordinary man's acceptance of ordinary truisms. For instance, one of the most obscure passages, in my very inadequate judgment, is that in which he explains how the mind is certain of an external object and not merely of an impression of that object; and yet apparently reaches it through a concept, though not merely through an impression. But the only point here is that he does explain that the mind is certain of an external object. It is enough for this purpose that his conclusion is what is called the conclusion of common sense; that it is his purpose to justify common sense; even though he justifies it in a passage which happens to be one of rather uncommon subtlety. The problem of later philosophers is that their conclusion is as dark as their demonstration; or that they bring out a result of which the result is chaos.

Unfortunately, between the man in the street and the Angel of the Schools, there stands at this moment a very high brick wall, with spikes on the top, separating two men who in many ways stand for the same thing. The wall is almost a historical accident; at least it was built a very long time ago, for reasons that need not affect the needs of normal men today; least of all the greatest need of normal men; which is for a normal philosophy. The first difficulty is merely a difference of form; not in the medieval but in the modern sense. There is first a simple obstacle of language; there is then a rather more subtle obstacle of logical method. But the language itself counts for a great deal; even when it is translated, it is still a foreign language; and it is, like other foreign languages, very often translated wrong. As with every other literature from another age or country, it carried with it an atmosphere which is beyond the mere translation of words, as they are translated in a traveller's phrase-book. For instance, the whole system of St. Thomas hangs on one huge and yet simple idea; which does actually cover everything there is, and even everything that could possibly be. He represents this cosmic conception by the word *Ens*; and anybody who can read any Latin at all, however rudely, feels it to be the apt and fitting word; exactly as he feels it in a French word in a piece of good French prose. It ought to be a matter of logic; but it is also a matter of language.

Unfortunately there is no satisfying translation of the word *Ens*. The difficulty is rather verbal than logical, but it is practical. I mean that when the translator says in English 'being', we are aware of a rather different atmosphere. Atmosphere ought not to affect these absolutes of the intellect; but it does. The new psychologists, who are almost eagerly at war with reason, never tire of telling us that the very terms we use are coloured by our subconsciousness, with something we meant to exclude from our consciousness. And one need not be so idealistically irrational as a modern psychologist, in order to admit that the very shape and sound of words do make a difference, even in the baldest prose, as they do in the most beautiful poetry. We cannot quite prevent the imagination from remembering irrelevant associations even in the abstract sciences like mathematics. Jones Minimus, hustled from history to geometry, may for an instant connect the Angles of the isosceles triangle with the Angles of the Anglo-Saxon Chronicle; and even the mature mathematician, if he is as mad as the psychoanalyst hopes, may have in the roots of his subconscious mind something material in his idea of a root. Now it unfortunately happens that the word 'being', as it comes to a modern Englishman, through modern associations, has a sort of hazy atmosphere that is not in the short and sharp Latin word. Perhaps it reminds him of fantastic professors in fiction, who wave their hands and say, "Thus do we mount to the ineffable heights of pure and radiant Being:" or, worse still, of actual professors in real life, who say, "All Being is Becoming; and is but the evolution of Not-Being by the law of its Being." Perhaps it only reminds him of romantic rhapsodies in old love stories; "Beautiful and adorable being, light and breath of my very being". Anyhow it has a wild and woolly sort of sound; as if only very vague people used it; or as if it might mean all sorts of different things.

Now the Latin word *Ens* has a sound like the English word *End*. It is final and even abrupt; it is nothing except itself. There was once a silly gibe against Scholastics like Aquinas, that they discussed whether angels could stand on the point of a needle. It is at least certain that this first word of Aquinas is as sharp as the point of a pin. For that also is, in an almost ideal sense, an End. But when we say that St. Thomas Aquinas is concerned fundamentally with the idea of Being, we must not admit any of the cloudier generalisations that we may have grown used to, or even grown tired of, in the sort of idealistic writing that is rather rhetoric than philosophy. Rhetoric is a very fine thing in its place, as a medieval scholar would have willingly agreed, as he taught it along with logic in the schools; but St. Thomas Aquinas himself is not at all rhetorical. Perhaps he is hardly even sufficiently rhetorical. There are any number of purple patches in Augustine; but there are no purple patches in Aquinas. He did on certain definite occasions drop into poetry; but he very seldom dropped into oratory. And so little was he in touch with some modern tendencies, that whenever he did write poetry, he actually put it into poems. There is another side to this, to be noted later. He very specially possessed the philosophy that inspires poetry; as he did so largely inspire Dante's poetry. And poetry without philosophy has only inspiration, or, in vulgar language, only wind. He had, so to speak, the imagination without the imagery. And even this is perhaps too sweeping. There is an image of his, that is true poetry as well as true philosophy; about the tree of life bowing down with a huge humility, because of the very load of its living fruitfulness; a thing Dante might have described so as to overwhelm us with the tremendous twilight and almost drug us with the divine fruit. But normally, we may say that his words are brief even when his books are long. I have taken the example of the word *Ens*, precisely because it is one of the cases in which Latin is plainer than plain English. And his style, unlike that of St. Augustine and many Catholic Doctors, is always a penny plain rather than twopence coloured. It is often difficult to understand, simply because the subjects are so difficult that hardly any mind, except one like his own, can fully understand them. But he never darkens it by using words without knowledge, or even more legitimately, by using words belonging only to imagination or intuition. So far as his method is concerned, he is perhaps the one real Rationalist among all the children of men.

This brings us to the other difficulty; that of logical method. I have never understood why there is supposed to be something crabbed or antique about a syllogism; still less can I understand what anybody means by talking as if induction had somehow taken the place of deduction. The whole point of deduction is that true premises produce a true conclusion. What is called induction seems simply to mean collecting a larger number of true premises, or perhaps, in some physical matters, taking rather more trouble to see that they are true. It may be a fact that a modern man can get more out of a great many premises, concerning microbes or asteroids than a medieval man could get out of a very few premises about salamanders and unicorns. But the process of deduction from the data is the same for the modern mind as for the medieval mind; and what is pompously called induction is simply collecting more of the data. And Aristotle or Aquinas, or anybody in his five wits, would of course agree that the conclusion could only be true if the premises were true; and that the more true premises there were the better. It was the misfortune of medieval culture that there were not enough true premises, owing to the rather ruder conditions of travel or experiment. But however perfect were the conditions of travel or experiment, they could only produce premises; it would still be necessary to deduce conclusions. But many modern people talk as if what they call induction were some magic way of reaching a conclusion, without using any of those horrid old syllogisms. But induction does not lead us to a conclusion. Induction only leads us to a deduction. Unless the last three syllogistic steps are all right, the conclusion is all wrong. Thus, the great nineteenth century men of science, whom I was brought up to revere ("accepting the conclusions of science", it was always called), went out and closely inspected the air and the earth, the chemicals and the gases, doubtless more closely than Aristotle or Aquinas, and then came back and embodied their final conclusion in a syllogism. "All matter is made of microscopic little knobs which are indivisible. My body is made of matter. Therefore my body is made of microscopic little knobs which are indivisible." They were not wrong in the form of their reasoning; because it is the only way to reason. In this world there is nothing except a syllogism—and a fallacy.

But of course these modern men knew, as the medieval men knew, that their conclusions would not be true unless their premises were true. And that is where the trouble began. For the men of science, or their sons and nephews, went out and took another look at the knobby nature of matter; and were surprised to find that it was not knobby at all. So they came back and completed the process with their syllogism; "All matter is made of whirling protons and electrons. My body is made of matter. Therefore my body is made of whirling protons and electrons." And that again is a good syllogism; though they may have to look at matter once or twice more, before we know whether it is a true premise and a true conclusion. But in the final process of truth there is nothing else except a good syllogism. The only other thing is a bad syllogism; as in the familiar fashionable shape; "All matter is made of protons and electrons. I should very much like to think that mind is much the same as matter. So I will announce, through the microphone or the megaphone, that my mind is made of protons and electrons." But that is not induction; it is only a very bad blunder in deduction. That is not another or new way of thinking; it is only ceasing to think.

What is really meant, and what is much more reasonable, is that the old syllogists sometimes set out the syllogism at length; and certainly that is not always necessary. A man can run down the three steps much more quickly than that; but a man cannot run down the three steps if they are not there. If he does, he will break his neck, as if he walked out of a fourth-story window. The truth about this false antithesis of induction and deduction is simply this; that as premises or data accumulated, the emphasis and detail was shifted to them, from the final deduction to which they lead. But they did lead to a final deduction; or else they led to nothing. The logician had so much to say about electrons or microbes that he dwelt most on these data and shortened or assumed his ultimate syllogism. But if he reasoned rightly, however rapidly, he reasoned syllogistically.

As a matter of fact, Aquinas does not usually argue in syllogisms; though he always argues syllogistically. I mean he does not set out all the steps of the logic in each case; the legend that he does so is part of that loose and largely unverified legend of the Renaissance;

that the Schoolmen were all crabbed and mechanical medieval bores.
But he does argue with a certain austerity, and disdain of ornament,
which may make him seem monotonous to anyone specially seeking
the modern forms of wit or fancy. But all this has nothing to do
with the question asked at the beginning of this chapter and needing
to be answered at the end of it; the question of what he is arguing
for. In that respect it can be repeated, most emphatically, that he is
arguing for common sense. He is arguing for a common sense which
would even now commend itself to most of the common people. He
is arguing for the popular proverbs that seeing is believing; that the
proof of the pudding is in the eating; that a man cannot jump down
his own throat or deny the fact of his own existence. He often maintains the view by the use of abstractions; but the abstractions are no
more abstract than Energy or Evolution or Space-Time; and they do
not land us, as the others often do, in hopeless contradictions about
common life. The Pragmatist sets out to be practical, but his practicality turns out to be entirely theoretical. The Thomist begins by being theoretical, but his theory turns out to be entirely practical.
That is why a great part of the world is returning to it today.

Finally, there is some real difficulty in the fact of a foreign language; apart from the ordinary fact of the Latin language. Modern
philosophical terminology is not always exactly identical with plain
English; and medieval philosophical terminology is not at all identical even with modern philosophical terminology. It is not really
very difficult to learn the meaning of the main terms; but their medieval meaning is sometimes the exact opposite of their modern
meaning. The obvious example is in the pivotal word "form". We
say nowadays, "I wrote a formal apology to the Dean", or "The
proceedings when we wound up the Tip-Cat Club were purely formal." But we mean that they were purely fictitious; and St. Thomas,
had he been a member of the Tip-Cat Club, would have meant just
the opposite. He would have meant that the proceedings dealt with
the very heart and soul and secret of the whole being of the Tip-
Cat Club; and that the apology to the Dean was so essentially apologetic that it tore the very heart out in tears of true contrition.
For "formal" in Thomist language means actual, or possessing the

real decisive quality that makes a thing itself. Roughly when he describes a thing as made out of Form and Matter, he very rightly recognises that Matter is the more mysterious and indefinite and featureless element; and that what stamps anything with its own identity is its Form. Matter, so to speak, is not so much the solid as the liquid or gaseous thing in the cosmos; and in this most modern scientists are beginning to agree with him. But the form is the fact; it is that which makes a brick a brick, and a bust a bust, and not the shapeless and trampled clay of which either may be made. The stone that broke a statuette, in some Gothic niche, might have been itself a statuette; and under chemical analysis, the statuette is only a stone. But such a chemical analysis is entirely false as a philosophical analysis. The reality, the thing that makes the two things real, is in the idea of the image and in the idea of the image-breaker. This is only a passing example of the mere idiom of the Thomist terminology; but it is not a bad prefatory specimen of the truth of Thomist thought. Every artist knows that the form is not superficial but fundamental; that the form is the foundation. Every sculptor knows that the form of the statue is not the outside of the statue, but rather the inside of the statue; even in the sense of the inside of the sculptor. Every poet knows that the sonnet-form is not only the form of the poem; but the poem. No modern critic who does not understand what the medieval Schoolman meant by form can meet the Schoolman as an intellectual equal.

VII

THE PERMANENT PHILOSOPHY

It is a pity that the word Anthropology has been degraded to the study of Anthropoids. It is now incurably associated with squabbles between prehistoric professors (in more senses than one) about whether a chip of stone is the tooth of a man or an ape; sometimes settled as in that famous case, when it was found to be the tooth of a pig. It is very right that there should be a purely physical science of such things; but the name commonly used might well, by analogy, have been dedicated to things not only wider and deeper, but rather more relevant. Just as, in America, the new Humanists have pointed out to the old Humanitarians that their humanitarianism has been largely concentrated on things that are *not* specially human, such as physical conditions, appetites, economic needs, environment and so on—so in practice those who are called Anthropologists have to narrow their minds to the materialistic things that are *not* notably anthropic. They have to hunt through history and pre-history something which emphatically is not *Homo Sapiens*, but is always in fact regarded as *Simius Insipiens*. *Homo Sapiens* can only be considered in relation to *Sapientia*; and only a book like that of St. Thomas is really devoted to the intrinsic idea of *Sapientia*. In short, there ought to be a real study called Anthropology corresponding to Theology. In this sense St. Thomas Aquinas, perhaps more than he is anything else, is a great anthropologist.

I apologise for the opening words of this chapter to all those excellent and eminent men of science, who are engaged in the real study of humanity in its relation to biology. But I rather fancy that they will be the last to deny that there has been a somewhat disproportionate disposition, in popular science, to turn the study of human beings into the study of savages. And savagery is not history: it is either the beginning of history or the end of it. I suspect that the greatest scientists would agree that only too many professors have thus been lost in the bush or the jungle; professors who wanted to study anthropology and never got any further than anthropophagy. But I have a particular reason for prefacing this suggestion of a higher anthropology by an apology to any genuine biologists who might seem to be included, but are certainly not included, in a protest against cheap popular science. For the first thing to be said about St. Thomas as an anthropologist, is that he is really remarkably like the best sort of modern biological anthropologist; of the sort who would call themselves Agnostics. This fact is so sharp and decisive a turning point in history, that the history really needs to be recalled and recorded.

St. Thomas Aquinas closely resembles the great Professor Huxley, the Agnostic who invented the word Agnosticism. He is like him in his way of starting the argument, and he is unlike everybody else, before and after, until the Huxleyan age. He adopts almost literally the Huxleyan definition of the Agnostic method; "To follow reason as far as it will go"; the only question is—where does it go? He lays down the almost startlingly modern or materialist statement; "Everything that is in the intellect has been in the senses". This is where he began, as much as any modern man of science, nay, as much as any modern materialist who can now hardly be called a man of science; at the very opposite end of enquiry from that of the mere mystic. The Platonists, or at least the Neo-Platonists, all tended to the view that the mind was lit entirely from within; St. Thomas insisted that it was lit by five windows, that we call the windows of the senses. But he wanted the light from without to shine on what was within. He wanted to study the nature of Man, and not merely of such moss and mushrooms as he might see through the window, and which he valued as the first enlightening experience of man. And starting from this point, he proceeds to climb the House of Man, step by step and story by story, until he has come out on the highest tower and beheld the largest vision.

In other words, he is an anthropologist, with a complete theory of Man, right or wrong. Now the modern Anthropologists, who called themselves Agnostics, completely failed to be Anthropologists at all. Under their limitations, they could not get a complete theory of Man, let alone a complete theory of nature. They began by ruling out something which they called the Unknowable. The incomprehensibility

was almost comprehensible, if we could really understand the Unknowable in the sense of the Ultimate. But it rapidly became
apparent that all sorts of things were Unknowable, which were exactly the things that a man has got to know. It is necessary to know
whether he is responsible or irresponsible, perfect or imperfect, per-
fectible or unperfectible, mortal or immortal, doomed or free, not in
order to understand God, but in order to understand Man. Nothing
that leaves these things under a cloud of religious doubt can possibly
pretend to be a Science of Man; it shrinks from anthropology as
completely as from theology. Has a man free will; or is his sense of
choice an illusion? Has he a conscience, or has his conscience any
authority; or is it only the prejudice of the tribal past? Is there
any real hope of settling these things by human reason; and has *that*
any authority? Is he to regard death as final; and is he to regard miraculous help as possible? Now it is all nonsense to say that these are
unknowable in any remote sense, like the distinction between the
Cherubim and the Seraphim, or the Procession of the Holy Ghost.
The Schoolmen may have shot too far beyond our limits in pursuing
the Cherubim and Seraphim. But in asking whether a man can
choose or whether a man will die, they were asking ordinary questions in natural history; like whether a cat can scratch or whether a
dog can smell. Nothing calling itself a complete Science of Man can
shirk them. And the great Agnostics did shirk them. They may have
said they had no scientific evidence; in that case they failed to produce even a scientific hypothesis. What they generally did produce
was a wildly unscientific contradiction. Most Monist moralists simply said that Man has no choice; but he must think and act heroically
as if he had. Huxley made morality, and even Victorian morality, in
the exact sense, supernatural. He said it had arbitrary rights above
nature; a sort of theology without theism.

I do not know for certain why St. Thomas was called the Angelic
Doctor: whether it was that he had an angelic temper, or the intel-
lectuality of an Angel; or whether there was a later legend that he
concentrated on Angels—especially on the points of needles. If so, I
do not quite understand how this idea arose; history has many examples of an irritating habit of labelling somebody in connection

with something, as if he never did anything else. Who was it who began the inane habit of referring to Dr. Johnson as 'our lexicographer'; as if he never did anything but write a dictionary? Why do most people insist on meeting the large and far-reaching mind of Pascal at its very narrowest point; the point at which it was sharpened into a spike by the spite of the Jansenists against the Jesuits? It is just possible, for all I know, that this labelling of Aquinas as a specialist was an obscure depreciation of him as a universalist. For that is a very common trick for the belittling of literary or scientific men. St. Thomas must have made a certain number of enemies, though he hardly ever treated them as enemies. Unfortunately, good temper is sometimes more irritating than bad temper. And he had, after all, done a great deal of damage, as many medieval men would have thought; and, what is more curious, a great deal of damage to both sides. He had been a revolutionist against Augustine and a traditionalist against Averrhoes. He might appear to some to have tried to wreck that ancient beauty of the city of God, which bore some resemblance to the Republic of Plato. He might appear to others to have inflicted a blow on the advancing and levelling forces of Islam, as dramatic as that of Godfrey storming Jerusalem. It is possible that these enemies, by way of damning with faint praise, talked about his very respectable little work on Angels: as a man might say that Darwin was really reliable when writing on coral-insects; or that some of Milton's Latin poems were very creditable indeed. But this is only a conjecture, and many other conjectures are possible. And I am disposed to think that St. Thomas really was rather specially interested in the nature of Angels, for the same reason that made him even more interested in the nature of Men. It was a part of that strong personal interest in things subordinate and semidependent, which runs through his whole system: a hierarchy of higher and lower liberties. He was interested in the problem of the Angel, as he was interested in the problem of the Man, because it was a problem; and especially because it was a problem of an intermediate creature. I do not pretend to deal here with this mysterious quality, as he conceives it to exist in that inscrutable intellectual being, who is less than God but more than Man. But it was this quality of a link in the chain, or a rung in the ladder, which mainly concerned the theologian, in developing his own particular theory of degrees. Above all, it is this which chiefly moves him, when he finds so fascinating the central mystery of Man. And for him the point is always that Man is not a balloon going up into the sky, nor a mole burrowing merely in the earth; but rather a thing like a tree, whose roots are fed from the earth, while its highest branches seem to rise almost to the stars.

I have pointed out that mere modern free-thought has left everything in a fog, including itself. The assertion that thought is free led first to the denial that will is free; but even about that there was no real determination among the Determinists. In practice, they told men that they must treat their will as free though it was not free. In other words, Man must live a double life; which is exactly the old heresy of Siger of Brabant about the Double Mind. In other words, the nineteenth century left everything in chaos; and the importance of Thomism to the twentieth century is that it may give us back a cosmos. We can give here only the rudest sketch of how Aquinas, like the Agnostics, beginning in the cosmic cellars, yet climbed to the cosmic towers.

Without pretending to span within such limits the essential Thomist idea, I may be allowed to throw out a sort of rough version of the fundamental question, which I think I have known myself, consciously or unconsciously since my childhood. When a child looks out of the nursery window and sees anything, say the green lawn of the garden, what does he actually know; or does he know anything? There are all sorts of nursery games of negative philosophy played round this question. A brilliant Victorian scientist delighted in declaring that the child does not see any grass at all; but only a sort of green mist reflected in a tiny mirror of the human eye. This piece of rationalism has always struck me as almost insanely irrational. If he is not sure of the existence of the grass, which he sees through the glass of a window, how on earth can he be sure of the existence of the retina, which he sees through the glass of a microscope? If sight deceives, why can it not go on deceiving? Men of another school answer that grass is a mere green impression on the mind; and that he can be sure of nothing except the mind. They declare that he can only be conscious of his own consciousness; which happens to be the one thing that we know the child is not conscious of at all. In that sense, it would be far truer to say that there is grass and no child, than to say that there is a conscious child but no grass. St. Thomas Aquinas, suddenly intervening in this nursery quarrel, says emphatically that the child is aware of *Ens*. Long before he knows that grass is grass, or self is self, he knows that something is something. Perhaps it would be best to say very emphatically (with a blow on the table), "There *is* an Is". That is as much monkish credulity as St. Thomas asks of us at the start. Very few unbelievers start by asking us to believe so little. And yet, upon this sharp pin-point of reality, he rears by long logical processes that have never really been successfully overthrown, the whole cosmic system of Christendom.

Thus, Aquinas insists very profoundly, but very practically, that there *instantly* enters, with this idea of affirmation, the idea of contradiction. It is instantly apparent, even to the child, that there cannot be both affirmation and contradiction. Whatever you call the thing he sees, a moon or a mirage or a sensation or a state of consciousness, when he sees it, he knows it is not true that he does not see it. Or whatever you call what he is supposed to be doing, seeing or dreaming or being conscious of an impression, he knows that if he is doing it, it is a lie to say he is not doing it. Therefore there has already entered *something* beyond even the first fact of being; there follows it like its shadow the first fundamental creed or commandment; that a thing cannot be and not be. Henceforth, in common or popular language, there is a false and true. I say in popular language, because Aquinas is nowhere more subtle than in pointing out that being is not strictly the same as truth; seeing truth must mean the appreciation of being by some mind capable of appreciating it. But in a general sense there has entered that primeval world of pure actuality, the division and dilemma that brings the ultimate sort of war into the world; the everlasting duel between Yes and No. This is the dilemma that many sceptics have darkened the universe and dissolved the mind, solely in order to escape. They are those who maintain that there is something that is both Yes and No. I do not know whether they pronounce it Yo.

The next step following on this acceptance of actuality or certainty, or whatever we call it in popular language, is much more difficult to explain in that language. But it represents exactly the point
at which nearly all other systems go wrong, and in taking the third
step abandon the first. Aquinas has affirmed that our first sense of
fact is a fact; and he cannot go back on it without falsehood. But
when we come to look at the fact or facts, as we know them, we observe that they have a rather queer character; which has made many
moderns grow strangely and restlessly sceptical about them. For instance, they are largely in a state of change, from being one thing to
being another; or their qualities are relative to other things; or they
appear to move incessantly; or they appear to vanish entirely. At this
point, as I say, many sages lose hold of the first principle of reality,
which they would concede at first; and fall back on saying that there
is nothing except change; or nothing except comparison; or nothing
except flux; or in effect that there is nothing at all. Aquinas turns
the whole argument the other way, keeping in line with his first
realisation of reality. There is no doubt about the being of being,
even if it does sometimes look like becoming; that is because what
we see is not the fullness of being; or (to continue a sort of colloquial
slang) we never see being being as much as it can. Ice is melted into
cold water and cold water is heated into hot water; it cannot be all
three at once. But this does not make water unreal or even relative;
it only means that its being is limited to being one thing at a time.
But the fullness of being is everything that it can be; and without it
the lesser or approximate forms of being cannot be explained as
anything; unless they are explained away as nothing.

This crude outline can only at the best be historical rather than
philosophical. It is impossible to compress into it the metaphysical
proofs of such an idea; especially in the medieval metaphysical language. But this distinction in philosophy is tremendous as a turning
point in history. Most thinkers, on realising the apparent mutability
of being, have really forgotten their own realisation of the being,
and believed only in the mutability. They cannot even say that a
thing changes into another thing; for them there is no instant in the
process at which it is a thing at all. It is only a change. It would

be more logical to call it nothing changing into nothing, than to say (on these principles) that there ever was or will be a moment when the thing is itself. St. Thomas maintains that the ordinary thing at any moment is something; but it is not everything that it could be. There is a fullness of being, in which it could be everything that it can be. Thus, while most sages come at last to nothing but naked change, he comes to the ultimate thing that is unchangeable, because it is all the other things at once. While they describe a change which is really a change in nothing, he describes a changelessness which includes the changes of everything. Things change because they are not complete; but their reality can only be explained as part of something that is complete. It is God.

Historically, at least, it was round this sharp and crooked corner that all the sophists have followed each other while the great Schoolman went up the high road of experience and expansion; to the beholding of cities, to the building of cities. They all failed at this early stage because, in the words of the old game, they took away the number they first thought of. The recognition of something, of a thing or things, is the first act of the intellect. But because the examination of a thing shows it is not a fixed or final thing, they inferred that there is nothing fixed or final. Thus, in various ways, they all began to see a thing as something thinner than a thing; a wave; a weakness; an abstract instability. St. Thomas, to use the same rude figure, saw a thing that was thicker than a thing; that was even more solid than the solid but secondary facts he had started by admitting as facts. Since we know them to be real, any elusive or bewildering element in their reality cannot really be unreality; and must be merely their relation to the real reality. A hundred human philosophies, ranging over the earth from Nominalism to Nirvana and Maya, from formless evolutionism to mindless quietism, all come from this first break in the Thomist chain; the notion that, because what we see does not satisfy us or explain itself, it is not even what we see. That cosmos is a contradiction in terms and strangles itself; but Thomism cuts itself free. The defect we see, in what is, is simply that it is not all that is. God is more actual even than Man; more actual even than Matter; for God with all His powers at every instant is immortally in action.

A cosmic comedy of a very curious sort occurred recently; involving the views of very brilliant men, such as Mr. Bernard Shaw and the Dean of St. Paul's. Briefly, freethinkers of many sorts had often said they had no need of a Creation, because the cosmos had always existed and always would exist. Mr. Bernard Shaw said he had become an atheist because the universe had gone on making itself from the beginning or without a beginning; Dean Inge later displayed consternation at the very idea that the universe could have an end. Most modern Christians, living by tradition where medieval Christians could live by logic or reason, vaguely felt that it was a dreadful idea to deprive them of the Day of Judgment. Most modern agnostics (who are delighted to have their ideas called dreadful) cried out all the more, with one accord, that the self-producing, self-existent, truly scientific universe had never needed to have a beginning and could not come to an end. At this very instant, quite suddenly, like the look-out man on a ship who shouts a warning about a rock, the *real* man of science, the expert who was examining the facts, announced in a loud voice that the universe *was* coming to an end. He had not been listening, of course, to the talk of the amateurs; he had been actually examining the texture of matter; and he said it was disintegrating: the world was apparently blowing itself up by a gradual explosion called energy; the whole business would certainly have an end and had presumably had a beginning. This was very shocking indeed; not to the orthodox, but rather specially to the unorthodox; who are rather more easily shocked. Dean Inge, who had been lecturing the orthodox for years on their stern duty of accepting all scientific discoveries, positively wailed aloud over this truly tactless scientific discovery; and practically implored the scientific discoverers to go away and discover something different. It seems almost incredible; but it is a fact that he asked what God would have to amuse Him, if the universe ceased. That is a measure of how much the modern mind needs Thomas Aquinas. But even without Aquinas, I can hardly conceive any educated man, let alone such a learned man, believing in God at all without assuming that God contains in Himself every perfection including eternal joy; and does not require the solar system to entertain him like a circus.

To step out of these presumptions, prejudices and private disappointments, into the world of St. Thomas, is like escaping from a scuffle in a dark room into the broad daylight. St. Thomas says, quite straightforwardly, that he himself believes this world has a beginning and end; because such seems to be the teaching of the Church; the validity of which mystical message to mankind he defends elsewhere with dozens of quite different arguments. Anyhow, the Church said the world would end; and apparently the Church was right; always supposing (as we are always supposed to suppose) that the latest men of science are right. But Aquinas says he sees no particular reason, in reason, why this world should not be a world without end; or even without beginning. And he is quite certain that, if it were entirely without end or beginning, there would still be exactly the same logical need of a Creator. Anybody who does not see that, he gently implies, does not really understand what is meant by a Creator.

For what St. Thomas means is not a medieval picture of an old king; but this second step in the great argument about *Ens* or Being; the second point which is so desperately difficult to put correctly in popular language. That is why I have introduced it here in the particular form of the argument that there must be a Creator even if there is no Day of Creation. Looking at Being as it is now, as the baby looks at the grass, we see a second thing about it; in quite popular language, it *looks* secondary and dependent. Existence exists; but it is not sufficiently self-existent; and would never become so merely by going on existing. The same primary sense which tells us it is Being, tells us that it is not perfect Being; not merely imperfect in the popular controversial sense of containing sin or sorrow; but imperfect as Being; less actual than the actuality it implies. For instance, its Being is often only Becoming; beginning to Be or ceasing to Be; it implies a more constant or complete thing of which it gives in itself no example. That is the meaning of that basic medieval phrase, "Everything that is moving is moved by another"; which, in the clear subtlety of St. Thomas, means inexpressibly more than the mere Deistic "somebody wound up the clock" with which it is probably often confounded. Anyone who thinks deeply will see that motion has about it an essential incompleteness, which approximates to something more complete.

The actual argument is rather technical; and concerns the fact that potentiality does not explain itself; moreover, in any case, unfolding must be of something folded. Suffice it to say that the mere modern evolutionists, who would ignore the argument, do not do so because they have discovered any flaw in the argument; for they have never discovered the argument itself. They do so because they are too shallow to see the flaw in their own argument; for the weakness of their thesis is covered by fashionable phraseology, as the strength of the old thesis is covered by old-fashioned phraseology. But for those who really think, there is always something really unthinkable about the whole evolutionary cosmos, as they conceive it; because it is something coming out of nothing; an ever-increasing flood of water pouring out of an empty jug. Those who can simply accept that, without even seeing the difficulty, are not likely to go so deep as Aquinas and see the solution of his difficulty. In a word, the world does not explain itself, and cannot do so merely by continuing to expand itself. But anyhow, it is absurd for the Evolutionist to complain that it is unthinkable for an admittedly unthinkable God to make everything out of nothing, and then pretend that it is *more* thinkable that nothing should turn itself into everything.

We have seen that most philosophers simply fail to philosophise about things because they change; they also fail to philosophise about things because they differ. We have no space to follow St. Thomas through all these negative heresies; but a word must be said about Nominalism, or the doubt founded on the things that differ. Everyone knows that the Nominalist declared that things differ too much to be really classified; so that they are only labelled. Aquinas was a firm but moderate Realist, and therefore held that there really are general qualities; as that human beings are human, and other paradoxes. To be an extreme Realist would have taken him too near to being a Platonist. He recognized that individuality is real, but said that it coexists with a common character making some generalisation possible; in fact, as in most things, he said exactly what all common sense would say, if no intelligent heretics had ever disturbed it.

Nevertheless, they still continue to disturb it. I remember when Mr. H. G. Wells had an alarming fit of Nominalist philosophy; and poured forth book after book to argue that everything is unique and untypical; as that a man is so much an individual that he is not even a man. It is a quaint and almost comic fact, that this chaotic negation especially attracts those who are always complaining of social chaos, and who propose to replace it by the most sweeping social regulations. It is the very men who say that nothing can be classified, who say that everything must be codified. Thus Mr. Bernard Shaw said that the only golden rule is that there is no golden rule. He prefers an iron rule; as in Russia.

But this is only a small inconsistency in some moderns as individuals. There is a much deeper inconsistency in them as theorists in relation to the general theory called Creative Evolution. They seem to imagine that they avoid the metaphysical doubt about mere change by assuming (it is not very clear why) that the change will always be for the better. But the mathematical difficulty of finding a corner in a curve is not altered by turning the chart upside down, and saying that a downward curve is now an upward curve. The point is that there is no point in the curve; no place at which we have a logical right to say that the curve has reached its climax, or revealed its origin, or come to its end. It makes no difference that they choose to be cheerful about it, and say, "It is enough that there is always a beyond"; instead of lamenting, like the more realistic poets of the past, over the tragedy of mere Mutability. It is not enough that there is always a beyond; because it might be beyond bearing. Indeed the only defence of this view is that sheer boredom is such an agony, that any movement is a relief. But the truth is that they have never read St. Thomas, or they would find, with no little terror, that they really agree with him. What they really mean is that change is not mere change; but is the unfolding of something; and if it is thus unfolded, though the unfolding takes twelve million years, it must be there already. In other words, they agree with Aquinas that there is everywhere potentiality that has not reached its end in act. But if it is a definite potentiality, and if it can only end in a definite act, why then there is a Great Being, in whom all potentialities already exist as a plan of action. In other words, it is impossible even to say that the change is for the better, unless the best exists somewhere, both before and after the change. Otherwise it is indeed mere change, as the blankest sceptics or the blackest pessimists would see it. Suppose two entirely new paths open before the progress of Creative Evolution. How is the evolutionist to know which Beyond is the better; unless he accepts from the past and present some standard of the best? By their superficial theory everything can change; everything can improve, even the nature of improvement. But in their submerged common sense, they do not really think that an ideal of kindness could change to an ideal of cruelty. It is typical of them that they will sometimes rather timidly use the word Purpose; but blush at the very mention of the word Person.

St. Thomas is the very reverse of anthropomorphic, in spite of his shrewdness as an anthropologist. Some theologians have even claimed that he is too much of an agnostic; and has left the nature of God too much of an intellectual abstraction. But we do not need even St. Thomas, we do not need anything but our own common sense, to tell us that if there has been from the beginning anything that can possibly be called a Purpose, it must reside in something that has the essential elements of a Person. There cannot be an intention hovering in the air all by itself, any more than a memory that nobody remembers or a joke that nobody has made. The only chance for those supporting such suggestions is to take refuge in blank and bottomless irrationality; and even then it is impossible to prove that anybody has any right to be unreasonable, if St. Thomas has no right to be reasonable.

In a sketch that aims only at the baldest simplification, this does seem to me the simplest truth about St. Thomas the philosopher. He is one, so to speak, who is faithful to his first love; and it is love at first sight. I mean that he immediately recognised a real quality in things; and afterwards resisted all the disintegrating doubts arising from the nature of those things. That is why I emphasise, even in the first few pages, the fact that there is a sort of purely Christian humility and fidelity underlying his philosophic realism. St. Thomas could as truly say, of having seen merely a stick or a stone, what St.

Paul said of having seen the rending of the secret heavens, "I was not disobedient to the heavenly vision". For though the stick or the stone is an earthly vision, it is through them that St. Thomas finds his way to heaven; and the point is that he is obedient to the vision; he does not go back on it. Nearly all the other sages who have led or misled mankind do, on one excuse or another, go back on it. They dissolve the stick or the stone in chemical solutions of scepticism; either in the medium of mere time and change; or in the difficulties of classification of unique units; or in the difficulty of recognising variety while admitting unity. The first of these three is called debate about flux or formless transition; the second is the debate about Nominalism and Realism, or the existence of general ideas; the third is called the ancient metaphysical riddle of the One and the Many. But they can all be reduced under a rough image to this same statement about St. Thomas. He is still true to the first truth and refusing the first treason. He will not deny what he has seen, though it be a secondary and diverse reality. He will not take away the numbers he first thought of, though there may be quite a number of them.

He has seen grass; and will not say he has not seen grass, because it today is and tomorrow is cast into the oven. That is the substance of all scepticism about change, transition, transformism and the rest. He will not say that there is no grass but only growth. If grass grows and withers, it can only mean that it is part of a greater thing, which is even more real; not that the grass is less real than it looks. St. Thomas has a really logical right to say, in the words of the modern mystic, A. E.: "I begin by the grass to be bound again to the Lord".

He has seen grass and grain; and he will not say that they do not differ, because there is something common to grass and grain. Nor will he say that there is nothing common to grass and grain, because they do really differ. He will not say, with the extreme Nominalists, that because grain can be differentiated into all sorts of fruitage, or grass trodden into mire with any kind of weed, therefore there can be no *classification* to distinguish weeds from slime or to draw a fine distinction between cattle-food and cattle. He will not say with the extreme Platonists, on the other hand, that he saw the perfect fruit in his own head by shutting his eyes, *before* he saw any difference between grain and grass. He saw one thing and then another thing, and then a common quality; but he does not really pretend that he saw the quality before the thing.

He has seen grass and gravel; that is to say, he has seen things really different; things not classified together like grass and grain. The first flash of fact shows us a world of really strange things; not merely strange to us, but strange to each other. The separate things need have nothing in common except Being. Everything is Being; but it is not true that everything is Unity. It is here, as I have said, that St. Thomas does definitely, one might say defiantly, part company with the Pantheist and Monist. All things are; but among the things that are is the thing called difference, quite as much as the thing called similarity. And here again we begin to be bound again to the Lord, not only by the universality of grass, but by the incompatibility of grass and gravel. For this world of different and varied beings is especially the world of the Christian Creator; the world of created things, like things made by an artist; as compared with the world that is only one thing, with a sort of shimmering and shifting veil of misleading change; which is the conception of so many of the ancient religions of Asia and the modern sophistries of Germany. In the face of these, St. Thomas still stands stubborn in the same obstinate objective fidelity. He has seen grass and gravel; and he is not disobedient to the heavenly vision.

To sum up; the reality of things, the mutability of things, the diversity of things, and all other such things that can be attributed to things, is followed carefully by the medieval philosopher, without losing touch with the original point of the reality. There is no space in this book to specify the thousand steps of thought by which he shows that he is right. But the point is that, even apart from being right he is real. He is a realist in a rather curious sense of his own, which is a third thing, distinct from the almost contrary medieval and modern meanings of the word. Even the doubts and difficulties about reality have driven him to believe in more reality rather than less. The *deceitfulness* of things which has had so sad an effect on so many sages, has almost a contrary effect on this sage. If things deceive us, it is by being more real than they seem. As ends in themselves they always deceive us; but as things tending to a greater end, they are even more real than we think them. If they seem to have a relative unreality (so to speak) it is because they are potential and not actual; they are unfulfilled, like packets of seeds or boxes of fireworks. They have it in them to be more real than they are. And there is an upper world of what the Schoolman called Fruition, or Fulfillment, in which all this relative relativity becomes actuality; in which the trees burst into flower or the rockets into flame.

Here I leave the reader, on the very lowest rung of those ladders of logic, by which St. Thomas besieged and mounted the House of Man. It is enough to say that by arguments as honest and laborious, he climbed up to the turrets and talked with angels on the roofs of gold. This is, in a very rude outline, his philosophy; it is impossible in such an outline to describe his theology. Anyone writing so small a book about so big a man, must leave out something. Those who know him best will best understand why, after some considerable consideration, I have left out the only important thing.

VIII

THE SEQUEL TO ST. THOMAS

It is often said that St. Thomas, unlike St. Francis, did not permit in his work the indescribable element of poetry: As, for instance, that there is little reference to any pleasure in the actual flowers and fruit of natural things, though any amount of concern with the buried roots of nature. And yet I confess that, in reading his philosophy, I have a very peculiar and powerful impression analogous to poetry. Curiously enough, it is in some ways more analogous to painting, and reminds me very much of the effect produced by the *best* of the modern painters, when they throw a strange and almost crude light upon stark and rectangular objects, or seem to be groping for rather than grasping the very pillars of the subconscious mind. It is probably because there is in his work a quality which is Primitive, in the best sense of a badly misused word; but anyhow, the pleasure is definitely not only of the reason, but also of the imagination.

Perhaps the impression is connected with the fact that painters deal with things without words. An artist draws quite gravely the grand curves of a pig; because he is not thinking of the *word* pig. There is no thinker who is so unmistakably thinking about things and not being misled by the indirect influence of words, as St. Thomas Aquinas. It is true in that sense that he has not the advantage of words, any more than the disadvantage of words. Here he differs sharply, for instance, from St. Augustine who was, among other things a wit. He was also a sort of prose poet, with a power over words in their atmospheric and emotional aspect; so that his books abound with beautiful passages that rise in the memory like strains of music; the *illi in vos saeviant;*[1] or the unforgettable cry, "Late I have loved thee, O Ancient Beauty!" It is true that there is little or nothing of this kind in St. Thomas; but if he was without the higher uses of the mere magic of words, he was also free from that abuse of it, by mere sentimentalists or self-centred artists, which can become merely morbid and a very

[1] This may be translated as "let them rage against you."

black magic indeed. And truly it is by some such comparison with the purely introspective intellectual, that we may find a hint about the real nature of the thing I describe, or rather fail to describe; I mean the elemental and primitive poetry that shines through all his thoughts; and especially through the thought with which all his thinking begins. It is the intense rightness of his sense of the relation between the mind and the real thing outside the mind.

That *strangeness* of things, which is the light in all poetry, and indeed in all art, is really connected with their otherness; or what is called their objectivity. What is subjective must be stale; it is exactly what is objective that is in this imaginative manner strange. In this the great contemplative is the complete contrary of that false contemplative, the mystic who looks only into his own soul, the selfish artist who shrinks from the world and lives only in his own mind. According to St. Thomas, the mind acts freely of itself, but its freedom exactly consists in finding a way out to liberty and the light of day; to reality and the land of the living. In the subjectivist, the pressure of the world forces the imagination inwards. In the Thomist, the energy of the mind forces the imagination outwards, but because the images it seeks are real things. All their romance and glamour, so to speak, lies in the fact that they are real things; things *not* to be found by staring inwards at the mind. The flower is a vision because it is not only a vision. Or, if you will, it is a vision because it is not a dream. This is for the poet the strangeness of stones and trees and solid things; they are strange because they are solid. I am putting it first in the poetical manner, and indeed it needs much more technical subtlety to put it in the philosophical manner. According to Aquinas, the object becomes a part of the mind; nay, according to Aquinas, the mind actually becomes the object. But, as one commentator acutely puts it, it only becomes the object and does not create the object. In other words, the object *is* an object; it can and does exist outside the mind, or in the absence of the mind. And *therefore* it enlarges the mind of which it becomes a part. The mind conquers a new province like an emperor; but only because the mind has answered the bell like a servant. The mind has opened the doors and windows, because it is the natural activity of what is inside the house to find out what is outside the house. If the mind is sufficient to itself, it is insufficient for itself. For this feeding upon fact *is* itself; as an organ it has an object which is objective; this eating of the strange strong meat of reality.

Note how this view avoids both pitfalls; the alternative abysses of impotence. The mind is not merely receptive, in the sense that it absorbs sensations like so much blotting-paper; on that sort of softness has been based all that cowardly materialism, which conceives man as wholly servile to his environment. On the other hand, the mind is not purely creative, in the sense that it paints pictures on the windows and then mistakes them for a landscape outside. But the mind is active, and its activity consists in following, so far as the will chooses to follow, the light outside that does really shine upon real landscapes. That is what gives the indefinably virile and even adventurous quality to this view of life; as compared with that which holds that material inferences pour in upon an utterly helpless mind, or that which holds that psychological influences pour out and create an entirely baseless phantasmagoria. In other words, the essence of the Thomist common sense is that two agencies are at work; reality and the recognition of reality; and their meeting is a sort of marriage. Indeed it is very truly a marriage, because it is fruitful; the only philosophy now in the world that really is fruitful. It produces practical results, precisely because it is the combination of an adventurous mind and a strange fact.

M. Maritain has used an admirable metaphor, in his book *Theonas*, when he says that the external fact *fertilises* the internal intelligence, as the bee fertilises the flower. Anyhow, upon that marriage, or whatever it may be called, the whole system of St. Thomas is founded; God made Man so that he was capable of coming in contact with reality; and those whom God hath joined, let no man put asunder.

Now, it is worthy of remark that it is the only working philosophy. Of nearly all other philosophies it is strictly true that their followers work in spite of them, or do not work at all. No sceptics work sceptically; no fatalists work fatalistically; all without exception work on the principle that it is possible to assume what it is not possible to believe. No materialist who thinks his mind was made up for him, by mud and blood and heredity, has any hesitation in making up his mind. No sceptic who believes that truth is subjective has any hesitation about treating it as objective.

Thus St. Thomas's work has a constructive quality absent from almost all cosmic systems after him. For he is already building a house, while the newer speculators are still at the stage of testing the rungs of a ladder, demonstrating the hopeless softness of the unbaked bricks, chemically analysing the spirit in the spirit-level, and generally quarrelling about whether they can even make the tools that will make the house. Aquinas is whole intellectual aeons ahead of them, over and above the common chronological sense of saying a man is in advance of his age; he is ages in advance of our age. For he has thrown out a bridge across the abyss of the first doubt, and found reality beyond and begun to build on it. Most modern philosophies are not philosophy but philosophic doubt; that is, doubt about whether there can be any philosophy. If we accept St. Thomas's fundamental act or argument in the acceptance of reality, the further deductions from it will be equally real; they will be things and not words. Unlike Kant and most of the Hegelians, he has a faith that is not merely a doubt about doubt. It is not merely what is commonly called a faith about faith; it is a faith about fact. From this point he can go forward, and deduce and develop and decide, like a man planning a city and sitting in a judgment-seat. But never since that time has any thinking man of that eminence thought that there is any real evidence for anything, not even the evidence of his senses, that was strong enough to bear the weight of a definite deduction.

From all this we may easily infer that this philosopher does not merely touch on social things, or even take them in his stride to spiritual things; though that is always his direction. He takes hold of them, he has not only a grasp of them, but a grip. As all his controversies prove, he was perhaps a perfect example of the iron hand in the velvet glove. He was a man who always turned his full attention to anything; and he seems to fix even passing things as they pass. To him even what was momentary was momentous. The reader feels that any small point of economic habit or human accident is for the moment almost scorched under the converging rays of a magnifying lens. It is impossible to put in these pages a thousandth part of the decisions on details of life that may be found in his work; it would be like reprinting the law-reports of an incredible century of just judges and sensible magistrates. We can only touch on one or two obvious topics of this kind.

I have noted the need to use modern atmospheric words for certain ancient atmospheric things; as in saying that St. Thomas was what most modern men vaguely mean by an Optimist. In the same way, he was very much what they vaguely mean by a Liberal. I do not mean that any of his thousand political suggestions would suit any such definite political creed; if there are nowadays any definite political creeds. I mean, in the same sense, that he has a sort of atmosphere of believing in breadth and balance and debate. He may not be a Liberal by the extreme demands of the moderns for we seem always to mean by the moderns the men of the last century, rather than this. He was very much of a Liberal compared with the most modern of all moderns; for they are nearly all of them turning into Fascists and Hitlerites. But the point is that he obviously preferred the sort of decisions that are reached by deliberation rather than despotic action; and while, like all his contemporaries and coreligionists, he has no doubt that true authority may be authoritative, he is rather averse to the whole savour of its being arbitrary. He is much less of an Imperialist than Dante, and even his Papalism is not very Imperial. He is very fond of phrases like "a mob of free men" as the essential material of a city; and he is emphatic upon the fact that law, when it ceases to be justice, ceases even to be law.

If this work were controversial, whole chapters could be given to the economics as well as the ethics of the Thomist system. It would be easy to show that, in this matter, he was a prophet as well as a philosopher. He foresaw from the first the peril of that mere reliance on trade and exchange, which was beginning about his time; and which has culminated in a universal commercial collapse in our time. He did not merely assert that Usury is unnatural, though in saying that he only followed Aristotle and obvious common sense, which was never contradicted by anybody until the time of the commercialists, who have involved us in the collapse. The modern world began by Bentham writing the Defence of Usury, and it has ended after a hundred years in even the vulgar newspaper opinion finding Finance indefensible. But St. Thomas struck much deeper than that. He even mentioned the truth, ignored during the long idolatry of trade, that things which men produce only to sell are likely to be worse in quality than the things they produce in order to consume. Something of our difficulty about the fine shades of Latin will be felt when we come to his statement that there is always a certain *inhonestas* about trade. For *inhonestas* does not exactly mean dishonesty. It means approximately "something unworthy," or, more nearly perhaps, "something not quite handsome." And he was right; for trade, in the modern sense, does mean selling something for a little more than it is worth, nor would the nineteenth century economists have denied it. They would only have said that he was not practical; and this seemed sound while their view led to practical prosperity. Things are a little different now that it has led to universal bankruptcy.

Here, however, we collide with a colossal paradox of history. The Thomist philosophy and theology, quite fairly compared with other philosophies like the Buddhist or the Monist, with other theologies like the Calvinist or the Christian Scientist, is quite obviously a working and even a fighting system; full of common sense and constructive confidence; and therefore normally full of hope and promise. Nor is this hope vain or this promise unfulfilled. In this not very hopeful modern moment, there are no men so hopeful as those who are today looking to St. Thomas as a leader in a hundred crying questions of craftsmanship and ownership and economic ethics. There is undoubtedly a hopeful and creative Thomism in our time. But we are none the less puzzled by the fact that this did not immediately follow on St. Thomas's time. It is true that there was a great march of progress in the thirteenth century; and in some things, such as the status of the peasant, matters had greatly improved by the end of the Middle Ages. But nobody can honestly say that Scholasticism had greatly improved by the end of the Middle Ages. Nobody can tell how far the popular spirit of the Friars had helped the later popular medieval movements; or how far this great Friar, with his luminous rules of justice and his lifelong sympathy with the poor, may have indirectly contributed to the improvement that certainly occurred. But those who followed his method, as distinct from his moral spirit, degenerated with a strange rapidity; and it was certainly not in the Scholastics that the improvement occurred. Of some of the Scholastics we can only say that they took everything that was worst in Scholasticism and made it worse. They continued to count the steps of logic; but every step of logic took them further from common sense. They forgot how St. Thomas had started almost as an agnostic; and seemed resolved to leave nothing in heaven or hell about which anybody could be agnostic. They were a sort of rabid rationalists, who would have left no mysteries in the Faith at all. In the earliest Scholasticism there is something that strikes a modern as fanciful and pedantic; but, properly understood, it has a fine spirit in its fancy. It is the spirit of freedom; and especially the spirit of free will. Nothing seems more quaint, for instance, than the speculations about what would have happened to every vegetable or animal or angel, if Eve had chosen *not* to eat the fruit of the tree. But this was originally full of the thrill of choice; and the feeling that she might have chosen otherwise. It was this detailed detective method that was followed, without the thrill of the original detective story. The world was cumbered with countless tomes, proving by logic a thousand things that can be known only to God. They developed all that was really sterile in Scholasticism, and left for us all that is really fruitful in Thomism.

There are many historical explantions. There is the Black Death, which broke the back of the Middle Ages; the consequent decline in clerical culture, which did so much to provoke the Reformation. But I suspect that there was another cause also; which can only be stated by saying that the contemporary fanatics, who controverted with Aquinas, left their own school behind them; and in a sense that school triumphed after all. The really narrow Augustinians, the men who saw the Christian life only as the narrow way, the men who could not even comprehend the great Dominican's exultation in the blaze of Being, or the glory of God in all his creatures, the men who continued to insist feverishly on every text, or even on every truth, that appeared pessimistic or paralysing, these gloomy Christians

could not be extirpated from Christendom; and they remained and
waited for their chance. The narrow Augustinians, the men who
would have no science or reason or rational use of secular things,
might have been defeated in controversy, but they had an accumulated passion of conviction. There was an Augustinian monastery
in the North where it was near to explosion.

Thomas Aquinas had struck his blow; but he had not entirely settled the Manichees. The Manichees are not so easily settled; in the
sense of settled forever. He had insured that the main outline of the
Christianity that has come down to us should be supernatural but
not anti-natural; and should never be darkened with a false spirituality to the oblivion of the Creator and the Christ who was made
Man. But as his tradition trailed away into less liberal or less creative
habits of thought, and as his medieval society fell away and decayed
through other causes, the thing against which he had made war
crept back into Christendom. A certain spirit or element in the
Christian religion, necessary and sometimes noble but always needing to be balanced by more gentle and generous elements in the
Faith, began once more to strengthen, as the framework of Scholasticism stiffened or split. The Fear of the Lord, that is the beginning
of wisdom, and therefore belongs to the beginnings, and is felt in
the first cold hours before the dawn of civilisation; the power that
comes out of the wilderness and rides on the whirlwind and breaks
the gods of stone; the power before which the eastern nations are
prostrate like a pavement; the power before which the primitive
prophets run naked and shouting, at once proclaiming and escaping
from their god; the fear that is rightly rooted in the beginnings of
every religion, true or false: the fear of the Lord, that is the beginning of wisdom; but not the end.

It is often remarked, as showing the ironical indifference of rulers
to revolutions, and especially the frivolity of those who are called the
Pagan Popes of the Renaissance, in their attitude to the Reformation, that when the Pope first heard of the first movements of Protestantism, which had started in Germany, he only said in an off hand
manner that it was "some quarrel of monks". Every Pope of course
was accustomed to quarrels among the monastic orders; but it has

always been noted as a strange and almost uncanny negligence that
he could see no more than this in the beginnings of the great sixteenth century schism. And yet, in a somewhat more recondite
sense, there is something to be said for what he has been blamed for
saying. In one sense, the schismatics had a sort of spiritual ancestry
even in mediaeval times.

It will be found earlier in this book; and it *was* a quarrel of monks.
We have seen how the great name of Augustine, a name never mentioned by Aquinas without respect but often mentioned without
agreement, covered an Augustinian school of thought naturally lingering longest in the Augustinian Order. The difference, like every
difference between Catholics, was only a difference of emphasis. The
Augustinians stressed the idea of the impotence of man before God,
the omniscience of God about the destiny of man, the need for holy
fear and the humiliation of intellectual pride, more than the opposite
and corresponding truths of free will or human dignity or good
works. In this they did in a sense continue the distinctive note of St.
Augustine, who is even now regarded as relatively the determinist
doctor of the Church. But there is emphasis and emphasis; and a
time was coming when emphasising the one side was to mean flatly
contradicting the other. Perhaps, after all, it did begin with a quarrel
of monks; but the Pope was yet to learn how quarrelsome a monk
could be. For there was one particular monk in that Augustinian
monastery in the German forests, who may be said to have had a
single and special talent for emphasis; for emphasis and nothing except emphasis; for emphasis with the quality of earthquake. He was
the son of a slatecutter; a man with a great voice and a certain
volume of personality; brooding, sincere, decidedly morbid; and his
name was Martin Luther. Neither Augustine nor the Augustinians
would have desired to see the day of that vindication of the Augustinian tradition; but in one sense, perhaps, the Augustinian
tradition was avenged after all.

It came out of its cell again, in the day of storm and ruin, and
cried out with a new and mighty voice for an elemental and emotional religion, and for the destruction of all philosophies. It had a
peculiar horror and loathing of the great Greek philosophies, and

of the scholasticism that had been founded on those philosophies. It had one theory that was the destruction of all theories; in fact it had its own theology which was itself the death of theology. Man could say nothing to God, nothing from God, nothing about God, except an almost inarticulate cry for mercy and for the supernatural help of Christ, in a world where all natural things were useless. Reason was useless. Will was useless. Man could not move himself an inch any more than a stone. Man could not trust what was in his head any more than a turnip. Nothing remained in earth or heaven, but the name of Chirst lifted in that lonely imprecation; awful as the cry of a beast in pain.

We must be just to those huge human figures, who are in fact the hinges of history. However strong, and rightly strong, be our own controversial conviction, it must never mislead us into thinking that something trivial has transformed the world. So it is with that great Augustinian monk, who avenged all the ascetic Augustinians of the Middle Ages; and whose broad and burly figure has been big enough to block out for four centuries the distant human mountain of Aquinas. It is not, as the moderns delight to say, a question of theology. The Protestant theology of Martin Luther was a thing that no modern Protestant would be seen dead in a field with; or if the phrase be too flippant, would be specially anxious to touch with a barge-pole. That Protestantism was pessimism; it was nothing but bare insistence on the hopelessness of all human virtue, as an attempt to escape hell. That Lutheranism is now quite unreal; more modern phases of Lutheranism are rather more unreal; but Luther was not unreal. He was one of those great elemental barbarians, to whom it is indeed given to change the world. To compare those two figures bulking so big in history, in any philosophical sense, would of course be futile and even unfair. On a great map like the mind of Aquinas, the mind of Luther would be almost invisible. But it is not altogether untrue to say, as so many journalists have said without caring whether it was true or untrue, that Luther opened an epoch; and began the modern world.

He was the first man who ever consciously used his consciousness; or what was later called his Personality. He had as a fact a rather strong personality. Aquinas had an even stronger personality; he had a massive and magnetic presence; he had an intellect that could act like a huge system of artillery spread over the whole world; he had that instantaneous presence of mind in debate, which alone really deserves the name of wit. But it never occured to him to use anything except his wits, in defence of a truth distinct from himself. It never occured to Aquinas to use Aquinas as a weapon. There is not a trace of his ever using his personal advantages, of birth or body or brain or breeding, in debate with anybody. In short, he belonged to an age of intellectual unconsciousness, to an age of intellectual innocence, which was very intellectual. Now Luther did begin the modern mood of depending on things not merely intellectual. It is not a question of praise or blame; it matters little whether we say that he was a strong personality, or that he was a bit of a big bully. When he quoted a Scripture text, inserting a word that is not in Scripture, he was content to shout back at all hecklers: "Tell them that Dr. Martin Luther will have it so!" That is what we now call Personality. A little later it was called Psychology. After that it was called Advertisement or Salesmanship. But we are not arguing about advantages or disadvantages. It is due to this great Augustinian pessimist to say, not only that he did triumph at last over the Angel of the Schools, but that he did in a very real sense make the modern world. He destroyed Reason; and substituted Suggestion.

It is said that the great Reformer publicly burned the *Summa Theologica* and the works of Aquinas; and with the bonfire of such books this book may well come to an end. They say it is very difficult to burn a book; and it must have been exceedingly difficult to burn such a mountain of books as the Dominican had contributed to the controversies of Christendom. Anyhow, there is something lurid and apocalyptic about the idea of such destruction, when we consider the compact complexity of all that encyclopaedic survey of social and moral and theoretical things. All the close-packed definitions that excluded so many errors and extremes; all the broad and balanced judgments upon the clash of loyalties or the choice of evils; all the liberal speculations upon the limits of government or the proper conditions of justice; all the distinctions between the use and abuse of private property; all the rules and exceptions about the great evil of war; all the allowances for human weakness and all the provisions for human health; all this mass of medieval humanism shrivelled and curled up in smoke before the eyes of its enemy; and that great passionate peasant rejoiced darkly, because the day of the Intellect was over. Sentence by sentence it burned, and syllogism by syllogism; and the golden maxims turned to golden flames in that last and dying glory of all that had once been the great wisdom of the Greeks. The great central Synthesis of history, that was to have linked the ancient with the modern world, went up in smoke and, for half the world, was forgotten like a vapour.

For a time it seemed that the destruction was final. It is still expressed in the amazing fact that (in the North) modern men can still write histories of philosophy, in which philosophy stops with the last little sophists of Greece and Rome; and is never heard of again until the appearance of such a third-rate philosopher as Francis Bacon. And yet this small book, which will probably do nothing else, or have very little other value, will be at least a testimony to the fact that the tide has turned once more. It is four hundred years after; and this book, I hope (and I am happy to say I believe) will probably be lost and forgotten in the flood of better books about St. Thomas Aquinas, which are at this moment pouring from every printing-press in Europe, and even in England and America. Compared with such books it is obviously a very slight and amateurish production; but it is not likely to be burned, and if it were, it would not leave even a noticeable gap in the pouring mass of new and magnificent work, which is now daily dedicated to the *philosophia perennis*; to the Everlasting Philosophy.

The text of this book has been set in Bembo by the Neumann Press of Long Prairie, Minnesota. Printed on Glatfelter Offset paper by Thomson Shore, Dexter, Michigan. Cover and jacket design by Darlene Lawless.